걸프 사태

# 미국 동향 3

_____

걸프 사태

미국 동향 3

## | 머리말

　걸프 전쟁은 미국의 주도하에 34개국 연합군 병력이 수행한 전쟁으로, 1990년 8월 이라크의 쿠웨이트 침공 및 합병에 반대하며 발발했다. 미국은 초기부터 파병 외교에 나섰고, 1990년 9월 서울 등에 고위 관리를 파견하며 한국의 동참을 요청했다. 88올림픽 이후 동구권 국교 수립과 유엔 가입 추진 등 적극적인 외교 활동을 펼치는 당시 한국에 있어 이는 미국과 국제사회의 지지를 얻기 위해서라도 피할 수 없는 일이었다. 결국 정부는 91년 1월부터 약 3개월에 걸쳐 국군의료지원단과 공군수송단을 사우디아라비아 및 아랍 에미리트 연합 등에 파병하였고, 군·민간 의료 활동, 병력 수송 임무를 수행했다. 동시에 당시 걸프 지역 8개국에 살던 5천여 명의 교민에게 방독면 등 물자를 제공하고, 특별기 파견 등으로 비상시 대피할 수 있도록 지원했다. 비록 전쟁 부담금과 유가 상승 등 어려움도 있었지만, 걸프전 파병과 군사 외교를 통해 한국은 유엔 가입에 박차를 가할 수 있었고 미국 등 선진 우방국, 아랍권 국가 등과 밀접한 외교 관계를 유지하며 여러 국익을 창출할 수 있었다.

　본 총서는 외교부에서 작성하여 30여 년간 유지한 걸프 사태 관련 자료를 담고 있다. 미국을 비롯한 여러 국가와의 군사 외교 과정, 일일 보고 자료와 기타 정부의 대응 및 조치, 재외동포 철수와 보호, 의료지원단과 수송단 파견 및 지원 과정, 유엔을 포함해 세계 각국에서 수집한 관련 동향 자료, 주변국 지원과 전후복구사업 참여 등 총 48권으로 구성되었다. 전체 분량은 약 2만 4천여 쪽에 이른다.

2024년 3월

한국학술정보(주)

# | 일러두기

· 본 총서에 실린 자료는 2022년 4월과 2023년 4월에 각각 공개한 외교문서 4,827권, 76만 여 쪽 가운데 일부를 발췌한 것이다.

· 각 권의 제목과 순서는 공개된 원본을 최대한 반영하였으나, 주제에 따라 일부는 적절히 변경하였다.

· 원본 자료는 A4 판형에 맞게 축소하거나 원본 비율을 유지한 채 A4 페이지 안에 삽입 하였다. 또한 현재 시점에선 공개되지 않아 '공란'이란 표기만 있는 페이지 역시 그대로 실었다.

· 외교부가 공개한 문서 각 권의 첫 페이지에는 '정리 보존 문서 목록'이란 이름으로 기록물 종류, 일자, 명칭, 간단한 내용 등의 정보가 수록되어 있으며, 이를 기준으로 0001번부터 번호가 매겨져 있다. 이는 삭제하지 않고 총서에 그대로 수록하였다.

· 보고서 내용에 관한 더 자세한 정보가 필요하다면, 외교부가 온라인상에 제공하는 『대한 민국 외교사료요약집』 1991년과 1992년 자료를 참조할 수 있다.

# | 차례

## 정 리 보 존 문 서 목 록

| 기록물종류 | 일반공문서철 | 등록번호 | 2012090486 | 등록일자 | 2012-09-17 |
|---|---|---|---|---|---|
| 분류번호 | 772 | 국가코드 | US/XF | 보존기간 | 영구 |
| 명 칭 | 걸프사태 : 미국 의회 동향, 1990-91. 전5권 | | | | |
| 생 산 과 | 북미1과 | 생산년도 | 1990~1991 | 담당그룹 | |
| 권 차 명 | V.1 1990.8-9월 | | | | |
| 내용목차 | * 걸프사태 관련 미국 의회에서의 각종 논의, 법안, 결의안, 청문회 개최 동향 등<br><br>* 9.10 상원, 페르시아만 사태 관련한 우방국 책임 분담에 관한 수정안 통과 | | | | |

0001

# 외 무 부

종  별 :

번  호 : USW-3913                                   일  시 : 90 0828 1634

수  신 : 장 관 ( 미북, 미안, 중근동)

발  신 : 주 미 대사

제  목 : 이락 사태- 의회 반응 ( 1)

1. 이락사태와 관련한 미군의 상뒤 파병이 미 국민, 의회 및 외국 정부로 부터 폭넓은 지지를 받고 있는 상황에서 BUSH 대통령은 금 8.28(화) 백악관에서 의회 지도부 및 외교, 군사 관련 의원들과 면담, 행정부 정책에 대한 강력한 지원을 촉구함.

2. 금일 회담은 이락.사태 이후 BUSH 와 의회인사들과의 첫 회동인바, BUSH 대통령은 정치적 운신의 폭이 최상에 도달하여 있는 현 시점을 이용, 에너지 문제를 포함한 국내 경제문제, 군사전략 및 BURDEN-SHARING 을 포함한 외국의 지원촉구 방안등 외교 전략에 관하여 대화를 나누는것으로 알려짐.

3. 내주 여름 휴가에서 돌아올 의원들은 사우디주둔 미군유지 비용, 미국의 장기적 전략 및 미국인 인질 문제들과 관련, 활발한 논의를 전개할 것으로 사료되는바, 미군의 해외 파병과 관련한 대통령의 권한을 규정한 WAR POWERS RESOLUTION 에 대한 논의 또한 불가피하게 재개될 것으로 전망됨.

4. 미의원들은 그간 이락사태에 대한 미 행정부의 입장에 대하여 전폭적 지지를 보여 왔으나 동사태가 장기화될경우 미국내 정치, 경제적 사안들과 관련, 행정부의 이락 정책에 대한 비난이 증가될 것으로 사료됨.

5. 한편, SAM NUNN 군사 위원장, WARNER 간사를 포함한 7명의 상원의원들은 사우디 파견 미군기지를 방문 하였으며, 방문후 가진 기자회견에서 NUNN 위원장은 이집트를 포함한 아랍제국들의 사우디 파병 증원을 유도, 미국과 이락간의 정면 군사적 충돌의 가능성을 저하시킬것을 BUSH 행정부에 촉구 하였음.

6. 이락 사태관련 미 의회의 반응을 일련번호보고 예정임.

첨부: WAR POWERS RESOLUTION ( USW(F)- 1963 ) (4매)

(대사 박동진- 국장)

| 미주국 | 1차보 | 2차보 | 미주국 | 중아국 | 통상국 | 정문국 | 안기부 | 대책반 |
|--------|--------|--------|--------|--------|--------|--------|--------|--------|
|        |        |        |        |        |        |        |        |        |

외신 1과  통제관

0002

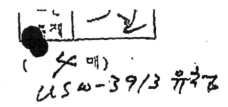
## CHAPTER 33—WAR POWERS RESOLUTION

### CHAPTER REFERRED TO IN OTHER SECTIONS

This chapter is referred to in title 22 section 3426.

### § 1541. Purpose and policy

#### (a) Congressional declaration

It is the purpose of this chapter to fulfill the intent of the framers of the Constitution of the United States and insure that the collective judgment of both the Congress and the President will apply to the introduction of United States Armed Forces into hostilities, or into situations where imminent involvement in hostilities is clearly indicated by the circumstances, and to the continued use of such forces in hostilities or in such situations.

#### (b) Congressional legislative power under necessary and proper clause

Under article I, section 8, of the Constitution, it is specifically provided that the Congress shall have the power to make all laws necessary and proper for carrying into execution, not only its own powers but also all other powers vested by the Constitution in the Government of the United States, or in any department or officer thereof.

#### (c) Presidential executive power as Commander-in-Chief; limitation

The constitutional powers of the President as Commander-in-Chief to introduce United States Armed Forces into hostilities, or into situations where imminent involvement in hostilities is clearly indicated by the circumstances, are exercised only pursuant to (1) a declaration of war, (2) specific statutory authorization, or (3) a national emergency created by attack upon the United States, its territories or possessions, or its armed forces.

(Pub. L. 93-148, § 2, Nov. 7, 1973, 87 Stat. 555.)

#### EFFECTIVE DATE

Section 10 of Pub. L. 93-148 provided that: "This joint resolution [enacting this chapter] shall take effect on the date of its enactment [Nov. 7, 1973]."

#### SHORT TITLE

Section 1 of Pub. L. 93-148 provided that: "This joint resolution [enacting this chapter] may be cited as the 'War Powers Resolution'."

#### ADHERENCE TO WAR POWERS RESOLUTION

Pub. L. 96-342, title X, § 1008, Sept. 8, 1980, 94 Stat. 1123, provided that: "Whereas, the National Command Authority must have the capacity to carry out any military mission which is essential to the national security of the United States having in its hands in the Rapid Deployment Force an increased capability to extend the reach of our military power in an expedited manner; and whereas, without the significant safeguard of the War Powers Resolution (Public Law 93-148) [this chapter], United States foreign and defense policies could be subject to misinterpretation; it is therefore the sense of the Congress that the provisions of the War Powers Resolution be strictly adhered to and that the congressional consultation process specified by such Resolution be utilized strictly according to the terms of the War Powers Resolution."

### § 1542. Consultation; initial and regular consultations

The President in every possible instance shall consult with Congress before introducing United States Armed Forces into hostilities or into situations where imminent involvement in hostilities is clearly indicated by the circumstances, and after every such introduction shall consult regularly with the Congress until United States Armed Forces are no longer engaged in hostilities or have been removed from such situations.

(Pub. L. 93-148, § 3, Nov. 7, 1973, 87 Stat. 555.)

## § 1543. Reporting requirement

**(a) Written report; time of submission; circumstances necessitating submission; information reported**

In the absence of a declaration of war, in any case in which United States Armed Forces are introduced—

(1) into hostilities or into situations where imminent involvement in hostilities is clearly indicated by the circumstances;

(2) into the territory, airspace or waters of a foreign nation, while equipped for combat, except for deployments which relate solely to supply, replacement, repair, or training of such forces; or

(3) in numbers which substantially enlarge United States Armed Forces equipped for combat already located in a foreign nation;

the President shall submit within 48 hours to the Speaker of the House of Representatives and to the President pro tempore of the Senate a report, in writing, setting forth—

(A) the circumstances necessitating the introduction of United States Armed Forces;

(B) the constitutional and legislative authority under which such introduction took place; and

(C) the estimated scope and duration of the hostilities or involvement.

**(b) Other information reported**

The President shall provide such other information as the Congress may request in the fulfillment of its constitutional responsibilities with respect to committing the Nation to war and to the use of United States Armed Forces abroad.

**(c) Periodic reports; semiannual requirement**

Whenever United States Armed Forces are introduced into hostilities or into any situation described in subsection (a) of this section, the President shall, so long as such armed forces continue to be engaged in such hostilities or situation, report to the Congress periodically on the status of such hostilities or situation as well as on the scope and duration of such hostilities or situation, but in no event shall he report to the Congress less often than once every six months.

(Pub. L. 93-148, § 4, Nov. 7, 1973, 87 Stat. 555.)

SECTION REFERRED TO IN OTHER SECTIONS

This section is referred to in section 1544 of this title.

## § 1544. Congressional action

**(a) Transmittal of report and referral to Congressional committees; joint request for convening Congress**

Each report submitted pursuant to section 1543(a)(1) of this title shall be transmitted to the Speaker of the House of Representatives and to the President pro tempore of the Senate on the same calendar day. Each report so transmitted shall be referred to the Committee on Foreign Affairs of the House of Representatives and to the Committee on Foreign Relations of the Senate for appropriate action. If, when the report is transmitted, the Congress has adjourned sine die or has adjourned for any period in excess of three calendar days, the Speaker of the House of Representatives and the President pro tempore of the Senate, if they deem it advisable (or if petitioned by at least 30 percent of the membership of their respective Houses) shall jointly request the President to convene Congress in order that it may consider the report and take appropriate action pursuant to this section.

**(b) Termination of use of United States Armed Forces; exceptions; extension period**

Within sixty calendar days after a report is submitted or is required to be submitted pursuant to section 1543(a)(1) of this title, whichever is earlier, the President shall terminate any use of United States Armed Forces with respect to which such report was submitted (or required to be submitted), unless the Congress (1) has declared war or has enacted a specific authorization for such use of United States Armed Forces, (2) has extended by law such sixty-day period, or (3) is physically unable to meet as a result of an armed attack upon the United States. Such sixty-day period shall be extended for not more than an additional thirty days if the President determines and certifies to the Congress in writing that unavoidable military necessity respecting the safety of United States Armed Forces requires the continued use of such armed forces in the course of bringing about a prompt removal of such forces.

**(c) Concurrent resolution for removal by President of United States Armed Forces**

Notwithstanding subsection (b) of this section, at any time that United States Armed Forces are engaged in hostilities outside the territory of the United States, its possessions and territories without a declaration of war or specific statutory authorization, such forces shall be removed by the President if the Congress so directs by concurrent resolution.

(Pub. L. 93-148, § 5, Nov. 7, 1973, 87 Stat. 556.)

SECTION REFERRED TO IN OTHER SECTIONS

This section is referred to in sections 1545, 1546 of this title.

## § 1545. Congressional priority procedures for joint resolution or bill

**(a) Time requirement; referral to Congressional committee; single report**

Any joint resolution or bill introduced pursuant to section 1544(b) of this title at least thirty calendar days before the expiration of the sixty-day period specified in such section shall be referred to the Committee on Foreign Affairs of the House of Representatives or the Committee on Foreign Relations of the Senate, as the case may be, and such committee shall report one such joint resolution or bill, together with its recommendations, not later than twenty-four calendar days before the expiration of the sixty-day period specified in such section, unless such House shall otherwise determine by the yeas and nays.

**(b) Pending business; vote**

Any joint resolution or bill so reported shall become the pending business of the House in

*1963-2*

question (in the case of the Senate the time for debate shall be equally divided between the proponents and the opponents), and shall be voted on within three calendar days thereafter, unless such House shall otherwise determine by yeas and nays.

### (c) Referral to other House committee

Such a joint resolution or bill passed by one House shall be referred to the committee of the other House named in subsection (a) of this section and shall be reported out not later than fourteen calendar days before the expiration of the sixty-day period specified in section 1544(b) of this title. The joint resolution or bill so reported shall become the pending business of the House in question and shall be voted on within three calendar days after it has been reported, unless such House shall otherwise determine by yeas and nays.

### (d) Disagreement between Houses

In the case of any disagreement between the two Houses of Congress with respect to a joint resolution or bill passed by both Houses, conferees shall be promptly appointed and the committee of conference shall make and file a report with respect to such resolution or bill not later than four calendar days before the expiration of the sixty-day period specified in section 1544(b) of this title. In the event the conferees are unable to agree within 48 hours, they shall report back to their respective Houses in disagreement. Notwithstanding any rule in either House concerning the printing of conference reports in the Record or concerning any delay in the consideration of such reports, such report shall be acted on by both Houses not later than the expiration of such sixty-day period.

(Pub. L. 93-148, § 6, Nov. 7, 1973, 87 Stat. 557.)

### § 1546. Congressional priority procedures for concurrent resolution

#### (a) Referral to Congressional committee; single report

Any concurrent resolution introduced pursuant to section 1544(c) of this title shall be referred to the Committee on Foreign Affairs of the House of Representatives or the Committee on Foreign Relations of the Senate, as the case may be, and one such concurrent resolution shall be reported out by such committee together with its recommendations within fifteen calendar days, unless such House shall otherwise determine by the yeas and nays.

#### (b) Pending business; vote

Any concurrent resolution so reported shall become the pending business of the House in question (in the case of the Senate the time for debate shall be equally divided between the proponents and the opponents) and shall be voted on within three calendar days thereafter, unless such House shall otherwise determine by yeas and nays.

#### (c) Referral to other House committee

Such a concurrent resolution passed by one House shall be referred to the committee of the other House named in subsection (a) of this section and shall be reported out by such committee together with its recommendations within fifteen calendar days and shall thereupon become the pending business of such House and shall be voted upon within three calendar days, unless such House shall otherwise determine by yeas and nays.

#### (d) Disagreement between Houses

In the case of any disagreement between the two Houses of Congress with respect to a concurrent resolution passed by both Houses, conferees shall be promptly appointed and the committee of conference shall make and file a report with respect to such concurrent resolution within six calendar days after the legislation is referred to the committee of conference. Notwithstanding any rule in either House concerning the printing of conference reports in the Record or concerning any delay in the consideration of such reports, such report shall be acted on by both Houses not later than six calendar days after the conference report is filed. In the event the conferees are unable to agree within 48 hours, they shall report back to their respective Houses in disagreement.

(Pub. L. 93-148, § 7, Nov. 7, 1973, 87 Stat. 557.)

### § 1547. Interpretation of joint resolution

#### (a) Inferences from any law or treaty

Authority to introduce United States Armed Forces into hostilities or into situations wherein involvement in hostilities is clearly indicated by the circumstances shall not be inferred—

(1) from any provision of law (whether or not in effect before November 7, 1973), including any provision contained in any appropriation Act, unless such provision specifically authorizes the introduction of United States Armed Forces into hostilities or into such situations and states that it is intended to constitute specific statutory authorization within the meaning of this chapter; or

(2) from any treaty heretofore or hereafter ratified unless such treaty is implemented by legislation specifically authorizing the introduction of United States Armed Forces into hostilities or into such situations and stating that it is intended to constitute specific statutory authorization within the meaning of this chapter.

#### (b) Joint headquarters operations of high-level military commands

Nothing in this chapter shall be construed to require any further specific statutory authorization to permit members of United States Armed Forces to participate jointly with members of the armed forces of one or more foreign countries in the headquarters operations of high-level military commands which were established prior to November 7, 1973, and pursuant to the United Nations Charter or any treaty ratified by the United States prior to such date.

#### (c) Introduction of United States Armed Forces

For purposes of this chapter, the term "introduction of United States Armed Forces" includes the assignment of members of such armed forces to command, coordinate, participate in the movement of, or accompany the

/963 — 3

regular or irregular military forces of any foreign country or government when such military forces are engaged, or there exists an imminent threat that such forces will become engaged, in hostilities.

(d) Constitutional authorities or existing treaties unaffected; construction against grant of Presidential authority respecting use of United States Armed Forces

Nothing in this chapter—

(1) is intended to alter the constitutional authority of the Congress or of the President, or the provisions of existing treaties; or

(2) shall be construed as granting any authority to the President with respect to the introduction of United States Armed Forces into hostilities or into situations wherein involvement in hostilities is clearly indicated by the circumstances which authority he would not have had in the absence of this chapter.

(Pub. L. 93-148, § 8, Nov. 7, 1973, 87 Stat. 558.)

§ 1548. Separability of provisions.

If any provision of this chapter or the application thereof to any person or circumstance is held invalid, the remainder of the chapter and the application of such provision to any other person or circumstance shall not be affected thereby.

(Pub. L. 93-148, § 9, Nov. 7, 1973, 87 Stat. 559.)

*Robert D. Hormats*

# A Bush Doctrine for the '90s

By committing American forces in concert with those of other nations, and by launching a massive diplomatic initiative to muster international support, President Bush has established an important doctrine for post-Cold War U.S. policy—protect American interests with maximum possible international participation.

For three decades American presidents have mainly paid lip service to enlisting foreign support for U.S. military actions overseas. President Bush has made this an operating principle.

This is both wise and necessary. The Soviet threat can no longer justify new U.S. engagement overseas. Expensive or extensive U.S. military initiatives will come under heavy public scrutiny, especially in light of pressing domestic needs.

Americans will insist that U.S. defense commitments to a region not exceed U.S. interests there and that the commitment of U.S. allies not fall short of their interests. Convincing Americans that the United States should continue to play a global leadership role—much less send troops to protect Western or other interests—will be difficult if other nations who benefit from U.S. actions do not contribute proportionally.

Making the Bush Doctrine work will require complicated diplomacy and coalition building.

U.S. officials will need to define the issues at stake—and American interests—in terms broad enough to command support from close allies as well as from nations that are not traditional followers of the United States. In the case of Iraq's invasion of Kuwait, some nations responded to U.S. diplomacy because they abhorred the precedent of territorial conquest; some feared Saddam Hussein gaining a stranglehold on world oil; some recognized the profound geopolitical consequences of a collapse of the balance of power in the area.

In addition, the United States will need increasingly to enlist the Soviet Union as part of the solution rather than, as during the Cold War, see it as part of the problem. Moscow participated as a responsible member of the international community by condemning Iraq. In so doing it strengthened American diplomacy vis-à-vis Baghdad and enabled several of its Third World friends to support the United States in the U.N.

Washington also will need to engage the U.N. Security Council, now unblocked by the end of the superpower impasse, in practical and forceful actions to prevent and resolve disputes. By mobilizing the U.S.S.R., China and many developing nations to vote sanctions against Iraq, and basing its troop commitment to the region solidly on the U.N. Charter, the United States bolstered the legitimacy of its military presence in the Gulf and facilitated the decision of Arab League members to support Saudi Arabia. U.N.-bestowed legitimacy should help Americans normally uncomfortable with sending troops abroad to see this action as consistent with larger international principles.

Making the doctrine work now and in the future will require the president to articulate a convincing rationale for U.S. military involvement. U.S. policy will lose domestic support if the rationale for it becomes confused in the public mind. That in turn would cause allies to question U.S. resolve, distance themselves from U.S. leadership and seek their own deals.

To hold together a military and diplomatic coalition of nations with conflicting interests and priorities, U.S. officials will need to conduct intimate consultations and intelligence sharing with a wider range of governments than ever before. It will also need to launch public affairs programs to explain its position to citizens of countries where public views are not as supportive of the United States as their governments.

These measures will be necessary to prevent other nations from negotiating arrangements that undermine the U.S. position as well as to convince them that the United States will not undermine theirs. American forces will need to coordinate with myriad foreign armies, navies and air forces. U.S. commanders had difficulty doing this with the British and French in World War II. It will be much more difficult for U.S. officers in the Gulf or other hot spots to do so with a multitude of non-U.S. and non-NATO counterparts, yet they must if this doctrine is to work.

Finally, the doctrine will require the United States to balance its desire to act quickly and forcefully with its desire to maintain international support. On occasion, acting boldly will encourage other nations to follow—as in the U.S. troop commitment to Saudi Arabia. But at times Washington might decide to refrain from, modify or delay certain actions on grounds that they jeopardize the coalition it has assembled or the international legitimacy of its policy. This issue has been raised by the U.S. blockade of Iraq. Similarly, the United States might be called on to take positions in behalf of certain principles—such as nonintervention—in circumstances where its immediate interests are not directly at stake in order to be in a stronger position to obtain international support when American interests are at stake.

Complications notwithstanding, the Bush Doctrine, effectively implemented, will strengthen domestic support for U.S. leadership in the 1990s by encouraging other nations to stand with it in promoting common interests.

*The writer is vice chairman of Goldman Sachs International.*

: USW(F)-

: 장 관                                    발신 : 주미대사       등[ ]

:                                              (    매  )

0008

# New Isolationism, Same Old Mistake

By Joshua Muravchik

WASHINGTON

So far, the chief critics of President Bush's bold military action in the Middle East are not liberals but conservatives such as Patrick Buchanan, Robert Novak and Edward Luttwak — yesterday's most redoubtable hawks and interventionists.

The sudden disappearance of the cold-war has pulled the rationale out from under the internationalist foreign policy that America has pursued for 40 years. With a victory over Communism behind us, why care what happens to the Emirate of Kuwait?

One answer is all, but the larger answer that has resonated in President Bush's statements is collective security. No longer divided automatically along East-West lines, the community of nations is joining to repulse an unmistakable act of aggression — just as President Woodrow Wilson hoped it would when he dreamed up the League of Nations. When we recognize in Mr. Bush's policy the heritage of that liberal Democratic president, whose name is synonymous with woolly-headed idealism, we begin to understand why the Buchanans, Nunns and Novaks are alarmed.

They see themselves not as isolationists but as realists. They don't want to spend American treasure and lives unless clear American interests are at stake. With the collapse of Soviet power, however, the difference between realism and isolationism is evaporating. When America is the world's only superpower, nothing threatens us directly.

All plausible threats are indirect and most are a lot more remote than the prospect of a belligerent, anti-Western tyrant gaining hegemony over the world petroleum trade. That even such stakes as these leave the conservative realists skeptical of visionary schemes. Thanks in part to their prudence, within 20 years we were fighting for our lives.

In our collective memory, Wilson's idealism shares blame equally with isolationism. for that disaster. The system of collective security that he sired came crashing down as soon as it was tested by the Japanese in Manchuria and then by Mussolini in Abyssinia. But was Wilson's vision faulty? Or did the fault lie with the isolationists who, by keeping America out of the League of Nations, made collective security a hollow shell while the aggressors gathered strength?

Today's United Nations-sponsored mission to restore Kuwait's independence is giving the idea of collective security a new trial. Thanks to forceful American leadership, the effort is likely to succeed. Without it, the U.N. would be as feckless as the League was in the 1930's.

American action shows how close to isolationist their sensibility is.

The last time America found itself in such an impregnable situation was in the immediate aftermath of World War I. The Kaiser had been defeated. New democracies were being erected on the ruins of old empires. Mussolini and Hitler were a couple of marginal eccentrics. Bolshevism scared some people, but most regarded it as an aberration. No wonder our isolationists succeeded in defeating Wilson's

---

### Our last bout with that approach ended at Pearl Harbor.

---

time when the U.S. can relinquish the prerogative of acting unilaterally to defend its interests or principles is not yet on the horizon.

But where Mr. Bush is right, as was Wilson, is on the principle of investing America's power in the effort to fashion an environment congenial to our long-term safety by enforcing a modicum of lawfulness in relations among states. An implicit assumption is that we cannot know what threats may lurk in the post-Communist world any more than we could foresee in 1920 the strength of Nazism or Communism. A corollary is that our abdication will encourage such threats to grow.

The realist-isolationists would rather bask in our status as the sole surviving superpower and avoid the risk and expense of policing the world. There will be time enough to act, they will say, when some local quarrel or bully grows large enough to present a clear danger to us. And so there was after the attack on Pearl Harbor, too.                          □

Joshua Muravchik is resident scholar at the American Enterprise Institute.

1961-2

August 28, 1990
NYT

원 본

# 외 무 부

종 별 :

번 호 : USW-3925                     일 시 : 90 0829 1400

수 신 : 장관( 미북,미안,중근동)

발 신 : 주미대사

제 목 : 이락사태-의회 반응(2)

1.작 8.28(화) 에 있는 BUSH 대통령의 미의원들에 대한 브리핑에 이어, 미상,하원은 8.31(금) 부터 4일간 양원 지도부 인사가 이끄는 두그룹의 의원단을 사우디, 바레인 및 이집트에 파견할 예정임.

2.민주,공화 양당 의원들로 구성될 동 의원단은 행정부와의 긴밀한 협의아래 이루어지는 것으로 의원들의 개별 방문이 미칠 사우디 주둔군에대한 불편 최소화 및미 정책에관한 일관된 노선 유지의 필요성에대한 고려에서 행하여 지는 것임.

3.하원 의원단은 RICHARD GEPHARDT 원내 총무를 단장으로 30여명의 의원, 상원 의원단은 CLAIBORNE PELL 외무 위원장이 이끄는 10명의 의원들로 구성될 것으로 알려짐.

(대사 박동진- 국장)

---

미주국     1차보     미주국     중아국

PAGE 1                                      90.08.30   05:51 CG

외신 1과 통제관

0009

원 본

# 외 무 부

종 별 :

번 호 : USW-3926                          일 시 : 90 0829 1400

수 신 : 장관( 미북, 미안, 중근동)

발 신 : 주미대사

제 목 : 이락사태- 의회 반응( 3)

1. 미 상원 외무위 공화당 간사 RICHARD LUGAR(인디아나) 의원은 작 8.28. 기자 간담회를 통해 동 아시아 7개국 순방결과에 대하여 설명한후 가진 질의응답에서 이락사태에대한 한국정부의 대미정책 지원에 관하여 언급 하였는바, 골자는 아래와 같음.

가. 노 대통령은 중동에서의 미국의 군사 전략지원을 위하여 한국 국적의 수송선(CARGOTRANSPORT PLANE) 을 제공할 것이라고 발표 함.

나. 한국 정부는 이락 제재 UN 결의안에 대하여 즉각적인 지지를 표명하였으며 미국에대한 뚜렷한 지지를 인정받기를 희망하였음. 주한미대사는 이에 대하여 한국 국적선이 태극마크를 부착한채 미군지원에 동원 된다면 소기의 성과를 거둘수 있을것이라고 언급 하였음.

2. LUGAR 의원은 아울러 화학무기를 보유하고 핵무기 개발을 추진하는 후세인의존재가 중동지역의 안정에 장애가 되는 까닭에 미국의 대이락 전략목표에 후세인 제거가 포함되어야 한다고 주장하였음.

첨부:한국 관련 질의 응답 ( USW(F)-1968 (1매)

(대사 박동진-국장)

| 미주국 | 차관 | 1차보 | 2차보 | 미주국 | 중아국 | | | | |
|--------|------|-------|-------|--------|--------|--|--|--|--|

외신 1과  통제관

0010

Q     To what extent in your travels did you see the perception that the situation in the Middle East is a conflict between the US and Iraq more than we would wish it perceived that way?  And then what do you think should be done (relative to ?) that?

SEN. LUGAR:  I found universally, in all seven stops, that the conflict was perceived as a United Nations effort.  It was not perceived as a US-versus-Iraq affair.  And the question almost always came back to the interests of the particular country in how aggressive it would be in supporting the UN or in making a visible sign of support for the United States.

Now, by the time we got to Korea, for example, seventh stop, almost two weeks later, the President of Korea, Roh Tae Woo, just prior to my visit with him had announced that a cargo transport plane -- a Korean plane on a Korean vessel be helped in transport -- would be made available to the general operation.

They had quickly supported the UN sanctions there, but they wanted a visible show of support for the United States and they wanted to make that known.  Our ambassador encouraged that they paint the plane clearly in Korean colors and fly (?) it to the United States and make it manifest that they had that kind of support.  They made no comment on that, but nevertheless, they're making something available.

| 관리<br>번호 | 90-1646 |
|---|---|

외 무 부

종 별 : 지급

번 호 : USW-4000

일 시 : 90 0904 1825

수 신 : 장관(미북)민안,중근동)

발 신 : 주 미 대사

제 목 : 이락 사태-의회 반응(4)

1. 미 하원 외무위(FASCELL 위원장)는 금 9.4(화) BAKER 국무장관을 참석시킨 가운데 이락사태에 관한 청문회를 개최함.

2. BAKER 장관은 모두 증언에서 이락 사태가 미국뿐 아니라 국제 사회 전체의 안정과 질서를 해치는 중대한 사태임을 강조하고 동 사태에 임하는 미 행정부의 정책 목표와 외교, 경제, 군사 전략및 외교적 노력에 관하여 설명함(주요 내용 전문 FAX 송부함)

-주요 증언 내용

A 가) 이락 사태의 본질

-이락의 쿠웨이트 점령은 냉전 체제 이후, 세계 질서 구상에 정치적인 시금석이 될것임.

-전략적 차원에서 미국은 혼란 상태의 중동 지역에서 이락의 무력 사용과 미국에 대한 협박은 문제 해결의 올바른 방안이 아님을 입증하여야함.

-경제적으로 전세계가 중동의 석유 자원에 의존하고 있음을 재 인식해야함.

나)이락 사태에 대한 미국의 정책 목표

-쿠웨이트로부터 이락군의 즉각적이며 무조건의 완전한 철수

-합법적 쿠웨이트 정권의 복귀

-이락, 쿠웨이트 잔류 미국인 인질의 보호

-페르시아만의 안보와 안정

3. 베이커 장관의 증언후 가진 질의 응답 요지는 아래임.

가)질의

-미국의 정책 목표에 후세인 축출과 쿠웨이트 왕정의 복귀 포함 여부(HIMILTON)

-미국의 단기적 정책 목표인 이락군의 쿠웨이트 철수가 이루어진다고 할경우,

---

| 미주국 | 장관 | 차관 | 1차보 | 2차보 | 미주국 | 중아국 | 청와대 | 안기부 |
|---|---|---|---|---|---|---|---|---|

90.09.05    08:28

외신 2과 통제관 FE

0012

이락의 화학, 핵무기들을 포함한 군사력을 제어할 방도(SOLARZ)

　-사우디 주둔 미군 병력 유지 비용 분담 문제(GILMAN)

　-중장기적 에너지 정책 수립의 필요성(TORRICELLI)

　-WAR POWERS RESOLUTION 발효 여부(GEJDENSON)

나)답변

　-후세인 축출 여부는 기본적으로 이락 국민들이 결정할 문제임.

　-이락의 군사력 제어 방안및 미국의 정책 목표 성취는 중동 지역에서의 새로운 안보 구조(SECURITY STRUCTURE)를 통해 모색될것임.

　-우방국들과의 방위비 분담 논의는 책임 분담(RESPONSIBILITY SHARING)의 차원에서 고려되는것이며 미국만이 우방국 서로간의 책임 분담을 조정할수 있는 입장에 있는 국가임.

　-WAR POWERS RESOLUTION 은 행정부와 의회가 전쟁 행위에 대하여 공동 책임을 진다는 기본 정신하에서 논의되어야한다는점에는 동의함.

4. 당관 관찰

가. 이락 사태에 관한 동 청문회는 미 의회가 하기 휴회에서 돌아온후 처음으로 개최하는것으로서, 참석한 의원들은 한결같이 현재까지의 미 행정부의 노력(특히, 유엔을 통한 국제적 지지 유도)에 찬사를 보냄.

나. 베이커 장관은 이락 사태가 기본적으로 외교적 노력을 통하여 해결되어야 한다는점(SECURITY STRUCTURE 구상등)을 누차 강조하였으며, 미 행정부의 노력이 성공하기 위하여 미 의회와 행정부간의 긴밀한 협조가 필요함을 강조하였음.

다. 그러나 참석 의원들은 동 사태에 대한 미 행정부의 장기적 정책 모표(중동 지역의 안보및 석유 수급의 안정)와 에너지 정책및 WAR POWERS RESOLUTION 에 대한 논란 여지를 제기함으로서 이락 사태에 대한 의회의 제반 관심 사항을 노정시켰음.

5. 이락 사태에 관하여 미 의회에서는 9.5(수) 상원 외교위 9.11(화) 상원 군사위 주최 청문회가 예정되어 있음.

　첨부베이커 증언 USW(F)-2069

　(대사 박동진-국장)

　90.12.31 까지

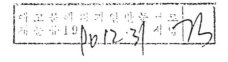

PAGE 2

0013

Embargoed until 2:00 pm Tuesday September 4, 1990

USW[月~2069
수신: 장관 (미북·미안·중르동)
발신: 주미대사
제목:                    (14매)

## America's Stake in the Persian Gulf Crisis

Statement

By

The Honorable James A. Baker, III

Before

The House Foreign Affairs Committee

Tuesday,

September 4, 1990

2069—1

0014

I have come here today to speak to you -- and through you to the American people -- about the conflict in the Persian Gulf and what it means for the United States.

I would like to use my statement today to place this crisis in a larger context. The entire world has mobilized to redress aggression against a small country in a distant place. Already, we're paying higher prices when we pull up to the local gas pump. And thousands of our finest young men and women now stand guard in the heat of the Persian Gulf.

The President has made it plain we have a straightforward responsibility to the American people: Openly and clearly, we have a duty to state what is at stake as a result of Saddam Hussein's invasion of Kuwait. We have a duty to tell our people what our immediate goals are in this conflict. And we have a duty to explain how we plan to achieve those goals in order to further our long-run interests in the Gulf and beyond.

The Stakes

Let me start by discussing what's at stake.

First, Iraq's unprovoked aggression is a political test of how the post-Cold War world will work. Amidst the revolutions sweeping the globe and the transformation of East-West

2069 -2

0015

relations, we stand at a critical juncture in history. The Iraqi invasion of Kuwait is one of the defining moments of a new era -- an era full of promise but also one replete with new challenges. While the rules of the road developed during the Cold War did, in the end, preserve East-West peace in Europe, the task now is to build an enduring peace that is global in scope, not limited just to Europe and not rooted in confrontation and tension.

If we are to build a stable and more comprehensive peace, we must respond to the defining moments of this new era, recognizing the emerging dangers lurking before us. We are entering an era in which ethnic and sectarian identities could easily breed new violence and conflict. It is an era in which new hostilities and threats could erupt as misguided leaders are tempted to assert regional dominance before the ground rules of a new order can be accepted.

Accordingly, we face a simple choice: Do we want to live in a world where aggression is made less likely because it is met with a powerful response from the international community, a world where civilized rules of conduct apply? Or are we willing to live in a world where aggression can go unchecked, where aggression succeeds because we cannot muster the collective will to challenge it?

Sadly, Saddam Hussein's attack on Kuwait will not be the last act of aggression that international society will face. So long as ruthless aggressors remain, the reality of international life is that such predatory designs will emerge

2069-3

0016

from time to time. But the current crisis is a first
opportunity to limit such dangers, to reinforce the standards
for civilized behavior found in the United Nations Charter, and
to help shape a more peaceful international order built on the
promise of recent trends in Europe and elsewhere. We must
seize this opportunity to solidify the ground rules of the new
order.

Second, from a strategic standpoint, we must show that
intimidation and force are not successful ways of doing
business in the volatile Middle East -- or anywhere else. The
combination of unresolved regional conflicts, turbulent social
and political changes, weapons of mass destruction, and much of
the world's energy supplies makes the Middle East particularly
combustible. No one is immune from conflicts in the Middle
East. And no one can feel safe when the danger of war
escalating in the Middle East is so high.

If we want to encourage peaceful change and preserve the
security of all our friends in the area, we must remain a
reliable partner for peace. We must help demonstrate that
Saddam Hussein's violent way is an anachronism, not the wave of
the future.

Third, and perhaps most obviously, what is at stake
economically is the dependence of the world on access to the
energy resources of the Persian Gulf. The effects on our
economy and our people are already being felt. But this is not
about increases in the price of a gallon of gas at your local

0017

service station.  It is not just a narrow question of the flow
of oil from Kuwait and Iraq.  It is about a dictator who acting
alone and unchallenged could strangle the global economic
order, determining by fiat whether we all enter a recession, or
even the darkness of a depression.

A sustained oil price spiral -- similar to what happened in
1973 and again in 1979 -- could easily cause higher inflation
and interest rates worldwide, sending us all into a sustained
recessionary slide.  The burden could become particularly great
for the new democracies of Eastern Europe, threatening to undo
the revolutions of 1989.  It would also be painfully felt in
the poorer countries of Central America, South Asia, and Africa
-- threatening those who are now embracing market-oriented
reforms and striving to improve living standards for their
impoverished millions.

Simply put, these are the stakes raised by Iraq's invasion
against Kuwait.  How have we and the international community
responded to them?

Our Objectives

For the United States, the President has identified four
immediate goals:

One, the immediate, complete, and unconditional withdrawal
of all Iraqi forces from Kuwait as mandated in United Nations
Security Council Resolution 660;

0018

Two, the restoration of Kuwait's legitimate government;

Three, the protection of the lives of American citizens held hostage by Iraq, both in Iraq and in Kuwait; and

Four, a commitment to the security and stability of the Persian Gulf.

Our strategy is to lead a global political alliance to isolate Iraq -- politically, economically, and militarily. In this way, we aim to make Iraq pay such a high price for its aggression that it will be forced to withdraw from Kuwait and release Americans and others held hostage. This in turn will allow the restoration of Kuwait's legitimate government. It will also improve the opportunities for long-term security and stability in the Persian Gulf in a way that builds on the unprecedented international consensus that has already been formed.

Implementing the Strategy

Our strategy has moved on two mutually-supporting tracks toward these aims. Let me summarize our efforts.

Diplomatically, we have worked from the beginning to foster a coordinated international response to Iraq's aggression. The results have been extraordinary and unprecedented. Five unanimous United Nations Security Council resolutions have been passed. And Iraq is now isolated.

0019

We are gratified by the responsible and productive work we
have been able to undertake with the other Permanent Members --
Britain, France, the Soviet Union, and the People's Republic of
China -- as well as the support the Arab League and the
Non-Aligned Movement have provided.

In particular, the Soviet Union has proven a responsible
partner, suggesting new possibilities for active superpower
cooperation in resolving regional conflicts. The President
will work to further strengthen our ties of partnership when he
meets President Gorbachev in Helsinki this Sunday. In taking
the long view, we should remember what this conflict would have
looked like if old-style zero-sum thinking was still driving
Soviet policy in the Gulf.

NATO, the EC, and the West European Union have pitched in
magnificently. Our NATO ally, Turkey, should also be singled
out for its fast, effective, and courageous cooperation.
Finally, a broad regional coalition -- including Egypt, Saudi
Arabia, Kuwait, the Gulf states, and Syria -- have done much to
foster a international cohesion.

In this regard, let me make a larger point: From the early
days of this Administration, we have made a concerted effort --
with our friends in Asia and Europe, with the Soviets, and with
organizations like NATO and the EC -- to focus on the explosive
dangers inherent in regional conflicts. In response to Iraq's
invasion, we have drawn upon the new international ties being
shaped by this strategy.

0020

The Kuwaitis themselves deserve our compassion and
respect. They have suffered a brutal invasion, their country
pillaged, their lives traumatized. There has been a tragic
loss of life, and thousands of Kuwaitis have fled to
neighboring states, escaping in many cases with only the
clothes on their back.

The Kuwaitis, however, are fighting back heroically. They
are not collaborating with the Iraqi occupiers. All elements
of Kuwaiti society -- from religious conservatives to secular
liberals -- have voiced support for the restoration of the
government. An indigenous Kuwaiti resistance has emerged. It
carries on the struggle against Iraqi aggression from inside
Kuwait. Moreover, the government of Kuwait in exile is
providing financial aid to support our military effort and to
help alleviate economic disruptions that have occurred in such
states as Egypt.

In short, Kuwait has been occupied, not conquered.

The political coalition, bound by the principle that Saddam
Hussein must be denied the fruits of aggression, has created an
economic embargo under UN auspices that is solidly in place.
Iraq's import-dependent economy is beginning to feel the
strain, and international pressures will continue to grow over
time as shortages mount. Sanction busters may be tempted by
the lure of financial profits, but Security Council Resolution
665 which permits enforcement by appropriate means should
ensure that Iraq's opportunities to export its oil and import
key materials will be severely constrained over time. 0021

Saddam Hussein aggression has exacted a broad range of
economic costs for countries across both the region and globe.
The destruction of the Kuwaiti economy by Iraqi invaders has
caused major economic dislocations for our friends in the
region, notably Egypt and Turkey. Other countries with fragile
economies, especially in Eastern Europe, are bearing heavy
costs. The need to offset the burden of our own military
efforts must also be addressed.

As the President announced last Thursday, we have initiated
an action plan to meet these needs. Our friends around the
world are responding. Saudi Arabia is meeting a large share of
the fuel costs for this effort. And other Gulf states are
providing fuel and financial resources to the affected states.

The President has also asked Secretary Brady and myself to
to go to key nations in the Gulf, Europe, and Asia to help
mobilize and coordinate the international effort. We will
attempt to ensure that the costs and responsibilities are
shared equitably and that our various efforts complement one
another. The aim is to address the vital needs of affected
parties and to maintain the solidarity of the international
coalition.

Time can be on the side of the international community.
Diplomacy can be made to work.

2069-9

0022

On the military track, over twenty-five countries are now supplying men and materiel in support of the Security Council resolutions. US military objectives are to deter an Iraqi attack on Saudi Arabia and to insure the effective implementation of the United Nations sanctions. Our military forces are also there to protect American lives and to provide an effective and decisive military response should Iraq escalate its aggression to active combat with the multinational force.

Once the present danger passes, however, we must not let its lessons go unheeded. We have a responsibility to assure the American people that a decade from now, their sons and daughters will not be put in jeopardy because we failed to work toward long-run solutions to the problems of the Gulf.

The historic international consensus we have built can become a solid foundation for successfully meeting our immediate objectives and building a safer future. It can foster a future Gulf environment that will protect our interests and help us avoid having to make this kind of massive diplomatic and military effort again.

In the long run, we seek a stable Gulf in which the nations of that region and their peoples can live in peace, free of the fear of coercion. We seek a region in which change can occur and legitimate security concerns can be preserved peacefully. And we seek a region in which energy supplies flow freely.

0023

We will need to work together with governments in the Gulf and outside of it to build a more durable order.  We will want to ensure that our friends in the area have the means to deter aggression and defend themselves, making it less necessary to send American men and women to help them.  And we will work with the rest of the regional and international community to prevent further Iraqi expansionism as well as Iraqi efforts to acquire and produce weapons of mass destruction.

Resolution of today's threat should also become a springboard for a sustained international effort to curb the proliferation of chemical, biological, and nuclear weapons and ballistic missiles in the region and elsewhere.  It can become a springboard for revived efforts to resolve the conflicts which lie at the root of such proliferation, including the festering conflict between Israel and its Palestinian and Arab neighbors.

It is not enough to demonstrate that aggression and intimidation don't pay; we must show that a pathway to reconciliation and peace does exist, and that it can be found with good will and good faith on all sides.

The Implications for America's Role in the World

Mr. Chairman, let me conclude by placing Saddam Hussein's invasion of Kuwait in historical perspective.

0024

For over four decades, the central fact of international relations was the conflict between East and West. The Cold War reverberated across the globe, affecting everyone everywhere. Much of America's foreign policy was either driven by, or derivative of, our efforts to contain Stalinist aggression.

Now, the central dispute of the post-war period -- the East-West conflict over the future of Europe -- has been transformed. Last year's people power revolutions in Central and Eastern Europe swept away the dictatorships of the past. In their place, the people are finding freedom. Europe is becoming whole and free, and Germany will be united in peace and freedom.

An enlightened Soviet leadership has encouraged peaceful, democratic change as the only legitimate road to progress. This Administration has actively engaged the new thinkers and reformers in the Soviet Union. Together, we are finding common interests that will unite East and West. Partnership is replacing conflict.

As I have said many times before, America's role in this sea change in world politics is straightforward: We must leave behind not only the Cold War but also the conflicts that preceded it.

And this is why -- as the President has said from the outset -- Iraq's aggression cannot stand.

0025

The line in the sands of Arabia is also a line in time.  By crossing into Kuwait, Saddam Hussein took a dangerous step back in history.  Maybe he thought the world would consider Kuwait expendable, that we would think of it as just a small, faraway country of which we knew and cared little.  Possibly he remembered the 1930s when the League of Nations failed to respond effectively to Mussolini's aggression against Abyssinia, what is today Ethiopia.  Clearly, Saddam Hussein thought his crime would pay.

But the world has decided otherwise.  He must not be allowed to hold on to what he stole.

The President has made our position clear:  The world must stand united to defend the principles enshrined in the United Nations Charter.

In this effort, America must lead and our people must understand that.  We remain the one nation that has the necessary political, military, and economic instruments at our disposal to catalyze a successful collective response by the international community.

Geographically, we stand apart from much of the world, separated by the Atlantic and the Pacific.  But politically, economically, and strategically, there are no oceans, and in a world without oceans, a policy of isolationism is no option at all.  Only American engagement can shape the peaceful world our people so deeply desire.

0026

We believe this▆▆ rdinated and comprehens     international
isolation of Iraq is the only peaceful path to meeting the
objectives set by the President.  Our efforts will, however,
take time and that is what we ask most of the American people:
Stand firm.  Be patient.  And remain united so that together we
can show that aggression does not pay.

2069-14

주 미 대 사 관

번호 : USW(F) - 2070

수신 : 장관 (미북, 미안, 중근동)

발신 : 주미대사

제목 : 이락사태 - 의회반응 (표지포함 8매)

연 : USW(F) - 2069

금 9.4 (화) 하원 외무위 주관 이락사태에 관한

청문회시 주요 결의 응답 요지을 별첨 송부함. 끝

0028

04 Sept. 90
Congressional Section/
Chris Moore

The House Committee on Foreign Affairs held a hearing today on
the Persian Gulf situation; James Baker III, Secretary of State,
was the only witness (see attached written testimony). The
following is a brief summary of the major points discussed during
the question and answer session.

U.S. Objectives in Securing Stability/Security in Persian Gulf

Under questioning from Rep. Lee Hamilton (D-IN), Secretary Baker
stated that the U.S. is committed to stability in the Gulf region
and that "out of necessity" this involves extending the U.S.
commitment to other nations bseides Saudi Arabia and Kuwait.

When Hamilton asked whether the Administration is seeking to
remove Hussein from power, Baker responded that this is not a
"stated" objective of the U.S. but that if the Iraqi people were
to vote to remove Hussein from office, "it would not make us
terribly unhappy."

When Rep. Stephen Solarz (D-NY) asked whether the Administration
is in agreement with the Arab states that have called for Iraq to
make reparation payments to Kuwait, Baker responded that it is
not one of the Administration's present objectives but that the
U.S. would be sympathetic to this goal as well as to reparations
for "individuals" affected by the Iraqi invasion of Kuwait.

Baker later elaborated on the new security structure the
Administration is seeking at the conclusion of the Persian Gulf
Crisis:

1. Major Arab participation in a security alliance.
2. A roll-back of Iraq's chemical capability.
3. Containment of Iraq's nuclear capability.

When asked by Rep. Pete Kostmayer (D-PA) how long the present
stalemate would continue, Baker responded that the Administration
has not put a time frame on its operation.

Egypt's Military Debt

Baker told the committee that Egyptian President Mubarak has
provided outstanding leadership during this crisis and that his
country needs to be helped financially by other governments in an
effort to alleviate the injuries suffered because of the economic
embargo against Iraq.

2070-2                                        0029

## Burdensharing

In response to Rep. Benjamin Gilman's (R-NY) question "Who's sharing the burden?" Baker said that 26 countries are helping the United States militarily share the "responsibility" of defending peace in the Middle East while the Administration has begun the process of soliciting non-military aid from other nations who are not in a position to participate militarily. Baker mentioned that Treasury Secretary Nicholas Brady is in Asia to talk to Japan, South Korea and Taiwan about their role in the initiative.

## Soviet Union's role in Persian Gulf Initiative

While Baker conceded that it is "inappropriate" for anyone to be aiding the Iraqis militarily, he said the Administration "could not have gotten to this point" without the enlightened leadership of the Soviet Union. Baker said he plans to discuss the role of Soviet military advisers in Iraq at a meeting later this week.

## War Powers Act (WPA)

Baker affirmed the Administration's opposition to the 60-day clause in the WPA and said that "in the absence of remedial legislation" the Administration would uphold its position that the clause is unconstitutional. Chairman Dante Fascell (D-FL) commented that the Congress can act on this matter but deferred debate on this topic until future hearings.

2070-3 끝

0030

관리
번호 91-1670

# 외 무 부

종 별 : 지 급

번 호 : USW-4023                                일 시 : 90 0905 1639

수 신 : 장관(미북,미안,중근동,기정)

발 신 : 주 미 대사

제 목 : 이락사태-의회 반응(5)

연:USW-4000

1. 금 9.5 10:00 시 상원외교위는 BAKER 국무장관을 출석시킨가운데 걸프만에서의 미국의 정책이라는 제하의 청문회를 개최하였음.

2. 금일 청문회시 BAKER 장관의 증언(하원 청문회 증언문과 동일)및 답변내용은 작일 하원 외무위 주관 청문회와 크게 상이한바는 없으나 궁극적 안정과 세력 균형을 정착시키기위한 새로운 지역안보체제의 구축이 필요함을 재강조하였음. 아울러 동장관은 동안보체제는 지역내 질서 구축, 침략저지를 목적으로하고 특히 이락의 팽창주의와 대량 살륙무기 개발을 저지하는 성격의 체제가 되어야하나 형태에 대해서는 상금 구체적으로 검토한적은 없으며, 핵무기 사용(NUCLEAR COUNTER BALANCE)을 전제로한 NATO 와는 다른 형태가 될수 밖에 없을것이라고 언급함.

3. BAKER 장관은 이라크 침공사태에 대한 평화적인 해결에 주력하고 있으며광범위한 경제 제재조치가 종국적으로 실효를 거두리라고 기대하고 있으나, 동조치가 실효를 거두기 위해서는 대국민과 의회의 계속적인 지지가 필요함을 강조하였음.

4. 의원들의 질의에서는 국제 기구인 유엔의 역할 재인식과 세계 에너지 수급안정 방안, 이락사태해결에 대한 소련의 역할, 팔레스타인 문제를 포함한 광범위한 문제해결 강구 가능성, 사태가 장기화될 경우 미행정부의 입지 약화를 방지하기 위한 고려에서 WAR POWERS RESOLUTION 논의 필요성이 지적되었음.

5. 상기 관련, 주요 질의 응답 요지는 별전 FAX USW(F)-2081 송부함.

(대사 박동진-국장)

예고:90.12.31 까지

| 미주국<br>대책반 | 장관 | 차관 | 1차보 | 2차보 | 미주국 | 중아국 | 청와대 | 안기부 |
|---|---|---|---|---|---|---|---|---|

번호: USF(W)-2◼︎
수신: 장관 (미북. 미안. 중근동)  , 발신: 주미대사      "첨부"
제목: 이락사태 - 의회반응 (청문회 론의·송답요지)
(1 때)

Despite reports that the Administration is planning a NATO-clone
security structure once the Persian Gulf Crisis is resolved,
Secretary of State James Baker III told members of the Senate
Foreign Relations Committee today that the Administration has "no
particular model in mind." Baker said his allusion yesterday to
NATOs peacekeeping ability in post-war Europe was just an allegory
and was not meant to signal that the Administration intends to
support a "NATO of the Middle East."

Baker said the Administration is still in the "very, very
preliminary" stages of thinking about any future security apparatus
in the Middle East. He said it is too early to say what role, if
any, the U.S. will play in maintaining peace in the Middle East,
but did say that a continued U.S. naval presence is a possibility.

In a day of mostly praise for the Administration's Persian Gulf
policy, the only sour note came when Sen. Joseph Biden (D-DE)
called the Administration's objective of reinstating Kuwait's
government at the time of the Iraqi invasion "a mistake." Baker
responded to Biden's and Chairman Claiborne Pell's (D-RI)
questioning on whether the U.S. should make reinstatement of the
emir of Kuwait its policy by pointing out that government
liberalization efforts had been made before the invasion and that
it is up to the Kuwaiti people to decide this issue.

The Administration's burden-sharing efforts were also discussed at
today's hearing. Sen. John Kerry (D-MA) lamented that other
nations have sent little ground troop support and asked whether
the U.S. should put the overall Persian Gulf effort directly under
U.N. supervision. Baker countered that the Administration is not
seeking direct U.N. supervision "at this juncture" and that he sees
a "good chance" of other countries sending additional ground
troops.

On financial burden-sharing, or, to use Baker's term,
"responsibility-sharing," Baker said the Administration will have
a better idea of what countries will be able to contribute and
where the money will go once he and Treasury Secretary Nicholas
Brady complete their trips to discuss the Persian Gulf situation
with other nations. Baker later said his planned trip to the
Middle East is not a "fund-raising trip" but that money would
certainly be part of the agenda.

Baker also said he would be discussing the role of Soviet military
advisors in Iraq with members of the Soviet delegation he will be
meeting with this weekend in Helsinki.

0032

# 페르시아湾 事態에 관한
# 베이커 美 国務長官 議会 證言 内容

90.9

外 務 部

0033

베이커 美 國務長官은 美下院 外務委( 9 . 4 ) 및
上院 外交委( 9 . 5 ) 聽聞會에 各各 出席, 페르시아灣
事態에 입하는 美國의 政策 目標와 戰略 및 外交的
努力에 관해 證言하였는바, 그 主要内容을 報告드립니다

## 主要 證言 内容

o 페르시아灣 事態 關聯, 美國의 利害關係 説明

  - 冷戰 以後의 新 國際秩序 形成期의 試金石인
    今番 事態를 통해 유엔 憲章 等의 基本 規範
    強化 必要

  - 中東이나 余他 어느 곳에서도 脅迫과 武力으로
    問題 解決에 成功할 수 없음을 보여주어야 할
    戰略的 考慮

  - 中東 石油에 대한 世界的 依存度에 비추어 사담
    후세인에 의한 世界 經濟秩序 破壞 行爲 防止

o 美國의 短期的 政策 目標 再強調

  - 쿠웨이트로부터 이라크軍의 即刻的이고 完全한
    無條件 撤收

  - 쿠웨이트 正統 政府의 復歸

0034

- 이라크, 쿠웨이트 殘留 美國人 人質의 生命 保護

- 페르시아灣의 安保와 安定 確保

o 事態 解決을 위한 美國의 外交的. 軍事的 措置가 成功的인 것으로 評價

o 美國의 國際的 役割의 重要性 强調 및 地域紛爭 解決을 위한 一致된 國際的 努力 必要性 强調

- 友邦國들에 대한 公平한 責任과 費用 分擔 要請

- 이를위해 베이커 國務長官 自身과 브래디 財務長官이 韓國 等 友邦國을 巡訪 豫定임

## 質疑 応答時 答辯 内容

o 후세인 逐出 與否는 이라크 國民들이 決定할 問題

o 中東地域의 窮極的 安定과 平和定着을 위한 새로운 地域 安保體制 構築 必要性 言及

- 美 海軍의 持續的인 페르시아灣 駐屯 必要性 示唆

o 友邦國들과의 費用分擔 論議는 責任分擔 차원에서 考慮되는 것임을 强調하고 美國만이 友邦國間의 責任分擔 調整役을 遂行할 수 있다고 言及

0035

$\boxed{\text{評 価}}$

o 부쉬 行政府가 페르시아灣에서 長期的 目標 및 戰略을 樹立하지 못하고 있으며 美國의 介入 必要性을 國民에게 納得시키지 못하고 있다는 批判에 대한 行政府의 立場 表明

o 議會의 超黨的 支持 確認을 통한 부쉬 行政府의 政策 妥當性 再確認 및 立場 强化

o 베이커 長官은 蘇聯의 協調에 讚辭를 보내면서 外交的 努力을 통한 事態의 解決을 强調하였는바 向後 蘇聯의 보다 積極的인 協力을 誘導하기 위한 努力을 倍加할 것으로 展望

   - 9.9(日) 헬싱키 美.蘇 頂上會談時 페灣 事態 早速 解決을 위한 蘇聯의 積極的 參與 要請 豫想

                                              - 끝 -

┌──────────┐
│ 원    본 │
└──────────┘

# 외 무 부

종    별 : 긴 급

번    호 : USW-4128                     일    시 : 90 0911 2337

수    신 : 장관(미북,미안,중근동,기정)

발    신 : 주 미 대사

제    목 : 이락사태-의회 반응(6)

1. 미상원 군사위(NUNN 위원장)는 금 9.11 CHENEY 국방장관, POWELL 합참의장을 참석시킨 가운데 페르시아만의 위기에 임하는 미 행정부의 군사 전략에 관한 청문회를 개최함.(CHENEY 장관및 POWELL 합참의장 모두 발언문 FAX 송부)

2.4 시간여에 걸친 금일 청문회에서 참석한 의원들은 우방국들의 방위비 책임분담, 사우디 주둔 미군 병력의 수준, 파병 미군에 대한 재정적 보상책, 주둔군의 명령체계등에 관하여 질문함.

3. 당관 관찰

가. 이락 사태에 임하는 미행정부의 군사 전략에 관하여, 공식적으로는 처음으로 개최된 금일 청문회에서 CHENEY 국방장관은 페르시아만 파병 미군 병력 수준이 14 만명에 이르며, 동 지역에서의 긴급 사태에 대비하여 병력이 당분간 증강될 계획임을 밝힘.

나. 많은 의원들은 우방국들이 구두로 성의만 표명할뿐 실질적인 기여가 결여되어 있음(일본, 독일 지칭)을 누차 지적하고, 심한 불만을 표명함으로서 금후 동맹국에 대한 미 의회 차원의 압력이 고조될것임을 시사함.

첨부 USW(F)-2177

(대사 박동진-국장)

·90.12.31 까지

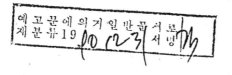

PAGE 1                                              90.09.12    13:39

외신 2과  통제관 FE

0037

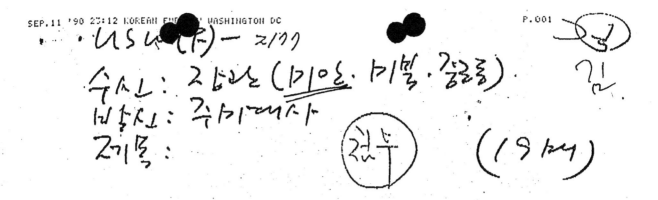

STATEMENT BY

HONORABLE RICHARD B. CHENEY

SECRETARY OF DEFENSE

BEFORE THE

SENATE ARMED SERVICES COMMITTEE

ON

OPERATION DESERT SHIELD

11 SEPTEMBER 1990

*Not for Publication*
*Until Released by the Committee*

0038

Mr. Chairman, members of the committee, it is a pleasure to appear before you this afternoon to discuss the recent events in the Persian Gulf region.  Today, United States military forces are involved in one of the most significant multinational operations that has occurred in the past 40 years.  The long-term implications of this operation for our military force structure, strategy, US presence and security relationships in the region, and economic security are equally significant.

The events of this crisis are well known.  On August 2nd, Iraqi armed forces, without provocation or warning, invaded the sovereign nation of Kuwait.  Facing negligible resistance from its much smaller neighbor, Iraq's tanks stormed through Kuwait in blitzkrieg fashion in a few short hours.  Witnesses report hundreds of casualties.  The invasion was clearly "naked aggression."

International indignation and condemnation was immediate.  The United Nations Security Council voted overwhelmingly to condemn the invasion and demand the Iraqis immediate and total withdrawal.

President Bush acted quickly and decisively.  Immediately after the invasion, he ordered an embargo of all trade with Iraq and, together with many other nations, announced sanctions that

2177 - 2

froze all Iraqi assets in this country and protected Kuwait's
assets.

On August 6th, four days after the invasion of Kuwait, I
briefed King Fahd about the threat from Iraq and the military
capabilities we could provide to help deter further Iraqi
aggression and to help defend Saudi Arabia.  King Fahd's
decisive and courageous decision to request foreign assistance
speaks to the seriousness of the situation.  In our discussion,
King Fahd talked about his personal respect for President Bush
and great trust in the United States.  He spoke of his faith in
our commitment to help defend his country, to stay until the job
was done, and when the job was done and we were asked to leave,
in fact, to leave.  This trust in America, held by many
countries, is key to our ability to help achieve a more secure
and stable world.

After unparalleled international consultation and exhausting
every alternative, President Bush on August 7th ordered the
deployment of US forces to Saudi Arabia to protect vital US
interests.  In doing so, he set forth clear, straightforward
objectives to:

    • deter and, if necessary, repel further Iraqi
      aggression;

    • effect the immediate, complete, and unconditional
      withdrawal of all Iraqi forces from Kuwait;

. restore the legitimate government of Kuwait; and

. protect the lives of American citizens.

This kind of clarity about what we seek to achieve is key to the effective, appropriate use of military forces.

With that same commitment to clarity of purpose, President Bush has kept Congress fully informed about our efforts, and we intend to continue doing so.

Failure to counter Iraq's aggression and territorial gains would have severe consequences for US interests. In the short-term, Iraq could manipulate and cause destabilizing uncertainty in the international oil market, force up prices to crippling levels, threaten regional states, and begin the process of building a strong and widespread political base. With the conquest of Kuwait, Saddam Hussein has direct control of the capacity to produce five million barrels of oil a day and a potentially strong influence over production of the rest of the Arabian Peninsula, which is another seven million barrels a day. This would give Saddam Hussein an extremely powerful oil weapon. With this weapon, he could coerce oil importing nations in Europe, Japan, and even the United States, which depend increasingly on Gulf oil.

Over the long-term, Iraq would be much stronger militarily.

Given its additional resources, Iraq could expand its vast
arsenal of conventional and non-conventional weaponry -- soon to
include nuclear weapons. His military strength, coupled with
enhanced economic and political power, would give Saddam Hussein
even greater coercive power over his neighbors on oil and other
issues.

The deployment of US forces to the region has gone
exceptionally well, and the level of multinational cooperation
is unprecedented. Today we have well over 100,000 soldiers,
sailors, airmen, and marines in the region. We have elements of
several Army divisions, numerous Air Force fighter and strategic
aircraft squadrons, a Marine Expeditionary Force and its
supporting units, Special Operations Forces, two carrier battle
groups, a battleship, and other naval assets in the Persian
Gulf, Indian Ocean, and Red Sea.

The United States is not alone in this important mission.
At the invitation of the Governments of Saudi Arabia and Kuwait,
military forces from 25 other countries are participating in the
land-based DESERT SHIELD operation and maritime enforcement of
the UN-directed economic sanctions.

These multinational forces face a formidable threat. Iraq
has elements of 11 divisions in Kuwait, totaling 173,680 troops,
over 1500 tanks, 1000 armored personnel carriers, and 778
artillery pieces. An additional 11 Iraqi divisions are deployed

2/99 — 5

in southern Iraq in support of those forces in Kuwait for a total of about 250,000 troops in the Kuwaiti theater. These are battle-hardened units, with leadership that has demonstrated a proclivity to use any and all forms of warfare, against civilian as well as military targets.

Even outside the immediate area, we recognize that terrorism is potentially a significant weapon in the Iraqi arsenal, and on September 4th Iraq was put back on the Department of State's list of states aiding and abetting terrorism. During this period of heightened tension, the terrorist threat to our forces in Saudi Arabia and to US personnel and interests worldwide is, and will remain, high. Pro-Iraqi demonstrations in major cities continue to fuel anti-American sentiment. US officials have received bomb threats, death threats, and verbal warnings from international terrorist organizations. Though no specific credible threats have yet been identified, it is imperative that we take adequate precautions to protect our interests worldwide. The Department of Defense, working closely with other US government agencies, is taking measures to enhance the protection of our servicemen and U.S. civilians overseas, as well as here in the United States.

Current operations in the Persian Gulf involve the first involuntary call-up of Selected Reserve units and individuals under the Total Force Policy established in 1973. Under this policy, Reserve components provide a high percentage of the

*2/17 — 6*

total capability in a number of specific functional mission
areas.  Initially, there were sufficient volunteers to support
this operation.  By August 22nd, prior to the Presidential call-
up of Selected Reserves, approximately 11,500 volunteer
reservists were serving on active duty under orders.

The scope of DESERT SHIELD requires an involuntary call-up
of Reservists to provide various capabilities, many of which
reside in the National Guard and Reserve components.  Mission
areas being fulfilled by Reservists include airlift, port
security, cargo handling, and medical support.  By August 31st,
more than 8,800 Reservists had been called up and 7,600
volunteers were still on active duty.  I anticipate that by the
end of September, close to 50,000 Reservists will be called.

Mr. Chairman, as you and your colleagues who have visited
the region can verify, much has been accomplished in the month
since President Bush ordered the deployment of US forces to
assist in the defense of Saudi Arabia and enforcement of
economic sanctions.  We can be proud of the speed and efficiency
with which the military undertook its mission and set up
defensive positions.  I dare say this type of operation would
not have been possible ten years ago.

Fortunately, predecessors of mine in the Pentagon, military
commanders, and Congress had the foresight to plan and program
for a Persian Gulf contingency.  While operating in this area of

제77 — 7

0044

the world with its long logistic lines, harsh environmental
conditions, and minimal infrastructure will always be extremely
difficult, we are better organized, trained, and equipped than
we would have been ten years ago.  In December 1982, members of
this committee approved an Administration proposal to establish
the US Central Command.  This command, with its full attention
devoted to the region we call Southwest Asia, has proven
invaluable both during the Iran-Iraq war and the current crisis.
Since 1980 we have done extensive planning and conducted
training and exercises, including our major biennual exercise
BRIGHT STAR in Egypt and other regional states, for desert
warfare.

Important programs, such as expanding airlift capacity with
C-5Bs and KC-10s, expanding sealift with the fast sealift ships,
and the Ready Reserve Fleet, afloat prepositioning in the Indian
Ocean and elsewhere, military construction and prepositioning
ashore in the region, and procurement of specialized equipment
such as that for water production were implemented.  Although
most of these programs improve our capability for regional
contingencies in general, during the last 11 years we have spent
over $20 billion on programs directly related to Southwest Asia
-- primarily for construction in the region and prepositioning
ashore and afloat.  During the same time we spent over ten times
that figure to build and maintain the forces we are using in
Desert Shield.  These investments, while costly, have proven
extremely worthwhile.

2177 — 8

The United States is expending considerable resources to support this operation.  By the end of fiscal year 1990, we will have spent more than $2.7 billion in additional costs over and above budgeted funds.  We expect these incremental costs to total about $15 billion in FY 1991, if the crisis continues for the entire fiscal year.  If conflict occurs, these costs would multiply many-fold.

The additional expenses of $1 billion per month are only one-third of our total costs associated with the military response.  The other two-thirds is made up of $1 billion per month associated with our substantial investment in the forces deployed, and about $1 billion in normal baseline operating costs.

President Bush has firmly endorsed the concept of burdensharing for this crisis and announced his Economic Action Plan to solicit contributions from other countries for their fair share of the burden.  Last week the President sent Secretaries Baker and Brady to the Persian Gulf region, Europe, and East Asia to discuss sharing responsibility with our friends and allies.  Our response to the Persian Gulf crisis has enjoyed broad support from the American people and Congress, and we have demonstrated our willingness to bear our fair share of the burden.  We recognize, however, that for the American people and

2/77 – 9

0046

Congress to sustain this effort, they must see that others are contributing their share as well.

In most cases, other countries are sharing the responsibility, and sharing it willingly. Secretaries Baker and Brady had successful and fruitful discussions in the countries they visited. Kuwait, for example, agreed to contribute $2.5 billion to the United States for military defensive purposes, and $2.5 billion in economic aid to states most affected by the crisis. Saudi Arabia and the United Arab Emirates also contributed significant amounts, including direct support for our military forces deployed to the region.

The question often asked is, "How long will we be there?" I cannot give a definitive answer. We were invited by the Saudi Arabian government to help defend the Kingdom, as were other nations, and we will be present as long as it takes to achieve our mutual objectives. When that is done, or when Saudi Arabia asks, we will leave. Likewise, we have been invited to use facilities in other Gulf countries, and when we are asked to leave we will do so.

Our relationship with Saudi Arabia was founded on trust, as exemplified by the historic meeting between President Franklin D. Roosevelt and King Abdul Aziz, held aboard the USS Quincy in the Suez Canal in February 1945. It would be difficult to overestimate the importance of this meeting in US-Saudi relations; King Abdul Aziz later called the meeting "the high point of my entire life" and said that "the hope of the Arabs is based upon the expectation that the United States will support them."

The strong American commitment to this region has been reaffirmed by every Administration since. Harry Truman told King Abdul Aziz in 1950 that any threat to Saudi Arabia was "a matter of immediate concern" to the United States. The first U.S. military advisory mission to Saudi Arabia was established in 1943 and our naval forces have been in the Persian Gulf since 1948.

In the future, our relationships with the Gulf states will undoubtedly change. Indeed, they already have. Facing this threat together and conducting DESERT SHIELD operations will shape our security relations for years to come. We will be working with the regional states to make arrangements for them to be able to defend themselves better and to receive reinforcement troops if that ever becomes necessary again in the future. It is imperative, therefore, that we take steps to ensure that countries like Saudi Arabia are never again in such a vunerable position requiring such a massive U.S. deployment. Accordingly, we will be consulting with you in the future on how we can strengthen our regional allies, both in terms of hardware and interoperability of command and control with U.S. forces. We will need you help and support.

Mr. Chairman, we--Congress and the Administration--have worked together in the past to prepare our forces for the possibility of the type of operation in which we are now engaged. We look forward to your support in continuing this partnership as we take the necessary actions to protect US interests, seek peaceful, lasting solutions to regional problems, and build long-term security relationships with our friends in the region.

September 11, 1990 10:23 AM

2/17 — 1 2

STATEMENT OF

GENERAL COLIN L. POWELL, USA

CHAIRMAN OF THE JOINT CHIEFS OF STAFF

BEFORE THE

SENATE COMMITTEE ON ARMED SERVICES

ON

"OPERATION DESERT SHIELD"

11 September 1990

2개 — 13

0050

Mr. Chairman, members of the Committee, I am pleased to have this opportunity to discuss the military aspects of U.S. actions in the Persian Gulf region.

As Secretary Cheney indicated in his statement, U.S. forces are in the Persian Gulf region to support the President's national policy objectives. Our military objectives are to deter further aggression by Iraq, and to enforce the mandatory Chapter 7 sanctions of the UN Charter and UN Security Council Resolutions 661, 662 and 665. In accomplishing these objectives, we are working very closely with allied and friendly nations-- today, over 25 in number--who have sent or are in the process of sending military forces to the region. Saddam Hussein is facing a multi-national military force. This multi-national force will be capable of a successful defense if Iraqi forces invade Saudi Arabia. It will also have the capability to respond should Iraqi forces invade any other nation in the area.

Because of the tremendous distances involved, we phased our overall operation for the defense of Saudi Arabia. In the initial phase naval, air superiority and light ground forces moved swiftly to provide an immediate deterrent presence. In the second phase attack aircraft, additional fighter aircraft, and maritime forces were deployed. In the current phase, we are building up heavy ground forces and additional air, maritime and sustainment forces to insure a successful defense of Saudi Arabia.

With respect to enforcing the UN sanctions, a multi-national naval force, consisting of U.S. naval forces and naval forces from twelve other allied nations--with additional forces from four other nations en route--is

2/77 - / 4

intercepting maritime vessels in the relevant ocean areas to determine their destination and whether they are in compliance with the UN sanctions regarding prohibited cargo. U.S. Navy support for this operation includes 11 ships in the Persian Gulf, 23 ships in the North Arabian Sea, and 13 ships in the Red Sea. To date, we have intercepted over 750 ships and we have boarded and diverted four ships that were not in compliance with UN sanctions, including two Iraqi ships.

U.S. investment in forces and equipment capable of deploying quickly to any part of the world has paid off. The movement of U.S. forces to Saudi Arabia and surrounding Gulf Coast countries is the largest rapid deployment of U.S. forces since World War II. We moved more forces and equipment in the first three weeks of Desert Shield than we moved during the first three months of the Korean War. This massive deployment of troops and equipment is the equivalent of moving and sustaining a city the size of Chattanooga, Tennessee.

Desert Shield has also convincingly demonstrated the value of a full range of balanced forces. In Desert Shield we have needed and deployed light forces, maritime forces, heavy forces, tactical and strategic air forces, mobility and sustainment forces.

As you know, we had to move as quickly as possible. As a result, Operation Desert Shield has taxed U.S. airlift and sealift to the maximum. The Military Airlift Command's organic fleet of aircraft is fully employed, with nearly 90 percent currently dedicated to Desert Shield missions. The remaining aircraft continue to support DOD's other worldwide requirements.

According to established plans, for the first time in history we activated a portion of the Civil Reserve Air Fleet (CRAF). CRAF Stage I made 38 civil aircraft available for DOD use. If required, Stage II and III can make an additional 78 and 277 aircraft available. To date, airlift has deployed over 75,000 people and over 65,000 tons of equipment. Moreover, the extent of Strategic Air Command's tanker support has been impressive--all combat aircraft deploying to the region required multiple aerial refuelings.

More than 180,000 tons of cargo has been sealifted to the area of operations -- with an additional 55 ships loading or en route. All eight of the Navy's fast sealift ships are supporting the deployment. As of today, seven of these ships have completed the 15 day journey and offloaded their cargoes in Saudi Arabia. Nine Maritime Prepositioning Ships (MPS-2 and MPS-3) from Diego Garcia and Guam have unloaded. These ships carried combat equipment and 30 days of supplies for the I Marine Expeditionary Force. Forty-one Ready Reserve Force (RRF) ships have been ordered activated and thirty-two are ready for sea. We are exploring options to increase our sealift capability, including getting ships from our allies.

Committee members will be pleased to hear that in all of these lift efforts, the U.S. Transportation Command has performed superbly. Coordinating the largest rapid lift in America's history has not been an easy task, but the new unified command has proven its worth.

You are aware that on 23 August, the President invoked, for the first time, the provisions of section 673b, Title 10, United States Code, the Selected Reserve Callup Authority. This augmentation of the Active Armed

217—16

Forces provides us with the capability to perform certain critical military activities. The Reserves and National Guard are an integral part of our Armed Forces. Currently we are ordering to active duty units and individuals to perform a wide variety of tasks both in this country and in and around the Arabian Peninsula.

We are all aware of the personal sacrifices being made by the reservists being called up. I assure you that we will only call those we need, and will retain them for only the period of service that is absolutely necessary to accomplish the mission. The most immediate need is for Army logistics forces to sustain the growing combat power in the theater of operations. We also will be calling up Air Force, Navy and Coast Guard units and individuals to support strategic lift and enhance the flow of forces and supplies to the U.S. Central Command (USCENTCOM) area. Finally, individual Army and Navy reservists are being called up to backfill critical medical specialists who have deployed to meet theater medical requirements.

In addition to those called up under the Presidential Callup Authority, many more reservists and guardsmen have supported this operation on a volunteer basis, logging thousands of air miles in support of strategic airlift, aerial refueling and tactical reconnaissance requirements, and pitching in to assist where needed in the deployment process. These are patriotic men and women, totally dedicated to our national defense. In short, our Total Force policy is working well in Operation Desert Shield.

All of the U.S. forces in Operation Desert Shield are organized as a joint force under the Central Command's Commander in Chief (USCINCCENT),

General H. Norman Schwarzkopf. This joint force includes Army, Navy, Air Force and Marine Corps component commanders.

Major U.S. forces deployed to the Middle East come under the operational control of USCINCCENT when they enter the USCENTCOM area of responsibility. USCINCCENT has primary responsibility for Operation Desert Shield and is supported by the other combatant commands and numerous federal departments and agencies. General Schwarzkopf's naval component commander commands both U.S. naval forces for the defense of Saudi Arabia and U.S. naval forces for the multi-national Maritime Intercept Force.

General Schwarzkopf's mission is "to deploy forces to the U.S. Central Command area of responsibility and take actions in concert with host nation forces, friendly regional forces and other, allies to defend against an Iraqi attack on Saudi Arabia and be prepared to conduct other operations as directed." General Schwarzkopf is coordinating closely with the military forces of Saudi Arabia and the other allied forces in theater.

U.S. forces in Saudi Arabia and in other Arab countries are part of a command arrangement that has established an effective coalition of Arab and Western forces. These forces are organized along national lines with national forces being assigned separate areas of operations. National Force Commanders are maintaining close coordination and cooperation on all issues.

2/77—/8

Host nation support has been outstanding. Saudi Arabia and other Gulf states have provided unprecedented use of airfields, port facilities, beddown locations, heavy equipment transport, and water for all allied forces.

A large Iraqi military force remains in Kuwait. It has the capability to attack Saudi Arabia with very little warning. As of this week, approximately 173,000 Iraqi troops with over 1,500 tanks continue to occupy positions in Kuwait. Moreover, 11 Iraqi divisions are deployed in southern Iraq in position to support the Iraqi forces in Kuwait.-

U.S. military forces in the Persian Gulf are well trained and well supported. Together with the military forces of participating Arab and Western countries, these forces will be capable of defending Saudi Arabia from an Iraqi attack and enforcing the UN sanctions.

217-19

0056

| 관리<br>번호 | 90-1930 |
|---|---|

# 외 무 부

종 별 : 긴 급

번 호 : USW-4129                          일 시 : 90 0911 2337

수 신 : 장관(미북,미안,중근동,기정)

발 신 : 주 미 대사

제 목 : 이락사태-의회 반응(7)

　　1. 부쉬 대통령은 금 9.11 현지시간 2100 부터 40 분간 상. 하 양원 합동회의에서 이락사태의 현황과 예산 논의를 포함한 미 국내문제에 관하여 연설을 행함(전문 FAX 송부함)

　　2. 동 연설은 부쉬 취임후 두차례에 걸친 연초 국정연설 이후 처음 가진 이례적인것으로서 하기 휴회 직후 양원 합동회의의 형식을 빌어, 의회와 미 국민 전체에게 공식적으로 사태의 현황과 행정부의 정책을 종합 설명하고, 지지를 호소하기 위한 목적에서 계획된것임.

　　3. 연설 요지 아래임.

　　가. 이락사태

　　-어느때보다도 미국민의 애국심이 절실한 시기이며, 그동안의 국민과 의회의 지지에 감사함.

　　-페르시아만에서의 미국의 정책 목표는 쿠웨이트로부터 이락의 무조건 철수쿠웨이트 합법적 정부의 원상 회복, 페르시안만의 안보와 안정확보및 미국민의 안전 확보인바 동 목표에 대한 유엔을 비롯한 국제사회의 강한 지지가 있었음.

　　-9.9 미소 정상회담을 통하여 새로운 협조 체제(NEW PARTNERSHIP)가 시작되므로서 새로운 세계 질서 수립이 미국의 중요한 정책 목표가 되었으며, 이락사태가 신세계 질서(NEW WORLD ORDER)에 대한 첫번째 도전으로서 미국은 강력한의지를 가지고 이와같은 도전에 임해야함.

　　-신뢰받을수 있는 미국의 지도력이 절실히 요구되는 현재의 국제 사회하에서 미국이 치루어야할 희생은 적지 않다고 보며, 국제 사회도 이에 동참하여야할것임.

　　-페르시아만 지역 안정의 보장, 우방국의 방위 협조, 화학, 생화학 무기및 핵무기 확산 방지를 위해 동 지역에 대한 미국의 장기적 개입이 필요함.

| 미주국<br>대책반 | 장관 | 차관 | 1차보 | 2차보 | 미주국 | 중아국 | 청와대 | 안기부 |
|---|---|---|---|---|---|---|---|---|

PAGE 1

나. 국내 사항

-이락 사태등 국제 사회에서 지도력을 발휘하기 위하여 미국 내에서의 단합된 지도력의 과시가 필요하바, 예산 적자등 미국 경제 안정을 위해 의회와 행정부의 긴밀한 협조가 필요함.

-상기 목적을 위해 의회는

. 성장에 근거한 증세 입법화

. 안정된 국방예산 확보를 위한 중장기 방위 계획 수립

. 국내 에너지 증산과 절감책에 대한 입법화

. 향후 5 년간 5 천억불 상당의 재정 적자 해소안 입법조치및 새로운 수입원 확보를 포함한 적자 감축안 입법화 조치를 취해야함.

(대사 박동진-국장)

90.12.31 까지

수신: 장관 (미북, 미안, 중근동)

발신: 주미대사

제목: 8ush       THE WHITE HOUSE

대통령 대 의회 연설    OFFICE OF THE PRESS SECRETARY

USW(F)-2176

(기밀)

EMBARGOED FOR RELEASE
UNTIL 9:00 P.M. EDT
TUESDAY, SEPTEMBER 11, 1990


TEXT OF REMARKS BY THE PRESIDENT
TO THE JOINT SESSION OF CONGRESS

U.S. CAPITOL
WASHINGTON, DC

SEPTEMBER 11, 1990

MR. PRESIDENT, MR. SPEAKER, MEMBERS OF THE CONGRESS,
DISTINGUISHED GUESTS, FELLOW AMERICANS, THANK YOU.

WE GATHER TONIGHT, WITNESS TO EVENTS IN THE PERSIAN GULF AS
SIGNIFICANT AS THEY ARE TRAGIC.  IN THE EARLY MORNING HOURS OF
AUGUST 2ND, FOLLOWING NEGOTIATIONS AND PROMISES BY IRAQ'S
DICTATOR SADDAM HUSSEIN NOT TO USE FORCE, A POWERFUL IRAQI ARMY
INVADED ITS TRUSTING AND MUCH WEAKER NEIGHBOR, KUWAIT.  WITHIN
THREE DAYS, 120,000 IRAQI TROOPS WITH 850 TANKS HAD POURED INTO
KUWAIT, AND MOVED SOUTH TO THREATEN SAUDI ARABIA.  IT WAS THEN I
DECIDED TO CHECK THAT AGGRESSION.

AT THIS MOMENT, OUR BRAVE SERVICEMEN AND WOMEN STAND WATCH IN
THAT DISTANT DESERT AND ON DISTANT SEAS, SIDE BY SIDE WITH THE
FORCES OF MORE THAN TWENTY OTHER NATIONS.

THEY ARE SOME OF THE FINEST MEN AND WOMEN OF THE UNITED STATES OF
AMERICA.  AND THEY'RE DOING ONE TERRIFIC JOB.

THESE VALIANT AMERICANS WERE READY AT A MOMENT'S NOTICE TO LEAVE
THEIR SPOUSES, THEIR CHILDREN, TO SERVE ON THE FRONT-LINE
HALF-WAY AROUND THE WORLD.  THEY REMIND US WHO KEEPS AMERICA
STRONG.  THEY DO.

IN THE TRYING CIRCUMSTANCES OF THE GULF, THE MORALE OF OUR
SERVICEMEN AND WOMEN IS EXCELLENT.  IN THE FACE OF DANGER, THEY
ARE BRAVE, WELL-TRAINED AND DEDICATED.

A SOLDIER, P.F.C. WADE MERRITT OF KNOXVILLE, TENNESSEE, NOW
STATIONED IN SAUDI ARABIA, WROTE HIS PARENTS OF HIS WORRIES, HIS
LOVE OF FAMILY, AND HIS HOPES FOR PEACE.  BUT WADE ALSO WROTE:
"I AM PROUD OF MY COUNTRY AND ITS FIRM STAND AGAINST INHUMANE
AGGRESSION.  I AM PROUD OF MY ARMY AND ITS MEN . . . I AM PROUD
TO SERVE MY COUNTRY."

LET ME JUST SAY, WADE, AMERICA IS PROUD OF YOU.  AND GRATEFUL TO
EVERY SOLDIER, SAILOR, MARINE AND AIRMAN SERVING THE CAUSE OF
PEACE IN THE PERSIAN GULF.

I ALSO WANT TO THANK THE CHAIRMAN OF THE JOINT CHIEFS OF STAFF,
GENERAL POWELL, THE CHIEFS, OUR COMMANDER IN THE PERSIAN GULF,
GENERAL SCHWARTZKOPF, AND THE MEN AND WOMEN OF THE DEPARTMENT OF
DEFENSE -- WHAT A MAGNIFICENT JOB YOU ARE DOING.

I WISH I COULD SAY THEIR WORK IS DONE.  BUT WE ALL KNOW IT IS
NOT.

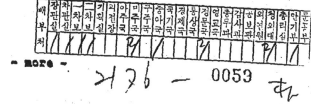

- more -

2176 - 0053

2

SO IF EVER THERE WAS A TIME TO PUT COUNTRY BEFORE SELF AND
PATRIOTISM BEFORE PARTY, THAT TIME IS NOW.  LET ME THANK ALL
AMERICANS, ESPECIALLY THOSE IN THIS CHAMBER, FOR YOUR SUPPORT FOR
OUR FORCES AND THEIR MISSION.

THAT SUPPORT WILL BE EVEN MORE IMPORTANT IN THE DAYS TO COME.

SO TONIGHT, I WANT TO TALK TO YOU ABOUT WHAT IS AT STAKE -- WHAT
WE MUST DO TOGETHER TO DEFEND CIVILIZED VALUES AROUND THE WORLD,
AND MAINTAIN OUR ECONOMIC STRENGTH AT HOME.

OUR OBJECTIVES IN THE PERSIAN GULF ARE CLEAR, OUR GOALS DEFINED
AND FAMILIAR:

--    IRAQ MUST WITHDRAW FROM KUWAIT COMPLETELY, IMMEDIATELY --
AND WITHOUT CONDITION.

--    KUWAIT'S LEGITIMATE GOVERNMENT MUST-BE-RESTORED.

--    THE SECURITY AND STABILITY OF THE PERSIAN GULF
MUST-BE-ASSURED.

--    AMERICAN CITIZENS ABROAD MUST-BE- PROTECTED.

THESE GOALS ARE NOT OURS ALONE.  THEY HAVE BEEN ENDORSED BY THE
U.N. SECURITY COUNCIL FIVE TIMES IN AS MANY WEEKS.  MOST
COUNTRIES SHARE OUR CONCERN FOR PRINCIPLE.  AND MANY HAVE A STAKE
IN THE STABILITY OF THE PERSIAN GULF.  THIS IS NOT, AS SADDAM
HUSSEIN WOULD HAVE IT, THE UNITED STATES AGAINST IRAQ.  IT IS
IRAQ AGAINST THE WORLD.

AS YOU KNOW, I'VE JUST RETURNED FROM A VERY PRODUCTIVE MEETING
WITH SOVIET PRESIDENT GORBACHEV.  I AM PLEASED THAT WE ARE
WORKING TOGETHER TO BUILD A NEW-RELATIONSHIP.  IN HELSINKI, OUR
JOINT STATEMENT AFFIRMED TO THE WORLD OUR SHARED RESOLVE TO
COUNTER IRAQ'S THREAT TO PEACE.  LET ME QUOTE:  "WE ARE UNITED IN
THE BELIEF THAT IRAQ'S AGGRESSION MUST-NOT-BE-TOLERATED.  NO
PEACEFUL INTERNATIONAL ORDER IS POSSIBLE IF LARGER STATES CAN
DEVOUR THEIR SMALLER NEIGHBORS."

CLEARLY, NO LONGER CAN A DICTATOR COUNT ON EAST-WEST
CONFRONTATION TO STYMIE CONCERTED U.N. ACTION AGAINST AGGRESSION.

A NEW PARTNERSHIP OF NATIONS HAS BEGUN.

WE STAND TODAY AT A UNIQUE AND EXTRAORDINARY MOMENT.  THE CRISIS
IN THE PERSIAN GULF, AS GRAVE AS IT IS, ALSO OFFERS A RARE
OPPORTUNITY TO MOVE TOWARD AN HISTORIC PERIOD OF COOPERATION.
OUT OF THESE TROUBLED TIMES, OUR FIFTH OBJECTIVE -- A NEW WORLD
ORDER -- CAN EMERGE: A NEW ERA -- FREER FROM THE THREAT OF
TERROR, STRONGER IN THE PURSUIT OF JUSTICE, AND MORE SECURE IN
THE QUEST FOR PEACE.  AN ERA IN WHICH THE NATIONS OF THE WORLD,
EAST AND WEST, NORTH AND SOUTH, CAN PROSPER AND LIVE IN HARMONY.

A HUNDRED GENERATIONS HAVE SEARCHED FOR THIS ELUSIVE PATH TO
PEACE, WHILE A THOUSAND WARS RAGED ACROSS THE SPAN OF HUMAN
ENDEAVOR.  TODAY THAT NEW WORLD IS STRUGGLING TO BE BORN.  A
WORLD QUITE DIFFERENT FROM THE ONE WE'VE KNOWN.  A WORLD WHERE
THE RULE OF LAW SUPPLANTS THE RULE OF THE JUNGLE.  A WORLD IN
WHICH NATIONS RECOGNIZE THE SHARED RESPONSIBILITY FOR FREEDOM AND
JUSTICE.  A WORLD WHERE THE STRONG RESPECT THE RIGHTS OF THE
WEAK.

THIS IS THE VISION I SHARED WITH PRESIDENT GORBACHEV IN HELSINKI.
HE, AND OTHER LEADERS FROM EUROPE, THE GULF AND AROUND THE WORLD,
UNDERSTAND THAT HOW WE MANAGE THIS CRISIS TODAY, COULD SHAPE THE
FUTURE FOR GENERATIONS TO COME.

- MORE -                        2176          0060

3

THE TEST WE FACE IS GREAT -- AND SO ARE THE STAKES.  THIS IS THE
FIRST ASSAULT ON THE NEW WORLD WE SEEK, THE FIRST TEST OF OUR
METTLE.  HAD WE NOT RESPONDED TO THIS FIRST PROVOCATION WITH
CLARITY OF PURPOSE; IF WE DO NOT CONTINUE TO DEMONSTRATE OUR
DETERMINATION; IT WOULD BE A SIGNAL TO ACTUAL AND POTENTIAL
DESPOTS AROUND THE WORLD.

AMERICA AND THE WORLD MUST DEFEND COMMON VITAL INTERESTS.  AND WE
WILL.

AMERICA AND THE WORLD MUST SUPPORT THE RULE OF LAW.  AND WE WILL.

AMERICA AND THE WORLD MUST STAND UP TO AGGRESSION.  AND WE WILL.

AND ONE THING MORE -- IN PURSUIT OF THESE GOALS AMERICA WILL NOT
BE INTIMIDATED.

VITAL ISSUES OF PRINCIPLE ARE AT STAKE.  SADDAM HUSSEIN IS
LITERALLY TRYING TO WIPE A COUNTRY OFF THE FACE OF THE EARTH.

WE DO NOT EXAGGERATE.

NOR DO WE EXAGGERATE WHEN WE SAY: SADDAM HUSSEIN WILL FAIL.

VITAL ECONOMIC INTERESTS ARE AT RISK AS WELL.  IRAQ ITSELF
CONTROLS SOME TEN PERCENT OF THE WORLD'S PROVEN OIL RESERVES.
IRAQ PLUS KUWAIT CONTROLS TWICE THAT.  AN IRAQ PERMITTED TO
SWALLOW KUWAIT WOULD HAVE THE ECONOMIC AND MILITARY POWER, AS
WELL AS THE ARROGANCE, TO INTIMIDATE AND COERCE ITS NEIGHBORS --
NEIGHBORS WHO CONTROL THE LION'S SHARE OF THE WORLD'S REMAINING
OIL RESERVES.  WE CANNOT PERMIT A RESOURCE SO VITAL TO BE
DOMINATED BY ONE SO RUTHLESS.  AND WE WON'T.

RECENT EVENTS HAVE SURELY PROVEN THAT THERE IS NO SUBSTITUTE FOR
AMERICAN LEADERSHIP.  IN THE FACE OF TYRANNY, LET NO ONE DOUBT
AMERICAN CREDIBILITY AND RELIABILITY.

LET NO ONE DOUBT OUR STAYING POWER.  WE WILL STAND BY OUR
FRIENDS.

ONE WAY OR ANOTHER, THE LEADER OF IRAQ MUST LEARN THIS
FUNDAMENTAL TRUTH.

FROM THE OUTSET, ACTING HAND-IN-HAND WITH OTHERS, WE'VE SOUGHT TO
FASHION THE BROADEST POSSIBLE INTERNATIONAL RESPONSE TO IRAQ'S
AGGRESSION.  THE LEVEL OF WORLD COOPERATION AND CONDEMNATION OF
IRAQ IS UNPRECEDENTED.

ARMED FORCES FROM COUNTRIES SPANNING FOUR CONTINENTS, ARE THERE
AT THE REQUEST OF KING FAHD OF SAUDI ARABIA TO DETER AND IF NEED
BE, TO DEFEND AGAINST ATTACK.  MUSLIMS AND NON-MUSLIMS, ARABS AND
NON-ARABS, SOLDIERS FROM MANY NATIONS, STAND
SHOULDER-TO-SHOULDER, RESOLUTE AGAINST SADDAM HUSSEIN'S
AMBITIONS.

WE CAN NOW POINT TO FIVE UNITED NATIONS SECURITY COUNCIL
RESOLUTIONS THAT CONDEMN IRAQ'S AGGRESSION. THEY CALL FOR IRAQ'S
IMMEDIATE AND UNCONDITIONAL WITHDRAWAL, THE RESTORATION OF
KUWAIT'S LEGITIMATE GOVERNMENT, AND CATEGORICALLY REJECT IRAQ'S
CYNICAL AND SELF-SERVING ATTEMPT TO ANNEX KUWAIT.

FINALLY, THE U.N. HAS DEMANDED THE RELEASE OF ALL FOREIGN
NATIONALS HELD HOSTAGE AGAINST THEIR WILL, AND IN CONTRAVENTION
OF INTERNATIONAL LAW.  IT IS A MOCKERY OF HUMAN DECENCY TO CALL
THESE PEOPLE "GUESTS."  THEY ARE HOSTAGES, AND THE WHOLE WORLD
KNOWS IT.

- more -                                       0061

4

PRIME MINISTER MARGARET THATCHER SAID IT ALL: "WE DO NOT BARGAIN
OVER HOSTAGES. WE WILL NOT STOOP TO THE LEVEL OF USING HUMAN
BEINGS AS BARGAINING (CHIPS). EVER."

OF COURSE, OUR HEARTS GO OUT TO THE HOSTAGES AND THEIR FAMILIES.
BUT OUR POLICY CANNOT CHANGE. AND IT WILL NOT CHANGE. AMERICA
AND THE WORLD WILL NOT BE BLACKMAILED.

WE ARE NOW IN SIGHT OF A UNITED NATIONS THAT PERFORMS AS
ENVISIONED BY ITS FOUNDERS. WE OWE MUCH TO THE OUTSTANDING
LEADERSHIP OF SECRETARY-GENERAL PEREZ DE CUELLAR. THE U.N. IS
BACKING UP ITS WORDS WITH ACTION. THE SECURITY COUNCIL HAS
IMPOSED MANDATORY ECONOMIC SANCTIONS ON IRAQ, DESIGNED TO FORCE
IRAQ TO RELINQUISH THE SPOILS OF ITS ILLEGAL CONQUEST. THE
SECURITY COUNCIL HAS ALSO TAKEN THE DECISIVE STEP OF AUTHORIZING
THE USE OF ALL MEANS NECESSARY TO ENSURE COMPLIANCE WITH THESE
SANCTIONS.

TOGETHER WITH OUR FRIENDS AND ALLIES, SHIPS OF THE UNITED STATES
NAVY ARE TODAY PATROLLING MIDEAST WATERS. THEY HAVE ALREADY
INTERCEPTED MORE THAN SEVEN HUNDRED SHIPS TO ENFORCE THE
SANCTIONS. THREE REGIONAL LEADERS I SPOKE WITH JUST YESTERDAY
TOLD ME THAT THESE SANCTIONS ARE WORKING. IRAQ IS FEELING THE
HEAT.

WE CONTINUE TO HOPE THAT IRAQ'S LEADERS WILL RECALCULATE JUST
WHAT THEIR AGGRESSION HAS COST THEM. THEY ARE CUT OFF FROM WORLD
TRADE. UNABLE TO SELL THEIR OIL. AND ONLY A TINY FRACTION OF
GOODS GETS THROUGH.

AT HOME, THE MATERIAL COST OF OUR LEADERSHIP CAN BE STEEP.
THAT'S WHY SECRETARY OF STATE BAKER AND TREASURY SECRETARY BRADY
HAVE MET WITH MANY WORLD LEADERS TO UNDERSCORE THAT THE BURDEN OF
THIS COLLECTIVE EFFORT MUST BE SHARED. WE ARE PREPARED TO DO OUR
SHARE AND MORE TO HELP CARRY THAT LOAD; WE INSIST OTHERS DO THEIR
SHARE AS WELL.

THE RESPONSE OF MOST OF OUR FRIENDS AND ALLIES HAS BEEN GOOD. TO
HELP DEFRAY COSTS, THE LEADERS OF SAUDI ARABIA, KUWAIT AND THE
UNITED ARAB EMIRATES HAVE PLEDGED TO PROVIDE OUR DEPLOYED TROOPS
WITH ALL THE FOOD AND FUEL THEY NEED. GENEROUS ASSISTANCE WILL
ALSO BE PROVIDED TO STALWART FRONT-LINE NATIONS, SUCH AS TURKEY
AND EGYPT.

I AM ALSO HEARTENED TO REPORT THAT THIS INTERNATIONAL RESPONSE
EXTENDS TO THE NEEDIEST VICTIMS OF THIS CONFLICT -- THE REFUGEES.
FOR OUR PART, WE HAVE CONTRIBUTED $28 MILLION FOR RELIEF EFFORTS.
THIS IS BUT A PORTION OF WHAT IS NEEDED. I COMMEND, IN
PARTICULAR, SAUDI ARABIA, JAPAN, AND SEVERAL EUROPEAN NATIONS WHO
HAVE JOINED US IN THIS HUMANITARIAN EFFORT.

THERE IS AN ENERGY-RELATED COST TO BE BORNE AS WELL.
OIL-PRODUCING NATIONS ARE ALREADY REPLACING LOST IRAQI AND
KUWAITI OUTPUT. MORE THAN HALF OF WHAT WAS LOST HAS BEEN MADE
UP. WE ARE GETTING SUPERB COOPERATION. IF PRODUCERS, INCLUDING
THE UNITED STATES, CONTINUE STEPS TO EXPAND OIL AND GAS
PRODUCTION, WE CAN STABILIZE PRICES AND GUARANTEE AGAINST
HARDSHIP. ADDITIONALLY, WE AND SEVERAL OF OUR ALLIES ALWAYS HAVE
THE OPTION TO EXTRACT OIL FROM OUR STRATEGIC PETROLEUM RESERVES,
IF CONDITIONS WARRANT. AS I HAVE POINTED OUT BEFORE,
CONSERVATION EFFORTS ARE ESSENTIAL TO KEEP OUR ENERGY NEEDS AS
LOW AS POSSIBLE. WE MUST THEN TAKE ADVANTAGE OF OUR ENERGY
SOURCES ACROSS THE BOARD: COAL, NATURAL GAS, HYDRO AND NUCLEAR.
OUR FAILURE TO DO THESE THINGS HAS MADE US MORE DEPENDENT ON
FOREIGN OIL THAN EVER BEFORE. FINALLY, LET NO ONE EVEN
CONTEMPLATE PROFITEERING FROM THIS CRISIS.

0062

- more -

-176 -4

**5**

I CANNOT PREDICT JUST HOW LONG IT WILL TAKE TO CONVINCE IRAQ TO
WITHDRAW FROM KUWAIT.  SANCTIONS WILL TAKE TIME TO HAVE THEIR
FULL INTENDED EFFECT.  WE WILL CONTINUE TO REVIEW ALL OPTIONS
WITH OUR ALLIES, BUT LET IT BE CLEAR:  WE WILL NOT LET THIS
AGGRESSION STAND.

OUR INTEREST, OUR INVOLVEMENT IN THE GULF, IS NOT TRANSITORY.  IT
PRE-DATED SADDAM HUSSEIN'S AGGRESSION, AND WILL SURVIVE IT.  LONG
AFTER ALL OUR TROOPS COME HOME, THERE WILL BE A LASTING ROLE FOR
THE UNITED STATES IN ASSISTING THE NATIONS OF THE PERSIAN GULF.
OUR ROLE, WITH OTHERS, IS TO DETER FUTURE AGGRESSION.  OUR ROLE
IS TO HELP OUR FRIENDS IN THEIR OWN SELF-DEFENSE.  AND SOMETHING
ELSE: TO CURB THE PROLIFERATION OF CHEMICAL, BIOLOGICAL,
BALLISTIC MISSILE AND ABOVE ALL, NUCLEAR TECHNOLOGIES.

LET ME ALSO MAKE CLEAR THAT THE UNITED STATES HAS NO QUARREL WITH
THE IRAQI PEOPLE.  OUR QUARREL IS WITH IRAQ'S DICTATOR, AND WITH
HIS AGGRESSION.  IRAQ WILL NOT BE PERMITTED TO ANNEX KUWAIT.
THAT'S NOT A THREAT, OR A BOAST, THAT'S JUST THE WAY IT'S GOING
TO BE.

OUR ABILITY TO FUNCTION EFFECTIVELY AS A GREAT POWER ABROAD
DEPENDS ON HOW WE CONDUCT OURSELVES HERE AT HOME.  OUR ECONOMY,
OUR ARMED FORCES, OUR ENERGY DEPENDENCE, AND OUR COHESION ALL
DETERMINE WHETHER WE CAN HELP OUR FRIENDS AND STAND UP TO OUR
FOES.

FOR AMERICA TO LEAD, AMERICA MUST REMAIN STRONG AND VITAL.  OUR
WORLD LEADERSHIP AND DOMESTIC STRENGTH ARE MUTUAL AND
REINFORCING; A WOVEN PIECE, AS STRONGLY BOUND AS OLD GLORY.

TO REVITALIZE OUR LEADERSHIP CAPACITY, WE MUST ADDRESS OUR BUDGET
DEFICIT -- NOT AFTER ELECTION DAY, OR NEXT YEAR, BUT NOW.

HIGHER OIL PRICES SLOW OUR GROWTH, AND HIGHER DEFENSE COSTS WOULD
ONLY MAKE OUR FISCAL DEFICIT PROBLEM WORSE.  THAT DEFICIT WAS
ALREADY GREATER THAN IT SHOULD HAVE BEEN -- A PROJECTED $232
BILLION FOR THE COMING YEAR.  IT MUST -- IT WILL -- BE REDUCED.

TO MY FRIENDS IN CONGRESS, TOGETHER WE MUST ACT THIS VERY MONTH
-- BEFORE THE NEXT FISCAL YEAR BEGINS OCTOBER FIRST -- TO GET
AMERICA'S ECONOMIC HOUSE IN ORDER.  THE GULF SITUATION HELPS US
REALIZE WE ARE MORE ECONOMICALLY VULNERABLE THAN WE EVER SHOULD
BE.  AMERICANS MUST NEVER AGAIN ENTER ANY CRISIS -- ECONOMIC OR
MILITARY -- WITH AN EXCESSIVE DEPENDENCE ON FOREIGN OIL AND AN
EXCESSIVE BURDEN OF FEDERAL DEBT.

MOST AMERICANS ARE SICK AND TIRED OF ENDLESS BATTLES IN THE
CONGRESS AND BETWEEN THE BRANCHES OVER BUDGET MATTERS.  IT IS
HIGH TIME WE PULLED TOGETHER -- AND GET THE JOB DONE RIGHT.  IT IS
UP TO US TO STRAIGHTEN THIS OUT.

THIS JOB HAS FOUR BASIC PARTS.

FIRST:  THE CONGRESS SHOULD, THIS MONTH, WITHIN A BUDGET
AGREEMENT, ENACT GROWTH-ORIENTED TAX MEASURES  -- TO HELP AVOID
RECESSION IN THE SHORT TERM; AND TO INCREASE SAVINGS, INVESTMENT,
PRODUCTIVITY AND COMPETITIVENESS FOR THE LONGER TERM.  THESE
MEASURES INCLUDE EXTENDING INCENTIVES FOR RESEARCH AND
EXPERIMENTATION; EXPANDING THE USE OF IRAs FOR NEW HOMEOWNERS;
ESTABLISHING TAX-DEFERRED FAMILY SAVINGS ACCOUNTS; CREATING
INCENTIVES FOR THE CREATION OF ENTERPRISE ZONES AND INITIATIVES
TO ENCOURAGE MORE DOMESTIC DRILLING; AND, YES, REDUCING THE TAX
RATE FOR CAPITAL GAINS.

- more -

0063

6

SECOND: THE CONGRESS SHOULD, THIS MONTH, ENACT A PRUDENT
MULTI-YEAR DEFENSE PROGRAM -- ONE THAT REFLECTS NOT ONLY THE
IMPROVEMENT IN EAST-WEST RELATIONS, BUT OUR BROADER
RESPONSIBILITIES TO DEAL WITH THE CONTINUING RISKS OF OUTLAW
ACTION AND REGIONAL CONFLICT. EVEN WITH OUR OBLIGATIONS IN THE
GULF, A SOUND DEFENSE BUDGET CAN HAVE SOME REDUCTION IN REAL
TERMS, AND WE ARE PREPARED TO ACCEPT THAT. BUT TO GO BEYOND SUCH
LEVELS, WHERE CUTTING DEFENSE WOULD THREATEN OUR VITAL MARGIN OF
SAFETY, IS SOMETHING I WILL NEVER ACCEPT.

THE WORLD IS STILL DANGEROUS. SURELY THAT IS NOW CLEAR.
STABILITY IS NOT SECURE. AMERICAN INTERESTS ARE FAR-REACHING.
INTER-DEPENDENCE HAS INCREASED. THE CONSEQUENCES OF REGIONAL
INSTABILITY CAN BE GLOBAL. THIS IS NO TIME TO RISK AMERICA'S
CAPACITY TO PROTECT HER VITAL INTERESTS.

THIRD: THE CONGRESS SHOULD, THIS MONTH, ENACT MEASURES TO
INCREASE DOMESTIC ENERGY PRODUCTION AND ENERGY CONSERVATION -- IN
ORDER TO REDUCE DEPENDENCE ON FOREIGN OIL. THESE MEASURES SHOULD
INCLUDE MY PROPOSALS TO INCREASE INCENTIVES FOR DOMESTIC OIL AND
GAS-EXPLORATION, FUEL-SWITCHING, AND TO ACCELERATE THE
DEVELOPMENT OF ALASKAN ENERGY RESOURCES, WITHOUT DAMAGE TO
WILDLIFE.

AS YOU KNOW, WHEN THE OIL EMBARGO WAS IMPOSED IN THE EARLY
1970'S, THE UNITED STATES IMPORTED ALMOST SIX MILLION BARRELS OF
OIL PER DAY. THIS YEAR, BEFORE THE IRAQI INVASION, U.S. IMPORTS
HAD RISEN TO NEARLY EIGHT MILLION BARRELS PER DAY. WE HAD MOVED
IN THE WRONG DIRECTION. NOW WE MUST ACT TO CORRECT THAT TREND.

FOURTH: THE CONGRESS SHOULD, THIS MONTH, ENACT A FIVE-YEAR
PROGRAM TO REDUCE THE PROJECTED DEBT AND DEFICITS BY $500 BILLION
-- THAT IS, BY HALF A TRILLION DOLLARS. IF, WITH THE CONGRESS,
WE CAN DEVELOP A SATISFACTORY PROGRAM BY THE END OF THE MONTH, WE
CAN AVOID THE AXE OF "SEQUESTER" -- DEEP ACROSS-THE-BOARD CUTS
THAT WOULD THREATEN OUR MILITARY CAPACITY AND RISK SUBSTANTIAL
DOMESTIC DISRUPTION.

I WANT TO BE ABLE TO TELL THE AMERICAN PEOPLE, WE HAVE TRULY
SOLVED THE DEFICIT PROBLEM. FOR ME TO DO THAT, A BUDGET
AGREEMENT MUST MEET THESE TESTS:

--  IT MUST INCLUDE THE MEASURES I'VE RECOMMENDED TO INCREASE
ECONOMIC GROWTH AND REDUCE DEPENDENCE ON FOREIGN OIL.

--  IT MUST BE FAIR. ALL SHOULD CONTRIBUTE, BUT THE BURDEN
SHOULD NOT BE EXCESSIVE FOR ANY ONE GROUP OF PROGRAMS OR PEOPLE.

--  IT MUST ADDRESS THE GROWTH OF GOVERNMENT'S HIDDEN
LIABILITIES.

--  IT MUST REFORM THE BUDGET PROCESS, AND FURTHER: IT MUST BE
REAL.

I URGE CONGRESS TO PROVIDE A COMPREHENSIVE FIVE-YEAR DEFICIT
REDUCTION PROGRAM TO ME AS A COMPLETE LEGISLATIVE PACKAGE -- WITH
MEASURES TO ASSURE THAT IT CAN BE FULLY ENFORCED. AMERICA IS
TIRED OF PHONEY DEFICIT REDUCTION, OR PROMISE-NOW,
SAVE-LATER-PLANS. ENOUGH IS ENOUGH. IT IS TIME FOR A PROGRAM
THAT IS CREDIBLE AND REAL.

--  FINALLY, TO THE EXTENT THAT THE DEFICIT REDUCTION PROGRAM
INCLUDES NEW REVENUE MEASURES, IT MUST AVOID ANY MEASURE THAT
WOULD THREATEN ECONOMIC GROWTH OR TURN US BACK TOWARD THE DAYS OF
PUNISHING INCOME TAX RATES. THAT IS ONE PATH WE SHOULD NOT HEAD
DOWN AGAIN.

- more -                                          0064

7

I HAVE BEEN PLEASED WITH RECENT PROGRESS, ALTHOUGH IT HAS NOT
ALWAYS SEEMED SO SMOOTH.

BUT NOW IT IS TIME TO PRODUCE.

I HOPE WE CAN WORK OUT A RESPONSIBLE PLAN.  BUT WITH OR WITHOUT
AGREEMENT FROM THE BUDGET SUMMIT, I ASK BOTH HOUSES OF THE
CONGRESS TO ALLOW A STRAIGHT UP-OR-DOWN VOTE ON A COMPLETE $500
BILLION DEFICIT REDUCTION PACKAGE -- NOT LATER THAN SEPTEMBER 28.

IF THE CONGRESS CANNOT GET ME A BUDGET, THEN AMERICANS WILL HAVE
TO FACE A TOUGH, MANDATED SEQUESTER.

I AM HOPEFUL, IN FACT I AM CONFIDENT, THE CONGRESS WILL DO WHAT
IT SHOULD.  AND WE IN THE EXECUTIVE BRANCH WILL DO OUR PART.

IN THE FINAL ANALYSIS, OUR ABILITY TO MEET OUR RESPONSIBILITIES
ABROAD DEPENDS UPON POLITICAL WILL AND CONSENSUS AT HOME.  THIS
IS NEVER EASY IN DEMOCRACIES -- WHERE WE GOVERN ONLY WITH THE
CONSENT OF THE GOVERNED.  AND ALTHOUGH FREE PEOPLE IN A FREE
SOCIETY ARE BOUND TO HAVE THEIR DIFFERENCES, AMERICANS
TRADITIONALLY COME TOGETHER IN TIMES OF ADVERSITY AND CHALLENGE.

ONCE AGAIN, AMERICANS HAVE STEPPED FORWARD TO SHARE A TEARFUL
GOODBYE WITH THEIR FAMILIES BEFORE LEAVING FOR A STRANGE AND
DISTANT SHORE.  AT THIS VERY MOMENT, THEY SERVE TOGETHER WITH
ARABS, EUROPEANS, ASIANS AND AFRICANS IN DEFENSE OF PRINCIPLE AND
THE DREAM OF A NEW WORLD ORDER.  THAT IS WHY THEY SWEAT AND TOIL
IN THE SAND AND THE HEAT AND THE SUN.

IF THEY CAN COME TOGETHER UNDER SUCH ADVERSITY; IF OLD
ADVERSARIES LIKE THE SOVIET UNION AND THE UNITED STATES CAN WORK
IN COMMON CAUSE; THEN SURELY WE WHO ARE SO FORTUNATE TO BE IN
THIS GREAT CHAMBER -- DEMOCRATS, REPUBLICANS, LIBERALS,
CONSERVATIVES -- CAN COME TOGETHER TO FULFILL OUR
RESPONSIBILITIES HERE.

THANK YOU, GOOD NIGHT, AND GOD BLESS AMERICA.

# # #

0065

관리
번호 70-1931

# 외 무 부

종 별 : 긴 급

번 호 : USW-4130                                          일 시 : 90 0911 2337

수 신 : 장관(미북,미안,중근동,기정)

발 신 : 주 미 대사

제 목 : 이락사태-의회 반응(8)

연 USW-4129

금일 부쉬 대통령 연설에 대한 의회 반응및 당관 평가를 하기 보고함.

1. 금일 연설을 통해 부쉬 대통령은 중동 사태가 미-소 정상회담등을 바탕으로 시도되는 새로운 세계 질서 모색에 대한 첫 도전임을 강조하고 신질서 유지에 있어서의 미국의 지도력의 필요성을 강력히 피력함.

2. 미 상하 양원의원들은 미주 공화 소속을 불문하고, 금일 저녁 부쉬 대통령의 특별 연설에 대해 매우 긍정적인 반응을 보였는바, GEPHARDT 민주당 하원 원내 총무는 금번 중동 사태와 관련, 부쉬 대통령의 정책을 높이 평가하면서 초당적인 지지를 재확인하였음(ASPEN 하원 군사위원장도 동 연설을 종합적이고도 매우 유익한 것이라고 평가)

3. 금일 연설은 미 행정부의 대이락 정책에 대한 정리, 요약의 의미를 가지고 있으나, 문제 해결을 위한 새로운 방안 제시에는 미흡한바 있다는 민주당측 반응도 있었음.

4. 부쉬 대통령은 동 연설에서 금번 사태 해결을 위하여는 지난주 HELSINKI에서 개최된 미.소 정상회담의 결과를 바탕으로, 전국제 사회의 단합된 참여가매우 중요한것임을 재강조하였는바, 미 의회 의원들도 연설후 보인 반응을 통하여 미국의 젊은 이들은 목숨의 위협을 무릅쓰고 중동의 사막에 투입되었으므로관련 우방국들로서는 최소한 재정적 희생(FINANCIAL SACRIFICE)은 감수해야할것임을 강조함.

5. 부쉬 대통령은 금일 연설에서 금번 사태 해결과 관련, 미국민 및 의회의초당적 지지에 사의를 표하고, 금번 사태가 장기화될 경우 초래될수 있늘 제반어려움에 대해서도 인내심을 가지고 극복해 나갈것을 호소함으로서 금번 사태 해결을 경제제재

미주국    장관    차관    1차보    2차보    미주국    중아국    청와대    안기부
대책반

90.09.12    13:41
외신 2과 통제관 FE
0066

조치를 통한 장기적 해결 방안을 모색하고 있음을 시사하였음.

(대사 박동진-국장)

90.12.31 까지

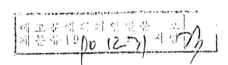

| 관리 | | |
|---|---|---|
| 번호 | Po-1P43 | |

# 외 무 부

종   별 :

번   호 : USW-4146                    일   시 : 90 0912 1755

수   신 : 장관(미북,미안,중근동,기정)

발   신 : 주 미 대사

제   목 : 이락 사태-의회 반응(9)

1. 이락의 쿠웨이트 침공 이래 6 주일이 지난 현재 상. 하 양원 외무위및 상원 군사위가 청문회를 개최하여 금번 사태에 관한 의회의 입장을 개진하였으며, 한편 9.11 부쉬 대통령도 양원 합동회의에서의 대 국민 연설을 통해 미 행정부의 입장을 종합적으로 밝혔는바, 현시점에서 당지 언론및 여론 조사, 특히 의회 인사들의 발언 내용에 나타난 미 우방국의 책임 분담 논의(BURDEN-SHARING)에대한 당관 관찰과 분석을 하기 보고함.

2. 페르시아만 사태 관련 책임 분담 논의

가. 배경

1)이락 사태의 장기화

페르시아만 주둔 미군의 장기화 조짐과 미 행정부의 동지역 안정을 위한 장기적 개입 공언에 따라 엄청난 전비 확보 방안의 일환으로서 방위 비용 분담 논의가 활발하게 거론되기 시작함.

2)국제 사회의 지지 확보 조치

이락 사태에 개입하는 미국의 정치적 명분을 제고하기 위한 방안으로서 우방국의 참여 강조의 필요성

3)산적된 미 국내 경제적 문제

재정적자와 경제 침체등 국내 경제적 어려움을 겪고 있는 미국으로서, 이락사태로 인한 추가 비용 부담에 대한 예산상의 경감책 강구

4)주요 우방국 기여도에 대한 불만

그간 미국의 활발한 외교로 상당수의 우방국이 책임 분담을 약속 하고는 있으나, 해외 주둔 미군 병력이 대규모로 배치되어 있으며, 대미 주요 무역 흑자국인 독일, 일본등이 중동 석유에 대한 의존도가 높은데도 불구하고 이락 사태에 대한 기여도가

---

미주국    차관    1차보    2차보    미주국    중아국    청와대    안기부

외신 2과  통제관 BT
0068

기대에 미치지 못하고 있다는 인식

　5)책임 분담 논의와 관련 한국이 거론되는 소이

　0 중동 석유 자원에 대한 의존도가 높은 국가

　0 과거 3-4 년간 대미 무역 흑자를 기록한 국가라는 인식과 최근 남북한 총리 회담 및 한국의 북방 정책의 성공적 추진등이 미 주요 언론의 보도 (사설 및 OP-ED 기사등)를 통해 한반도 긴장완화가 다소 과장되게 미국 여론에 부영되고 있는점.

　0 한국은 독일, 일본 다음으로 다수의 미군 병력이 주둔하고 있는 국가이며한미 상호간에 전통 우방임을 강조하여온 관계

　0 아울러, 이락에 대한 아국의 경제, 통상면에서의 이해 관계(건설 수주등)가 동 사태에 임하는 아국 정부의 입장을 미온화 시키고 있다는 미 정책 결정자들의 인식

　나. 아국 관계 논의 현황및 전망

　1)책임 분담 논의 계속

　현재까지의 우방국 책임 분담과 관련한 아국에 대한 언급은 주로 독일, 일본의 기여도에 대한불만의 연장 선상에서 이해될수 있으나, 금 9.12 하원 본회의에서의 주 일본 미군 유지 비용에 대한 일본 정부의 추가 부담을 골자로 하는 BONIOR 수정안이나, 9.10 상원 본회의에서 채택된 DECONCINI 결의안등의 논의 과정에서 감지될수 있듯이 미군이 주둔하고 있는 국가에 대한 이락 사태와 관련한 방위비 분담 논의는 산발적으로 계속될것으로 사료됨.

　2) 우방국과의 교섭에 대한 의회의 강력한 지지

　금후에도 사태의 장기화와 사태의 악화 여하에 따라 대 우방국 방위 분담 요구는 미 의회의 초당적 지지를 바탕으로 점차 고조될것으로 전망됨.

　3. 상기 언급한 DECONCINI 결의안은 별전 보고함.

　(대사 박동진-국장)

　90.12.31 까지

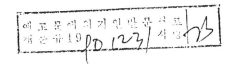

외 무 부

관리
번호 : ㅏ0-1ㅏ42

종 별 :

번 호 : USW-4147                          일 시 : 90 0912 1755

수 신 : 장관(미북,미안,중근동,기정)

발 신 : 주 미 대사

제 목 : 이락사태-의회 반응(10)

연 USW-4146

1. 연호 2 항 관련, 미 상원은 9.10 본회의 재무, 우정및 행정 지출 법안 논의시 DENNIS CDCONCINI(민주-아리조나), ALFONSE D'AMATO(공-뉴욕)및 JESSE HELMS(공-노스캐롤라이나)의원이 제안한 페르시아만 사태 관련한 우방국 책임 분담에 관한 수정안을 만장일치로 통과 시켰음.

2. 동 결의안의 골자는 아래임.

가. 책임 분담 논의 의회 보고 의무화

페르시아만 지역에 얽힌 국제적인 이 해 관계를 공동으로 방위하기 위하여, 미 대통령은 우방국들의 적절한 책임 분담을 진지하게 논의해야하며, 동 논의과정의 상세 진전 상황을 90.11.31 까지 의회에 보고해야함.

나. 책임 분담 논의 비 협조국에 대한 제재 조치 경고

적절한 책임 역할 논의에 비 협조적인 국가에 대해서는 미국과의 쌍무 관계에 지대한 악영향을 초래할것을 경고해야하며, 법적인 지원 조치가 필요시 의회에 요청할것.

3. 수정안 제안 취지를 설명하는 가운데, DECONCINI 의원은 독일과 일본의 책임 분담에 대한 기여가 미진함에 강한 불만을 표명하고 파키스탄, 방글라데시등 후진국들도 지상 병력을 파견하는 만큼, 페르시아만의 석유에 다분히 의존하고 있는 한국도 병력 파견, 운송 수단 제공등의 조치등을 통해 책임 분담에 참여할수 있을것이라고 언급함.

4. 동 수정안은 법적인 구속력이 없는 SENSE OF SENOTE 의 형식으로 채택된바, 참고 바라며, 전문 FAX 송부함.

첨부 USW(F)-2188

| 미주국 | 차관 | 1차보 | 2차보 | 미주국 | 중아국 | 정와대 | 안기부 |
|---|---|---|---|---|---|---|---|

PAGE 1

(대사 박동진-국장)
90.12.31 까지

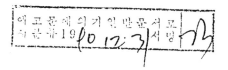

PAGE 2

0071

AMENDMENT NO. ____                    Calendar No. ____

Purpose: To express the sense of the Senate regarding burden-sharing in the Persian Gulf.

IN THE SENATE OF THE UNITED STATES—101st Cong., 2d Sess.

## H.R. 5241

Making appropriations for the Treasury Department, the United States Postal Service, the Executive Office of the President, and certain Independent Agencies, for the fiscal year ending September 30, 1991, and for other purposes.

Referred to the Committee on _____
                    and ordered to be printed

Ordered to lie on the table and to be printed

AMENDMENT intended to be proposed by Mr. DeConcini,

Viz:

1    On page 114, after line 22, add the following new

2 section:

3    SEC. ___. (a) The Senate finds that—

4        (1) democracy and freedom of the independent

5    Arab nations have been threatened by the invasion

6    and illegal annexation of Kuwait by the Government

7    of the Republic of Iraq;

8        (2) the safety of American citizens and those of

9    other countries have been directly threatened by the

2/88—1

0072

1    decision of the Government of Iraq to move them

2    and use them as "human shields" at strategic de-

3    fense and industrial installations;

4    (3) the stability of world oil production and

5    marketing has been threatened by the illegal Iraqi

6    seizure of Kuwaiti ports and oil production facilities;

7    (4) the United Nations has condemned Iraq's in-

8    vasion of Kuwait, has voted to impose an economic

9    embargo on Iraq, and has declared null and void the

10    annexation of Kuwait;

11    (5) the United Nations Security Council has ap-

12    proved the use of appropriate military force by indi-

13    vidual nations to enforce United Nations sanctions;

14    (6) the President of the United States has taken

15    the lead in unifying world opinion and directing

16    international efforts against the Iraqi aggression and

17    in defense of Saudi Arabia and the other Gulf states;

18    (7) a majority of Arab nations have condemned

19    Iraq's actions and have supported Arab military and

20    diplomatic efforts to defend the Gulf states and to

21    ensure Iraq's withdrawal from Kuwait;

22    (8) the United States is deploying tens of thou-

23    sands of American troops and military hardware to

24    the Persian Gulf in defense of the strategic interests

25    of the United States in the region.

2-/ 8권 — 2

1 ~~defense forces considerable risk of attack and~~ at

2 costs estimated to be in excess of $~~25~~ 40 million a day,

3 during a time of an increasing budget deficit;

4      (9) a principle position of the United States and

5 its NATO and major non-NATO allies is one of bur-

6 densharing in the collective defense of the Western

7 alliance;

8      (10) the Senate and the American people are

9 deeply concerned about the need for a reduced

10 budget deficit and improved economic growth; and

11      (11) President George Bush has announced his

12 intention to develop an economic action plan under

13 which nations benefitting from the economic embar-

14 go and the military actions in the Persian Gulf assist

15 those nations which are committing their military

16 personnel and materiel to support these United Na-

17 tions actions.

18 (b) It is the sense of the Senate that—

19      (1) the President of the United States *should* be con-

20 gratulated for taking the diplomatic initiative to en-

21 courage other nations to share the international fi-

22 nancial burden of the defense of Saudi Arabia; and

23      (2) the President of the United States—

2/88 - 3

0074

1    (A) in consultation with the allies of the

2    United States in the Persian Gulf defense oper-

3    ation, should—

4        (i) take steps to ensure that United

5    States allies are sharing an appropriate por-

6    tion of the collective defense of their inter-

7    ests in the Gulf;

8        (ii) take steps to ensure that those

9    allies who are precluded from any overt

10   military participation in the Gulf, or who

11   decide against participating in these defen-

12   sive actions, or who only provide minimal

13   participation are assuming an appropriate

14   financial share of the collective defense

15   commensurate with their national means;

16   and

17       (iii) take steps to ensure that those oil

18   producing nations which may benefit from

19   increased individual oil production and

20   world oil prices as a result of the embargo

21   of Iraqi and Kuwaiti oil proportionally

22   share the burden of the costs of the embar-

23   go, either directly with those nations pro-

24   viding the defense, or by equivalent "in-

25   kind" payments, or by assuming some of

2/88 - 4

the other international financial burdens of the major defense-providing nations;

(B) in concert with the Secretary of State, the Secretary of Defense, the Secretary of the Treasury, and the Director of the Office of Management and Budget, shall consult with Congress on the steps the President is taking to meet the goals enumerated in subparagraph (A) and shall provide a report to the ~~congressional~~ Congress ~~leadership~~ no later than November 30, 1990, detailing the progress of such steps to date;

(C) during his consultations with other international leaders, should consider stressing, among other points, that failure by any country to actively contribute in the most appropriate manner for that country could have a detrimental impact on its bilateral relationship with the United States; and

(D) should also inform Congress of any legislative initiatives which need to be taken to meet the goals enumerated in subparagraphs (A) through (C).

2788-5

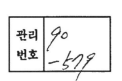

# 외 무 부

종 별 : 지 급

번 호 : USW-4215                                    일 시 : 90 0917 1759

수 신 : 장관(미안,미북,중근동,아일,기정)

발 신 : 주 미 대사

제 목 : 이락사태 관련 미의회 동향(11)

1. 하원 외무위 아태소위(SOLARZ 위원장)는 오는 9.19(수)오전 09:30 이락 사태와관련, 아시아 각국의 반응에 관한 청문회를 개최할 예정임.(국무성 SOLOMON 동아태 차관보 증언 예정)

2. 상기 청문회 개최관련, 금 9.17(월)오후 당관 임성준 참사관은 아태 소위 STANLEY ROTH 수석 전문위원을 방문, 관련 사항을 탐문한바 요지 아래 보고함.

가. 금번 이락사태 발생으로 인하여 아시아 각국도 많은 영향을 받고 있는바, 금번 청문회는 이들 제국을 3 가지 CATEGORY 로 분류하여 REVIEW 할것임.

나. 첫째 CATEGORY 는 금번 사태로 인하여 매우 어려움을 겪고 있는 서남아4 개국(방글라데시, 인도, 파키스탄, 스리랑카)과 필리핀의 상황을 검토할것인바, 필리핀의 경우 55,000 명의 근로자 대책, 유가상승으로인한 국내경제 악화, 수출(약 1 억불)타격등 가장 어려움을 겪고 있으며, 이들 국가에 대한 지원방안이 제시될것임.

다. 둘째 CATEGORY 는 역할분담(BURDEN-SHARING)문제인바, 주된 초점은 일본의 지원방안에 모아질것인바, 대만, 한국등도 경제적으로 비교적 여유가 있는 국가이므로 거론될 것으로 생각됨.

라. 셋째, CATEGORY 는 금번 사태로 인한 유가상승등으로 이득을 보고 있는국가도 있는데, 브르나이, 인도네시아가 여기에 속하며, 이들국가의 금번 사태관련 기여 방안이 거론될것임.

3. 동위원은 최근 일본과 서독이 미의회를 비롯한 여론의 비판대상이 되고 있는것은 분담공약 내용(40 억불)이 빈약한것 보다는 분담문제에 관한 정부태도가 사우디나 쿠웨이트 왕정에 비하여 분명하지 않았고 발표시기도 다소 늦어진데기인한것으로 본다고 하면서, 금후 아국정부가 계획하고 있는 지원 내용은 규모의 대소를 불문하고 신속히 발표하는것이 도움이 될것이라는 개인적인 견해를

---

미주국    차관    1차보    2차보    아주국    미주국    중아국    청와대    안기부

표명하였음. (대사 박동진국장)
   예고:90.12.31 까지

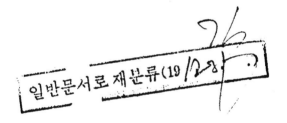

PAGE 2

0078

```
관리
번호 90-2057
```

외 무 부

종 별 : 지급

번 호 : USW-4228　　　　　　　　일 시 : 90 0918 1620

수 신 : 장관(미안,미북,아일,기정)

발 신 : 주 미 대사

제 목 : BONIOR수정안 반응

　　　　연:USW-4158

　　　　대:WUS-3063

　　1. 대호 미하원에서의 BONIOR 수정안 채택에 따른 상원 토의전망 및 행정부반응등에 대한 미의회 및 행정부 관계자 의견을 하기 종합 보고함.

　　가. BONIOR 수정안 제출 및 채택배경

　　(MARK KOYANAGI 보니어 의원 보좌관)

　　O BONIOR 수정안은 페르시아만 사태 발발 이전인 금년 7 월에 준비한 것으로 일본의 경제력이 미국내 경제에 심각한 타격을 주고있는 상황에서 미국이 일본의 방위를 위해 재정지출을 한다는 사실에 대해 반대해온 BONIOR 의원의 평소 생각을 반영한것임.

　　O BONIOR 의원이나 KOYANAGI 보좌관 자신도 동 수정안이 채택될것으로 기대하지 않고 있었으나, 페르시아만 사태와 관련한 일본정부의 미온적 조치에 대한 불만표시로 동수정안이 채택된것으로 보고 있음.

　　나.BONIOR 수정안 상원 심의 전망

　　O BONIOR 수정안과 동일 내용의 법안이 상원에 제출된바 없고, BONIOR 수정안에 대한 상원내 논의 일정도 계획된바 없음.

　　-BONIOR 의원과 동일주 출신인 DONALD RIEGLE 상원의원이 동일내용의 법안제출을 고려한바 있었으나 상금 제출치않았음.

　　O FY 91 국방예산 수권법안에 대한 상. 하원 협의회의 심의시 BONIOR 수정안이 채택될 가능성은 희박한것으로 전망됨(상원군사위 FREEDMAN 전문위원 및 KOYANAGI 보니어 의원 보좌관)

　　- 동수정안 하원 채택이후 일본 정부가 페르시아만 사태 분담금으로 30 억불을

---

미주국　　장관　　차관　　2차보　　아주국　　미주국　　외연원　　청와대　　안기부

외신 2과　통제관 FE

0079

추가로 공약함에 따라 <u>미의회내 일본에 대한 강경한 입장이 완화된 상황임.</u>

- 동 수정안에 대해 찬성 부표한 의원중 상당수가 동 수정안 내용에 찬성한것이라기 보다는 <u>일본정부에 대한 각성 (WAKE-UP CALL)을 촉구한것임.</u>

0 다만, 상원내 일각에서는 일본이 폐만 사태 분담금 40 억불지원 공약이 아직도 충분치 않다는 견해가 있는바, 일본의 폐만 사태 분담금 증액 차원에서 동문제가 거론될 가능성도 배제치 어려움(채택 가능성은 희박)

다. 국무부등 행정부 반응(9.13 PITZWATER 백악관 대변인 기자 브리핑 및 DE VILLA FRANCA 국무부 담당관)

0 BONIOR 수정안은 미의회내 일본에 대한 <u>일반적 감정을 표시한</u> 것일뿐 일본의 방위문제에 대해 미의회가 어떤 결정을 내린것으로 보기는 어려움.

0 동 수정안 통과는 주일 미군 문제 자체보다도 일본으로 하여금 폐만 비용부담을 많이하게 하려는데 기인함.

0 일본내에서 외무성등 대외문제 관련 부서는 폐만 비용부담이 적극적이었으나 대장성등 타부서가 반대해왔던 것으로 보이며, 그런 의미에서 동수정안 같은 WAKE-UP CALL 이 필요했던것으로 볼수 있음.

2. 당관 관찰 및 평가

0 BONIOR 수정안 채택이 전기한바와같이 주일 미군에 대한 일본의 방위분담비용에 대한 불만이나 미국의 동맹국 군사협력정책의 변경에 따른 것이 아닌 일시적인 미의회의 의견을 반영함.

0 다만, 미의회내 동맹국에 대한 방위분담 증액 압력이 상존하고 있는 상황에서, BONIOR 수정안과같은 극단적인 방위 비용의 동맹국 부담안이 채택되었다는점은 향후 방위분담 문제 심의시 동맹국에게 불리하게 작용하게될것임.

0 상기 BONIOR 수정안과유사한 내용의 법안이 주한미군에 대해서도 입안될 가능성은 현재로서는없는것으로 보이나 (북한의 직접적 위협에 대한 의회내 인식), 없는것으로 보이나(북한의 직접적 위협에 대한 의회내 인식향후 의회내 재정적자 해소 논의,한반도 정세 변화 가능성,주요 우방국의 기여확대에 대한우방국의 기여확대에 대한 기대심리등으로 주한미군에 대한 논의의 개연성은 상존하고 있음.

(대사 박동진-국장)

예고:90.12.31 일반

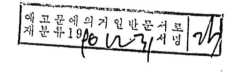

관리
번호 R-1768

# 외 무 부

종 별 : 지급

번 호 : USW-4245                     일 시 : 90 0918 2010

수 신 : 장관(미북,미안,중근동,  기정)

발 신 : 주 미 대사

제 목 : 이락 사태 관련 미 의회 동향(12)

　　　연 USW-4215

　　1. 금 9.18 하원 외무위 인권 및 국제기구 소위(위원장 GUS YATRON, 민-펜실바니아)는 JOHN KELLY 국무부 중동 담당 차관보 및 HENRY ROWEN 국방부 국제 안보 담당 차관보를 출석시킨 가운데 페 만 사태에 관한 청문회를 개최하였음.

　　2. 상기 차관보들은 증언에서 미국의 대 페만 사태 해결을 위한 외교적 노력과 성과를 설명하고, 동맹국들의 비용 분담 노력(총 지원금액 200 억불)을 높이 평가하였음.

　　3. 동 청문회 질의 응답시 TOM LANTOS 의원(민-칼리포니아)은 페만 사태에 대한 한국정부의 지원 규모에 대해 질문한바 ROWEN 국방부 차관보는 구체적 수치는 갖고 있지 않으나 한국정부로부터 상당한 규모의 지원(A VERY SIGNIFICANT CONTRIBUTION)이 올것으로 기대하고 있다고 답변하였으며, MEL LEVINE 의원(민-캘리포니아)은 250 억불 상당의 대우디 무기 수출 결정과 관련, 동 배경에 대해서는 이해를 하나 인도 시기가 2 년이나 걸리는 군사 장비에 대해서도 판매 결정을 지금 내리고자 하는 행정부측 입장에 대해 우려를 표명하였음.

　　4. 상기 청문회 증언문은 별첨 FAX 송부함.

　　첨부 USW(F)-2273

　　(대사 박동진-국장)

예고문에
개분류 12

미주국　장관　차관　1차보　2차보　아주국　미주국　미주국　중아국
중아국　외연원　청와대　안기부　대책반

〈첨부〉

USW(F) — 2203

수신: 장관 (미북. 미안. 음근문)

발신: 주미대사.

제목: 하원 인권 및 국제기가구 소위 청문회 (페만사태)

### ASSISTANT SECRETARY JOHN H. KELLY'S APPEARANCE BEFORE THE HOUSE FOREIGN AFFAIRS SUBCOMMITTEE ON EUROPE AND THE MIDDLE EAST

### SEPTEMBER 18, 1990 AT 2:00 P.M.

### AMERICAN LEADERSHIP IN THE MIDDLE EAST

0082

- 2 -

I AM PLEASED TO APPEAR BEFORE THE SUBCOMMITTEE.

BETWEEN SEPTEMBER 5 AND 17, I ACCOMPANIED SECRETARY BAKER ON
A VISIT TO EIGHT COUNTRIES IN THE MIDDLE EAST AND EUROPE. I
WANT TO TELL YOU AT THE OUTSET THAT IN EVERY COUNTRY WE VISITED,
AMERICAN LEADERSHIP WAS ACKNOWLEDGED, APPRECIATED, AND
RECOGNIZED AS ESSENTIAL FOR RESOLUTION OF THE GULF CRISIS.

THERE IS GRATITUDE FOR THE AMERICAN MILITARY PRESENCE ON THE
ARABIAN PENINSULA. THERE IS RECOGNITION OF THE SACRIFICES BEING
MADE BY THE MEN AND WOMEN OF THE AMERICAN ARMED FORCES. THERE
IS SOLIDARITY THAT IRAQI AGGRESSION MUST NOT STAND AND THERE IS
WILLINGNESS TO SHARE THE RESPONSIBILITIES FOR IMPLEMENTATION OF
THE UNITED NATIONS SECURITY COUNCIL RESOLUTIONS.

POLITICALLY THIS WAS ACKNOWLEDGED IN ARAB CAPITALS, BY NATO
AND THE EUROPEAN COMMUNITY, AND IN THE JOINT STATEMENT ISSUED BY
PRESIDENTS BUSH AND GORBACHEV IN HELSINKI. MILITARILY THIS IS
RECOGNIZED BY THE DECISIONS OF MANY NATIONS TO CONTRIBUTE FORCES
TO THE EFFORT IN THE GULF. ECONOMICALLY THE SHARED
RESPONSIBILITY IS MANIFESTED BY PLEDGES OF UP TO TWENTY BILLION
DOLLARS TO HELP SHARE THE COSTS OF THE AMERICAN DEFENSE
CONTRIBUTION AND TO CUSHION THE ECONOMIC SHOCK FOR THOSE
COUNTRIES HURT MOST BY IRAQI AGGRESSION.

TODAY, SEVEN WEEKS AFTER THE INVASION OF KUWAIT, IRAQI
OCCUPATION FORCES REMAIN DUG IN THROUGHOUT THAT COUNTRY, AND
CONTINUE TO THREATEN THE SECURITY OF SAUDI ARABIA AND
NEIGHBORING STATES. IRAQ CONTINUES TO HOLD HOSTAGE HUNDREDS OF
THOUSANDS OF FOREIGN NATIONALS, INCLUDING ABOUT 1,440    0083
AMERICANS. MANY U.S. CITIZENS HAVE BEEN INCARCERATED TO BE USED

- 3 -

SINCE IRAQ'S INVASION OF KUWAIT, THE CIVILIZED WORLD HAS
SPOKEN WITH A NEARLY UNANIMOUS VOICE IN ITS DETERMINATION THAT
IRAQI AGGRESSION MUST BE CONTAINED AND REVERSED. AS PRESIDENT
BUSH SAID SEPTEMBER 11 IN HIS ADDRESS TO A JOINT SESSION OF
CONGRESS, THIS WILL REQUIRE PATIENCE AND STRONG WILL.

I LAST APPEARED BEFORE THIS SUBCOMMITTEE ON JULY 31, AT A
TIME WHEN IRAQI THREATS AND INTIMIDATION HAD RAISED TENSIONS IN
THE REGION TO VERY HIGH LEVELS. I SAID THEN THAT ADMINISTRATION
POLICY WAS "TO DO ALL WE CAN TO SUPPORT OUR FRIENDS WHEN THEY
ARE THREATENED AND TO PRESERVE STABILITY" IN THE AREA.

TWO DAYS LATER, THE IRAQI GOVERNMENT DEMONSTRATED THE DEPTHS
OF ITS IRRESPONSIBILITY AND ITS CONTEMPT FOR CIVILIZED STANDARDS
OF BEHAVIOR BY CARRYING OUT AN UNPROVOKED ACT OF AGGRESSION
AGAINST KUWAIT.

IN THE WEEKS SINCE THEN, THE WORLD HAS MOBILIZED TO REVERSE
IRAQ'S AGGRESSION. THE UNITED STATES HAS CARRIED OUT A MASSIVE
MILITARY DEPLOYMENT OF PERSONNEL AND MATERIAL TO THE GULF
REGION. WE HAVE BEEN JOINED IN OUR MILITARY EFFORTS BY MANY
OTHER STATES. TODAY, OVER TWENTY NATIONS HAVE RESPONDED TO
REQUESTS FROM SAUDI ARABIA AND KUWAIT FOR ASSISTANCE TO DETER
FURTHER IRAQI ACTS OF AGGRESSION BY CONTRIBUTING GROUND, AIR, OR
MARITIME FORCES.

0084

- 4 -

WE ALSO HAVE BEEN ACTIVE ON THE DIPLOMATIC FRONT AS WE HAVE
MOLDED AN INTERNATIONAL CONSENSUS TO DETER FURTHER IRAQI
AGGRESSION. WE HAVE MET WITH AN EXCEPTIONALLY HIGH DEGREE OF
INTERNATIONAL COOPERATION IN THIS EFFORT. THE UNITED NATIONS
SECURITY COUNCIL HAS PASSED SEVEN RESOLUTIONS ON THE GULF
CRISIS. THREE MEETINGS OF THE ARAB LEAGUE HAVE PRODUCED STRONG
CONDEMNATION OF IRAQI BEHAVIOR. AT LEAST 98 COUNTRIES HAVE
ANNOUNCED PUBLICLY THAT THEY SUPPORT UN SECURITY COUNCIL
RESOLUTION 661 ESTABLISHING MANDATORY SANCTIONS AGAINST IRAQ AND
HAVE TAKEN, OR WILL TAKE, STEPS TO IMPLEMENT THAT RESOLUTION. A
NUMBER OF NATIONS ARE PROVIDING FINANCIAL AND ECONOMIC SUPPORT
TO THOSE STATES ENDURING PARTICULAR ECONOMIC SACRIFICES DUE TO
THEIR ADHERENCE TO THE SANCTIONS. OPEC NATIONS SUCH AS SAUDI
ARABIA, THE UNITED ARAB EMIRATES, AND VENEZUELA HAVE AGREED TO
INCREASE PRODUCTION TO OFFSET THE LOSS OF IRAQI AND KUWAITI OIL
EXPORTS.

IRAQ TODAY STANDS AS AN INTERNATIONAL PARIAH, AN OUTLAW
ISOLATED FROM THE ARAB LEAGUE MAJORITY AND CONDEMNED BY THE
INTERNATIONAL COMMUNITY. THE IRAQI ECONOMY IS FEELING THE BITE
OF SANCTIONS. THAT BITE WILL BECOME MORE PAINFUL IN THE WEEKS
AND MONTHS AHEAD. IRAQ LOSES APPROXIMATELY 2.7 MILLION BARRELS
A DAY IN LOST OIL EXPORTS OR MORE THAN 2.4 BILLION DOLLARS PER
MONTH FROM ITS INABILITY TO SELL IRAQI OIL ON THE INTERNATIONAL
MARKET.

0085

– 5 –

## DIPLOMATIC STRATEGY:

THE PRESIDENT HAS CLEARLY DEFINED OUR OBJECTIVES:  THE
IMMEDIATE, COMPLETE AND UNCONDITIONAL WITHDRAWAL OF ALL IRAQI
FORCES FROM KUWAIT; RESTORATION OF KUWAIT'S LEGITIMATE
GOVERNMENT; THE SECURITY AND STABILITY OF THE GULF REGION; AND
THE PROTECTION OF THE LIVES OF AMERICAN AND OTHER FOREIGN
CITIZENS HELD HOSTAGE BY IRAQ.

WE HAVE WIDE INTERNATIONAL SUPPORT FOR THIS POSITION.  WHEN
I ACCOMPANIED THE SECRETARY ON HIS RECENT TRIP, I HEARD ARAB AND
EUROPEAN LEADERS AGREE STRONGLY WITH THIS DETERMINATION.

THE JOINT COMMUNIQUE ISSUED BY PRESIDENT BUSH AND SOVIET
PRESIDENT GORBACHEV AT THE CONCLUSION OF THEIR SEPTEMBER 9
MEETING IN HELSINKI STRESSES THAT "NOTHING SHORT OF THE COMPLETE
IMPLEMENTATION OF THE UNITED NATIONS SECURITY COUNCIL
RESOLUTIONS IS ACCEPTABLE." DURING THE SECRETARY'S VISIT TO
NATO HEADQUARTERS ON SEPTEMBER 10, OUR EUROPEAN ALLIES WERE
UNITED IN REJECTING THE IDEA OF A PARTIAL SOLUTION.

GIVEN THE INFLEXIBLE IRAQI POSITION, OUR DIPLOMATIC STRATEGY
MUST FOCUS ON SUSTAINING THE INTERNATIONAL SENSE OF FIRMNESS,
THE UNITY OF PURPOSE, AND THE SENSE OF COHESION THAT HAVE
CONFRONTED SADDAM HUSSEIN.  WE MUST WORK TO MAINTAIN AND
STRENGTHEN SANCTIONS AGAINST IRAQ WHILE INCREASING MULTINATIONAL
MILITARY FORCES IN THE AREA TO DETER FURTHER IRAQI ACTS OF
AGGRESSION.

0086

– 6 –

RESPONSIBILITY-SHARING:

WE MUST ASSURE THAT THE MILITARY AND ECONOMIC BURDEN OF
DETERRING AGGRESSION WHILE THE SANCTIONS TAKE EFFECT ARE SHARED
EQUITABLY.  AS THE PRESIDENT SAID ON AUGUST 30, "IT IS IMPORTANT
THAT THE CONSIDERABLE BURDEN OF THE EFFORT BE SHARED BY THOSE
BEING DEFENDED, AND THOSE WHO BENEFIT FROM THE FREE FLOW OF
OIL.  INDEED, ANYONE WHO HAS A STAKE IN INTERNATIONAL ORDER HAS
AN INTEREST THAT ALL OF US SUCCEED....WE'RE MORE THAN WILLING TO
BEAR OUR FAIR SHARE OF THE BURDEN.... BUT WE ALSO EXPECT OTHERS
TO BEAR THEIR FAIR SHARE."

WE MUST ALSO ASSURE THAT THOSE STATES, SUCH AS EGYPT AND
TURKEY, WHOSE ECONOMIES HAVE BEEN HIT PARTICULARLY HARD BY
ADHERENCE TO THE SANCTIONS ARE GIVEN THE FINANCIAL ASSISTANCE
NECESSARY TO HELP THEM WEATHER THE STORM CREATED BY IRAQI
AGGRESSION.

JORDAN'S ECONOMY STANDS TO LOOSE PROPORTIONATELY MORE THAN
ANY OTHER NATION AS A RESULT OF STRICT ADHERENCE TO UNSC
RESOLUTION 661.  FOR THIS REASON, WE HAVE WORKED BILATERALLY
DURING THE BAKER/BRADY MISSIONS AND AT THE UN TO GENERATE
SUPPORT FOR JORDAN, PROVIDING THAT JORDAN VIGOROUSLY ENFORCES
SANCTIONS.  INDICATIONS ARE THAT JORDAN IS APPLYING SANCTIONS;
THERE HAS BEEN IMPROVEMENT.

HOWEVER, ON THE POLITICAL LEVEL, JORDAN'S PERFORMANCE STILL
PRESENTS DIFFICULTIES.  WE ARE SHOCKED BY THE RALLY OF RADICAL
ARAB FORCES HELD THIS WEEKEND IN AMMAN AND PARTICULARLY BY ITS
HARSH ANTI-AMERICAN TONE.  THAT JORDAN WOULD LENDS ITS NAME TO
AN EVENT OF THIS SORT IS, FRANKLY, VERY DISAPPOINTING.

0087

- 7 -

WE FIND IT HARD TO UNDERSTAND WHY SOME OF THE SAME FORCES
WHO WERE DRIVEN OUT OF JORDAN IN 1970 BECAUSE THEY UNDERMINED
JORDANIAN STABILITY ARE TODAY ASSEMBLING IN AMMAN TO DECLARE
THEIR SUPPORT FOR SADDAM HUSSEIN.

THE JORDANIAN GOVERNMENT HAS INFORMED US THAT IT OPPOSES
IRAQI ACQUISITION OF TERRITORIES BY FORCE IN KUWAIT; WE WOULD
HOPE THAT IT WOULD LOOK FOR WAYS TO STRENGTHEN THAT OPPOSITION,
RATHER THAN UNDERMINE IT.

HOSTAGES IN IRAQ:

IRAQ STILL CONTINUES TO HOLD ABOUT 1440 AMERICAN CITIZENS
HOSTAGE, AS WELL AS HUNDREDS OF THOUSANDS OF OTHER FOREIGNERS.

ABOUT THREE WEEKS AGO, I WAS AT ANDREWS AIR FORCE BASE TO
MEET THE FIRST PLANE BRINGING HOME WOMEN AND CHILDREN FROM OUR
EMBASSY IN KUWAIT.  I SAW FAMILIES WHO HAD DISPLAYED GREAT
COURAGE, BUT WHO ALSO REMAINED FULL OF ANXIETY FOR RELATIVES
LEFT BEHIND.  THESE FEELINGS ARE SHARED BY THOUSANDS OF FAMILIES
ACROSS THE UNITED STATES AND THE WORLD WHO HAVE RELATIVES STILL
TRAPPED IN IRAQ AND KUWAIT.  THE U.S. EMBASSY IN KUWAIT REMAINS
OPEN, AND OUR FLAG STILL FLIES, TO DEMONSTRATE THE COMMITMENT OF
THE AMERICAN GOVERNMENT AND PEOPLE TO DO ALL WE CAN TO PROTECT
OUR FELLOW CITIZENS AND SECURE THEIR SAFE RETURN HOME.  THE MEN
AND WOMEN SERVING AT OUR EMBASSY IN KUWAIT AND OUR EMBASSY IN
BAGHDAD HAVE BEEN AN INSPIRATION TO US ALL.  THEY HAVE DISPLAYED
COURAGE AND RESILIENCE UNDER SOME OF THE MOST TRYING CONDITIONS
IMAGINABLE.  I KNOW ALL MEMBERS OF THE COMMITTEE JOIN ME IN  0088
SALUTING THE PERFORMANCE OF OUR FELLOW AMERICANS WHO REMAIN IN
BAGHDAD AND KUWAIT.

- 8 -

WE AND THE CIVILIZED WORLD DEMAND THAT IRAQ COMPLY WITH UN
SECURITY COUNCIL RESOLUTION 664. WE DEMAND THAT THE IRAQI
GOVERNMENT FACILITATE THE IMMEDIATE DEPARTURE OF ALL FOREIGN
NATIONALS WISHING TO LEAVE IRAQ AND KUWAIT.

CONCLUSION:

THE INTERNATIONAL REACTION TO THE IRAQI INVASION OF KUWAIT
IS TRULY UNPRECEDENTED. THE UNITED STATES AND THE SOVIET UNION,
EMERGING FROM THE COLD WAR, HAVE TAKEN A COMMON STAND. THE ARAB
LEAGUE MAJORITY, THE MAJORITY OF THE ORGANIZATION OF THE ISLAMIC
CONFERENCE, THE EUROPEAN COMMUNITY, NATO, THE ORGANIZATION OF
AMERICAN STATES, THE ORGANIZATION OF AFRICAN UNITY, AND MEMBERS
OF THE ASSOCIATION OF SOUTH EAST ASIAN NATIONS HAVE SPOKEN OUT
FORCEFULLY AGAINST IRAQI AGGRESSION. THIS IS TRULY
INTERNATIONAL COHESION -- AND THIS COHESION EXISTS BECAUSE THE
CAUSE IS JUST. THE UNITED STATES IS LEADING, BUT THE UNITED
STATES IS NOT ALONE. THE UNITED NATIONS SECURITY COUNCIL HAS
VOTED SEVEN RESOLUTIONS. ON THE ISSUE OF IRAQI AGGRESSION,
THERE IS NO EAST OR WEST; THERE IS NO NORTH OR SOUTH. THERE IS
UNITY THAT ECHOES PRESIDENT BUSH'S STATEMENT "IRAQI AGGRESSION
WILL NOT STAND."

0089

Statement

by


The Honorable Henry S. Rowen
Assistant Secretary of Defense for
International Security Affairs


Before
The House Foreign Affairs Committee


September 18, 1990

0090

MR. CHAIRMAN:

THANK YOU FOR THE OPPORTUNITY TO APPEAR TODAY TO TESTIFY ON THE
GULF CRISIS. I WILL KEEP MY REMARKS BRIEF SO YOU AND OTHER
MEMBERS CAN HAVE MORE TIME FOR QUESTIONS.

SEVEN WEEKS AGO, AT THE REQUEST OF KING FAHD, PRESIDENT BUSH
ORDERED THE DEPLOYMENT OF U.S. FORCES TO SAUDI ARABIA TO PROTECT
VITAL U.S. INTERESTS. OUR OBJECTIVES ARE TO:

1. ASSURE THE SECURITY AND STABILITY IN THE REGION;

2. EFFECT THE IMMEDIATE, COMPLETE, AND UNCONDITIONAL
WITHDRAWAL OF ALL IRAQI FORCES FROM KUWAIT;

3. RESTORE THE LEGITIMATE GOVERNMENT OF KUWAIT; AND

4. PROTECT THE LIVES OF AMERICAN CITIZENS IN THE REGION.

IN SUPPORT OF THESE OBJECTIVES WE HAVE UNDERTAKEN AN
UNPRECEDENTED MILITARY EFFORT. WE NOW HAVE OVER 150,000
SOLDIERS, SAILORS, AIRMEN, AND MARINES IN THE GULF THEATER. THE
MOVEMENT OF U.S. FORCES HAS GONE VERY WELL. WE HAVE ELEMENTS OF
SEVERAL ARMY DIVISIONS, NUMEROUS AIR FORCE FIGHTER AND STRATEGIC
AIRCRAFT SQUADRONS, A MARINE EXPEDITIONARY FORCE, SPECIAL
OPERATIONS FORCES, THREE CARRIER BATTLE GROUPS, A BATTLESHIP,

0091

AND OTHER NAVAL ASSETS IN THE PERSIAN GULF, INDIAN OCEAN, AND
RED SEA.

THIS FAST DEPLOYMENT IS THE RESULT OF OUR RECOGNIZING THE
IMPORTANCE OF THE GULF FOR MANY YEARS AND THE PREPARATIONS WE
MADE. AS YOU KNOW, THE GULF HOLDS OVER 70 PERCENT OF THE WORLD
OIL RESERVES AND IS THE SOURCE FOR 33 PERCENT OF WESTERN OIL
PRODUCTION CAPACITY. THIS SOURCE OF ENERGY IS CRITICAL NOT ONLY
TO THE U.S. BUT ALSO THE WORLD ECONOMY.

OUR PREPARATIONS OVER THE YEARS ENTAILED HAVING A NAVAL FORCE IN
THE GULF; ACCESS AGREEMENTS FOR BASES BOTH EN-ROUTE TO THE
REGION, IN DIEGO GARCIA FOR INSTANCE AS LONG AGO AS 1966, AND IN
THE REGION; EQUIPMENT PREPOSITIONED IN SHIPS AND ON LAND; JOINT
PLANNING AND EXERCISES WITH FRIENDLY REGIONAL STATES; AND THE
CREATION OF THE U.S. CENTRAL COMMAND. SALES OF U.S.-MADE WEAPON
SYSTEMS HAS ALSO ASSURED COMPATIBILITY AND INTEROPERABILITY
WHILE THE BUILDING OF OVERSIZED FACILITIES BY FRIENDLY REGIONAL
COUNTRIES HAS ENABLED THEM TO ACCOMMODATE U.S. AND OTHER
MILITARY FORCES IN THIS CRISIS.

WE HAVE MUCH COMPANY IN THIS ENTERPRISE. AT THE INVITATION OF
THE GOVERNMENTS OF KUWAIT, SAUDI ARABIA AND OTHER GULF NATIONS,
MILITARY FORCES FROM 26 COUNTRIES ARE PARTICIPATING IN THE LAND-
BASED DESERT SHIELD OPERATION AND MARITIME ENFORCEMENT OF THE   0092
U.N.-IMPOSED ECONOMIC SANCTIONS. IN THE LAST FEW DAYS, WE HAVE
WITNESSED INCREASED COMMITMENTS BY THE U.K., FRANCE, AND EGYPT

AMONG OTHERS.  ALL MEMBERS OF THE GULF COOPERATION COUNCIL --
SAUDI ARABIA, KUWAIT, BAHRAIN, QATAR, OMAN, AND THE UAE -- HAVE
DONE THEIR PART IN THE COLLECTIVE EFFORT BY OFFERING BOTH TROOPS
AND MATERIELS.

LEFT UNCOUNTERED, THE IRAQI ARMY COULD HAVE SEIZED THE SAUDI OIL
FIELDS.  EVEN WITHOUT DOING THAT, IRAQ WOULD HAVE DOMINATED THE
ARABIAN PENINSULA.  IN THE SHORT-TERM, IRAQ COULD HAVE
DESTABILIZED AND MANIPULATED THE OIL MARKET, BRINGING DISRUPTION
IN PRODUCTION AND INCREASE IN PRICES.  IN THE LONGER-TERM,
SADDAM COULD HAVE CONSOLIDATED HIS CONTROL, EXPANDED HIS
MILITARY ARSENALS BY USING THE INCREASED REVENUE, AND THREATENED
THE ECONOMIC LIVELIHOOD OF ALL OIL-IMPORTING NATIONS.  MOST
DANGEROUSLY, ARMED WITH NEW ECONOMIC, POLITICAL, AND MILITARY
WEAPONS, SADDAM HUSSEIN WOULD HAVE BEEN ABLE TO ESTABLISH IRAQ
AS THE LEADING POWER IN THE REGION.  THUS, STOPPING SADDAM
HUSSEIN IS IMPERATIVE; THE OUTCOME OF THIS CRISIS WILL DEFINE
ACCEPTABLE INTERNATIONAL BEHAVIOR FOR THE AGGRESSORS IN POST-
COLD WAR ERA.

MR. CHAIRMAN, AS YOU KNOW, THE COST OF PROVIDING THE FORCES IN
OPERATION DESERT SHIELD IS ABOUT $3 BILLION PER MONTH, OF WHICH
$1 BILLION IS INCREMENTAL EXPENSES.  IN ADDITION, FRONTLINE
COUNTRIES SUCH AS TURKEY, EGYPT, AND JORDAN FACE SERIOUS
ECONOMIC LOSSES DUE TO THE ECONOMIC EMBARGO.  OTHER NATIONS ARE
HURT AS WELL.  THE PRESIDENT HAS ANNOUNCED AN ECONOMIC ACTION    0093
PLAN TO SEEK CONTRIBUTIONS FROM OTHER COUNTRIES.  OUR ALLIES ARE

RESPONDING. THEIR CONTRIBUTIONS TOTAL $20 BILLION; ABOUT HALF
OF THAT IS TO OFFSET U.S. COSTS AND HALF FOR THE FRONTLINE
STATES. SPECIFICALLY, THE GULF STATES HAVE OFFERED $12 BILLION
TO OUR PLAN; JAPAN HAS QUADRUPLED ITS INITIAL CONTRIBUTION AND
OFFERED $4 BILLION; GERMANY HAS OFFERED $2 BILLION; AND THE EC
HAS PLEDGED $2 BILLION. THESE CONTRIBUTIONS COME IN THE FORM OF
CASH AND IN-KIND GOODS AND SERVICES. THIS SUPPORT --
DIPLOMATICALLY, MILITARILY, AND FINANCIALLY-- SHOWS THE HIGH
COMMITMENT OF MANY NATIONS TO THIS ENTERPRISE.

LOOKING AHEAD, THE QUESTION IS OFTEN ASKED, "HOW LONG WILL WE BE
THERE?" I CANNOT GIVE A DEFINITIVE ANSWER. WE WERE INVITED
ALONG WITH MANY OTHER NATIONS BY THE SAUDIS AND OTHER
GOVERNMENTS TO HELP DEFEND THEIR COUNTRIES, AND WE WILL BE THERE
AS LONG AS IT TAKES TO ACHIEVE OUR MUTUAL OBJECTIVES. WHEN THAT
IS DONE, OR WHEN THE COUNTRIES ASK, WE WILL LEAVE.

IN THE FUTURE, WE WILL NEED TO WORK WITH OUR FRIENDS IN THE GULF
TO STRENGTHEN THEIR DEFENSE CAPABILITIES AND BOLSTER THEIR
ABILITIES TO RECEIVE REINFORCEMENTS IF THAT EVER BECOMES
NECESSARY AGAIN. WE NEED TO ENSURE THAT THE COUNTRIES OF THIS
AREA ARE NOT IN SUCH A VULNERABLE POSITION THAT A MASSIVE U.S.
DEPLOYMENT IS REQUIRED. TO ACCOMPLISH THAT TASK, MR. CHAIRMAN,
WE WILL NEED TO CONSULT WITH YOU AND MEMBERS OF THIS COMMITTEE,
AND WE WILL NEED YOUR HELP AND SUPPORT.

THANK YOU.                                                      0094

관리
번호 PO-1961

# 외 무 부

종    별 : 지급
번    호 : USW-4259                    일    시 : 90 0919 1817
수    신 : 장관(미북,미안,중근동,서남아,기정)
발    신 : 주 미 대사
제    목 : 이락 사태 의회 반응(13)

연 USW-4215

1. 금 9.19(수) 하원 아태 소위 청문회(위원장 STEVEN SOLARZ 민-뉴욕)는 "페만 사태에 대한 아시아의 반응" 이라는 제하의 청문회를 개최하였음. 동 청문회는 2 부로 나뉘어져 진행되었으며, 1 부에서는 국무부 근동및 서남아 담당 부차관보 TERESITA SCHAFFER 를 출석 시킨 가운데 서남아 4 개국(방글라데시, 인도,파키스탄, 스리랑카)의 동 사태에 대한 반응및 동 4 개국의 난민 문제, 경제적지원 방안등이 논의되었고, 2 부에서는 SOLOMON 국무부 아태 담당 차관보 및 ROBERT FAUVER 경제기획담당 부차관보가 출석한 가운데 일본, 한국, 호주등으로부터의 기여 문제및 필리핀에 대한 지원 방안등이 논의되었음. 아태 소위 소속 의원 대부분은 본회의 의사 일정 관계로 동 청문회에 참석치 않았는바, 제 1 부에는 JIM LEACH 공화당 간사, 제 2 부에는 DONALD LUKENS 의원만이 각각 참석하였음.

2. 동 청문회 1 부에서 SCHAFFER 부차관보는 증언문을 통해 인디아, 파키스탄, 방글라데시, 스리랑카등 서남아 4 개국이 PERSIA 만 사태로 인한 난민 문제 및 경제 제재 참여에 따른 경제적 타격등으로 큰 어려움을 겪고 있는 사정을 각국별로 설명하고, 미 행정부는 난민관계 국제기구와 협력하에 난민수송문제를 해결하고 있으며, 이집트, 요르단및 터어키등 전선 3 개국 지원문제 다음으로 동 4 개국에 대한 경제지원책 고려하고 있음을 밝혔음.

또한 질의응답시 난민 관련 국제기구의 자금 사정 및 난민수송 현황, 미국군등 다국적군의 사우디 주둔에 대한 각국 입장에 대한 질의가 있었는바, SCHAFFER 부차관보는 난민관계 국제기구의 자금사정은 나쁘지않으며 ( INT'L ORGANIZATION FOR MIGRATION 에 38 백만불의 자금이 있으며 이중 20 백만불은 미정부 지원액임)난민수송문제는 IMO 의 주도로도 이루어지고 있으나, 각국이 자국난민을

| 미주국 | 장관 | 차관 | 아주국 | 미주국 | 중아국 | 청와대 | 안기부 | | |
|--------|------|------|--------|--------|--------|--------|--------|--|--|

수송하고 있고, 외국군의 사우디 파병문제에 대해 인도정부는 군사적 조치는 유엔 체제하에서 다루어져야 된다는 입장을 갖고 있다고 답변함.

3. 동청문회 2 부에서 있었던 SOLOMON 차관보의 증언 및 주요 질의 응답요지는 별전 보고함.

　　첨부:SCHAFFER 부차관보 증언문 USW(F)-2291 (14 매)

　　(대사 박동진-국장)

　　예고:90.12.31 까지

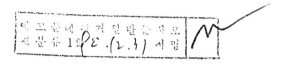

Testimony of Teresita C. Schaffer
Deputy Assistant Secretary of State
Bureau of Near Eastern and South Asian Affairs
Department of State
Before the Sub-Committee
On Asian and Pacific Affairs
House Foreign Affairs Committee

September 19, 1990

Mr. Chairman, Members of the Subcommittee--

Thank you for this opportunity to discuss the effects of the Gulf Crisis on the countries of South Asia. Saddam Hussein's march into Kuwait August 2 has struck a devastating blow against some of the poorest countries of the world in South Asia.

The hardest hit countries are those with large populations of guest workers in Iraq and Kuwait. India estimates that there were between 170,000 and 200,000 Indians in Kuwait and Iraq on August 2. Estimates of the numbers of Bangladeshis range from 100,000 to 140,000. There were an estimated 100,000 each of Sri Lankans and Pakistanis. These people had found, in the opportunity to be guest workers in the oil rich Gulf States, a way to provide for their families, and a way to contribute hard currency to their home economies. In Bangladesh, for example, remittances from Iraq and Kuwait made up 8 percent of the country's precious annual hard currency for imports.

For the fragile economies of South Asia, large foreign exchange revenue losses have a multiplier effect that could last well into the 21st Century. Many of these countries had just begun healthy growth trends, with reduced inflation and some job creation. The foreign exchange from remittances provided a balance of payments cushion that allowed for the import of necessary technologies for industrial growth.

2291-2

0098

The South Asian countries have limited natural resources and, as in the 1970s, they will be among the hardest hit by the rise in oil prices. India, which formerly imported 40 percent of its oil from Kuwait, says that every one dollar increase in the price of oil will cost India 225 million dollars a year. As we all know, the rise in oil prices has a ripple effect on other industries. Shipping costs, traditionally high in this remote part of the world, have already increased by 10 percent, reducing the competitiveness of South Asian goods in their distant principal export markets -- North America and Europe

Implementation of sanctions will also affect exports. In addition to India's dependence on Iraqi oil, India's exports to Iraq and Kuwait amounted to 300 million dollars annually and Iraq was a major market for teas from Sri Lanka and Bangladesh. All four countries are honoring sanctions. Tangible evidence of this is that following the imposition of sanctions, Bangladesh and Sri Lanka both cancelled multi-million dollar tea sales to Iraq.

This crisis will complicate the efforts by the South Asian countries to reform their economies. Bangladesh has just signed an IMF enhanced economic support facility; continued implementation of Pakistan's ESAF is under negotiation. Sri Lanka is in the middle of a three year IMF agreement. The ability of these countries to meet their obligations under IMF agreements is now placed in doubt. India is grappling with a deteriorating balance of payments. All of the countries are negotiating at the

2291 - 3

GATT. Prior to the crisis, they were facing up to the difficult economic decisions that offered them hope of full participation in the world market economy. It would be tragic if their programs fell apart because of the economic burden placed upon them by this crisis.

## THE REPATRIATION EFFORTS

Now, let me address what has become one the largest, most abrupt humanitarian relocation efforts ever attempted. Jordanian officials report that more than 540,000 people have entered Jordan from Iraq and Kuwait since August 2. The situation in Jordan has stabilized, at least temporarily, with more people now leaving than arriving. The 60,000 or so displaced persons currently in Jordan are receiving adequate food, water, shelter and medical care. The most spartan camp, Shalaan I (often shown in media reports) is being emptied as people are moving to new camps prepared with latrines, piped water, electricity and medical facilities.

Our information on displaced persons in Turkey, Saudi Arabia and Iran is more sketchy. Unlike Jordan, where international voluntary organizations are involved in relief operations, Turkey, Saudi Arabia and Iran are relying mainly on domestic relief organizations. Turkey has allowed ten thousand Bangladeshis to enter and set up a special holding camp where they await repatriation flights organized by the International Organization for Migration and the European Community. More are to be allowed

2291 -4

0100

in at a rate of about 2000 per day. A UN assessment team has
looked at foreign nationals transiting Iran. As many as 40,000 of
these are South Asians who are transiting from Turkey to their
home countries.

The U.S Government has made 28 million dollars available for
relief and repatriation efforts -- 5 million dollars has been
given to UN and international relief agencies as well as
contributions to the Jordanian and Turkish Red Crescent
Societies; Ten million dollars was given to the International
Organization for Migration for repatriation efforts. Foodstuffs
donated to the World Food Program, originally budgeted at 13
million dollars have, due to lower than budgeted foodgrain costs,
come to slightly over 11 million dollars. This is excess to
current World Food Program requirements in the Gulf. The
foodstuffs are being stored and/or diverted to Liberia pending
additional need in the Gulf. Several U.S. military flights are
scheduled to deliver 3,000 additional tents and other relief
supplies.

Repatriation of the evacuees continues to be a major economic
burden. The International Organization for Migration (IOM) has
already received pledges of 38 million dollars in response to its
request for 60 million dollars. IOM has repatriated more than
15,000 people from Jordan to Bangladesh, Sri Lanka, the
Philippines and Pakistan with another 35,000 people scheduled to
move by the end of September. In addition, IOM has booked 25
charters to repatriate 5000 Bangladeshis who fled to Turkey.

2281

India, which is financing most of the cost of repatriation of its own nationals, says the total cost of its airlift may reach 300 million dollars.

But the initial costs of repatriating the workers will only be a fraction of what it will cost to absorb the workers when they arrive home. All of the countries with large numbers of workers in the Gulf already suffer from high unemployment rates of thirty percent and more. Unemployment compensation and welfare are virtually unknown. We estimate Pakistan's costs for resettlement at 75 million dollars during the next fiscal year. All the affected countries will need to work this unexpected influx of people into their development planning, and our own aid programs will need to be flexible enough to help this process along.

This is the bad news. The good news is that despite the economic costs of the crisis and well-founded concerns for the welfare of citizens still in Iraq and Kuwait, the countries of South Asia have, without exception, supported international efforts to force Iraq to comply with United Nations Security Council Resolution 661. All of the countries are abiding by sanctions. Some have sent troops. In short, the extraordinarily high level in international cooperation on the crisis is visible in the South Asian countries' response to it.

Now I'd like to discuss the specific impact of the crisis on these four countries.

2291-6

# INDIA

The Persian Gulf crisis came at a time when India already faced serious fiscal and balance of payments difficulties, leaving it with little cushion to deal with increased energy costs, loss of remittances from the Gulf and foregone export earnings and debt repayments from Iraq and Kuwait.  India which purchased 40-45 percent of its imported petroleum from Kuwait and Iraq prior to August 2 has found new sources albeit at higher prices, and the country now faces an import bill for the year of $6 billion compared with $4 billion in 1989.

Indirect effects of increased petroleum prices are significant.  Demand for petroleum, which is consumed largely in power generation, is quite inelastic in the short run.  Inevitable increased costs of transportation, intermediate goods and other factors of production will make Indian exports less competitive, and the vigorous rate of export growth of recent years will surely decline if the world economy suffers a downturn as a result of the Gulf crisis.

Indian exports to Iraq and Kuwait amounted to $300 million annually before the imposition of sanctions.  However Iraq also owes India $800 million for completed construction projects in Iraq and had the real potential for even higher levels of revenues from future projects.

2281 -7

Remittances of $500-600 million from 200 thousand Indians in Iraq and Kuwait are, of course, completely eliminated, but understandably frightened Indian expats throughout the Gulf are returning home.

India may avoid negative growth, but the 5 percent real GDP growth of the past three years is likely to decline to the 3 percent range or lower in the next year. Inflation for the year --a political issue before the Iraqi invasion-- will push into double digits, perhaps reaching 15 percent. Foreign exchange reserves under pressure before August 2 stand at $3 billion (less than 40 days worth of imports) with no potential positive offset.

PAKISTAN

The Gulf crisis both hits hard at worker remittances from the Gulf states, and exacerbates Pakistan's looming trade deficit. Pakistan had been making progress in economic growth and reform, beginning in the 1980's when it generally achieved strong economic growth with moderate inflation. Recognizing its economic weaknesses, the government started a structural adjustment program with the IMF and the World Bank in 1988/89. It took some steps to improve the investment climate and attract foreign investors.

The Gulf crisis threatens the progress made to date and stifles incentives to continue economic reform measures. The

2291 —8

immediate, direct effects of the crisis are large. Pakistan is
likely to lose up to $150 million for the rest of this year in
lost remittances from workers previously in Iraq and Kuwait, and
up to $300 million next year. Increased oil prices mean a roughly
$600 million hike in the oil import bill for 1990/91, assuming a
per barrel price of 31 dollars. By enforcing the sanctions of
U.N. Resolution 661, Pakistan stands to lose about $50 million in
exports to Iraq and Kuwait in 1990-91. The cost of repatriating
and resettling Pakistani citizens may run about $75 million.
Pakistan announced September 12 that all Pakistani evacuees in
Jordan, Turkey, Saudi Arabia, and Iran had been repatriated and
that the majority of the 30,000 who remained in Kuwait were there
by choice.

Pakistan has sent about 2,000 troops to the Gulf and
announced it will enforce the sanctions, despite criticism of this
policy during the politically sensitive run-up to elections on
October 24. All Kuwaiti investments in Pakistan have been frozen
and loan repayments ceased. All trade between Pakistan and Iraq
and Kuwait has ceased. A credit line issued to Iraq for the
purchase of Pakistani equipment has been cut off. Iraqi aircraft
(including stolen Kuwaiti aircraft) and ships have been denied
access to Pakistani airspace and waters. Pakistan has asked us
and other donors to help offset the impact of the Gulf crisis.

BANGLADESH

For Bangladesh, the Gulf Crisis comes at a time when the

2291 —9

0105

government has just completed year-long negotiations on an IMF
Enhanced Structural Adjustment Facility. This agreement contains
tough reforms designed to put the economy, which partially
derailed in 1989, back on track. The donor group, concerned about
economic trends in Bangladesh, had, at their annual pledging
session last Spring, given only tentative approval to Bangladesh's
efforts to restore fiscal responsibility and called for a mid-term
review in November to review progress. An already tight
Bangladesh budget passed in June made no allowance for annual
losses of 300 million dollars in remittances, 40 million dollars
from increased oil prices, 25 million dollars in lost exports to
Iraq and Kuwait and a 150 million dollar repatriation and
resettlement bill. To put this in perspective, these additional
costs of 500 million dollars represent almost 25 percent of
Bangladesh's budgeted revenues for FY 91. Gross Domestic Product
growth rates, estimated at more than five percent for FY 90 may
slip to two to three percent. The balance of payments, just
recently restored to an acceptable state, is likely to drop below
the safety levels again.

Bangladesh has begun to take measures to address these
costs. Domestic gasoline prices were raised and conservation
measures implemented. New foreign exchange restrictions were
implemented. Bangladesh has canvassed the international community
asking for assistance with repatriation efforts and hopes to
recoup some of the expenses it incurred chartering repatriation
flights. They are discussing their needs with donor groups. We
expect Bangladeshi representatives in their annual discussions

2231—10

0106

with the World Bank and the IMF that are taking place in Washington this month to be active in encouraging early release of economic support payments. They may seek assistance from the IMF compensatory financing facility. Bangladesh may be able to find ways of speeding up utilization of its two billion dollar aid pipeline -- a pipeline that has been a matter of concern for donors for quite some time.

Despite these costs, Bangladesh has condemned Iraq's invasion, stalwartly imposed sanctions and sent over 2000 troops to the Gulf.

SRI LANKA

From the outset, Sri Lanka has cited economic hardship as a basis for relief from sanctions. Before fully embracing sanctions on August 28, it argued that UN Article 50 provided relief from compliance. It also argued that tea, its principal export to Iraq, was a humanitarian foodstuff and therefore exempt from coverage. We forcefully contested this view both in Washington and in Colombo. Nevertheless, Sri Lanka did not agree to full compliance until after departure of the Iraqi freighter Zanubia, partly laden with Sri Lankan tea. The Zanubia was later interdicted and turned back in the Gulf.

Sri Lanka is now observing sanction, however, with heavy costs to its economy at a time when it is waging an expensive war

2281-11

against ruthless Tamil separatists. Sri Lanka will lose $35 million in remittances this year, and $50 million in 1991, from the 100,000 Sri Lankans working in Kuwait. If oil prices remain in the $24 - $26 dollar range, oil costs will increase by more than $20 million this year, and $40 million in 1991, also depleting reserves. It has also lost an important market for tea which could cost it $20 million this year alone. Alternative markets are being explored. Sri Lanka may approach the IMF Compensatory fund for relief from export losses.

These losses will increase Sri Lanka's current account deficit by an estimated 20 percent this year, and 25 percent in 1991. To maintain its current level of economic growth, Sri Lanka estimates that it will need $200 million more in concessional assistance over the next two years, and options are limited: First, it could reduce foreign exchange reserves; however, reserves are already at low levels. Secondly, the government could request more balance of payments support from the international community--however, debt service is already one fourth of export earnings, so more loans are not an attractive option. Thirdly, the government could reduce imports of food, investment, and other goods, but this could have serious political and economic consequences.

More elusive are the social and economic costs of the 100,000 Sri Lankans in Kuwait if they all return home. The workers

2291 -12

represent three percent of the island's total labor force. With
unemployment high, social programs strained by military
expenditures, and great numbers of people already displaced by
intense fighting on the island, these costs will have to be great.

THE USG RESPONSE

I have tried to outline the magnitude of the economic impact
of the Gulf crisis on the countries of South Asia. Prior to the
crisis, all of these countries were moving, albeit at different
paces, toward more private sector, market oriented economies that
could compete in the global market. We are very concerned that in
their efforts to cushion the effects of the Gulf Crisis, the
countries of South Asia could backslide on some of the reforms
already achieved or postpone planned reforms. We do not think
that this is the time to move backward.

We have significant aid programs in each of the South Asian
countries. These programs are based on each country's needs and
performance. The economic reforms and development we have helped
these countries to achieve can make the economic blow of this
crisis less devastating.

The U.S. Government has responded and will be responding to
the short term repatriation costs. We are also reviewing with the
affected countries the need for assistance with short term
resettlement of displaced persons in their home countries and
their long term re-integration into their home economies. This is

2281－13

a complex process, potentially affecting many aspects of a
country's development program.  Especially for the short term
portion of it, there will probably be a special role for the
voluntary organizations and UN agencies to play.  But we will also
be examining how available U.S. Government resources can best be
used to support these countries' development.

As you are aware, we hope that the international community
will contribute generously to efforts to help those countries most
in need.  We are actively encouraging support from all countries
and our representatives are participating in discussions in the
multilateral development banks.  This is all part of the cost of
our collective decision to stop Iraqi aggression and a cost that
must be shared by all who benefit from this decision.

2291-14

0110

관리
번호 PO-1766

# 외 무 부

종 별 : 긴 급

번 호 : USW-4260                                    일 시 : 90 0919 1817

수 신 : 장관(미북,미안,중근동,아일)

발 신 : 주 미 대사

제 목 : 이락사태 의회 반응(14)

연:USW-4215

1. 금 9.19(수)하원 아태소위 청문회시 SOLOMON 차관보의 증언의 주요내용은 하기와같음.

0 동아태지역 국가는 이락에 대한 경제제재 조치에 신속히 동참하였으며, 일본등 여러 동맹국이 경제적, 군사적으로 책임분담 방안을 발표하였음.

0 유엔 안보리 재재결의에서 중국 및 말레이지아 협조가 긴요하였으며 유엔의 제재 조치에 유엔 비회원국인 한국을 포함 전 동아태지역 국가(북한및 베트남제외)가 참여하였음.

0 페만사태 책임분담에 있어 일본은 40 억불이라는 상당한 규모의 지원방안을 발표했으며, 이는 일본정부내 의견조정, 재원확보 방안등 여러현실적 요소를 고려하면 시기적으로 늦었다고 보기는 어려움. 일본은 여러국제문제에 있어 미국의 동반자이며 지도적인 역할을 수행하는 방향으로 변하고 있음. 금번 페만사태에 있어서 일본으로 부터 재정적 지원뿐만아니라 비군사적 인력제공 및 수송분야에서도 적극적인 참여를 기대함.

0 한국은 금번 사태가 국제안보에 미치는 영향 및 침략저지라는 국제법원칙수호의 중요성을 잘인식하고 있으며, 사우디 주둔 외국군 수송에 최초로 수송 수단을 제공한 국가임. 한국정부는 페만사태 책임분담 방안을 고려중에 있음.

0 한국정부의 조치가 사태진전에 맞추어 취해질 것인지여부에 관심을 (실제증언시 동부분을 발언하지 않았음)갖고 있음. (별첨증언문 PP12-13 참조)

0 페만 사태로 인해 필리핀, 태국이 큰 경제적 어려움을 격고 있으며, 동국가들을 위해 원유의 안정적 공급 및 원조제공 필요성이 있음.

0 금번 페만 사태는 아태지역 국가들에게 일개국의 침략 행위가 미치는 전세계적

| 미주국 | 장관 | 차관 | 1차보 | 2차보 | 아주국 | 미주국 | 중아국 | 정문국 |
|--------|------|------|-------|-------|--------|--------|--------|--------|
| 청와대 | 안기부 | | | | | | | |

대책반

PAGE 1                                              90.09.20    09:01

외신 2과 통제관 FE

0111

영향을 새로이 인식시켰으며, 각국의 경제 및 안보문제를 전세계적 차원에서 보게하는 계기가 되었음.

2. SOLOMON 차관보 증언에 대한 질의 응답시에는 일본의 책임분담 규모의 적정성 및 동시행시기와 한국군의 사우디 파병문제가 주로 논의된바 동 요지 하기 보고함.

(일본의 책임분담)

(질) 일본의 책임분담 규모가 적정(FAIR SHARE)한것인지 ?(솔라즈 의원)

(답) 책임분담규모의 적정성 판단은 매우 어려우며, 사태발전, 세계경제변화에 따라 달라질것이나, 일본정부는 적정 규모의 지원을 하고자하는 정치적 의지가 있음.

(질) 일본의 책임분담 규모가 영국등 유럽국가 규모에 비해 크다고 보는지(솔라즈 의원)

(답) 영국등 군대를 파견한 국가에 대해 동파병을 절대적인 화폐가치로 평가하기는 어려우나 금년말 이전까지의 일본의 분담규모는 영국보다 크리라고 생각함.(FAUVER 부차관보)

(질) 일본정부가 사우디 주둔군 비용으로 제공하는 20 억불은 언제, 어떻게사용되는지 (솔라즈 의원)

(답)일본정부는 20 억불중 약 10 억불은 금년도 기존 예산에서 충당하고, 나머지 10 억불은 일본 의회에 추가로 배정 요청하는것으로 알고 있으며, 일본의금년도 회계년도말(91.3 말)이전까지 전액 사용될것임.동자금의 대부분은 사우디 미군주둔 비용으로 사용될것이며 일부분이 타국 주둔군 용으로 사용되리라고 봄.

(질) 전선국가 지원금 20 억불은 어떻게 사용되며, 어떠한 형태의 원조가 될것인지 (솔라즈 의원)

(답) 20 억불중 6 억불은 COMMODITY LOAN 형태로 3 개 전선국가에 배정키로결정되었으며 나머지 14 억불중에서도 대부분이 동 3 개국에 지원될것임. 동원조는 UNTIED AID 로서 매우 양허적인 (CONCESSIONARY TERMS)조건이 될것임.

(한국군 파병문제)

(질) 오늘 워싱턴 포스트에 미국 정부가 4.5 억불을 한국정부에 요청하고 한국정부는 1.5 억불분담을 고려중이라고 하는데 사실여부는(솔라즈 의원)

(답) 현재 양국정부간에 협의가 진행중이며, 동수치는 밝힐수 없지만(비밀 사항으로 추후 통보)신문 보도와 유사하다고 말할수 있음. 한국을 제일먼저 수송수단을 제공한 국가이며 경제원조를 고려하고 있음.

PAGE 2

0112

(질) 이락내 한국교민수는 (솔라즈 의원)

(답) 사태발발시에는 약 1,300 명이 있었으나 거의 철수하고 현재 약 400 명이 있는것으로 알고 있음.

(질) 한국은 침략에 대한 집단 조치의 혜택을 본 나라로서 상징적의미로 파병할계획이 있는지 (솔라즈 의원)

(답) 한국민은 과거 역사를 잘알고 있으며, 북한으로부터의 침략위협은 줄어들지 않은 상황임. 한국정부는 페만사태 책임분담 방안을 강구중에 있음.

(질) 월남파병당시 북한으로부터의 안보 위협과 현재 비교하면(솔라즈 의원)

(답) 1960 년대에 비해 현재 북한으로부터의 위협이 더크다고 봄.

(질) 소련은 북한을 지지하고 있지 않은바, 북한으로부터의 위협은 감소되었다고 봄. 한국은 한국전 당시 외국군의 도움을 얻었고 미국원조와 희생의 수혜자로서 사우디에 파병하지 않는것은 매우 실망스러운 것임 (LUKENS 의원)

(답변 없음)

(질) 한국 정부가 파병하는것이 도움이 될것으로 보는지 (솔라즈 의원)

(답) 한국 파병문제는 매우 복합적이고 미묘한 성격을 띠고 있음. 주한미군의 일부 감군이 결정되었고 북한의 위협이 상존하고 있음.

(질) 나 자신보다 북한의 위협을 잘알고 있는 의원은 없다고 보며, 한국전 당시 터어키는 자신의 안보 위협이 있었음에도 불구하고 파병하였음. 한국정부가소수의 군대를 파견하더라도 안보상 심각한 위해가 없다고 보며 상징적으로 다국적군에 기여한다는 것은 정치적으로 한국에 도움이 될것임. 침략에 대한 국제적 집단 조치의 확립이라는 차원에서도 한국에 도움이 될것임. 개인 견해로는 한국정부가 1 개 여단을 파견하는것이 1.5 억불을 제공하는것보다 좋다고 생각함.

(답)노태우 대통령은 명백히 미국이 취하고 있는 집단적 조치에 지지를 하고 있으나, 한국군 파병문제에 관해서는 복합적인 고려가 필요할것임. 그것은 북한에 잘못된 신호를 줄수 있는바 신중한 검토가 필요함.

(질) 미국정부는 한국군 파병문제를 검토한적이 있는지 (솔라즈 의원)

(답) 현재로서는 검토한바 없으며 주한미군 감축 결정이 고려되어야 할것임.

(질) 미국정부는 한국군 파병문제를 검토해야할것임. 다국적군에 참여하는것은 집단 조치를 지지한다는 측면에서 군사적이라기 보다는 정치적임. 새로운 국제질서에서 침략은 받아들여질수 없다는 원칙을 확고히 하는것이 중요함.

PAGE 3

(답변 없음)

(기타 질문사항)

(질) 폐만 사태에 대한 유엔 안보리 조치에서 중국의 태도는 어떠했는지, 장애가 되었는지 (솔라즈 의원)

(답) 중국은 이락에 대한 무기수출 금지를 했으며 유엔안보리 결의안 채택에 매우 중요한 역할을 하였음.

(질) 만약 유엔 안보리가 헌장 42 조에 의한 집단 조치를 심의할 경우, 중국이 VETO 할것인지 (솔라즈 의원)

(답) 가상적인 질문에 답변키 어려움.

3. 동청문회 SOLOMON 증언문은 별첨 FAX 송부함.

첨부: 동증언문 ( USW(F)-2292 )

(대사 박동진-국장)

예고:90.12.31 까지

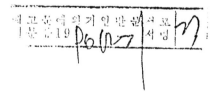

PAGE 4

0114

USW (F) - 2292

수신: 장관 ( 미북. 미안. 품은동 . 아일 )

발신: 주미대사

제목: 하원 아태 소위 청문회 Ⅱ ( 페만사태 )

Testimony of Assistant Secretary Richard H. Solomon
Before the House Foreign Affairs Committee
Subcommittee on Asian and Pacific Affairs
September 19, 1990

2292-1

Mr. Chairman, I appreciate this opportunity to appear before your Subcommittee to review the East Asian contribution to our efforts to reverse Iraqi aggression, and the effects the crisis in the Gulf is having on the economies of the region.

In the seven weeks since Saddam Hussein's army invaded and occupied Kuwait, the world community, including most of the countries of Asia, has displayed an unprecedented degree of cooperation in the effort to respond to Iraqi aggression. Political support from the countries of the region -- particularly from China and Malaysia -- was crucial to the rapid passage of US-backed resolutions in the UN. East Asian and Pacific countries were among the first to announce their adherence to the full range of UN sanctions against Iraq. Japan and some of our other allies and friends in the Asia-Pacific region have announced substantial economic assistance to the front line states of Jordan, Egypt, and

2292 - 2

0116

Turkey. They also have contributed financial and material resources to the multinational force in the Gulf; and Australia has contributed military assets as well.

While the effects of Iraqi aggression have naturally been felt most severely in the Middle East, we should keep in mind that this is a crisis of truly global proportions. We have already begun to witness a negative economic impact on some of the more fragile East Asian economies, particularly the Philippines. Thailand, while enjoying a stronger economy, also will be hard hit. The price of oil has risen sharply. East Asian countries have lost two important suppliers of crude and refined petroleum products: Iraq and Kuwait. East Asian exporters also have lost the Iraqi and Kuwaiti markets for their agricultural products and finished goods. Several East Asian countries stand to lose millions of dollars in worker remittances. The repatriation of these workers and their reintegration into their home societies will burden a number of Asian economies.

Our efforts to generate economic assistance for those countries adversely affected by the crisis must of necessity focus first on the front line states of Egypt, Jordan, and Turkey. But we have not neglected the needs of the Philippines or other East Asian states. In the following remarks I would

2292-3

like to address Asian support for our goals in the Gulf, as well as U.S. and Asian efforts to blunt the economic impact of the crisis in the East Asia-Pacific region.

RESPONSE TO THE GULF CHALLENGE:  UN DIPLOMACY AND SANCTIONS

East Asian and Pacific countries have displayed unprecedented unity in support of the seven UN Security Council resolutions and in implementing UN sanctions against Iraq. Obtaining China's early support for these Security Council resolutions was one of the keys to achieving a global response to this crisis.  Fellow Security Council member Malaysia also supported all of the resolutions, and co-sponsored the original resolution 660 condemning the Iraqi invasion and demanding that Iraq withdraw from Kuwait.

A number of East Asian and Pacific countries, including Japan, condemned the invasion and put their own sanctions in place even before the Security Council passed resolution 661 on August 6.  Since then, the entire region  -- with the sole exceptions of Vietnam and North Korea -- has indicated support for the sanctions and has abided by them.  Even non-UN member South Korea has done so.

2292-4

## RESPONSIBILITY SHARING

We are following a two-track approach to maintaining sanctions against Iraq. First, we must assure equitable sharing of the military and economic burdens of deterring aggression while the sanctions take effect. Second, we must assure that those states whose economies have been hardest hit by adherence to the sanctions are given financial support which will allow them to weather the loss of energy supplies, export markets, and worker remittances.

I can say without hesitation that we have received generous support from our Asian friends and allies in pursuing these two tracks, and we will continue to work with them to bolster our joint efforts in order to successfully counter Iraq's aggression. Let me first outline in some detail JAPAN'S response.

As I mentioned at the start, Japan responded quickly -- even before passage of UN resolution 660 -- to impose economic sanctions on Iraq and freeze Kuwaiti assets in Japan. The focus then turned to what Japan could do to assist in the multinational effort in the Persian Gulf.

232-5

0119

Early in the crisis, we indicated to all countries that we would welcome any and all contributions to the multinational effort. For constitutional, legal, and political reasons, with which you and the Committee are very familiar, the Japanese Government determined that it could not dispatch military forces to the Gulf region. For our part, we too knew that the possibility of reversing 45 years of Japanese legal constraints and public sentiment overnight was almost zero, so there was a recognition within the US Government from the beginning that Japan's contribution most probably would come in non-military areas.

We have been in constant contact with our Japanese allies from the very beginning of the crisis. We have expressed our view that as an economic superpower and a major player on the world scene, and as a country whose vital interests are at stake in the Persian Gulf, Japan's contribution should be substantial, timely, and visible.

Let us consider the first point -- whether Japan's response has been substantial. Japan has announced that it will contribute $2 billion to the multinational defense effort in the Gulf. Almost all of this will go to providing materiel and equipment for the multinational forces and paying for the charter of civilian aircraft and ships to transport equipment

2292-6

to the Gulf. (A small amount will be used to pay for support
of a 100-person Japanese medical team committed to the Gulf.)
This aid is untied; so goods can be purchased in Japan, the
United States, or anywhere. It will be used to procure
equipment, such as air conditioners and prefabricated housing,
to protect our troops against the desert heat; for generators;
vehicles; equipment for water supply and food storage; and
medical supplies.

From a policy point of view, Japan's contribution to the
multinational defense force is a policy breakthrough, with
important implications for the future. This is the first time
that Japan has provided financial assistance to defense efforts
outside Japan. Until now, Japan has provided only for its own
Self-Defense Forces and the support of US Forces stationed in
Japan. This has now changed. In addition, not all of this $2
billion defense contribution is going to support U.S. Forces;
part of it -- as yet undetermined -- will go to aid other
nations, with which Japan is not formally allied, participating
in the multinational defense effort. Again, this sets an
important policy precedent for the future.

Some goods procured under this $2 billion contribution
already are moving to the Gulf -- 800 4-wheel drive vehicles,
built to desert specifications. More equipment will be
coming. In addition, Japan has chartered ships and aircraft
which soon will begin moving goods to Saudi Arabia.

The second part of Japan's substantial financial contribution is another $2 billion for economic assistance to the countries most affected by the imposition of economic sanctions.  Of this amount, $600 million will be provided now as emergency assistance to Jordan, Turkey, and Egypt as commodity loans at a concessional interest rate of 1 percent repayable over 30 years.  This funding will be disbursed entirely within the next two months.  The remaining $1.4 billion will require a supplemental budget allocation in the Japanese Diet.  The details on this supplemental allocation are still being worked out, but we understand that most of it will also be provided to the three front-line states.

The third part of Japan's financial contribution is $22 million to assist in the refugee effort in Jordan.  Of this amount, Japan has allocated $8 million to the UN Disaster Relief Organization (UNDRO), $2 million to the International Red Cross, and $12 million to the International Organization on Migration.

This brings Japan's total contribution to date to over $4 billion.  Only Saudi Arabia and Kuwait have been more generous in their support.

2252-8

0122

The first test, of substantiality, clearly has been met.
The President has indicated that we are pleased by Japan's
important contribution.  We only ask that Japan -- and other
countries -- be prepared to provide additional assistance
should the situation warrant it.

What about the other two criteria -- timeliness, and the
visibility of Japan's effort?  It is the problem of timeliness
that has laid Japan open to most of the criticism over the past
few weeks.  From the beginning of this crisis, we have stressed
to Japan the importance of early action.  Quite frankly, Mr.
Chairman, we have stressed to the Japanese Government the need
for not only a timely, but also a demostrably visible response,
lest people conclude Japan was reluctant to shoulder its fair
share of the burdens and risks of the crisis.  I regret to say
that our prediction proved true.

Why did it take Japan over six weeks, from the time of
Iraq's invasion, to announce its broad response?  Speaker Foley
addressed this pointin a speech the other evening, and I will
borrow his wise observation that to explain the reasons why
something happens is not to apologize for it.

Nineteen ninety has been a year in which Japan has had to
reassess and fundamentally adjust its policies for economic

2292-9

0123

development and, since early August, for its security.  In a
conservative society which fundamentally values decision-making
by consensus, and in which governmental bureaucracies carry
considerably greater weight than in our system, these
adjustments have not been reflexively swift.

The crisis in the Gulf presented the Japanese Government
with a range of problems and choices it had not coped with
before as a leading world economic power.  It had to assess
constitutional and legal constraints; the reaction of the
opposition parties and the labor unions; public and press
reaction; concern over the Japanese hostages; and financial
concerns -- where the money could be found in Japan's budget to
pay for its contribution.  Working through these issues took a
certain amount of time.

As we had anticipated, American impatience began to grow as
Japan worked through its decision.  Last week Congress
expressed its concern on this subject.  Those of us who were
following these developments closely knew that the Japanese
Government was approaching a decision point, and that a public
announcement was just a few days away.  Congress expressed its
will on September 11, and when the Japanese made their
announcement on September 14, the impression was created that
Japan was responding to Congressional pressure, thus

292-10

0124

reinforcing the view that bashing Japan is the only way to produce a decision. In fact, based on the information available to me, I have found Japan's political leadership determined to play a responsive and responsible role as a partner of the United States in the Gulf crisis.

Finally, let us take a look at the third criterion -- visibility. We have often been accused of practicing "checkbook diplomacy" with Japan -- that is, we make the decisions and take the action, and Japan pays the bills. In this case, we have made it clear from the beginning that we want Japan and all countries to share the risks as well as the financial burdens of the challenge in the Gulf. For many years, the Japanese people have been content to let America worry about the world for them. What we and others -- including many of Japan's leaders -- have been seeking in recent years is a greater international role for Japan. As the President and Secretary Baker have pointed out many times, we seek a global partnership with our primary Asian ally .

Because Japan, by constitutional restriction, cannot send its military forces to the Gulf, it is all the more important that Japan participate actively and visibly in non-military ways. The dispatch of a Japanese medical team to the area is a welcome step. The efforts of Japanese companies to locate

2292-11

supplies, divert them from their regular markets and send them on an emergency basis to our forces in Saudi Arabia is also a recognized contribution. The provision of Japanese airplanes and ships to provide transportation is another visible way Japan has contributed to our efforts -- although the level of such cooperation to date has been less than we would like. We want to see more Japanese flag carriers on their way to the Gulf. Japan has made a major financial contribution to the refugee effort in Jordan, but what is needed is not only financial support but personnel and transportation resources as well. We have been heartened by recent comments by Japanese Government spokesmen that thousands of Japanese personnel may yet go to the Gulf in non-military roles.

As we have pointed out to our Japanese partners, the Gulf crisis is not an isolated regional conflict. It is a security challenge with profound implications for Japan's economic future and its role as a global partner of the United States and the industrial democracies. Japan's major financial contribution is welcomed, but we also are looking to the Japanese people, to the full extent they can, to become players in world affairs -- not just spectators.

Let me now turn to the support provided by others in the region. The REPUBLIC OF KOREA recognizes the importance of its

*2292-12*

stake in this challenge to global security, both economically
and in upholding the principle of resisting aggression. The
South Koreans were the first to offer transport services to us
and to the multilateral Arab force opposing Iraq.

Treasury Secretary Brady visited Seoul on September 7 to
discuss, among other issues, the need for increased financial
assistance to states whose economies are being adversely
affected by the Gulf crisis. Secretary Brady characterized his
meeting with President Roh as a success. The Korean President
applauded President Bush's decisive action in the Gulf and said
that Korea would be supportive of the collective effort. The
South Korean Government is now in the process of formulating a
response to requests on Gulf responsibility sharing, although
we are concerned that their actions are not keeping pace with
events in the region.

AUSTRALIA was quick to support the multinational force in
the Gulf. Within a week of the Iraqi invasion, Prime Minister
Hawke announced that Australia would contribute two guided
missile frigates and a support ship to the multinational
force. These forces already have been engaged in actively
enforcing the UN sanctions -- last week an Australian ship
assisted us in interdicting and boarding an Iraqi tanker in the
Gulf.

2292-13

Australia also announced support for UN sanctions against Iraq and Kuwait, even though this entails foregoing about $340 million per year in wheat sales, and may involve Iraq defaulting on $700 million in debt for past grain deliveries. Australia has donated $1.6 million to various international relief agencies to assist foreign nationals stranded in the Gulf. The Government of Australia also donated 60,000 tons of diverted wheat destined for Iraq to Egypt for refugee relief.

NEW ZEALAND also moved quickly to impose mandatory economic sanctions, a measure that will cost the country about USD 40-60 million in dairy and live sheep exports. New Zealand offered two fully crewed civilian aircraft to the UN Secretary General and a 40 person civilian medical team to the ICRC for use in Saudia Arabia.

The Royal New Zealand Air Force airlifted 16 tons of donated milk powder to Egypt for refugee relief and used the same aircraft for three flights ferrying refugees from camps in Jordan to their homes in Pakistan and the Philippines. New Zealand intends further airlift of South Asians with a military aircraft returning from England.

292-14

0128

Of the ASEAN countries, Indonesia and Malaysia have increased domestic oil production, and we expect that a portion of this will go to Asian countries that have lost Iraq and Kuwait as suppliers. INDONESIAN oil production is expected to increase by 50,000 b/d by the end of this year and by a similar amount in 1991 (a 7% increase overall). Press reports from Jakarta indicate that Indonesia may sell oil to the Philippines as part of an ASEAN Petroleum Security Agreement. MALAYSIA has announced that it will increase oil production by 55,000 b/d (a 10% increase) and has agreed to reserve two-thirds of this increase for the Philippines, Pakistan, Bangladesh, and India. Malaysia also has declared that it will donate food worth $100,000 for refugees fleeing Iraq and Kuwait.

THAILAND has not provided economic assistance to front line or other Asian states, and we would not expect it to be able to do so as it is one of the countries experiencing economic difficulties as a result of the Gulf crisis. The Thai have not supplied or been asked to supply cash/in kind support for the multinational force.

We have also initiated consultations with SINGAPORE and BRUNEI on how they can assist refugees stranded in the Middle

2292 - 15

East and contribute to easing the economic burden of the front
line states and the Philippines.

## THE ECONOMIC IMPACT OF THE CRISIS ON EAST ASIA AND THE PACIFIC

Implementing economic sanctions against Iraq imposes
diverse burdens on countries in the region - particularly the
loss of oil imports from Iraq and Kuwait, exports to Iraq and
Kuwait, and worker remittances and debt repayments from those
two countries. As I suggested above, our efforts at obtaining
assistance have focussed on support for the multinational force
and aid to the front line states. However, we will not neglect
the economic impact of the crisis on East Asia and the need for
aiding the hardest hit economies, particularly the Philippines.

Well before this crisis, energy analysts pointed out the
vulnerability of the East Asia and Pacific region -- with its
high dependence on imported oil and limited refining capacity
-- to a third oil shock originating in the Persian Gulf. All
the same, we have reason to believe that the economy of the
region can adjust over time to the effects of $30 per barrel of
oil. However, the economic impact varies from country to
country. Some particularly hard-hit economies will require
help from the world community. Others will be in a more
favorable economic position, allowing them to extend help.

2292-16

0130

The countries of East Asia hardest hit by the Gulf crisis are the Philippines and, to a lesser extent, Thailand. Besides being large net oil importers, both countries had thousands of workers in Iraq and Kuwait whose remittances were a significant source of overseas earnings, and who now represent a major evacuee/refugee burden. Both have lost the benefit of agricultural exports to Iraq and Kuwait. Despite these problems, Thailand is in relatively good position to absorb the economic shocks of the crisis. The small economies of the Pacific Island states, however, such as Fiji and Papua-New Guinea, are almost totally dependent on foreign oil and will be hard hit by energy price increases.

The Newly Industrialized Economies (NIEs) may experience somewhat slower GNP growth and higher inflation over the next two years; but they should weather this crisis. Japan has taken a range of measures since the oil shocks of the 1970s to reduce its dependence on imported oil, and with its 140 days of reserves and its budget and current account surpluses, the country seems well-positioned to ride out the short-term effects of the crisis.

Minor oil producers and IEA members Australia and New Zealand will be affected more by the loss of agricultural

2282-17

export markets than by the energy impacts of the crisis.  The
region's oil producers and refiners will experience mostly
positive impacts; but as they seek to diversify their export
markets, even they will be affected negatively by any slowdown
in their trading partners' economies.

The crisis in the Gulf hit a <u>PHILIPPINE</u> economy already
burdened with serious problems.  The July earthquake caused an
estimated $1 billion in damage.  The Philippine government is
also coping with nearly $28 billion in international debt.
Even before the crisis, projected GNP growth was halved to 3%
as a result of the earthquake and flood.  Official unemployment
stood at 9%.  A significant oil price increase, coupled with a
fall in the economic performance of developed country
importers, could cause growth in Philippine GNP to suffer a
further slowdown.

The more than 60,000 Filipino workers in Kuwait and Iraq
have provided something on the order of $150-160 million per
year in remittances.  We estimate a loss of up to $60 million
in remittances for the balance of CY 1990 and a loss of up to
$156 million in 1991 if the crisis continues.  Although it is
difficult to estimate the cost of repatriation and
resettlement, these activities will place an added burden on
the Philippine economy.

2292-18

The oil supply situation in the Philippines gives special cause for concern. Crude oil is the Philippines' largest single commodity import, accounting, in value terms, for 11% of total 1989 imports. Kuwait supplied around 23% (in volume) of Philippine crude imports during the first five months of 1990. Oil imports at higher prices will put a tremendous strain on the Philippine economy, which has made significant progress under the democratically elected Aquino government. While the annual oil bill may go up as much as $1 billion, the country must continue to service its massive foreign debt. The Philippines is looking to its ASEAN neighbors, to Saudi Arabia, and to Iran as sources of replacement energy supplies.

As a result of the Gulf crisis, THAILAND losing millions of dollars in terms of lost exports to Iraq, lost worker remittances, and increased fuel costs. Approximately 10,000 Thai workers labored in Kuwait and Iraq. In the period January-July 1990, Thailand sold 112,000 MT of rice to Iraq and 49,000 MT to Kuwait, worth $32 million and $13 million respectively. With total rice sales running 47% lower in volume terms than during the same period in 1989, the Thai can ill afford to lose these markets.

2292-19

As a net fuel importer, Thailand appears to be adjusting well to a loss of approximately 27,000 b/d from Iraq and Kuwait. The Thai Government has arranged with Iran for shipments equivalent to 15,000 b/d from September through December, at a "friendship price" $0.80 to $1.55 per barrel less than the spot price. Thailand is in better general financial and economic shape than the Philippines: it is experiencing the highest GNP growth rate in Asia (over 10% in 1989) and running a government budget surplus. According to one estimate, growth may slow to between 6% and 8% as a result of the crisis.

The NIEs (Korea, Taiwan, Singapore, and Hong Kong) import 100% of the oil they consume. Korea and Taiwan do have other local energy sources, such as coal and nuclear power, accounting for 46% and 28% respectively of their total primary energy requirements. However, the domestic economic impact of higher oil prices is not the only concern of these economies. The NIEs will face slower economic growth, higher general price levels, and weaker external accounts resulting from the combination of higher oil import prices at home and lower purchasing power in their trading partners (except for oil exporters). Inflation was already becoming a concern in Korea,,and now a $30/bl oil price could push inflation into *double digits*. Taiwan has already revised its 1990 GNP growth estimate down to 5.5% (vice 7.2% before the Iraqi invasion).

2292-20

0134

The NIEs, Japan, and Thailand should be able to weather an oil price hike, albeit after a year or two of slower economic growth and higher general price levels. In many respects, the present crisis is more manageable than the oil shocks of the 1970s. In fact, according to some analyses, an oil price hike could provide an incentive to these economies to increase in time productivity and energy-efficiency, thus making their economies even more competitive in foreign markets.

Higher oil prices represent higher export revenues for regional oil producers Indonesia, China, Malaysia and Brunei. At a $30/bl price, we estimate annual revenue increases of $5 billion for Indonesia, $2 billion for Malaysia, $2 billion for China, and $700 million for Brunei. There is a downside for even these countries, however. Their exports of manufactures may suffer from spillover effects of economic slowdown in the industrialized economies. China will lose foreign-exchange formerly earned by the more than 10,000 Chinese construction workers in Iraq and Kuwait. Malaysia will have to forego revenue from food exports to Iraq and Kuwait.

## The USG Response

Mr. Chairman, as I have suggested above, we are focusing first on the needs of the states in the Middle East most

2292-21

severely affected by the crisis -- Egypt, Turkey, and Jordan.
Nevertheless, we are well aware of the importance of addressing
this problem in the global terms that characterize this
challenge to the world community.  In this context I would like
to say a few words about what we have done on behalf of the
Philippines and what more could be done.

In practical terms, I believe that our approach to the
Philippines will take much the same form as those steps
outlined by Deputy Assistant Secretary Schaffer for South
Asia.  We will be working closely with international
organizations on the task of repatriating and reintegrating
workers.  We have already seen some Asian oil producers
increase domestic production to stabilize prices and offer to
provide the Philippines with supply alternatives to Iraq and
Kuwait.  We could explore a role for aid donors and
multilateral financial institutions.

In doing this, however, we must keep in mind that the
Philippines has embarked on an economic reform program in
cooperation with the IMF and other donors, including the United
States.  We would want any arrangements to aid the Philippines
to enhance the prospects for the success of this effort.

2292-22

0136

## HUMANITARIAN CONCERNS

Hundreds of thousands of foreign workers have lost their means of livlihood as a result of the Iraqi invasion of Kuwait. Many of these victims of conflict remain trapped in Iraq and Kuwait, hostages to Iraq's inhumane tactics of denying them exit or food rations. Others have managed to cross a border to safety; but having left all behind, they are in dire need of international humanitarian assistance. Most will require transportation to their home countries and, while they await space in the international airlift, the world must provide for their basic needs for water, food, shelter, and medical attention.

There are no good figures available on the number of Philippine workers currently in Iraq and Kuwait. Estimates range from 45,000 to 70,000 Filipinos. Approximately 10,000 Thai workers were in Iraq and Kuwait at the outset of the crisis. We understand that the Thai government has assisted in the departure of most of the Thai workers. We estimate that as many as 3,000 Filipino workers have left the region and that approximately 2,000 are in Jordan. The majority of Filipino workers stranded as a result of the crisis remain in Kuwait. At an earlier stage in the crisis, our Embassy in Kuwait aided the Philippine government in assisting its citizens stranded

2292-23

0137

there. We understand that food supplies and ▓▓▓▓▓ ▓▓▓ ▓▓
the refugees ▓▓ ▓he Jordanian camps are ██ate. We remain
concerned about the safety of Filipino and other workers still
in Iraq and Kuwait.

The International Organization for Migration is
coordinating the airlift of refugees, having received to date
$40 million for this purpose. In the ten day period
September 3-13, over 15,000 persons were moved, including
12,000 to Bangladesh and nearly 3,000 to Sri Lanka. Smaller
numbers were also moved to the Philippines, Thailand, and
Pakistan. Between September 13-23, we expect another 19,000
persons of all affected nationalities to depart.

The U.S. has pledged $28 million for relief efforts -- $10
million for transportation and up to $18 million for food,
shelter, and other necessities. I am glad to report that Asian
countries have contributed generously to the relief effort. In
his speech before the joint session of Congress, the President
singled out Japan for its $22 million contribution. As I
mentioned above, Australia will contribute $1.5 million to
assisting foreign nationals stranded as a result of the
crisis. Malaysia has leased a plane for the transport of
Bangladeshis from Turkey, and we will be discussing with Brunei
and Singapore their possible support for this effort.

2292-24

0138

The plight of Asian and other hostages in Iraq and Kuwait has focussed attention on the question of defining shipments of foodstuffs "in humanitarian circumstances," as permitted under UNSCR 661. Last week, the UN Security Council passed UNSCR 666 - a resolution which, while allowing food supplies to reach the innocent bystanders in this crisis, will deny them to Iraq.

The Philippines has turned to the Sanctions Committee to request relief, on an urgent basis, for their nationals trapped in Iraq and Kuwait. This request is in keeping with both the spirit and letter of UNSC resolution 661, and in agreement with the approach outlined above. We will continue to work closely with the Philippines in seeking a solution to this problem.

CONCLUSION

In conclusion, Mr. Chairman, I would say that this crisis has signalled to the Asia-Pacific community that acts of aggression half way around the world have an immediate and significant impact on the community's security and economic livelihood. The Pacific community has closed ranks in support of the UN sanctions and the multinational force with remarkable dispatch It is acting expeditiously to aid those countries -- in Asia and elsewhere -- hit by the economic shock waves

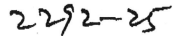

created by the crisis. More can be done, and we are in close
touch with Japan, South Korea, and other countries in East Asia
capable of providing further assistance. If anything positive
can be said about the Gulf crisis, it is that it has led the
nations of East Asia to see their economic and security
interests in global terms and to pull together in response to
the challenge created by Iraq's invasion of Kuwait.

2292-26

0140

# 외 무 부

종 별 :

번 호 : USW-4270          일 시 : 90 0919 1826

수 신 : 장관( 미북, 국연)사본: 주 유엔 대사(중계필)

발 신 : 주미대사

제 목 : 이락 사태 관련 유엔 역할

    1. 미하원 외무위 인권및 국제 기구 소위(YATRON위원장)와 국제 운용 소위(DYNALLY 위원장)는 공동으로 금 9.19 이락 사태와 관련한 유엔의 역할과 미국의 대 유엔정책에 관한 청문회를 개최함.

    2.금일 청문회에는 THOMAS PICKERING UN 주재 미대사와 JOHN BOLTON 국무부국제 기구 담당차관보가 참석, 증언하였는바, 주요 내용 아래보고함.

    - 탈 냉전 이후 문명 세계가 직면한 첫 시련이 이락 사태인바, 탈 냉전 이후 국제 법에 근거한 세계 질서 수립을 위해 유엔을 통한 문제 해결에 주력하고 있음.

    - 미 행정부의 유엔 전략은 회원국의 합의(CONSENSUS)와 공동 행동(ACTION)에주안점을 두고 있는바, 이락을 국제 사회에서 고립시키고, 동 사태의 평화적 해결을위해, 유엔 헌장에 근거한 모든 방안을 모색하고 있음. 동사태와 관련된 안보리의 일련의 결의는 미국의 성공적 유엔 전략의 성과라고 평가됨.

    -유엔 결의에 따른 대이락 제재 조치 성패 여부는,국제 사회에서의 침략행위에 대한 응징이 유효할것인가를 가늠하는 계기가 될것인바, 유엔 안보리는제재 조치를 보강하기 위한 보완 조치 또한 강구중임.

    -지역, 이념 및 빈부 격차에 따라 분열 되어 있던 유엔 회원국들이 단결하여 유엔을 활성화시키기 위한 조치로서 주목되는 사항은: 이락의 침략행위에 대한 소련의 공식 비난: 동 분쟁 해결에 공동 방안 모색을 위하여 안보리 상임 이사국들이 수시 회합: 안보리 상임 이사국의 고위 관리들간의 수시 접촉, :이사국과 기타 회원국들간의 진지한 대화 등을 거론할수있는바, 지역 분쟁을 유엔을 통해 외교적으로 해결하기위해서는 회원국들간의 뚜렷한 목적 의식과 인내심이 필요함.

    3.참석 의원들은 유엔 제재 조치 위반국에 대한 응징 방안, 동 사태로 인한 난민처우책등에 관해 관심을 표명하였으며 PICKERING 대사는 금일 청문회를

---

미주국    1차보    중아국    국기국    정와대    안기부

외신 1과 통제관

0141

이용하여유엔에서의 미국의 체납 분담금지불에 대한 의회의 승인을 촉구하였음.

　4. PICKERING 대사 증언 내용 별첨 팩시송부함.

　　첨부: USW(F)-2290

　　(대사 박동진-국장)

USW (F) ● 2290

수신: 장관 (미북, 중안, 중근동)
　　　　　　　사본: 주 뷰엔대사

발신: 주미대사
제목: 이락 사태 관련 UN 역할
　　　　USW-4270 유첨 (8부)

2290—1

For more than a year we in this Administration and in this
country have been describing the dramatic political challenges
in Europe, and between ourselves and the Soviets, as ushering
in a "post cold war" era.  Much of that discussion has been
conceptual.  More than any single event, Saddam Hussein's
brazen invasion of Kuwait will force it to be concrete.  It
will decide if this is to be a "new" old era reminiscent of the
1930's, in which aggression is tolerated -- and thus rewarded
-- or the beginning of a more promising age when aggressors are
forced to respect international law.  If we are to succeed much
will depend on our efforts in and through the United Nations.

I welcome this opportunity to comment on those efforts and
on the steps we have taken to build upon them in order to close
the vise on Saddam Hussein.  Since the Assistant Secretary for
International Organizations will address this committee on the
full spectrum of UN issues with which the Administration is now
engaged, I will confine my remarks to our Security Council
strategy on the Persian Gulf.

At its best, UN diplomacy delivers two results:  consensus,
and international action.  The events of the last six weeks
have indeed shown the UN at its best.  But that should not have
been surprising to those who have been following the UN and the
changing international scene closely.  The steps taken by the
Security Council were prefigured in the work of the Council for
the last two years.  What was surprising was the speed and
cohesiveness with which the Council moved.  The first meeting
of the Council was called within minutes of the news of the
invasion -- at about 10:30 pm eastern time in the evening of
the first of August.  The first resolution was passed within
six hours after the Council actually met, and it would have
been passed several hours sooner except for delay caused by one
member of the Council who required time in order to receive
instructions.  Four and a half days later, strict sanctions
were imposed when it became clear that Iraq's so-called
withdrawal was a sham.  Then when the annexation took place, it
was rapidly nullified; when Embassies and hostages were
threatened the Council took action; and within three weeks,
minimum force was authorized to enforce the sanctions at sea.

At the opening of this crisis the President identified four
immediate goals for our policy.  They continue to guide our
work:

2290-2

0144

-- first, the immediate, complete and unconditional withdrawal of all Iraqi forces from Kuwait as mandated in the United Nations Security Council Resolution 660 and the restoration of Kuwait's legitimate government;

-- second, the defense of Saudi Arabia;

-- third, the protection of the lives of American citizens held hostage by Iraq, both in Iraq and Kuwait;

-- fourth, a commitment to the security and stability of the Persian Gulf region.

To attain these goals the President emphasized a strategy of leading a global alliance to isolate and to use the full force of the UN Charter to get Iraq to reverse its aggression and invasion. To move this strategy forward we have used the diplomatic advantages of working through the United Nations. Just as a line has been drawn in the sands of Saudi Arabia against further aggression, we have drawn important lines at the Security Council to set down the requirements for a solution:

-- Resolution 660, adopted immediately after the invasion, demands complete and unconditional Iraqi withdrawal from Kuwait. It provides for a negotiation to settle the differences between Iraq and Kuwait, with the help of others including the Arab League.

-- Resolution 661, adopted after Iraq's refusal to withdraw, imposes comprehensive economic sanctions against Iraq to get it to withdraw from Kuwait and to allow the legitimate government of Kuwait to be restored. The only exceptions to these sanctions are supplies intended strictly for medical purposes, and in humanitarian circumstances, foodstuffs. The Council, acting alone or through its Sanctions Committee, must decide whether those circumstances exist.

-- Resolution 662 declared Iraq's annexation of Kuwait to be null and void.

2290-3

0145

Resolution 664 demanded that foreign nations in Iraq and Kuwait be allowed to depart and that Iraq take no action to jeopardize their safety or health.  It also nullified Iraq's order to close Embassies in Kuwait and withdraw the members of their diplomatic missions.

-- Resolution 665 provided authorization for states with maritime forces in the area to control shipping to ensure that the sanctions are respected.

-- Resolution 666 established a procedure for determining whether there is an urgent humanitarian need to justify particular shipments of foodstuffs to Iraq or Kuwait and an international mechanism for ensuring that relief supplies reach their intended beneficiaries.

-- Resolution 667 condemned Iraqi abduction of persons protected by diplomatic immunity and Iraqi violation of diplomatic premises, and committed members to immediate consultations toward adoption of further enforcement measures under Chapter 7 of the Charter.

Making these measures effective:  In numerous past cases, economic sanctions have not resulted in bringing effective pressure in the short term.  Either sanctions have not been comprehensive, allowing loopholes through which to circumvent them, or they have lacked universal support, opening channels for widescale leakage.  The members of the United Nations face a test in their readiness to plug the loopholes and stem the leakages.  Let me add that this test is important not just because we need to stop replenishments for Iraq.  The real test is whether the internatonal community will send a solid signal to Saddam Hussein that his aggression will not be tolerated.

Presidents Bush and Gorbachev have already staked out their position in Helsinki" "Our preference is to resolve the crisis peacefully, and we will be united against Iraq's aggression as long as the crisis exists.  However, we are determined to see this aggression end, and if the current steps fail to end it, we are prepared to consider additional ones consistent with the UN Charter.  We must demonstrate beyond any doubt that aggression cannot and will not pay.

229.-4

0146

The Security Council took a significant first step to back up sanctions when it gave authorization for naval forces to interdict vessels suspected of sanctions busting. Now we are working on two additional ways to make sanctions sustainable.

First, in order to ensure that an exception permitting shipment of medical supplies and, in humanitarian circumstances, foodstuffs, does not offer Saddam Hussein an escape from the noose of sanctions, we joined with other Members of the Security Council to create a sturdy mechanism for deciding when humanitarian circumstances exist and what should be done: shipment of good will not be allowed unless it is approved by the Sanctions Committee, and particular shipments that are approved should be distributed only for the essential needs of the civilian population and only under the supervision of a designated international agency. An Indian ship with food for Indian and other third country nations is now due to arrive with desperately needed relief supplies. We will be watching to see if Iraq allows these supplies to reach their intended beneficiaries under appropriate supervision.

Second, we recognize that the burden of applying sanctions falls unevenly on different countries. Article 50 of the UN Charter provides that states confronting special economic problems in applying sanctions can consult the Security Council about help in solving those problems. The President has identified Egypt, Jordan, and Turkey as special cases, and no doubt there are others. The Sanctions Committee has already acted to recommend measures to assist Jordan. We are working with our colleagues both on the Council and off to devise the speediest and most appropriate means of dealing with such needs. Naturally, we will want to be sure that beneficiaries are fully enforcing the sanctions themselves.

Looking Forward: Secretary Baker has said that we face a simple choice: whether we want to live in a world where aggression is less likely because it is met with a strong response or in a world where aggression succeeds because the nations of the world cannot muster the collective will to challenge it. We have an opportunity to reinforce the standards for civilized behavior found in the United Nations Charter and use the organization as an instrument to mobilize the collective will.

229.-5

Let us remember the consequences when the wrong choice is made. In 1936 Mussolini sent his Roman legions off to Ethiopia to conquer a new empire. Despite Haile Selassie's impassioned plea to the League of Nations, there was no collective international will for a strong response. Aggression seemed to succeed. This lesson was not lost on other nations harboring aggressive designs. It was an early step toward the worldwide conflagration which followed.

Most of the history of the United Nations has been marked by divisions -- between East and West, between North and South -- that have in recent years often pitted the United States against large majorities. Ideological debates served to divide the members but not to help find common ground. Against this background what helps to account for the remarkable response to the Iraqi invasion of Kuwait?

Increasingly in recent years we have been able to work within the Security Council to achieve a real sense of solidarity. Now members are more inclined to emphasize the interests that unify them rather than the disputes that divide them. Key factors in putting together a new way of working have been:

-- the shift in Soviet behavior toward a willingness to condemn acts of aggression, even if perpetrated by a longtime friend such as Iraq, and a readiness to resort to the mechanisms for collective action contained in the Charter.

-- the ability of the Permanent Members to have regular, business-like discussions on finding joint approaches to solutions of regional conflicts; these discussions have made possible parallel recommendations for action by Beijing, London, Moscow, Paris, and Washington.

-- the effective use of high level personal contacts among these capitals, certainly the contacts between Secretary Baker and Foreign Minister Shevardnadze were the key to unlocking agreement on authorizing sanctions and then naval action to ensure compliance with sanctions against Iraq.

229-6

0148

-- careful consultation with other members of the Security
Council and with other states having a role to play in specific
situations. For example, in the past weeks the non-aligned
members of the Council, who collectively could wield a veto
over Council actions, have played an important role.

-- deep concern among the smaller, non-aligned members of
the organization and the Council about the prospect of a member
state being swallowed up in an act of aggression.

-- a sense of solidarity, particularly in Africa, that
established frontiers, however disagreeable, cannot be changed
arbitrarily by force without creating a regime of anarchy and
destruction.

By its very nature such complex diplomatic activity
requires steadiness of purpose and patience. However
successful our initial efforts in New York, we must ensure
their effectiveness over time.

## U.S. Financial Responsibilities

Before ending let me raise with you a serious matter that
could hobble our ability to mount an effective UN response to
Iraq's aggression against Kuwait and to capitalize on progress
on other issues, including Cambodia. For the United States to
maintain a strong voice in a healthy United Nations we need
prompt positive action on the President's request to the
Congress to pay U.S. assessments and arrearages. If the new
era now being defined is to include greater respect for states'
obligations under the Charter, we must start by meeting our own
obligations.

Now that the world is treating the United Nations more
realistically, it is our belief that the states members of the
Organization should also be treating the UN more
realistically. This is related to what the organization is to
be asked to do in all facets of its activity. It will also
relate to the Organizations' funding. Now that we expect more
from the United Nations, and we have had much success in
holding the line on budgets, it is clear that we should meet
our regular assessments and obligations under the Charter and
deal effectively with the arrearages which have mounted up.

290-7

As the President's Representative in the United Nations, I am disturbed and chagrined by the fact we are now the largest debtor. Our leadership in the Security Council in recent weeks has not been made any easier by this fact. Our leadership in the coming General Assembly will suffer seriously by our inability to meet our obligations under the Charter. The United States expects members of the United Nations, including the Soviet Union and others, to uphold their treaty obligations. Unfortunately, in this key area, we are not doing so.

As you well know, President Bush has enthusiastically and wholeheartedly endorsed this objective. Last week Secretary Baker said "that we are faced with the first crisis of the first post-cold war era, and we are the biggest deadbeats in paying our dues to the United Nations. It is outrageous and we ought to have the President's budget request funded regardless of what it takes."

Let's made no bones about it, there is a great deal at stake here. Our failure to meet our financial obligations will affect us in the Persian Gulf. It affects us in Cambodia, it affects the Secretary General's progress in moving toward a referendum in the Western Sahara, the important peacemaking and peacekeeping effort in Central America and especially in El Salvador to mention only a few.

If the new era now being defined is to include greater respect for states' obligations under the Charter, then we need to do our own part to restore the financial health of the organization. The leadership of the United States in New York has been critical in bringing along the United Nations in recent weeks and months in the absolutely vital effort of developing a solid, collective international front against aggression. Now that we have this hard-won consensus, it would be tragic to lose it by failing to meet our financial obligations. Moreover, the financial obligations that go with this are miniscule compared to the major expenditures we and others will be making to take all of the other steps required to meet the challenge of aggression in this year. I have dwelt on this point at some length because I believe that it is our highest and most critical priority with the United Nations at the current time. I urge you to help us meet this challenge.

229 0 - 8

0150

# 외 무 부

종 별 :

번 호 : USW-4271 　　　　　　　　　　　일 시 : 90 0919 1828

수 신 : 장관(미북,미안, 중근동)

발 신 : 주미대사

제 목 : 이락 사태 의회 반응(15) (언론 보도 종합)

　1. 하원 외무위 구주및 중동 소위 청문회(9.18)

　0 민주당 소속 의원들은 부쉬 행정부가 이락 사태발발전 이락에 대하여 지나친 유화 정책을 취한 결과, 이락의 쿠웨이트 침공을 초래한 것이라고 하면서 증언에 나선 JOHN KELLY 국무성 중동 차관보를 공격하였음.

　0 특히 LEE HAMILTON(민-인디아나)소위원장은 KELLY 차관보가 지난 4.26 및 7.31 ( 사태 발발 2일전) 증언에서 만약 이락이 쿠웨이트를 침공하는 경우에도 미국이쿠웨이트를 방어하지는 않을것이라고 시사 하였던 사실을 들어 행정부의 잘못된 정책을 추궁하였음.

　0 한편 일부 의원들은 행정부가 금번 이락사태를 구실로 하여 의회와의 협의없이 엄청난 규모의 무기를 사우디에 판매하려 한다고 비난하고, 일부 긴급한 수량을 제외 하고는 의회와의 협의를 거쳐 판매해야할것이라고 주장함.

　2. 대 이락 선전 포고 관련 결의안 추진

　0 민주당 지도부는 이락 사태와 관련, 현재까지의 부쉬 행정부의 조치를 용인하는 동시 전투발발시 의회의 사전 동의를 얻어 군사력을 사용토록 하는 내용의 결의안추진을 계획중임.

　0 DANTE FASCELL 하원 외무 위원장은 대통령에게 어느 정도의 재량권은 주되 정식 선전 포고는 의회의 동의를 얻어야할것이라고 언급하여 상기 결의안 지지를 표명함.

　0 S. SOLARZ 아태 소위 위원장도 의회가 어떤 명확한 역할을 할수 있도록 초당적인 지지를 얻어 결의안을 채택한다면, 사담. 후세인에게도 명확한 멧세지가 될뿐아 니라 오판을 미연에 방지할수있다고 주장함.

　3. 동맹국 분담금 사용 절차

　0 국방부는 금번 이락 사태와 관련, 조성된 동맹국 분담금을 의회와의 사전

미주국　　1차보　　중아국　　정문국　　안기부　　법무부

PAGE 1 　　　　　　　　　　　　　　　　　　90.09.20　　08:48 BX

　　　　　　　　　　　　　　　　　　　　외신 1과 통제관

　　　　　　　　　　　　　　　　　　　0151

동의없이 사용할수 있도록 국방 헌금법안( NATIONAL DEFENSEGIFT FUND)을 의회에 제출함.

    0 이에 대하여 LES ASPIN 하원 군사위원장,JOHN MURTHA 하원 세출위 군사 소위원장등 관련 의원들은 국방부의 상기 법안에 반대 의사를 표명하고 여하한 경우에도 의회의 통제한에 예산집행이 이루어 져야할것이라고 주장함.

    (대사 박동진-국장)

| 관리<br>번호 | ro-(ryn |
|---|---|

# 외 무 부

종  별 : 지 급

번  호 : USW-4293

일  시 : 90 0920 1833

수  신 : 장관(미북,미안,중근동)

발  신 : 주 미 대사

제  목 : 이락 사태 의회 반응(16)

1. 9.19 하원 세출위 군사 소위는 CHENEY 국방장관및 POWELL 합참의장을 출석시켜 DESERT SHIELD 작전을 위한 추가 지출 법안 관련 청문회를 개최 하였음. 동 청문회는 비 공개로 진행되었으나, 청문회 직후 입수한 증언문을 별전 FAX 송부함.

2. 동 청문회에 관한 언론 보도에 의하면, 폐만 사태 동맹국 분담금 사용 절차에 관한 논의가 있었으며, CHENEY 국방장관은 동 분담금을 의회 동의 없이 행정부가 직접 사용할수 있도록 허가해 줄것을 요청하였으나 거부 되었다함.

   첨부 USW(F)-2313

   (대사 박동진-국장)

   90.12.31 까지

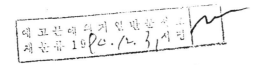

| 미주국 | 차관 | 1차보 | 미주국 | 중아국 | 청와대 | 안기부 | 대책반 |
|---|---|---|---|---|---|---|---|

PAGE 1

90.09.21    08:39

외신 2과  통제관 BT

0153

USW(F) — 2312                                      # 첨부

수신: 장관 ( 미북, 미안, 증근동)
발신: 주미대사

제목: 하원 세흘위 군사소위 청문회
( 페만 사태)                                      ( 14 매 )

# STATEMENT OF
# THE SECRETARY OF DEFENSE

# DICK CHENEY

# BEFORE THE

# HOUSE APPROPRIATIONS
# DEFENSE SUBCOMMITTEE

# IN CONNECTION WITH
# OPERATION DESERT SHIELD

# SEPTEMBER 19, 1990

0154

### STATEMENT OF SECRETARY OF DEFENSE DICK CHENEY
### IN CONNECTION WITH OPERATION DESERT SHIELD
### DEFENSE SUBCOMMITTEE OF THE HOUSE APPROPRIATIONS COMMITTEE
### SEPTEMBER 19, 1990

Mr. Chairman, members of the committee, thank you for this opportunity to discuss Operation DESERT SHIELD and the defense budget issues surrounding it.

Today, U.S. military forces are involved in one of the most significant multinational operations of the post-war period. The long-term implications of this operation for our military force structure, strategy, U.S. presence and security relationships in the region, and economic security are all significant.

### OPERATION DESERT SHIELD AND U.S. NATIONAL INTERESTS

The events of this crisis are well known. On August 2, Iraqi armed forces, without provocation or warning, invaded the sovereign nation of Kuwait. Facing negligible resistance from its much smaller neighbor, Iraq's tanks stormed through Kuwait in blitzkrieg fashion. Witnesses reported hundreds of casualties. The invasion was clearly "naked aggression."

International indignation and condemnation was immediate. The United Nations Security Council voted overwhelmingly to condemn the invasion and demand Iraq's immediate and total withdrawal.

President Bush acted quickly and decisively. Immediately after the invasion, he ordered an embargo of all trade with Iraq and, together with many other nations, announced sanctions that froze all Iraqi assets in this country and protected Kuwait's assets.

On August 6, four days after the invasion of Kuwait, I briefed King Fahd about the threat from Iraq and the military capabilities we could provide to help deter further Iraqi aggression and to help defend Saudi Arabia. King Fahd's decisive and courageous decision to request foreign assistance speaks to the seriousness of the situation. In our discussion, King Fahd talked about his personal respect for President Bush and his great trust in the United States. He spoke of his faith in our commitment to help defend his country, to stay until the job was done and, when the job was done and we were asked to leave, in fact to leave. This trust in America, held by many countries, is key to our ability to help achieve a more secure and stable world.

0155

After unparalleled international consultation and exhausting every alternative, on August 7 President Bush ordered the deployment of U.S. forces to Saudi Arabia to protect vital

American interests.  In doing so, he set forth clear,
straightforward objectives to:

   • Assure the security and stability of the Persian Gulf
area;
   • Effect the immediate, complete, and unconditional·
withdrawal of all Iraqi forces from Kuwait;
   • Restore the legitimate government of Kuwait; and
   • Protect the lives of American citizens abroad.

   This kind of clarity about what we seek to achieve is key
to the effective, appropriate use of our military forces.  With
that same commitment to clarity of purpose, President Bush has
kept Congress fully informed about our efforts, and we intend to
continue doing so.

   Failure to counter Iraq's aggression and territorial gains
would have severe consequences for U.S. interests.  In the
short-term, Iraq could manipulate and cause destabilizing
uncertainty in the international oil market, force up prices to
crippling levels, threaten regional states, and begin the
process of building a strong and widespread political base.
With the conquest of Kuwait, Saddam Hussein has direct control
of the capacity to produce five million barrels of oil a day and
a potentially strong influence over production of the rest of
the Arabian Peninsula, which is another seven million barrels a
day.  This would give Saddam Hussein an extremely powerful oil
·weapon.  With this weapon, he could coerce oil importing nations
in Europe, Japan, and even the United States, which depend
increasingly on Gulf oil.

   Over the long-term, Iraq also would be much stronger
militarily.  Given its additional resources, Iraq could expand
its vast arsenal of conventional and non-conventional weaponry--
possibly soon to include nuclear weapons.  His military
strength, coupled with enhanced economic and political power,
would give Saddam Hussein even greater coercive power over his
neighbors on oil and other issues.

### U.S. AND INTERNATIONAL ACTIONS IN RESPONSE TO IRAQI THREAT

   The deployment of U.S. forces to the region has gone
exceptionally well, and the level of multinational cooperation
is unprecedented.  Today we have over 150,000 soldiers, sailors,
airmen, and marines in the region.  We have elements of several
Army divisions, numerous Air Force fighter and strategic
aircraft squadrons, a Marine Expeditionary Force with its
supporting units, Special Operations Forces, three carrier
battle groups, a battleship, and other naval assets in the
Persian Gulf, Indian Ocean, and Red Sea.

   The United States is not alone in this important mission.
At the invitation of the governments of Saudi Arabia, Kuwait,
and other Gulf nations, military forces from over 25 other

0156

countries are participating in the land-based DESERT SHIELD
operation and the maritime enforcement of the UN-imposed
economic sanctions. Furthermore, we expect that contributions
from these other nations may increase over time. We were
particularly encouraged that Britain and France announced that
they will strengthen their forces participating in DESERT SHIELD
by one brigade each.

These multinational forces face a formidable threat. Iraq
has elements of 11 divisions in Kuwait, totaling 173,680 troops,
over 1,500 tanks, 1,000 armored personnel carriers, and 778
artillery pieces. An additional 11 divisions are deployed in
southern Iraq in support of those forces in Kuwait, for a total
of well over 250,000 Iraqi troops in the Kuwaiti theater. These
are battle-hardened units, with leadership that has demonstrated
a proclivity to use any and all forms of warfare, against
civilian as well as military targets.

Terrorism is potentially another significant weapon in
Saddam Hussein's arsenal, and on September 4 Iraq was put back
on the State Department's list of nations aiding and abetting
terrorism. During this period of heightened tension, the
terrorist threat to our forces in Saudi Arabia and to American
citizens and interests worldwide will likely remain high. Pro-
Iraqi demonstrations in major cities continue to fuel anti-
American sentiment. U.S. officials have received bomb threats,
death threats, and verbal warnings from international terrorist
organizations. Though no specific credible threats have yet
been identified, it is imperative that we take adequate
precautions to protect our interests worldwide. The Department
of Defense (DoD), working closely with other U.S. government
agencies, is adopting measures to enhance the protection of
American military personnel and civilians overseas, as well as
here in the United States.

Current operations in the Persian Gulf area involve the
first involuntary call up of Selected Reserve units and
individuals under the Total Force Policy established in 1973.
Under this policy, reserve components provide a high percentage
of the total capability in a number of functional areas.
Initially, there were sufficient reserve volunteers to support
this operation. By August 22, prior to the presidential call up
of Selected Reserves, approximately 11,500 volunteer reservists
were serving on active duty under orders.

The scope of DESERT SHIELD requires an involuntary call up
of reservists to provide various capabilities, many of which
reside in the National Guard and Reserve. Mission areas being
fulfilled by reservists include airlift, port security, cargo
handling, and medical support. By August 31, more than 8,800
reservists had been called up and 7,600 volunteers were still on
active duty. I anticipate that by the end of September, close
to 50,000 reservists will be called.

0157

2312-4

As you who have visited the region can verify, much has been accomplished since President Bush ordered the deployment of U.S. forces. We can be proud of the speed and efficiency with which our military undertook its mission. I dare say an operation of this scope and complexity would not have been possible a decade ago.

Fortunately, predecessors of mine in the Pentagon, military commanders, and Congress had the foresight to plan and program for a Persian Gulf contingency. Operating in this area of the world--with its long logistic lines, harsh environment, and minimal infrastructure--will always be extremely difficult; but compared to a decade ago, we now are better organized, trained, and equipped to do so. Our U.S. Central Command, with its full attention devoted to the region we call Southwest Asia, has proved invaluable during both the Iran-Iraq war and the current crisis. Since 1980 we have done extensive planning for desert warfare and conducted relevant training and exercises, including our major biennial exercise BRIGHT STAR in Egypt and other regional states.

## COSTS OF OPERATION DESERT SHIELD

We estimate that incremental costs associated with Operation DESERT SHIELD and increased fuel prices will total $2.7 billion for FY 1990. These costs will be offset--to the extent possible within individual appropriations--by deferring and canceling lower priority requirements, yielding $652 million. For these offsets we will work with Congress under existing notification and/or approval procedures. The Department also is proposing the transfer of $175 million in unobligated fund balances to accounts where needed. To cover the remaining $1.9 billion in incremental costs, President Bush has submitted to Congress a supplemental FY 1990 appropriations request.

The President's request also seeks approval of appropriations language to provide DoD explicit statutory authority to accept contributions from foreign sources under expedited procedures. This authority would enable the Secretary of Defense to accept contributions that now may only be accepted by the Treasury or the General Services Administration for transfer to DoD. This would increase our Department's flexibility in accepting and using contributions arising from Operation DESERT SHIELD. We further are requesting authority to enter into reciprocal agreements with foreign governments to provide logistics support, supplies, and services.

Regarding these requested new authorities, the DoD Comptroller will work with congressional staffs to devise a reporting mechanism to keep Congress fully informed on the 0158 status of contributions and related transfers to Defense accounts. The Comptroller also will establish a procedure to track and report to the Congress the receipt of in-kind support.

I urge your prompt approval of all elements of the
President's supplemental request.  Detailed justification of our
FY 1990 supplemental request has been provided separately, and
the Department is eager to assist you in any way it can.

For FY 1991 we estimate that incremental costs associated
with Operation DESERT SHIELD and increased fuel costs will total
about $15 billion, if the crisis continues for the entire fiscal
year.  If conflict occurs, these costs would be much higher.

President Bush has firmly endorsed the concept of
responsibility sharing for this crisis and announced his
Economic Action Plan to solicit contributions from other
countries for their fair share of this effort.  Last week
Secretaries Baker and Brady had successful and fruitful
discussions on responsibility sharing with our friends and
allies in the Persian Gulf region, Europe, and East Asia.  The
U.S. response to the Gulf crisis has enjoyed broad support from
the American people and Congress, and we have demonstrated our
willingness to bear our fair share of the sacrifices it
requires.  We recognize, however, that for the American people
and Congress to sustain this effort, they must see that others
are contributing their share as well.

In most cases, other countries are sharing the
responsibility, and sharing it willingly.  Pledged contributions
total about $20 billion in military and economic assistance;
about half of that is for the United States and half for the
frontline states most affected by the crisis.  Contributions
include $12 billion from the Gulf states, $4 billion from Japan,
$2 billion from Germany, and $2 billion from the Economic
Community.  These contributions come in the form of either cash
or in-kind support.  Overall, we are very pleased by the
diplomatic, military, and financial support that our allies and
friends are giving to this collective effort.

## LOOKING AHEAD

The question often asked about the Gulf crisis is, "How
long will we be there?"  I cannot give a definitive answer.  We
were invited by the Saudi Arabian government, as were other
nations, to help defend the Kingdom, and we will be present as
long as it takes to achieve our mutual objectives.  When that is
done, or when Saudi Arabia asks, we will leave.  Likewise, we
have been invited to use facilities in other Gulf countries; and
when we are asked to leave, we will.

In the future, our relationships with the Gulf states will
undoubtedly change.  Indeed, they already have.  Facing this
current threat together will shape our security relations for
years to come.  We will be working with the regional states to
make arrangements for them to be able to defend themselves
better and to receive reinforcement troops, if that ever becomes
necessary.  It is imperative that we take steps to ensure that

0159

countries like Saudi Arabia are never again in so vulnerable
position requiring such a massive U.S. deployment.  To this end,
we will be consulting with the Congress on how we can strengthen
our regional allies, both in terms of hardware and
interoperability of command and control with U.S. forces.  We
will need your help.

Over many years the President and Congress have worked
together to prepare U.S. forces for the possibility of an
operation like DESERT SHIELD.  We look forward to your support
in continuing this partnership--as we work to protect America's
interests, seek peaceful and lasting solutions to regional
problems, and build long-term security relationships with our
friends in the region.

0160

2712-7

STATEMENT OF

GENERAL COLIN L. POWELL, USA

CHAIRMAN OF THE JOINT CHIEFS OF STAFF

BEFORE THE

DEFENSE SUBCOMMITTEE OF THE·

HOUSE APPROPRIATIONS COMMITTEE

ON

"OPERATION DESERT SHIELD"


19 September 1990


0161

Mr. Chairman, members of the Committee, I am pleased to have this opportunity to discuss the military aspects of U.S. actions in the Persian Gulf region.

As Secretary Cheney indicated in his statement, U.S. forces are in the Persian Gulf region to support the President's national policy objectives. Our military objectives are to deter further aggression by Iraq, to defend Saudi Arabia should deterrence fail, and to enforce the mandatory Chapter 7 sanctions of the UN Charter and UN Security Council Resolutions 661, 662 and 665. In accomplishing these objectives, we are working very closely with allied and friendly nations-- today over 25 in number--who have sent or are in the process of sending military forces to the region. Saddam Hussein is facing a multi-national military force. This multi-national force will be capable of a successful defense if Iraqi forces invade Saudi Arabia. It will also have the capability to respond should Iraqi forces invade any other nation in the area.

Because of the tremendous distances involved, we phased our overall operation for the defense of Saudi Arabia. In the initial phase naval, air superiority and light ground forces moved swiftly to provide an immediate deterrent presence. In the second phase attack aircraft, additional fighter aircraft, and maritime forces were deployed. In the current phase, we are building up heavy ground forces and additional air, maritime and sustainment forces to insure a successful defense of Saudi Arabia.

With respect to enforcing the UN sanctions, a multi-national naval force, consisting of U.S. naval forces and naval forces from more than 15 allied and friendly nations, is intercepting maritime vessels in the relevant ocean areas to

0162

termine their destination and whether they are in compliance with the UN

nctions regarding prohibited cargo. As of this week, U.S. Navy support for this

eration includes 10 ships in the Persian Gulf, 28 ships in the North Arabian Sea,

d 8 ships in the Red Sea. To date, we have intercepted over 1,000 ships and we

ve boarded and diverted five ships that were not in compliance with UN

nctions, including two Iraqi ships.

U.S. investment in forces and equipment capable of deploying quickly to any

rt of the world has paid off. The movement of U.S. forces to Saudi Arabia and

rrounding Gulf Coast countries is the largest rapid deployment of U.S. forces

nce World War II. We moved more forces and equipment in the first three

eeks of Desert Shield than we moved during the first three months of the

orean War. This massive deployment of troops and equipment is the equivalent

f moving and sustaining a city the size of Chattanooga, Tennessee.

Desert Shield has also convincingly demonstrated the value of a full range of

alanced forces. In Desert Shield we have needed and deployed light forces,

aritime forces, heavy forces, tactical and strategic air forces, mobility and

istainment forces.

As you know, we had to move as quickly as possible. As a result, Operation

)esert Shield has taxed U.S. airlift and sealift to the maximum. The Military

irlift Command's organic fleet of aircraft is fully employed, with nearly 90

ercent dedicated to Desert Shield missions. The remaining aircraft continue to   0163

ipport DOD's other worldwide requirements. According to established plans, for

first time in history we activated a portion of the Civil Reserve Air Fleet

Stage II and III can make an additional 78 and 277 aircraft available. To date, the Military Airlift Command has deployed over 85,000 people and over 78,000 tons of equipment. Moreover, the extent of Strategic Air Command's tanker support has been impressive--all combat aircraft deploying to the region required multiple aerial refuelings.

More than 213,000 tons of cargo has been sealifted to the area of operations -- with an additional 72 ships loading or en route. All eight of the Navy's fast sealift ships are supporting the deployment. As of today, seven of these ships have completed the 15 day journey and offloaded their cargoes in Saudi Arabia and one ship is undergoing repairs at Rota, Spain. Nine Maritime Prepositioning Ships (MPS-2 and MPS-3) from Diego Garcia and Guam have unloaded. These ships carried combat equipment and 30 days of supplies for the I Marine Expeditionary Force. As of this week, 40 Ready Reserve Force (RRF) ships are activated and 37 are at sea or ready for sea. To increase our sealift capability, we have leased 18 U.S. and 13 foreign ships.

Committee members will be pleased to hear that in all of these lift efforts, the U.S. Transportation Command has performed superbly. Coordinating the largest rapid lift in America's history has not been an easy task, but the new unified command has proven its worth.

You are aware that on 23 August, the President invoked, for the first time, the provisions of section 673b, Title 10, United States Code, the Selected Reserve Callup Authority. This augmentation of the Active Armed Forces provides us 0164

. . .  . . . . . . . . . . . . certain critical military activities. The Reserves

ordering to active duty units and individuals to perform a wide variety of tasks both in this country and in and around the Arabian Peninsula.

We are all aware of the personal sacrifices being made by the reservists being called up. I assure you that we will only call those we need, and will retain them for only the period of service that is absolutely necessary to accomplish the mission. The most immediate need is for Army logistics forces to sustain the growing combat power in the theater of operations. We also will be calling up Air Force, Navy and Coast Guard units and individuals to support strategic lift and enhance the flow of forces and supplies to the U.S. Central Command (USCENTCOM) area. Finally, individual Army and Navy reservists are being called up to backfill critical medical specialists who have deployed to meet theater medical requirements.

In addition to those called up under the Presidential Callup Authority, many more reservists and guardsmen have supported this operation on a volunteer basis, logging thousands of air miles in support of strategic airlift, aerial refueling and tactical reconnaissance requirements, and pitching in to assist where needed in the deployment process. These are patriotic men and women, totally dedicated to our national defense. In short, our Total Force policy is working well in Operation Desert Shield.

All of the U.S. forces in Operation Desert Shield are organized as a joint force under the Central Command's Commander in Chief (USCINCCENT), General H. Norman Schwarzkopf. This joint force includes Army, Navy, Air Force and Marine Corps component commanders.

0165

Major U.S. forces deployed to the Middle East come under the operational control of USCINCCENT when they enter the USCENTCOM area of responsibility. USCINCCENT has primary responsibility for Operation Desert Shield and is supported by the other combatant commands and numerous federal departments and agencies.   General Schwarzkopf's naval component commander commands both U.S. naval forces for the defense of Saudi Arabia and U.S. naval forces for the multi-national Maritime Intercept Force.

General Schwarzkopf's mission is "to deploy forces to the U.S. Central Command area of responsibility and take actions in concert with host nation forces, friendly regional forces and other allies to defend against an Iraqi attack on Saudi Arabia and be prepared to conduct other operations as directed."   General Schwarzkopf is coordinating closely with the military forces of Saudi Arabia and the other allied forces in theater.

U.S. forces in Saudi Arabia and in other Arab countries are part of a command arrangement that has established an effective coalition of Arab and Western forces.   These forces are organized along national lines with national forces being assigned separate areas of operations.   National Force Commanders are maintaining close coordination and cooperation on all issues.

Host nation support has been outstanding.  Saudi Arabia and other Gulf states have provided unprecedented use of airfields, port facilities, beddown locations, heavy equipment transport, and water for all allied forces.

0166

A large Iraqi military force remains in Kuwait. It has the ...

173,000 Iraqi troops with over 1,500 tanks continue to occupy positions in Kuwait. Moreover, 11 Iraqi divisions are deployed in southern Iraq in position to support the Iraqi forces in Kuwait.

U.S. military forces in the Persian Gulf are well trained and well supported. I returned Saturday night from a visit to the area and I am pleased to report that while there are glitches here and there, on balance the operation is proceeding smoothly. I have complete confidence in the GIs that are manning the tanks, ships, and planes in the Gulf region. Together with the military forces of participating Arab and Western countries, these forces will be capable of defending Saudi Arabia from an Iraqi attack and enforcing the UN sanctions.

6    2312-14 끝    0167

# 외 무 부

종 별 :

번 호 : USW-4294     일 시 : 90 0920 1833

수 신 : 장관(미북,미안,중근동)

발 신 : 주미대사

제 목 : 이락사태 의회 반응(17) ( 언론 보도 종합)

연: USW-4271

1. 의회내 행정부 정책에 대한 비난 분위기 형성

0 페만사태 발발 직후 행정부에 초당적이고 전폭적인 지지 분위기에서 서서히 행정부 정책을 비판하는 분위기가 의회내 형성되기 시작하였음.

- 연호 9.18 하원 외무위 구주 및 중동소위 청문회시 국무부에 대해 이락 침공 가능성 오판 및 유화적태도 비난

- 이락과의 전쟁 발발시 의회의 사전 통제권한 확립을 위한 결의안 추진

2. 하원 세출위 대외활동 소위(9.19)

0 동 청문회시 EAGLEBURGER 국무부 부장관은 앞으로 국무부는 국제적 문제 해결에 대처하는 비용으로 미국 연방예산 사용을 억제하고 그대신 동맹국으로부터의 분담금을 요청하는 방향으로 나갈것임을 밝혔음.

0 이집트의 FMS차관 67억불 면제 관련, MRAZEK 의원(민주-뉴욕), MICKEY EDWARDS(공화-오크라호마) 등이 행정부 정책을 비판하였고 EAGLEBURGER 부장관은 이번 조치는 예외적인것으로 타국에 대해 선례가 될수 없다는 점을 강조함.

( 대사 박동진- 국장)

미주국     1차보     중아국     정문국     안기부

미ㅋㅋ

PAGE 1     90.09.21     09:43 BX

외신 1과 통제관

0168

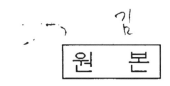

# 외 무 부

종 별 :

번 호 : USW-4335                                         일 시 : 90 0924 1837

수 신 : 장 관(미북,미안, 중근동)

발 신 : 주 미 대사

제 목 : 이락사태 의회 반응(18)(언론 보도 종합)

연: USW-4294

페만 사태의 국내정치적 잇슈화 조짐

0 페만 사태가 일단 주춤한 양상을 보임에 따라 의원들은 역대 행정부가 취해온 대이락정책 및 사태발발 직전의 행정부 조치에 대해 의문을 제기하고 있으며 행정부는 관계부처간 및 의회에대해 나름대로의 불만이 있음.

  - 백악관 관계자는 국무부 관리들이 페만사태 대응 조치에 대한 공을 독차지하려 한다고 비난하는 반면, 대사우디 무기수출 관련한 국방부의 조치에 대해 불만을 갖고 있음.

  - 행정부 관리들은 사태발발 직후 사우디까지 방문할정도로 행정부 정책에 강력한 지지를 냈던 의원들이 최근 들어 함구하고 있는데 대해 불쾌감을 표시

0 JIM LEACH 하원의원 (공화-아이오아)은 페만사태가 이락과의 전쟁으로 발전하지 않는한 상기불만표출 현상이 심화될것이라는 우려를 표명하였음.

0 한편, 지난 주 BAKER 국무장관은 페만 사태관련해서 거의 모습을 드러내지 않아 페만사태관련 정책에 있어서 국무장관의 영향력에 대한 의구심을 불러 일으킨반면, CHENEY 국방장관및 POWELL 합참의장은 DUGAN 공군참모총장 해임문제등에서 보여지듯이 역할이 증대되고 있는 것으로 보여짐.

  (대사 박동 진-국장)

---

미주국      1차보      미주국      중아국      정문국      안기부      통상국 대책반      2라반

PAGE 1                                                    90.09.25    09:32 WG

외신 1과 통제관

0169

<table>
<tr><td colspan="7" align="center">정 리 보 존 문 서 목 록</td></tr>
</table>

| 기록물종류 | 일반공문서철 | 등록번호 | 2012090487 | 등록일자 | 2012-09-17 |
|---|---|---|---|---|---|
| 분류번호 | 772 | 국가코드 | US/XF | 보존기간 | 영구 |

| 명 칭 | 걸프사태 : 미국 의회 동향, 1990-91. 전5권 | | | | |
|---|---|---|---|---|---|
| 생 산 과 | 북미1과 | 생산년도 | 1990~1991 | 담당그룹 | |
| 권 차 명 | V.2 1990.10-12월 | | | | |

| 내용목차 | * 걸프사태 관련 미국 의회에서의 각종 논의, 법안, 결의안, 청문회 개최 동향 등<br><br>* 10.1 하원, 이라크 침공에 대한 미국 정책 결의안(H-J, RES 658) 통과<br>   10.2 상원, 페르시안 사태 관련 Bush 대통령 조치에 대한 지지표명 결의안 통과<br>   10.28 하원 의원 81명, 페르시안사태 관련 연서 성명 발표<br>   11.16 Aspin 하원 군사위원장, 페르시안 사태 관련 주요 동맹국의 비용 분담에 관한 평가 보고서 발표 |
|---|---|

0001

# 외 무 부

종 별 :

번 호 : USW-4447

일 시 : 90 1001 1857

수 신 : 장 관 (미북, 미안,중근동,기정)

발 신 : 주 미 대사

제 목 : 이락사태 의회반응(19)

1. 금 10.1.(월)오후 하원은 '이락침공에 대한 미국정책'이라는 제하의 결의안(H-J,RES658)을 압도적 다수(380 찬성, 29 반대)로 통과시켰음.

2. 동 결의안의 주요내용은 미 행정부가 취해온 페만사태 관련정책 및 정책목표에 지지를 보내고 페만사태의 외교적 해결에 보다 더 노력할 것을 행정부에 당부하는내용이며, 동 결의안에 대한 제안 설명시 FASCELL 외무위 위원장은 동 결의안은 현재까지 행정부의 조치를 지지함으로써 대외정책 문제에 관해 의회도 행정부와 공히 책임을 지고있다는 점을 명백히 하고자 하는 것이며, 동결의안 내용이 현재까지 미 행정부 조치에 대해서만 언급 하였다고해서 행정부의 향후조치까지도 지지하는것은 아니며, 향후조치는 의회와의 긴밀한 협의하에 취해져야 할것이라는 의견을 표명하였으며, 대부분의 발언의원도 상기내용에 찬성하는 내용의 발언을 하였음.

3. 동 결의안은 합동 결의안(JOINT RESOLUTION)으로서 동일한 내용의 결의안이 상원에서 통과되면 대통령 서명을 거쳐 구속력을 갖게되며, 현재 상원에서는 페만사태관련 유사한 내용의 결의안을 공동결의안(CONCURRENT RESOLUTION, S CON RES .147)형식으로 심의중(10.2.본회의 심의 예정)에 있음을 참고바람.

4. 동결의안 은 별전 팩스 송부함.

첨부: USW (F)- 2453(10매)

(대사 박동진- 국장)

---

미주국    1차보    미주국    중아국    정문국    안기부    대책반    통상국

90.10.02    10:55 FC

외신 1과    통제관
0002

# 첨부

IRAQRES3

To Mr. NOH

USW (F) — 2453

수신: 장관 (미북. 미안. 중근동)

발신: 주미대사

제목: 페만사태 관련 하원결의안

[COMMITTEE PRINT]
September 27, 1990: 4 PM

101ST CONGRESS
2D SESSION

H. J. RES. 658

# IN THE HOUSE OF REPRESENTATIVES

Mr. _____ introduced the following joint resolution; which
was referred to the Committee on _____

# JOINT RESOLUTION

To support actions the President has taken with respect to Iraqi
aggression against Kuwait and to demonstrate United States
resolve.

0003

IRAQRES3

2

Whereas the Government of Iraq without provocation invaded and
occupied the territory of Kuwait on August 2, 1990, has
brutalized the population of Kuwait, has taken large numbers
of innocent hostages, and has disregarded the rights of
diplomats, all in clear violation of international law and
the norms of international conduct;

Whereas Iraq's actions have caused great suffering among the
hundreds of thousands of innocent people who have been
displaced by this crisis;

Whereas the President condemned Iraq's unprovoked and naked
aggression and undertook a series of actions, including
imposing comprehensive economic sanctions on Iraq and
freezing Iraqi and Kuwaiti assets in the United States;

Whereas the United Nations Security Council in a series of
resolutions condemned these actions as blatantly unlawful,
imposed mandatory economic sanctions (including maritime and
air embargoes) designed to compel Iraq to withdraw from
Kuwait, called on all states to take appropriate measures to
ensure that these sanctions are enforced, called for the
immediate release of all hostages, strongly condemned
aggressive acts perpetrated by Iraq against diplomatic
premises and personnel in Kuwait, and reaffirmed the right of
individual and collective self-defense in this situation;

Whereas the President, in response to requests from governments
in the region and in exercise of the inherent right of

0004

IRAQRES3

3

individual and collective self-defense as specified in the
Charter of the United Nations, has deployed United States
Armed Forces into and around the Arabian Peninsula as part of
a multinational force that includes Arab, Islamic,
nonaligned, North Atlantic Treaty Organization member, and
other states to deal with this armed aggression, to protect
American lives, and to assist in enforcement of sanctions and
the defense of friendly states in the region;
Whereas friends and allies have provided critical leadership in,
and support for, the international efforts to impose
sanctions on Iraq and otherwise oppose Iraqi aggression; and
Whereas these actions have thus far deterred Iraq from initiating
hostilities against other friendly states in the region or
against United States forces: Now, therefore, be it

1        Resolved by the Senate and House of Representatives of
2   the United States of America in Congress assembled,
3   SECTION 1. SHORT TITLE.
4        This resolution may be cited as the ``United States
5   Policy on Iraqi Aggression Resolution''.
6   SEC. 2. DECLARATION OF UNITED STATES OBJECTIVES AND POLICIES.
7        (a) UNITED STATES OBJECTIVES.--United States policy in
8   the Persian Gulf, as stated by the President and hereby
9   affirmed by the Congress, is directed toward--
10        (1) the immediate, unconditional, and complete
11   withdrawal of all Iraqi forces from Kuwait;

0005

IRAQRES]

4

1        (2) the restoration of Kuwait's legitimate
2     government;
3        (3) the security and stability of the Persian Gulf
4     region;
5        (4) the protection of American citizens abroad, and
6     the release of all those held hostage by Iraq; and
7        (5) the fostering of a new world order, freer from
8     the threat of terror, stronger in the pursuit of justice,
9     and more secure in the quest for peace.
10       (b) IMPORTANCE OF SECURITY AND STABILITY OF THE
11    REGION.--The United States and the international community
12    recognize the importance of the security and stability of the
13    Persian Gulf region and adequate access to its energy
14    resources. The United States and the international community
15    must continue to oppose Iraq's armed aggression against
16    Kuwait, a flagrant violation of international law which
17    threatens global economic security and constitutes a serious
18    challenge to international efforts to build a stable and
19    peaceful environment in the post-Cold War era.
20       (c) CONDEMNATION OF IRAQ--The United States and the
21    international community--
22       (1) should continue to condemn Iraq for its flagrant
23    aggression, its abysmal human rights record, its support
24    for international terrorism, its efforts to destabilize
25    the region, its taking of civilian hostages, its

0006

IRAQRES3

5

1   terrorism of diplomats and violations of diplomatic
2   premises, and its continuing efforts to develop and its
3   demonstrated willingness to use weapons of mass
4   destruction; and
5       (2) should hold Iraq and its leaders accountable for
6   such actions.
7   (d) SUPPORT FOR DEPLOYMENT OF UNITED STATES ARMED
8   FORCES.--The Congress--
9       (1) supports the deployment by the President of
10   United States Armed Forces to the Persian Gulf region in
11   response to Iraq's military aggression;
12       (2) expresses its appreciation to and support for the
13   members of the Armed Forces who have been deployed to
14   that region and to the members of the Ready Reserve and
15   the National Guard who have been ordered to active duty;
16   and
17       (3) declares its support for them as they perform
18   their vital role in the achievement of United States
19   objectives.
20   (e) UNITED STATES EFFORTS TO PROMOTE INTERNATIONAL
21   COOPERATION.--The Congress commends the President for his
22   successful efforts to promote international consensus and
23   cooperation in response to this crisis. The United States
24   should continue its efforts to--
25       (1) strengthen the international consensus against

0007

2453-5

IRAQRES3

6

1  Iraq's aggression, through broadening cooperation with
2  the Soviet Union, other members of the international
3  community, and the United Nations;
4      (2) obtain additional and substantial commitments of
5  air, sea, and ground forces from other nations in support
6  of the multinational forces deployed in the Persian Gulf
7  region in response to Iraq's aggression;
8      (3) obtain increased financial assistance and other
9  support from other nations for those multinational
10  forces;
11      (4) obtain substantial tangible international
12  assistance for those nations that have suffered financial
13  losses as a result of their support for the United
14  Nations trade embargo against Iraq; and
15      (5) obtain adequate international humanitarian
16  assistance for those foreign nationals who have fled Iraq
17  and Kuwait.
18  (E) OTHER UNITED STATES ACTIONS.--The United States
19  should also--
20      (1) continue to seek international consensus--
21          (A) to contain Iraq's conventional, chemical,
22  biological, and nuclear weapons and ballistic missile
23  programs, and
24          (B) to stop the export to Iraq of dual use
25  technology and military components, including

2453-6

0008

IRAQRES3

7

1    technology and components of direct or indirect

2    United States origin;

3    (2) continue to seek international consensus to

4    address regional problems of arms proliferation,

5    including conventional weapons, ballistic missiles, and

6    weapons of mass destruction (chemical, biological, and

7    nuclear weapons), and to seek to ensure that conventional

8    weapons transfers to the region reflect legitimate

9    security needs of the recipient nation;

10    (3) continue its stated policy to maintain Israel's

11    economic well-being and qualitative military advantage in

12    the Middle East (including through means such as

13    technology transfers and defense cooperation), and

14    continue its efforts to achieve an Arab-Israeli peace

15    settlement; and

16    (4) continue promoting respect for internationally

17    recognized human rights and the rule of law, and support

18    the development of democratic institutions, throughout

19    the region.

20  (g) SUPPORT FOR ACTIONS OF THE UNITED NATIONS.--

21    (1) COMMENDATION OF THE UNITED NATIONS.--The United

22    Nations should be commended for its timely, unified, and

23    strong response to Iraq's armed aggression against

24    Kuwait.

25    (2) COMMENDATION OF SECURITY COUNCIL MEMBERS.--The

0009

2453-7

IRAQRES3

8

1   member states of the United Nations Security Council who
2   formulated a coordinated and unprecedented international
3   policy response to Iraq's aggression through the adoption
4   of Resolutions 660, 661, 662, 664, 665, 666, 667, and 668
5   should also be commended.
6       (3) AFFIRMATION OF RESOLUTIONS.--The Congress affirms
7   its support for those Security Council resolutions.
8       (4) INTERNATIONAL IMPLEMENTATION OF RESOLUTIONS.--The
9   Congress calls on all nations to fully support and comply
10  with the resolutions adopted by the Security Council and
11  to strengthen the enforcement of the sanctions imposed by
12  the United Nations against Iraq.
13      (5) CONTINUATION OF DIPLOMATIC EFFORTS.--The United
14  States and other members of the international community
15  should continue efforts to achieve a diplomatic solution
16  to the crisis in the Persian Gulf region through
17  implementation of those resolutions.
18  SEC. 3. EFFORTS TO ACHIEVE UNITED STATES OBJECTIVES AND
19          POLICIES.
20  The Congress supports the President's emphasis on
21  diplomatic efforts, international sanctions, and negotiations
22  under the auspices of the United Nations to achieve the
23  United States objectives and policies set forth in section 2.
24  The United States shall continue to emphasize the use of
25  diplomatic and other nonmilitary means in order to achieve

0010

IRAQRES3

9

1    those objectives and policies, while maintaining credible

2    United States and multinational deterrent military force.

3    SEC. 4. WAR POWERS FINDINGS.

4        The Congress finds that--

5            (1) on August 9, 1990, the President reported to the

6    Congress that he had ordered the deployment of

7    substantial elements of the United States Armed Forces

8    into the Persian Gulf region in response to the threat

9    posed by the actions of Iraq;

10           (2) in this report, the President stated that the

11   report was being provided ``consistent with the War

12   Powers Resolution'';

13           (3) the War Powers Resolution requires, in sections

14   4(a)(2) and 4(a)(3), that the President report to the

15   Congress whenever, in the absence of a declaration of

16   war, United States Armed Forces are introduced into the

17   territory, airspace, or waters of a foreign nation while

18   equipped for combat (except for deployments which relate

19   solely to supply, replacement, repair, or training of

20   such forces) or are introduced in numbers which

21   substantially enlarge United States Armed Forces equipped

22   for combat already located in a foreign nation;

23           (4) the War Powers Resolution also requires, in

24   section 4(a)(1), that the President report to the          0011

25   Congress whenever, in the absence of a declaration of

IRAQRES3

10

1    war, United States Armed Forces are introduced into

2    hostilities or situations where imminent involvement in

3    hostilities is clearly indicated by the circumstances;

4         (5) consistent with that requirement, the President

5    declared in his August 9th report, ``I do not believe

6    involvement in hostilities is imminent''; and

7         (6) the President has consulted with the Congress and

8    has kept the Congress informed with regard to the

9    deployment of United States Armed Forces into the Persian

10   Gulf region.

2453-10

0012

# 외 무 부

종 별 :

번 호 : USW-4474 　　　　　　　　일 시 : 90 1002 1845

수 신 : 장관(미안,미국,중근동,기정)

발 신 : 주미대사

제 목 : 페만사태 관련 상원 결의안

　　연: USW-4447

　　1. 미상원은 금 10.2(화) 페만 사태와관련, 부쉬 대통령이 취한 조치에 대한 지지를 표명하는 결의안 ( S.CON.RES. 147) 을 96:3 으로 통과시켰음.

　　2. 동 결의안의 골자는 아래와같음.

　　가. 미 대통령이 유엔 결의안과 헌법규정에 따라 취한 행동에 지지를 표명하며, 향후 추가 조치도 이에 준하는 행동이어야 함.

　　나. 유엔 결의에 따른 대이락 제재조치에 국제사회의 참여를 촉구함.

　　3. 동 결의안의 표결에 앞선 논의에서 의원들은 페만 사태에 관한 미 의회의 역할 ( 특히 WAR POWERS RESOLUTION)을 강조하였음.

　　4. 연호 작 10.1. 하원결의안과 금일 상원 결의안을 통하여 페만 사태와 관련 미행정부 조치에관한 의회의 공식적인 지지 표명이 있었는바, 현재까지의 의회의 전폭적인 지지도와 별도로 WAR POWERS RESOLUTION 을 통한 의회의 역할을 둘러싸고 논의가 제기되고 있음이 주목됨.

　　5. 결의안 별첨 송부함

　　첨부: USW(F)-2465 (3 매)(대사 박동진-국장)

---

미주국　　미주국　　중아국　　정문국　　안기부

USW (주)- 24발
수신: 장관 (미안·미북·중근동·기정)
발신: 주미대사
제목: 테러사태 관련 상원결의안
USW - 4474 의 휴청.

D✓

# SENATE CONCURRENT RESOLUTION 147—SUPPORTING THE PRESIDENT'S ACTIONS WITH RESPECT TO IRAQI AGGRESSION AGAINST KUWAIT

Mr. MITCHELL (for himself, Mr. DOLE, Mr. PELL, Mr. NUNN, Mr. WARNER, Mr. BOREN, Mr. MOYNIHAN, and Mr. DeConcini) submitted the following concurrent resolution; which was placed on the calendar:

### S. CON. RES. 147

Whereas on August 2, 1990, the armed forces of Iraq invaded and occupied the State of Kuwait, took large numbers of innocent hostages, and disregarded the rights of diplomats, all in clear violation of the United Nations Charter and fundamental principles of international law;

Whereas the President condemned Iraq's aggression, imposed comprehensive United States economic sanctions upon Iraq, and froze Iraqi assets in the United States;

Whereas the United Nations Security Council, in a series of five unanimously approved resolutions, condemned Iraq's actions as unlawful, imposed mandatory economic sanctions designed to compel Iraq to withdraw from Kuwait, called on all states to take appropriate measures to ensure the enforcement of sanctions, called for the immediate release of all hostages, and reaffirmed the right of individual and collective self-defense; and

2465-1

Whereas, in response to requests from governments in the region exercising the right of collective self-defense as provided in Article 51 of the United Nations Charter, the President deployed United States Armed Forces in the Persian Gulf region as part of a multilateral effort: Now, therefore, be it

*Resolved by the Senate (the House of Representatives concurring),* That (a) the Congress strongly approves the leadership of the President in successfully pursuing the passage of United Nations Security Council Resolutions 660, 661, 662, 664, 665, 666, 687, and 670, which call for—

(1) the immediate, complete, and unconditional withdrawal of all Iraqi forces from Kuwait;

(2) the restoration of Kuwait's sovereignty, independence, and territorial integrity;

(3) the release and safe passage of foreign nationals held hostage by Iraq;

(4) the imposition of economic sanctions, including the cessation of airline transport, against Iraq; and

(5) the maintenance of international peace and security in the Persian Gulf region.

2465—2

0015

(b) The Congress approves the actions taken by the President in support of these goals, including the involvement of the United Nations and of the friendly governments. The Congress supports continued action by the President in accordance with the decisions of the United Nations Security Council and in accordance with United States constitutional and statutory processes, including the authorization and appropriation of funds by the Congress, to deter Iraqi aggression and to protect American lives and vital interests in the region.

(c) The Congress calls on all nations to strengthen the enforcement of the United Nations imposed sanctions against Iraq, to provide assistance for those adversely affected by enforcement of the sanctions, and to provide assistance to refugees fleeing Kuwait and Iraq.

Sec. 2. The Secretary of the Senate shall transmit a copy of this concurrent resolution to the President.

2465—3

0016

# 報 告 事 項

報告畢

1990. 10. 5
美 洲 局
北 美 課(28)

題 目 : 페灣 事態 關聯 美 議會 決議案 通過

미 상.하원은 10.1(월) 및 10.2(화) 페르시아만 사태 관련 미 행정부가 그간
취한 조치를 지지하는 결의안을 각각 통과시켰는 바, 동 결의안 주요내용 등
관련사항을 아래 보고 드립니다.

1. 결의안 요지

о 그간 미 행정부가 취해온 페르시아만 사태 관련 정책 및 정책목표에
지지를 표함.
  - 향후 추가 조치도 의회와의 협의 등 이에 준하는 행동을 기대

о 미 의회는 행정부에 페만 사태의 외교적 해결을 위해 보다 노력할 것을
당부함.

о UN 결의에 따른 대 이라크 제재조치에 국제사회의 동참을 촉구함.

2. 표결시 주요 발언 내용

о 미국의 주요 대외정책 문제에 관해 의회도 행정부와 공히 책임을 지고
있다는 점을 명백히 하고자 함.(Fascell 하원 외무위원장)

о War Powers Resolution과 관련한 미 행정부의 대 의회 협의 절차의 중요성
강조함.

0017

3. 참고 사항

ㅇ 미 하원 통과 결의안은 합동 결의안(Joint Resolution) 형식으로서 동일
   내용의 결의안이 상원에서 통과되면 대통령 서명을 거쳐 구속력을 갖게 됨.
   - 미 상원은 유사한 내용의 결의안을 공동 결의안(Concurrent Resolution)
     으로 심의 통과

0018

# 報　告　事　項

報 告 畢

1990. 10. 5
美 洲 局
北 美 課(28)

題 目 : 페灣 事態 關聯 美 議會 決議案 通過

---

미 상.하원은 10.1(월) 및 10.2(화) 페르시아만 사태 관련 미 행정부가 그간
취한 조치를 지지하는 결의안을 각각 통과시켰는 바, 동 결의안 주요내용 등
관련사항을 아래 보고 드립니다.

---

1. 결의안 요지

   o 그간 미 행정부가 취해온 페르시아만 사태 관련 정책 및 정책목표에
     지지를 표함.
     - 향후 추가 조치도 의회와의 협의 등 이에 준하는 행동을 기대

   o 미 의회는 행정부에 페만 사태의 외교적 해결을 위해 보다 노력할 것을
     당부함.

   o UN 결의에 따른 대 이라크 제재조치에 국제사회의 동참을 촉구함.


2. 표결시 주요 발언 내용

   o 미국의 주요 대외정책 문제에 관해 의회도 행정부와 공히 책임을 지고
     있다는 점을 명백히 하고자 함.(Fascell 하원 외무위원장)

   o War Powers Resolution과 관련한 미 행정부의 대 의회 협의 절차의 중요성
     강조함.

0019

3. 참고 사항

  ° 미 하원 동과 결의안은 합동 결의안(Joint Resolution) 형식으로서 동일
    내용의 결의안이 상원에서 통과되면 대통령 서명을 거쳐 구속력을 갖게 됨.
    - 미 상원은 유사한 내용의 결의안을 공동 결의안(Concurrent Resolution)
      으로 심의 통과

0020

# 報　告　事　項

1990.
美　洲　局
北　美　課(30)

報　告　畢

題　目 :　美 聯邦 政府豫算 危機 解決展望

1. 개　요

ㅇ 미 하원은 10.8. 계속 지출법안에 대한 부쉬 대통령의 거부권을 무효화
　시키기 위한 재적 2/3의 찬성 표결에 실패한후 양당 지도부간 절충을 거쳐
　포괄 예산안을 부분 수정하여 통과시킴으로써 미 연방정부의 예산 위기의
　해결 실마리가 마련되고 있는바, 관련 사항을 아래 보고드립니다.

2. 변동 내용

가. 포괄 예산안 부분 수정

ㅇ 당초 합의된 예산편성 원칙에는 변동이 없으나 사회보장 부분 감축을
　다소 완화하고 세금인상을 다소 늘려 타결을 봄.

나. 계속 지출법안 발효 가능성

ㅇ 일부 수정된 포괄 예산안 통과에 따라 10.9(화) 연방 공무원 출근시간
　이전 계속 지출법안의 통과 및 이에대한 부쉬 대통령의 서명이 예측되어
　연방정부의 기능정지 사태는 피할 수 있을 것으로 전망됨.　끝.

0021

# 외 무 부

종 별 :

번 호 : USW-4682　　　　　　　　　　일 시 : 90 1017 1935

수 신 : 장 관 ( 미북,미안,중근동)

발 신 : 주 미 대사

제 목 : 페만 사태 관련 상원 청문회

　　1. 금 10.17. 상원 외교위는 BAKER 국무장관을 출석시킨 가운데 '' US POLICY IN THE PERSION GULF '' 라는 제하의 청문회를 개최 하였음.

　　2. BEKER 장관은 증언문을 통해 1) 페만 사태에 대한 미 행정부의 4대 목표 (이라크의 무조건완전 철수, 쿠웨이트 정봉정부의 복귀, 미국 시민보호 및 페만의 안전보장)가 불변이며, 2) 동맹국과의 책임 분담하 (아국의 2.2 억불 지원CEUEL 언급) 에 외교적 , 경제적 GHEF을 통한 사태의 평화적해결에 우선적 노력을 기울이고 있 고, 3) 페만주둔 병력은 이라크의 사우디 침공을 억제하고 UN의 제재 조치의 효율적수행을 위해 배치 되었으며, 4)페만 사태의 부분적 해결은 향후 페만 지역의 안정성을 저해 시킬것인바, 시간이 걸리더라도 사태의 완전한 해결 모색이 필요 하다는 기존의 행정부 입장을 재확인 하였음.

　　3.동 청문회 질의 응답시에는 행정부의 정책에 대한 의원들의 지지 표명과 함께 군사력을 사용하게 될경우 미 의회와의 사전 협의 문제에 집중되었으며, BIDEN 상원의원은 페만 주둔미군 병력이 이라크의 사우디 침공을 억제하고 미국시민을 보호하며 UN 의 집단 행동에 참여하는 경우를 제외하고는 의회의 사전 협의 및 동의 없이는 군사력 사용을 금지하는 결의안을 제출할 생각이라고 밝혔음. 동 장관은 군사력사용에 대한 미 의회의 사전 동의 문제에 관해서는 명확한 답변을 하지 않고 과거와 같이 의회와 협의를 하겠다는 내용의 답변을 하였음.

　　4.금번 청문회시 한국에 대한 직접 언급된바는 없으나, JOHN KERRY (민주, 메사추세츠) 및 NANCY KASSEBANM (공화-켄사스) 의원은 페만 사태는 미국의 단독 군사 행동 보다는 한국 전시와 마찬가지로 UN 주도하의 집단 조치로 해결 되어야 한다는 입장을 표명하는 과정에서 언급 되었음.

　　5.금번 청문회는 페만 사태가 정체화 되고 있고 이스라엘과 팔레스타인 주민과의

---

미주국　　1차보　　미주국　　중아국　　정문국　　안기부

PAGE 1　　　　　　　　　　　　　　　　　90.10.18　　11:02 WG

외신 1과 통제관

0022

충돌사건 및 이라크측의 쿠웨이트 부분 철수제안등으로 폐만사태의 양상이 변화하고 있다는 의구심이 제기됨에 따라 폐만 사태에 대한 미 정부의 방침을 확고히 해야할 필요성에 따라 주선된것임.

　첨부: USW(F)- 2650 ( 15 매) (대사 박동진- 국장)

USW(F) ─ 26조

수신: 장관 (미북. 미안 )

발신: 주미대사

제목: 페만사태 관련
      상원 청문회

TESTIMONY

OF

THE HONORABLE JAMES A. BAKER, III

SECRETARY OF STATE

BEFORE THE

SENATE FOREIGN RELATIONS COMMITTEE

OCTOBER 17, 1990

〈첨부〉

Mr. Chairman:


Six weeks ago, it was my privilege to speak to this
Committee and through you, to the American people, about Iraq's
aggression against Kuwait.  At that time, I outlined the
President's goals:


First, the immediate, complete, and unconditional
withdrawal of all Iraqi forces from Kuwait as mandated in
United Nations Security Council Resolution 660;


Second, the restoration of Kuwait's legitimate government;


Third, the protection of the lives of American citizens
held hostage by Iraq, both in Iraq and in Kuwait; and


Fourth, a commitment to the security and stability of the
Persian Gulf.


I also described our strategy for achieving these goals.


0024

-2-

The key element of that approach is American leadership of a
global alliance that isolates Iraq -- politically,
economically, and militarily.

Today, I would like to discuss with you what we have done
to carry out that strategy since early September, including how
responsibilities are being shared and what results have been
achieved.

## Maintaining the Coalition

First, we have been working successfully through the United
Nations Security Council to isolate Iraq politically and to
impose penalties for its refusal to comply with the UN
resolutions.  That effort is continuing today as the Council
considers its tenth resolution on the Gulf.

Second, we have secured notable cooperation from the Soviet
nion.  We have described this conflict as the first real crisis
of the post Cold-War period.  The positive approach of the
Soviet Union has validated that label.  In their Helsinki Joint
Statement, President Bush and President Gorbachev declared,
"We are united in the belief that Iraq's aggression must not be
tolerated.  No peaceful international order is possible if
larger states can devour their smaller neighbors."

Since then, I have met with Foreign Minister Shevardnadze
on several occasions, both in Moscow and in New York, and have
talked to him on the phone frequently.  The Soviets continue to
support the objectives of the Security Council Resolutions.

0025

-3-

Third, from the beginning, we recognized that maintaining such an unprecedented international coalition would necessitate special efforts.  The United States could lead -- indeed, had to lead -- but we should not carry the responsibility alone. The principle of shared responsibility had to be observed.

We must jointly face the military threat.  But we must also act collectively to support the many nations observing the economic embargo or contributing forces for the defense of Saudi Arabia.  Iraq's pillage of Kuwait continues to displace hundreds of thousands of workers, straining the resources of neighboring states and the fragile economies of their homelands.

Immediately after testifying before this committee early last month, I left at the President's request to visit our major allies and partners in the Arabian Peninsula, the European Community, Italy, and Germany to put responsibility sharing into effect.  The Secretary of the Treasury led a similar mission to London, Paris, Tokyo, and Seoul.  This exercise in sharing responsibilities produced commitments of $20 billion in resources, equally divided between support for the front line states of Egypt, Turkey, and Jordan and assistance to the multinational military effort.  This includes support for a substantial portion of our incremental defense costs, now running about $1 billion per month.

2650-3

0026

-4-

I would summarize the results of our on-going efforts as
follows:

● Fifty-four nations have contributed or offered to
contribute militarily and/or economically to the Gulf
effort.

● The three Gulf states of Saudi Arabia, Kuwait, and the
United Arab Emirates have agreed to contribute more than
$12 billion to this effort in 1990.  All of the states in
the Gulf Cooperation Council (GCC) have contributed troops
to the multinational force in Saudi Arabia and are
providing access and services in support of U.S. forces.
Host nation support for our deployed forces includes the
free use of ports, logistical facilities, bases, and fuel.

● The U.K. is deploying over 6,000 combat troops, over 50
aircraft, and 12 warships.

● France has deployed over 4,000 combat troops, 30 aircraft,
and 12 warships.

● Japan has pledged $4 billion: $2 billion in support of the
military effort plus $2 billion in economic aid.  And we
hope to see that commitment fulfilled promptly and in a
form immediately usable.

● Germany has pledged $2 billion: $1 billion in support of
the military effort plus $1 billion in economic aid. 

0027

• The European Community has pledged $670 million in economic aid, along with member state commitments of an additional $1.3 billion.

• Italy has deployed 4 warships and 8 aircraft.

• Korea has pledged $220 million: $95 million in support of the military effort plus $125 million in economic aid.

To coordinate timely and effective economic assistance to the front line states, the President launched the Gulf Crisis Financial Coordinating Committee on September 25.  This group unites the major donors of Europe, Asia, and the Gulf under US chairmanship, with technical support from the IMF and World Bank.  We see it as an important vehicle for maintaining the international coalition.

The most important demonstration of America's commitment to bolstering the economic stability of our front-line allies is the President's proposal to cancel Egypt's FMS debt.  No other signal would send the same powerful message to our friends in the region that we are determined to stand by them, even on the toughest issues.  Last Thursday's assassination of the Speaker of Egypt's Parliament is a tragic reminder of how far Egypt's enemies are prepared to go to divert President Mubarak from his responsible and courageous course.  Strong Congressional endorsement of Egyptian debt cancellation would provide Egypt critical economic relief and send a powerful and timely signal that the United States stands by its friends.

0028

Mr. Chairman, the political and economic isolation of Iraq
has been achieved.  The costs and responsibilities for
enforcing this isolation are being fairly distributed.
Economic leakage is minimal.  The Iraqi economy will suffer
badly and the Iraqi war machine will be hurt, too.

The Military Track

A discussion of diplomacy and economic sanctions, however,
should not blind us to the other essential track of our policy:
the military build-up in the Gulf.  I have just detailed for
you the contributions made by our allies, including combat
units, aircraft, and warships.  In addition, Arab states such
as Egypt and Syria are sending major units.  There are now many
thousands of Arab and Muslim soldiers deployed with the
multinational forces in and around Saudi Arabia.  And, of
course, very large numbers of American marines, soldiers,
sailors, and airmen are there already.  All told, over twenty
five countries are now supplying men or materiel in support of
the Security Council resolutions.

Our military objectives are to deter an Iraqi attack on
Saudi Arabia and to ensure the effective implementation of the
UN sanctions.  Economic sanctions against an aggressor like
Saddam Hussein would never be effective unless the
international community could help ensure the security of those
nations, such as Saudi Arabia and Turkey, who must apply those

2650-6

0029

sanctions.  Our military forces are also there to protect
American lives and to provide an effective and decisive
response should Iraq escalate its aggression to active combat
with the multinational force.

Saddam Hussein must know that he lacks not only the
political and economic options of holding Kuwait but also the
military option to succeed with his aggression.  The political,
economic, and military aspects of our strategy reinforce each
other.

The Need for Time

As the strategy takes effect, we face a difficult task. We
must remain firm, not wavering from the goals we have set or
our focus on the blatant aggression committed by Iraq.  We must
exercise patience as the grip of sanctions tightens with
increasing severity.

Some may urge action for action's sake.  But the only truly
effective action we can take now is to continue to heighten
Iraq's political, economic, and military isolation.  Every day
-- in Washington, in New York, in the region -- we continue our
search for a peaceful solution.

Action that moves toward a partial solution would be
self-defeating appeasement.

2650-9

0030

And should there be any doubt about the awful consequences of a partial solution, I would urge a close look at what Saddam Hussein is doing to the people of Kuwait. Because Saddam Hussein controls access to the true story of Kuwait, this is a story that is not told frequently enough. So I commend the Congress' effort to secure eyewitness testimony of the brutalities now taking place.

It is the rape of Kuwait. Hospitals have been looted without regard for the sick. Parents have been tortured and executed in front of their children. Children have been tortured and executed in front of their parents. Even after his military conquest, Saddam has continued to make war on the people of Kuwait.

Let me be blunt: Saddam Hussein has invaded and tortured a peaceful Arab neighbor purely for self-aggrandizement. He is not raping Kuwait to advance the Palestinian cause.

We cannot allow this violent way to become the wave of the future in the Middle East. Saddam Hussein must fail if peace is to succeed. The prospects for a just and lasting peace between Israel and its Arab neighbors will be shattered if he prevails.

It is time to clear the air once and for all about the relationship between Saddam's aggression in Kuwait and other conflicts and problems in the region. I will put it to you simply: Does anyone seriously think that if this aggression

0031

succeeds, that prospects will be better for peace between
Israel and the Palestinians?  Can anyone seriously believe that
if Iraq wins this contest with the international community, it
will be easier to eliminate chemical weapons or biological
weapons or nuclear weapons in the region?

Of course not.

Every hope for peace in this conflict-ridden region depends
on stopping Iraq's aggression and ultimately reversing its
capacity for future aggression.

Defeating Aggression

Let me sum it up.

Since we met last, a great coalition of nations has
gathered to isolate Iraq and its dictator.  Where before his
aggression Saddam Hussein found allies of consequence, today he
finds none.  Where before the invasion, the Iraqi economy had
important international links, today it has none.  And where
once there were prospects for successful Iraqi aggression
against Saudi Arabia, today there are none.

Unity remains essential.  I do not believe we could have
come this far if most nations did not agree with President Bush
that we all have a stake in a world where conflicts are settled
peacefully.  And that unity, expressed in political, economic
and military terms, remains the best hope for a peaceful
solution to this conflict as well.  *650-9*

0032

Mr. Chairman, it is gratifying that the vast majority of
Americans have rallied behind the President in support of both
our goals and our strategy in the Persian Gulf.  Indeed, most
of the world has done so, as well.  Saddam Hussein cannot be
allowed to ruin the region.  He cannot be allowed to spoil this
time of hope in the world for a more secure and prosperous
future.  There is a morality among nations.  That morality must
prevail.

266-10

0033

# BIDEN PROPOSAL

## STATUTORY AUTHORIZATION

### A Joint Resolution

Providing statutory authorization for the deployment of
United States Armed Forces in the Persian Gulf region to
deter and, if necessary, defend against further Iraqi
aggression and to participate in multilateral efforts to
restore the sovereignty of Kuwait and promote the security
and stability of the region.


Resolved by the Senate and House of Representatives of the
United States of America in Congress assembled,


SEC. 1.  SHORT TITLE.

   This joint resolution may be cited as the "Collective
Security in the Persian Gulf Resolution".


SEC. 2.  FINDINGS AND PURPOSE.

   (a) Findings. - Congress finds that in response to the act
of aggression by Iraq against Kuwait, which began on August 2,
1990, the United States has -
      (1) participated in decisions of the United Nations
Security Council, as follows:
         (A) Resolution 660, demanding immediate and
unconditional withdrawal of Iraqi forces from Kuwait
and restoration of the sovereignty, independence, and
territorial integrity of that nation;
         (B) Resolution 661, imposing economic sanctions
against Iraq;
         (C) Resolution 662, declaring null and void
Iraq's annexation of Kuwait;
         (D) Resolution 664, demanding the release and
safe passage of innocent civilians;
         (E) Resolution 665, authorizing appropriate
measures to halt maritime shipping to and from Iraq
and Kuwait as necessary to enforce economic sanctions;
         (F) Resolution 666, directing that food supplied
to Iraq for humanitarian purposes be conveyed solely
through the United Nations;
         (G) Resolution 667, condemning Iraq for the
violation of diplomatic protections in Kuwait; and
         (H) Resolution 670, extending the economic
embargo to include material transported by aircraft.

      (2) acting in response to the request of threatened
nations and in accordance with the United Nations Charter,
deployed United States Armed Forces in Saudi Arabia and
elsewhere in the Persian Gulf region in conjunction with

2670-11

0034

-2-

military deployments by other United Nations member-states, in order to -
        (A) deter and, if necessary, defend against further Iraqi aggression; and
        (B) assist in enforcing economic sanctions against Iraq pursuant to United Nations Security Council Resolutions 661, 665, and 670.

    (b) Purpose. - Congress intends this joint resolution to constitute specific statutory authorization for continued United States military participation in collective security actions in the Persian Gulf region.

SEC. 3. GOALS OF UNITED STATES POLICY.

    (a) Immediate Goals. - The immediate goals of United States policy in the Persian Gulf region shall be:
        (1) unconditional withdrawal of Iraqi forces from Kuwait;
        (2) restoration of the sovereignty of Kuwait; and
        (3) protection of the lives of American citizens held hostage in Iraq and Kuwait.

    (b) Long-Term Goals. - Over the long term, United States policy in the Persian Gulf region shall seek to achieve:
        (1) the security and stability of the region; and
        (2) by unprecedented and effective use of the mechanisms of collective security action, the promotion of a new world order.

SEC. 4. PRINCIPLES GOVERNING UNITED STATES POLICY.

    United States participation in collective security actions relating to the Persian Gulf region shall be governed by the following principles:
        (1) Collective Responsibility. - The United States shall continue to emphasize adequate sharing, by countries of the region and of the industrialized world, of the responsibilities, including the costs of military deployments and participation in economic sanctions, associated with collective security actions in the Persian Gulf region.
        (2) Emphasis on United Nations. - The United States shall continue to emphasize and rely upon the procedures and instrumentalities of the United Nations system in order to sustain effective multilateral support for collective security actions in the Persian Gulf region.
        (3) Role of Regional and Other Forces. - The United States, having taken urgent measures to lead a collective security action in the Persian Gulf region, shall seek to promote -

2650-12

0035

-3-

      (A) greater participation in ground-force defense by countries of the region; and

      (B) greater sharing of responsibilities, among countries having vital interests in the region, for the deployment and support of armed forces needed for regional stability.

      (4) Compliance with the Law of Nations. - The United States shall, in cooperation with other nations, seek to achieve substantial compliance by Iraq with the Law of Nations, including:

      (A) the United Nations Charter;

      (B) the International Covenant on Civil and Political Rights;

      (C) the Convention on the Prevention and Punishment of the Crime of Genocide;

      (D) the Protocol for the Prohibition of the Use in War of Asphyxiating, Poisonous or Other Gases, and of Bacteriological Methods of Warfare;

      (E) the Treaty on the Non-Proliferation of Nuclear Weapons; and

      (F) the Convention on the Prohibition of the Development, Production and Stockpiling of Bacteriological (Biological) and Toxin Weapons and on Their Destruction.

Accordingly, the United States shall seek effective multilateral participation in such restrictions on trade with the current government of Iraq as may be necessary to ensure a cessation of transfers to that regime of military technology and equipment, including all material and technical assistance that could contribute to the development or employment of ballistic missiles and nuclear, biological, and chemical weapons.

2650-13

0036

-4-

SEC. 5.  AUTHORIZATION FOR USE OF FORCE.

(a) Authorization. - The President is authorized to
continue to deploy United States Armed Forces in the Persian
Gulf region -
        (1) to deter and, if necessary, defend against further
Iraqi aggression;
        (2) to respond as may be necessary, proportionate, and
effective to any acts of intended harm to American citizens
or nationals; and
        (3) to participate in collective security actions in
the event that the United Nations directs the use of
military force to counter threats to regional security
posed by the Iraqi regime.

(b) Further Authorization. -
        (1) Before initiating a use of force against Iraq
beyond those uses authorized by subsection (a), the
President shall -
                (A) consult and seek the advice of the Combined
Congressional Leadership Group created pursuant to
section 7 of this Resolution;
                (B) set forth to Congress and the American people
his explanation of the imperatives mandating such use
of force in the absence of a United Nations directive;
and
                (C) seek a declaration of war or other statutory
authorization.
        (2) In light of evolving developments in and relating
to the Persian Gulf, Congress shall from time to time
consider further measures of authorization; and
authorization for military action shall at no time be
inferred from the authorization or appropriation of funds
for the Department of Defense.


SEC. 6. REPORTS TO CONGRESS.

(a) Report on Principles and Goals. - Not later than
January 31, 1991, and every three months thereafter for so long
as United States Armed Forces continue to participate in
collective security actions in the Persian Gulf region, the
President shall transmit to the Speaker of the House of
Representatives and chairman of the Committee on Foreign
Relations of the Senate a report providing a detailed
description of such participation, the circumstances requiring
the continuation of such participation, and the results of
United States efforts undertaken in accord with the goals and
principles set forth in sections 3 and 4.

(b) Reports on Developments in the Persian Gulf Region. -
In the event of developments in the Persian Gulf region that

2650-14

-5-

involve or appear likely to involve the United States Armed
Forces in hostilities, the President shall, in accord with the
reporting requirements of the War Powers Resolution, report
fully and promptly to the Congress on the circumstances and the
implications thereof.

SEC. 7.   CONGRESSIONAL LEADERSHIP GROUP.

   (a) Establishment. - To facilitate congressional
deliberation and Executive-Legislative consultation on critical
decisions relating to United States participation in collective
security actions pursuant to this Resolution, there shall be
established in each House of Congress, as an exercise of the
rulemaking authority of that House, a Leadership Group which
shall be comprised as follows:
        (1) in the House of Representatives -
            (A) the Speaker, who shall serve as chairman;
            (B) the Majority and Minority Leaders;
            (C) the chairmen and ranking members of the
Committee on Foreign Affairs, the Committee on Armed
Services, and the Permanent Select Committee on
Intelligence; and
        (2) in the Senate -
            (A) the Majority Leader, who shall serve as
chairman;
            (B) the President pro tempore and the Minority
Leader;
            (C) the chairmen and ranking members of the
Committee on Foreign Relations, the Committee on Armed
Services, and the Select Committee on Intelligence.

   (b) Combined Congressional Leadership Group. - When the
chairmen of the two groups deem it appropriate and practical for
purposes of congressional deliberation or Executive-Legislative
consultation, they shall arrange for the two Groups to assemble
as a Combined Congressional Leadership Group, on which the two
chairmen shall act as co-chairmen.

   (c) Consultation Regarding the Use of Force. - The
President shall, unless urgent circumstances do not permit,
consult and seek the advice of the Combined Congressional
Leadership Group designated pursuant to this section, prior to
key decisions relating to the disposition or commitment of
United States Armed Forces authorized by this Resolution to be
deployed in the Persian Gulf region.

*2680-15*

외 무 부

종 별 : 지 급

번 호 : USW-4878               일 시 : 90 1030 1856

수 신 : 장관(미안,미북,중근동)

발 신 : 주 미 대사

제 목 : 페만 사태 관련 부쉬 대통령 앞 하원의원 연서 서한

1. 10.28 RONALD V. DELLUMS 하원 의원(민-칼리포니아)등 하원 의원 81 명은 페만 사태 관련한 연서 성명을 발표하였는바, 동 요지 하기 보고함.

0 페만 지역에 있어서의 전쟁 발발 가능성이 높아 지는데 대한 우려 표명과함께 전쟁 선포는 의회의 고유 권한임을 강조

0 페만 사태 해결을 위한 공격적 군사 행동에 반대하며, 유엔 체제 아래 비군사적 외교적 해결을 위해 모든 노력을 우선 경주해야할것임.

0 의회 휴회기간중 행정부측이 소수 의회 지도부와 협의 하는것은 의회의 전쟁 선포권의 대체 수단으로서 간주될수 없음.

2. 관찰 및 평가

가. 미의회는 페만 사태 관련 지금까지 행정부가 취해온 제반 조치에 대하여 긍정적인 평가를 해오고 있으나, 최근 사태의 장기화에 따라 일부 민주당계 의원들은 부쉬 행정부가 무력에 의한 해결 방안을 강구하려는 움직임에 대하여 우려를 표시하고 있으며, 상기 성명도 이와같은 우려 표명의 일환으로 발표된것으로 보임.

나. 특히 전쟁 선포 없이 대통령이 취할수 있는 군사적 행동의 범위(WAR POWERS ACT)에 관하여 의회와 행정부는 입장의 대립을 보여 오고있으며, 상기 성명에서도 서명 의원들은 전쟁 선포와 관련한 의회의 권한을 강조하고 있음.

다. 금 10.30 부쉬 대통령은 의회 지도부 인사들을 백악관으로 초치하여 최근 페만 사태 동향에 관하여 대의회 설명을 행한바, 의회 인사들은 행정부가 군사 공격에 앞서 경제 제재 조치와 외교적 해결 노력에 더욱 힘을 기울여 줄것을 당부 하였음.

라. 상기 성명 관련, SOLARZ 아태 소위원장실등 주요 의원 보좌관들의 견해를 타진하였던바, 일부 진보적 민주계 의원들 사이에 페만 사태가 전면 전쟁으로발발할것으로 우려하는 움직임이 있는것은 사실이나 상금도 대부분의

미주국     차관     1차보     미주국     중아국     정와대     안기부     대책반

의원들은부쉬 대통령의 정책을 지지하고 있으며 상기 성명이 이와같은 의회의 전반적
분위기에 영향을 미칠것으로 보지는 않는다는 견해를 피력하였음.
첨부 USW(F)-2850
(대사 박동진-국장)
90.12.31. 까지
난문서로 재분류(

USW(F) - 2850                                                                 서 천복

수신: 장관 (미안 7북. 품국동)
발신: 주미대사        **Congress of the United States**
제목: 페만 사태        **Washington, DC 20515**
       관련 의원 연서 성명  (3매)

### STATEMENT OF CONCERN

#### October 26, 1990

We, as Members of Congress, express our grave concern about the possibility of war in the Middle East.

Recent reports and briefings indicate that the United States has shifted from a defensive to an offensive posture and that war may be imminent. We believe that the consequences would be catastrophic -- resulting in the massive loss of lives, including 10,000 to 50,000 Americans. This would not be a "low intensity conflict." This could only be described as war. Under the U.S. Constitution, only the Congress can declare war.

We are emphatically opposed to any offensive military action. We believe the U.N.-sponsored embargo must be given every opportunity to work and that all multinational, non-military means of resolving the situation must be pursued. If, after all peaceful means to resolve the conflict are exhausted, and the President believes that military action is warranted, then under Article I, Section 8 of the Constitution, he must seek a declaration of war from the Congress.

Given that Congress is about to adjourn, possibly until next year, we are gravely concerned that the Administration may attempt an end-run around the Constitution. We understand a mechanism is being established by which a few Members of Congress will be monitoring the situation. This group should not be seen as a surrogate for the entire body of Congress. We firmly believe that consulting with this group in no way replaces the President's Constitutional obligation to seek a declaration of war before undertaking any offensive military action. We demand that the Administration not undertake any offensive military action without the full deliberation and declaration required by the Constitution.

0041

*News & Views*

*from*

# RON DELLUMS OF CALIFORNIA

### *8th Congressional District*

2136 Rayburn Building
Washington, D.C. 20515
(202) 225-2661

201 18th Street, Suite 105
Oakland, California 94617
(415) 763-0370

For Release:    Saturday, 27 Oct. 1990    Contact: R.H. (Max) Miller

### DELLUMS LEADS CONGRESSIONAL EFFORT TO HEAD OFF WAR WITH IRAQ

Washington, D.C.--Rep. Ronald V. Dellums (D.-8th C.D.-Calif.) today spearheaded a new Congressional effort to head off the increasing possibility of a war with Iraq in the near future. Dellums has condemned the Iraqi invasion of Kuwait from the outset, while urging the President repeatedly to work for a diplomatic solution through the United Nations that would ensure the full restoration of Kuwaiti sovereignty.

In a statement signed by 81 House Members that was given to House Speaker Thomas S. Foley and forwarded to the President, Dellums noted that the U.S. has militarily "shifted from a defensive to an offensive posture and that war may be imminent." Reaffirming the Congress's solemn, but ultimate war-making responsibility and power under Article I, Section 8 of the Constitution, the statement went on to say:

"Given that the Congress is about to adjourn, possibly until next year, we are gravely concerned that the Administration may attempt an end-run around the Constitution. We understand a mechanism is being established by which a few Members of Congress will be monitoring the situation. This group should not be seen as a surrogate for the entire body of Congress. We firmly believe that consulting with this group in no way replaces the President's Constitutional obligation to seek a declaration of war before undertaking any offensive military action. We demand that the Administration not undertake any offensive military action without the full deliberation and declaration required by the Constitution."

Dellums and approximately 20 of his Congressional colleagues plan to meet with Speaker Foley later this evening to reiterate "their grave concerns about this crisis which grows more ominous with each passing day." Dellums then went on to say:

"The purpose of our meeting with the Speaker is to make him fully aware that there is an active, aggressive peace movement within the Congress which is determined to seek and work for a non-violent, diplomatic resolution of this crisis. In an institutional context we will also urge him to stand forthrightly in defense of the Constitutional mandate that gives the Congress

0042

218  걸프 사태 미국 동향 3

/ "I am convinced ▦▦ the overwhelming majority of the
American people do no▦▦▦t war with Iraq and its ●▦ndant mass
killing and physical devastation. Twenty-five years ago, as a
citizen activist, I did everything possible to challenge the
illegality and immorality of the policies we were pursuing in
Indochina. Today, as a citizen Congressman, I intend to use my
institutional power under the Constitution, and the Bill of Rights
to challenge this Administration's seemingly inexorable march to
war and its disastrous consequences."

-30-

ZP50 -3

0043

외 무 부

원 본

종 별 :

번 호 : USW-4887

일 시 : 90 1031 1510

수 신 : 장 관 (민안,미북,중근동)

발 신 : 주 미 대사

제 목 : 페만사태 의회반응

연: USW-4878

1. 작 10.30. BUSH 대통령과 의회 양당 지도자들과의 페만사태 관련 회합과 관련, 의회는 행정부가 전쟁선포를 의회에 요청하든가, 혹은 군사행동을 취하기 전 의회의 동의를 구하는 양안에 대하여 BUSH 대통령의 확답을 얻는데 실패하였음.

2. MITCHELL 상원 원내총무는 의회 폐회직전 ADJOURNMENT RESOLUTION 을 통해, 페만사태와 관련 폐회중에도 의원들을 소집할수 있는 권한을 상.하원 지도부에 부여하였으며, 행정부와 긴밀한 협의를 위하여 양원 지도부, 외무위, 군사위, 정보위 위원장과 간사들 18명으로 특별 위원회를 구성한바 있음을 참고바람.

(대사 박동진- 국장)

---

미주국    1차보    미주국    중아국    정문국    안기부

PAGE 1

90.11.01    08:30 FC

외신 1과 통제관

0044

관리번호 90-677

# 외 무 부

종 별 : 지급

번 호 : USW-5072

일 시 : 90 1113 1843

수 신 : 장관(미안,미북,중근동)

발 신 : 주 미 대사

제 목 : 페만사태-의회 반응

1. 중간선거 이후 BUSH 대통령의 페만 주둔 미군병력 증강 결정에 따라 동 조치와 관련 BUSH 행정부의 페만 사태에 관한 논란이 가중되고 있는바, 양당 의회 지도부의 관련 동향을 아래와같이 보고함.

2. 양당의 상이한 입장 표출

가. 중간선거 이전 BUSH 행정부의 페만 정책에 대한 국민의 높은 지지도에 따라 민주당은 페만사태 문제를 선거 이슈로 활용치 않았으나, 최근 공화, 민주양당 지도부는 BUSH 대통령이 페만사태에 대하여 유엔과는 긴밀한 협조를 취한데비하여 미의회와 국민들과의 진지한 논의가 상대적으로 결여되어 있다는 점을 공통점으로 지적하고 있음.

나. 특히 민주당 지도부는 BUSH 행정부의 정책과 관련, 미국의 페만전략과 병력 증원에 대한 뚜렷한 목적에 대하여 국민에게 충분한 설명을 할것을 촉구하였음.(FOLEY 의장, GEPHARDT 원내총무 서한), 또한 , 상원 군사위원장 NUNN 및 외무위원장 PELL 은 미행정부의 페만 전략에 의문을 제기하면서 동지역에서의 미국의 구체적인 이익에 대한 뚜렷한 인식을 촉구하고 이에 대하여 국민에게 설명해 줄 의무가 대통령에게 있음을 주장하였음.

다. BUSH 대통령의 페만 정책에 대한 민주당 지도부의 일련의 비판에 대하여 상원 외무위 LUGAR 상원의원은 금 11.13(화)기자회견을 통하여 페만 사태의 평화적 해결을 위해서는 미국의 정책에 대한 국제적 신뢰도의 제고가 필요한바, 이를 위해 BUSH 대통령이 미병력 증강 사유에 대한 가능한 상세한 설명이 필요하다고 언급함. 아울러 국민을 대표하는 의회가 회동하여 동사태와 미전략 및 소요재원등에 대한 논의를 하고, 대통령의 정책에 대한 의회의 입장을 표명함이 미정책의 신뢰성 제고에 필수적임을 강조하였음.

---

| 미주국 | 차관 | 1차보 | 2차보 | 미주국 | 중아국 | 청와대 | 안기부 | 대책반 |
|---|---|---|---|---|---|---|---|---|

90.11.14    09:44
외신 2과   통제관 CF
0045

라. DOLE 공화당 상원 원내총무도 11.13. LUGAR 상원의원에 지지를 표명하면서 의회의 특별회기 소집에 찬성하였으나, MITCHEL 상원민주당 총무는 대통령이 전쟁수행 결정을 확실하게 표명한후에야 의회 소집이 의미가 있다고 말하면서 현단계에서의 특별회기소집에는 소극적인 입장을 보였음.

마. BUSH 행정부 입장

0 백악관 FITZWATER 대변인도 BUSH 대통령이 전쟁 수행 결정을 한바가 없으며 따라서 대의회 승인을 얻기 위한 의회 특별회기 소집에 반대 입장을 표명하였으며, 의회에 대하여는 계속 긴밀히 협의해 나갈것임을 밝혔음.

3. 관찰

가. 중간선거가 끝나고 의회가 휴회중인 현재, BUSH 대통령의 병력 증강 발표에 따라 다소 입장의 차이는 있다고 하더라도 양당 의회지도부는 행정부가 의회의 승인 없이 전쟁에 돌입할 가능성에 대해 깊은 우려를 표명하고 있으며, 행정부의 정책에 대하여 미의회와 국민들에 대한 납득할만한 설명이 있어야 한다는데 대체로 의견이 모아지고 있음.

나. 단지, 102 회기 개원 이전에 변칙적으로 의회를 소집하여 사태를 논의하자는 제안과 관련, 의회내에서의 많은 논란이 미정책 결정에 분열된 모습을 노정 시킴으로써, HUSSEIN 에 대하여 그릇된 메세지를 보낼 우려가 있다는 점 또한지적되고 있음이 주목됨.

다. 상기와같은 의회내 불만이 계속 노정될 것을 감안할때, BUSH 대통령은 101 회기 하기 휴회중 동사태와 관련한 의회 지도부와의 논의와 같은 형식으로,102 회기 개원 이전에도 수시로 대의회 지도부 설명회를 가짐으로서 의회의 상기와같은 요구에 대응해 나갈것으로 보임.

첨부:LUGAR 기자회견문 USW(F)-3029 (2 매)

(대사 박동진-국장)

예고:90.12.31 까지

외 무 부

종    별 :

번    호 : USW-5116                                    일    시 : 90 1115 1814

수    신 : 장관( 미북, 미안, 중근동, 기정)

발    신 : 주 미 대사

제    목 : 페만사태-의회 동향

1. BUSH 대통령은 최근 폐만 주둔 미군병력 증강과 관련, 행정부측이 이라크에 대한 공세 전쟁을 구상하고 있지 않느냐 하는 우려를 불식시키기 위해 작 11.14. 의회 지도부와 백악관 면담을 가졌음.

2. 동 면담시 BUSH 대통령은 의회 지도부에 대해 폐만 주둔 미군 병력의 증강에도 불구, 아직 이락에 대한 무력사용에 대해 어떤 결정을 내린바 없음을 강조하고, 무력사용 문제에 대해 어떤 결정을 내린바 없는 상황에서 의회측이 특별회기를 갖는것은 무의미 하다는 반대 입장을 밝혔음.

3. 동 면담시에 민주당 의회지도부는 UN 제재 조치가 소기의 성과를 거두기위해서는 좀더 시간이 필요하고, 기존정책의 변경을 UN 제재조치의 실요성이 판명된 이후에나 고려되어야 할것이라는 우려를 전달하였으며, 상기 면담에도 불구, 일부 의원들은 최근 폐만 주둔 미군병력 증강 조칭의 필요성에 대해 계속 의구심을 갖고 있는것으로 보도 되고 있음.

4. 관찰

O BUSH 행정부는 최근의 미군 병력 증강 조치는 무력사용 조치가 필요하다고 판단되는 시점에서 무력사용을 가능하게 하기위한 사전 조치로서 그 필요성을 옹호하고 있으나, 폐만사태 해결을 위해 무력을 사용할 필요성이 있느냐는 근본적 문제에 대해 의회나 일반 국민 사이에 일반적 합의가 없는 상황에서 금번 병력 증강 조치가 취해짐에 따라 민주당 의원들로 부터 강한 반발을 불러 일으켰음.

O 금번 병력 증강 조치에 대해 민주당 의원들이 강한 반발을 보인것은 무력사용을 통한 폐만사태 해결에 대한 우려 표명 이라는 점도 있으나, 의회와 행정부간의 WAR POWER 에 관한 다툼에서 행정부측이 의회와 아무런 사전 협의 없이 무력사용의 가능성을 높이는 조치를 취하였다는 절차적인 문제에서도 이유를 찾을수 있음.

| 미주국 | 차관 | 1차보 | 2차보 | 미주국 | 중아국 | 정와대 | 안기부 | 대책반 |
|--------|------|-------|-------|--------|--------|--------|--------|--------|

PAGE 1

90.11.16    09:04
외신 2과  통제관 BW
0047

(대사 박동진-국장)
90.12.31 까지

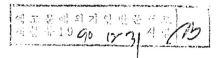

0048

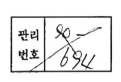

외 무 부

종 별 : 지 급

번 호 : USW-5198                                일 시 : 90 1120 1813

수 신 : 장관(미북,미안,중근동)

발 신 : 주 미 대사

제 목 : 페만사태-의회 반응

　　1. 11.16. LES ASPIN 하원 군사위 위원장은 페만사태 관련 주요 동맹국의 비용분담에 대한 평가 보고서를 발표하였음.

　　2. 상기 보고서는 페만 사태 비용분담을 약속한 전 국가를 대상으로 하지는않았으며, 페만사태 직접 관련국가 및 주요 선진국을 대상으로하여 평점을 부여한것임.

　　3. 상기 보고서중 한국관련 사항은 동보고서 첨부물인 동보고서에 포함되어있지 않은 국가의 분담내역 표상에 한국이 2.2 억불 지원을 발표했고, 군의료단 파견을 고려중이라고 기술한것이 전부이며, 당관이 동보고서 작성자인 하원군사위 WARREN NELSON 전문위원을 접촉한바, 동인은 한국의 비용 분담 규모는 만족스러우며 B 정도의 평점은 될것이라는 의견을 밝힌바 있음.

　　4. 상기 보고서 관련 보도자료 및 보고서 주요 부분은 별첨 FAX 송부하며 전문은 파편 송부예정임.

　　(대사 박동진-국장)

　　예고:90.12.31 까지

일반문서로 재분류(19 .  .  )

| 미주국 | 1차보 | 2차보 | 미주국 | 중아국 | 대책반 |
| --- | --- | --- | --- | --- | --- |

90.11.21   08:38
외신 2과  통제관 BT

0049

USW (F) — 3/3/
수신: 장관 (미복), 미안, 등근동)
발신: 주미 대사
제목: Aspin 군사위원장 보고서 - 페만사태 관련 (6매)

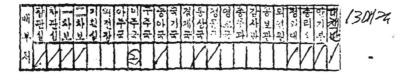

130/7

FOR RELEASE:    Friday, November 16, 1990,   AM newspapers
For further information, contact:  Lynn Reddy (202) 225-2191
                                   Warren Nelson (202) 225-2086

### ASPIN GRADES INTERNATIONAL PERFORMANCE IN THE MIDEAST

WASHINGTON -- Rep. Les Aspin (D-Wis.), chairman of the House
Armed Services Committee, today rated the contributions made to
the containment of Iraq by the world's nations, giving an A-plus
only to Turkey and Egypt.

Aspin gave a C to both Japan and Germany, saying neither
nation was doing anywhere near as much as it could to shoulder a
fair share of the burden of the confrontation.

"The American public is gritting its teeth over the
willingness of other nations to see this conflict through to the
last American," Aspin said in releasing his "Burdensharing Report
Card."

He said, "Other nations should know they are being judged by
the American public and commonly found wanting.  This report is
my effort to formalize the judgments that citizens are making on
their own."

                        MORE

                                                        0050

-2-

Aspin's report card also laid down a clear warning to other
nations about a potential American backlash if they fail to do
more, particularly in light of the decision to increase American
troop strength to make it possible to go on the offense.

"Before the President comes to Congress for support of
offensive operations, he'd better make sure the allies are making
an adequate contribution," Aspin said.  The report card also
dealt directly with the backlash issue.  It read:

While the world is busily debating whether the soft
Americans will sustain a confrontation when faced with
any substantial casualties, the world ought also to
consider the attitude of the American public should a
war erupt in which the casualties are overwhelmingly
American.  If Americans are critical today of the
relative unwillingness of others -- chiefly Europeans
and Japanese -- to share the burden of this
confrontation, imagine how critical -- even furious --
they are likely to be when they see few others paying
the bloodprice.  One should expect the American public
to demand that the Congress and the Administration
impose a heavy penalty on non-participants.

Aspin said the additional U.S. troops announced for
deployment to Saudi Arabia represented the "added danger that th
Administration might consider fighting alone.  That might be
doable militarily, but it is not politically.  The American
people won't stand for our allies sitting out the fighting while
Americans are dying."

The Aspin Burdensharing Report Card grades 19 nations and
groups of nations on their contributions.  It gives Fs to three
Arab nations -- Yemen, Libya and the Sudan -- for making
clandestine efforts to help Saddam Hussein evade the UN
sanctions.

In perhaps the most startling grades, Aspin gave only a B t
Saudi Arabia and a B-plus to Jordan.  He complained that the
Saudi financial contribution amounted to only about 10 weeks of
additional revenues earned by the Saudis as a result of soaring
oil prices.  Aspin's report comments: "Since the confrontation
with Saddam Hussein is now almost 15 weeks old, the Saudis have
already earned significantly more than they have pledged to the
effort.  Money does not grow on trees, but in Saudi Arabia it
does spew from derricks.  More should be expected of Riyadh."

As for Jordan, Aspin said King Hussein was doing far more
than anyone had a right to demand given the scale of the domesti

MORE

3/31 -2

0051

-3-

pressures he faces. He rapped Saudi Arabia and the Gulf Arabs for treating King Hussein "like a kickball and making it harder for him to help them! The goal here should be to encourage Jordan to help. Unfortunately, the Saudi propensity for punishing King Hussein for his initial non-compliance just makes it all the harder for him to be helpful in the future."

Turkey gets an A-plus for immediately enforcing the sanctions without any pressure from Washington and despite the immense cost to the Turkish economy. "The Turks don't stand to gain from this confrontation," Aspin said. "They are taking a nasty economic beating. While we complain about the lackadaisical Europeans who refused to be nudged, pushed or kicked to the frontlines, we shouldn't forget people like the Turks who have jumped into the trenches ahead of us."

The grades were not issued on military contributions alone. There were six criteria by which the nations were assessed:

o    Military participation

o    Financial contribution

o    Compliance with UN sanctions

o    Political support

o    Response time

o    Special factors involving a nation's ability to contribute and limitations on its contributions.

# # # #

3/31-3

0052

# PERSIAN GULF CRISIS
# REPORT CARD

| Student | Grade | Observations |
|---|---|---|
| France | B | One bad term paper |
| United Kingdom | B+ | She always has the most brilliant analysis |
| Germany | C | Distracted; could contribute more |
| Other Europe | C- | Class attendance is poor |
| Turkey | A+ | Superb performance with no prompting needed |
| USSR | B | Not yet quite up to full potential |
| Kuwait | A | Excellent despite family house burning down |
| Saudi Arabia | B | Underachiever; should really be tops in class |
| Egypt | A+ | Performing far beyond potential |
| Syria | B+ | Disruptive student now back in class |
| Jordan | B+ | Big problems at home; noisy family; coping well |
| Yemen | F | } |
| Libya | F | } Disruptive student; consider for expulsion |
| Sudan | F | } |
| Other Arabs | C | Often playing hooky |
| Iran | D | Self-centered; unable to work with others |
| Israel | — | Auditing class |
| Japan | C | Problems at home, but can still contribute more |
| United States | A- | Excellent start; floundering a bit now. |

3/31-K

0053

covering nations NOT described in this report

| NATION | MILITARY COMMITMENT | | | FINANCIAL COMMITMENT OR SACRIFICE (in $ millions) | EMBARGO COMPLIANCE |
|---|---|---|---|---|---|
| | TROOPS TO SAUDI ARABIA | AIRCRAFT TO SAUDI ARABIA | SHIPS TO REGION | | |
| Argentina | 125-150 (1) | 2 (1) | 2 | none | Yes |
| Australia | none | none | 2 | 1 | Yes |
| Bangladesh | 6,000 | none | none | 3,500 in losses | Yes |
| Belgium | none | none (2) | 4 | unk thru EC (3) | Yes |
| Bulgaria | none (4) | none | none | none | Yes |
| Canada | none | none (5) | 3 | 75 | Yes |
| Czechoslovak | 200 | none | none | none | Yes |
| Denmark | none | none | 1 | unk thru EC | Yes |
| Finland | none | none | none | 1-2 ? | Yes |
| Greece | none (7) | none | none (6) | unk thru EC | Yes |
| Iceland | none (7) | none (7) | none (7) | 2.5 | Yes |
| Italy | none | none (8) | 4 | 150 (8) | Yes |
| Luxembourg | none | none | none | unk thru EC | Yes |
| Morocco | 1,200 | none | none | none | Yes |
| Netherlands | none | offer 18 (9) | 3 | unk thru EC | Yes |
| Norway | none | none | 1 | none | Yes |
| Pakistan | 5,000 (10) | offered (10) | offered (10) | 1,100 in losses | Yes |
| Poland | none | none | offer 2 (11) | none | Yes |
| Portugal | none | none | 1 (12) | unk thru EC | Yes |
| Senegal | 490 | none | none | none | Yes |
| South Korea | none (13) | none | none | 220 | Yes |
| Spain | none | none | 4 | unk thru EC | Yes |
| Sweden | none | none | none | 1-2 ? | Yes |
| Taiwan | none | none | none | 30 | Yes |

ᅩ-161ᄃ

0054

Footnotes:

1. Argentina offered to send 125-150 Army personnel, 2 ships, 1 C-130 transport aircraft and 1 Boeing 707; ships are scheduled to arrive in the Gulf region in early November; ground and air assets are on hold pending invitation.

2. Belgium sent several C-130 transport aircraft to the region; at least 2 operated in Jordan ferrying refugees.

3. The EC has pledged $2 billion to the Gulf effort. We do not have information on the individual member contributions to that fund.

4. Bulgaria announce in late September it was prepared to send small military contingent (probably an engineer unit to clear land mines); no information on disposition.

5. Canada sent 18 F-18s and 2 C-130s to a base in Qatar from where they can fly in support of allied operations.

6. Greece did deploy 1 frigate to the Eastern Mediterranean.

7. Iceland has no military forces.

8. Italy sent 8 Tornados to a base in the UAE, from where they can fly in support of allied operations; unclear if Italy's pledge of $150 million is in addition to a contribution thru the EC.

9. The Dutch have offered to deploy 18 F-16s but Turkey declined to base them; continue to seek a base in the region.

10. Pakistan pledged 5,000 troops, initially were being deployed in the UAE, final disposition unclear.

11. Poland has offered a hospital ship and a cargo ship, preferably for transporting Egyptian and Moroccan forces; no information on actual deployment.

12. Portugal pledged 1 transport ship for Gulf movements, sent 1 frigate to the Mediterranean, and chartered 2 merchant ships to the U.S.

13. South Korea announced intention to send a military hospital unit; no information on actual deployment.

0055

홍

주　미　대　사　관

미국(정) 700-2687                                    1990. 11. 20.
수신 : 장　관
참조 : 미주국장, 중동아프리카국장
제목 : 페만사태 비용분담 보고서


　　　연 : USW - 5198


　　　연호 Les Aspin 하원 군사위원장이 발표한 페만사태 동맹국 비용분담에
대한 평가 보고서를 별첨 송부합니다.


첨부 : 동 보고서 및 관계 보도자료 1부.　　끝.

주　　　미　　　대　　　사

**65725**

0056

# NEWS RELEASE

## House Armed Services Committee

2120 Rayburn House Office Bldg.
Washington, D.C. 20515

FOR RELEASE:   Friday, November 16, 1990,   AM newspapers
For further information, contact:   Lynn Reddy (202) 225-2191
                                    Warren Nelson (202) 225-2086

### ASPIN GRADES INTERNATIONAL PERFORMANCE IN THE MIDEAST

WASHINGTON -- Rep. Les Aspin (D-Wis.), chairman of the House Armed Services Committee, today rated the contributions made to the containment of Iraq by the world's nations, giving an A-plus only to Turkey and Egypt.

Aspin gave a C to both Japan and Germany, saying neither nation was doing anywhere near as much as it could to shoulder a fair share of the burden of the confrontation.

"The American public is gritting its teeth over the willingness of other nations to see this conflict through to the last American," Aspin said in releasing his "Burdensharing Report Card."

He said, "Other nations should know they are being judged by the American public and commonly found wanting.  This report is my effort to formalize the judgments that citizens are making on their own."

MORE

0057

Aspin's report card also laid down a clear warning to other
nations about a potential American backlash if they fail to do
more, particularly in light of the decision to increase American
troop strength to make it possible to go on the offense.

"Before the President comes to Congress for support of
offensive operations, he'd better make sure the allies are making
an adequate contribution," Aspin said. The report card also
dealt directly with the backlash issue. It read:

> While the world is busily debating whether the soft
> Americans will sustain a confrontation when faced with
> any substantial casualties, the world ought also to
> consider the attitude of the American public should a
> war erupt in which the casualties are overwhelmingly
> American. If Americans are critical today of the
> relative unwillingness of others -- chiefly Europeans
> and Japanese -- to share the burden of this
> confrontation, imagine how critical -- even furious --
> they are likely to be when they see few others paying
> the bloodprice. One should expect the American public
> to demand that the Congress and the Administration
> impose a heavy penalty on non-participants.

Aspin said the additional U.S. troops announced for
deployment to Saudi Arabia represented the "added danger that the
Administration might consider fighting alone. That might be
doable militarily, but it is not politically. The American
people won't stand for our allies sitting out the fighting while
Americans are dying."

The Aspin Burdensharing Report Card grades 19 nations and
groups of nations on their contributions. It gives Fs to three
Arab nations -- Yemen, Libya and the Sudan -- for making
clandestine efforts to help Saddam Hussein evade the UN
sanctions.

In perhaps the most startling grades, Aspin gave only a B to
Saudi Arabia and a B-plus to Jordan. He complained that the
Saudi financial contribution amounted to only about 10 weeks of
additional revenues earned by the Saudis as a result of soaring
oil prices. Aspin's report comments: "Since the confrontation
with Saddam Hussein is now almost 15 weeks old, the Saudis have
already earned significantly more than they have pledged to the
effort. Money does not grow on trees, but in Saudi Arabia it
does spew from derricks. More should be expected of Riyadh."

As for Jordan, Aspin said King Hussein was doing far more
than anyone had a right to demand given the scale of the domestic

MORE

0058

pressures he faces. He rapped Saudi Arabia and the Gulf Arabs
for treating King Hussein "like a kickball and making it harder
for him to help them! The goal here should be to encourage
Jordan to help. Unfortunately, the Saudi propensity for
punishing King Hussein for his initial non-compliance just makes
it all the harder for him to be helpful in the future."

Turkey gets an A-plus for immediately enforcing the
sanctions without any pressure from Washington and despite the
immense cost to the Turkish economy. "The Turks don't stand to
gain from this confrontation," Aspin said. "They are taking a
nasty economic beating. While we complain about the
lackadaisical Europeans who refused to be nudged, pushed or
kicked to the frontlines, we shouldn't forget people like the
Turks who have jumped into the trenches ahead of us."

The grades were not issued on military contributions alone.
There were six criteria by which the nations were assessed:

o   Military participation

o   Financial contribution

o   Compliance with UN sanctions

o   Political support

o   Response time

o   Special factors involving a nation's ability to
    contribute and limitations on its contributions.

# # # #

0053

# BURDENSHARING

# REPORT

# CARD

# ON THE

# PERSIAN

# GULF

# CRISIS

## by Rep. Les Aspin

*House Armed Services Committee*
*2120 Rayburn Office Building*
*Washington, D.C. 20515*

*November 14, 1990*

0060

# PERSIAN GULF CRISIS
# REPORT CARD

| Student | Grade | Observations |
|---|---|---|
| France | B | One bad term paper |
| United Kingdom | B+ | She always has the most brilliant analysis |
| Germany | C | Distracted; could contribute more |
| Other Europe | C- | Class attendance is poor |
| Turkey | A+ | Superb performance with no prompting needed |
| USSR | B | Not yet quite up to full potential |
| Kuwait | A | Excellent despite family house burning down |
| Saudi Arabia | B | Underachiever; should really be tops in class |
| Egypt | A+ | Performing far beyond potential |
| Syria | B+ | Disruptive student now back in class |
| Jordan | B+ | Big problems at home; noisy family; coping well |
| Yemen | F | } |
| Libya | F | } Disruptive student; consider for expulsion |
| Sudan | F | } |
| Other Arabs | C | Often playing hooky |
| Iran | D | Self-centered; unable to work with others |
| Israel | — | Auditing class |
| Japan | C | Problems at home, but can still contribute more |
| United States | A- | Excellent start; floundering a bit now. |

0061

## Introduction

The current confrontation in the Persian Gulf between the world and Iraq is the first defining event of the new world after the Cold War. As such, it has a significance that far transcends the narrow albeit significant issue of the future of Kuwait and Saudi Arabia. The question for the new post-Cold War world is whether an international community no longer dominated by the East-West balance of terror will allow jungle law to define the new era or whether it is to be capable of enforcing some standard of behavior.

One option calls for the United States to act as the policeman of the world, collaring the bullies and thugs like Saddam Hussein. But that is a role the American public rejects. While we have always been willing to be part of a larger, multinational security effort, we are unwilling to arrogate to ourselves the burdens or the benefits of the solitary policeman's role.

With Europe and Japan fully recovered from the ravages of World War II, and with considerable wealth now found among the oil producing nations, the American public in recent years has demanded that the burdens of international security be more equitably shared. The confrontation in the Persian Gulf provides an appropriate time and place for judging how the world is doing in meeting the challenge and sharing the burden.

In this analysis, I propose to grade the performances of the other major players. For simplicity's sake, I have rated each country with a simple schoolhouse A-to-F grading system. This is not meant to trivialize an important issue, but rather to summarize and give greater clarity to an analysis that is necessarily nuanced and intricate.

## Grading standards

Before we can assess the performance of individual players, we need a set of grading guidelines. The most fundamental principle of the new world order must certainly be:

> All nations share the benefits of international security and stability and therefore must, commensurate with their capabilities, share the responsibility for maintaining that security and stability.

0062

The criteria by which I have assessed individual nations in this crisis flow from that fundamental principle. I have used six such criteria:

- Military participation;
- Financial contribution;
- Compliance with the UN sanctions;
- Political support;
- Response time; and
- Special factors involving the nation's capabilities and mitigating circumstances. This last criterion is necessary because we cannot assess nations based on how their contributions compare with those of other nations in absolute terms -- nations obviously vary in capabilities, constraints and what they have at stake. Furthermore, some should be donors in this crisis while others contribute by virtue of the severe losses they suffer in facing the threat.

A few general observations are needed to set the stage for the national assessments.

First, the United States was obviously one of the workhorses of the old order and has leapt into the traces again to lead the effort in this first test of the new order. The United States should certainly do its share but, frankly, it has been weakened by pulling far more than its fair share in the past and simply should not and cannot go on doing so. In the current crisis, it has deployed in the area far more troops than all of its partners combined. It is already paying the lion's share of the costs in treasure and will no doubt pay the lion's share in blood if it comes to combat.

While the world is busily debating whether the soft Americans will sustain a confrontation when faced with any substantial casualties, the world ought also to consider the attitude of the American public should a war erupt in which the casualties are overwhelmingly American. If Americans are critical today of the relative unwillingness of others -- chiefly Europeans and Japanese -- to share the burden of this confrontation, imagine how critical -- even furious -- they are likely to be when they see few others paying the bloodprice. One should expect the American public to demand that the Congress and the Administration impose a heavy penalty on non-participants.

Second, we should recognize that the much improved relationship between the United States and the Soviet Union is now promoting global solidarity rather than confrontation. For 40 years, the intense competition between the superpowers and the coalitions behind them stymied meaningful efforts at international cooperation. Now, for the first time, the United Nations has been able to leave those bloc politics behind and assume an active leadership role. The world Woodrow Wilson envisioned seven decades ago now has a chance of emerging into reality.

A third general observation regarding this crisis is that, for the most part, the Arab world has also risen above the bloc politics of the past to join actively in the opposition to the Iraqi aggression. Arab military and

0063

financial contributions to the multinational effort underscore the vital political message to Saddam Hussein that he is isolated -- even in his own backyard. There is little doubt that Saddam miscalculated on that score and was surprised to find such resolute opposition to his aggression among his Arab brethren. To Saddam's claim that the current crisis was generated by the United States with a fig leaf of international cover, the Arab community has responded forcefully that Saddam has broken not just international law but the Arab code, and that he must reverse his course.

On the other hand, the Arab nations of the Gulf did not comprehend the threat in July and failed to respond in the days before the August 2 invasion. The United States offered concrete military support to the Gulf nations when Saddam began his buildup in July. Only the United Arab Emirates accepted our offer -- and it quickly denied any connection between the crisis and our deployment of aircraft to the UAE. So, while the regional response after the attack was swift and clear, none of the governments showed the kind of pre-invasion resolve required to have had any hope of dissuading Saddam from invading Kuwait.

As a handy reference aid, one table at the end of this report summarizes the contributions made by the nations rated here. A second table summarizes the contributions of other nations not specifically cited in this report card. A third table lists all the ground forces so far committed to the theater. The three tables together give a compact yet comprehensive summary of how the world is responding in measurable terms.

The tables and text reflect where we are as of early November. In some cases, this report shows what has been delivered. In other cases, it shows what has been promised and awaits delivery. There is legitimate reason to question, for example, whether Japan's promised aid will materialize, but also good reason to expect more Saudi aid will surface.

A future report card measuring the fulfillment of promises and the extent of political, military and financial contributions is planned for a later date. This stands as a report card on the performance of the nations playing key roles three months into the international confrontation.

## Western Europe

We begin our assessments of individual nations by looking at Europe. For characterizing our grading curve for European countries thus far in this crisis, it would be difficult to improve on British Prime Minister Margaret Thatcher's own words:

> It is sad that at this critical time Europe has not fully measured up to expectations. The only countries in Europe which have done significantly more than the minimum are Britain and France. It's not what you say that counts but what you do. We cannot expect the United States to go on bearing major defense burdens worldwide, acting in effect as

0Q64

4

the world's policeman, if it does not get a positive and swift response from its allies when the crunch comes — particularly when fundamental principles as well as their own interests are just as much at stake.

That leads us logically to start with the nations Mrs. Thatcher singles out.

## France

Despite its special relationship with Iraq in the past, France has been a leader of the European response to the Iraqi aggression, especially following the intrusion of Iraqi forces into the French Embassy in Kuwait September 14. After that, President Francois Mitterrand immediately ordered 4,000 additional troops to Saudi Arabia and expelled Iraqi defense and intelligence officials from the Iraqi Embassy in Paris.

France now has almost 13,000 military personnel committed to the crisis and deployed in the general area. Paris has had to make its military contributions to the Gulf effort over the protests of domestic critics who reflect traditional French reluctance to participate in multinational military operations, especially outside Europe, and French aversion to integrating French units into multinational military structures. We find France's willingness in this case to commit its forces and integrate them into the multinational effort a welcome contribution and a further recognition of the greater degree of interdependence involved in the new world order.

The 5,000 French ground troops are lightly equipped -- they have armored fighting vehicles but no tanks or heavy artillery. They are, however, from the well trained and experienced Rapid Action Force.

France has also provided important political leadership in international organizations, encouraging the U.N. Security Council to act promptly in adopting its resolutions and pressing the European Community to increase its relief aid to the front-line states suffering from the crisis. However, President Mitterrand's late-September peace proposal undoubtedly encouraged Saddam Hussein to believe he could outlast us. Among other difficulties, the plan implied that if Saddam stated his *intention* to withdraw from Kuwait, the embargo could be loosened and negotiations could begin. Although President Mitterrand later said that Iraq must actually *complete* its withdrawal to trigger the loosening of the embargo and commencement of negotiations, damage had already been done. Still, Mitterrand's oral blunder was little different from President Bush's similar, inept speech broaching compromise.

How was the French response time? Their initial response was meager, a more robust response did not come until the Iraqi intrusion into the French Embassy in Kuwait, almost six weeks after the invasion. So, there is room for improvement here.

0065

French contributions to the multinational effort have been substantial, but are they completely commensurate with French capabilities? Probably not -- they can do more, and maybe they will. Averaging its performance against all six criteria, France gets a B.

## United Kingdom

Mrs. Thatcher's United Kingdom has responded to the crisis in similar fashion. British land, air and naval personnel pledged to the operation now number roughly 15,000. The core of the ground force is one of the best equipped units in the British Army, an armored brigade from Germany. The brigade's 7,000 troops will be joined by about 2,000 support personnel. The unit will add much needed heavy elements to the multinational forces. It has more than a hundred main battle tanks, almost fifty armored fighting vehicles, an artillery regiment with 155mm self-propelled guns, and a helicopter detachment.

Britain's ability to sustain its ground troops deployed to Saudi Arabia, however, is apparently not quite up to the challenge. The British armored Brigade reportedly will depend on the U.S. for its logistic support.

The British have also sent additional combat aircraft to the region to supplement those already assigned there. They now have about 40 combat aircraft in the area (Tornado ground attack and air defense fighters and Jaguar ground attack aircraft). They are also operating 12 ships in the area as well as some maritime patrol aircraft.

The British financial commitment to the effort is not as great as that of the French -- London has pledged $10.3 million in relief of the front-line states versus $40 million by Paris. Both are meager offers.

Britain's political support of the Gulf effort has been typically solid. It has been active in the U.N. Security Council and in building international consensus behind the allied coalition.

The British do not score high in response time. The armored brigade from Germany is only now completing its deployment in Saudi Arabia, having taken three months to get into place.

Like the French, the British could probably muster more wherewithal in support of the international effort in the Gulf. London has been steadier than Paris in its political resolve and has committed a heavier military force, but its financial support has been lighter and its response time has been somewhat longer. Give the British a B-plus.

## Germany

Turning to Germany, let's begin with what Bonn *has* done. In the military sphere, it has sent seven ships to the Eastern Mediterranean -- not the Gulf -- to replace U.S. ships diverted to the Gulf. It has offered the use of German air bases to help facilitate U.S. deployments to the Gulf.

0066

In the financial sphere, Bonn has pledged just over $2.1 billion, which, unlike the French and British contributions, meets Everett Dirksen's definition of real money. Half supports U.S. deployments in the Gulf, and half aids front-line states. The amount pledged to U.S. deployments will consist of the following: about $645 million worth of various military support equipment such as generators, cranes, radio and engineering equipment, water tanker vehicles, and defensive equipment for nuclear/biological/chemical (NBC) environments; about $130 million worth of NBC recon vehicles; and about $260 million to charter air and sealift for U.S. forces. Roughly half of the support equipment will come from the deactivated East German Army. In other words, a third of a billion of this contribution is a spoil of victory in the Cold War.

Now, let's look at what Germany has *not* done. We should first say that Chancellor Helmut Kohl is right. When visited by Secretary of State James Baker in mid-September, he said that, in putting soldiers on the line in Saudi Arabia, other countries are "acting on our behalf, and they are also defending our interests. . . . We are tops in the field of exports, but we are not fully assuming our responsibility" in the Persian Gulf.

Even in terms of Germany's financial contribution, it is not assuming its full responsibility. Germany is not only the world's leading exporter, it enjoys a 4 percent economic growth rate and a $55 billion current account surplus. It could certainly do more to offset the costs of those nations acting on its behalf, and could have certainly offered its contributions more promptly than waiting six weeks until Secretary Baker showed up at the front door soliciting funds.

In military terms, of course, Germany has not sent a single soldier, sailor or airman. Again, Chancellor Kohl strikes the right tone, saying in the same public forum with Secretary Baker, "Let me say very frankly that I am dismayed we are not completely free to act in the community of nations in a way we would like to act." The Chancellor was referring to constitutional constraints that many Germans argue bar deployment of German forces outside the NATO region, a limitation that the Federal Republic has honored throughout the post-war period. Chancellor Kohl is also pledged to seek, after all-German elections in December, a constitutional amendment relaxing the restriction on deploying German military forces overseas. But this is not a constitutional bar as explicit as Japan's Constitution. In fact, some even question if it might be just a convenient crutch on which to lean when Germany doesn't really want to do more.

The Cold War is over. The stark requirements of the new world order are upon us. Germany is eager to be in the forefront of that new world order when it involves German unification, where Chancellor Kohl questions no sacrifice and bears every burden. The future-looking attitude ought to be applied elsewhere.

Let's agree with Chancellor Kohl that Germany is not fully assuming its responsibility. Give Germany a C.

0067

### Other European allies

What about our other West European allies? Mrs. Thatcher was right -- the others have not done nearly as well as the British and French. They have enforced all aspects of the trade embargo. Our NATO allies have allowed us unrestricted use of our European bases to support our Gulf deployments. All European Community members have expelled Iraqi military personnel from their countries and restricted diplomatic activities for Iraqi Embassy officials. But all this is more in the category of minimal compliance than in the realm of burdensharing; expelling Iraqi spies is hardly a burden. Our European allies remain, on the whole, reluctant to become directly involved in defense efforts in the Gulf. They have provided strong political support. Still, given the fact that public opinion polls show overwhelming public support in Europe for demanding Saddam's withdrawal from Kuwait, that has been no burden either.[1]

The United States has recommended that its NATO allies consider sending ground units to join the multinational forces in Saudi Arabia. Thus far, however, military support from that quarter, other than the British and French, has been limited to naval deployments, a few combat aircraft, and overflight and landing rights.

Financial support from our European allies has been uneven. The European Community has pledged $2 billion to assist Egypt, Turkey and Jordan, $500 million of which was disbursed immediately after the pledge was made. Italy has pledged $150 million to the relief effort and Canada has offered $75 million for refugee aid and transportation of military forces to the area. Others have pledged much smaller amounts or made no pledge at all.

In sum, the bulk of our European allies have given solid (and painless) political support, passable economic support, and mere token military support. These dozen nations as a bloc, therefore, get a C-minus.

### Turkey

It is necessary to single out one NATO ally, Turkey, for special credit. Turkey has responded admirably -- and at considerable cost. Ankara promptly shut down the oil pipeline from Iraq that runs through Turkey to the Mediterranean Sea, thus closing off an important export avenue for Iraqi oil, along with almost 70 percent of Turkey's own oil supply. Iraq has reportedly impounded $1.5 billion in Turkish assets, and

---

[1] A mid-October poll showed 70 percent of the respondents in Britain, Germany, France, Italy and Spain supported the use of military force to end the occupation of Kuwait.

estimates are that Turkey will lose more than $4 billion in a year of sanctions. All of this is from a total Turkish economy of only about $100 billion.

The Turkish role may be more in negative terms -- that is, its economic losses -- than in positive terms. But that in itself makes it all the more laudable. The kinds of burdens Turkey has voluntarily shouldered are the kind most governments shy away from because political opponents can so readily use them to attack the government for shooting the country in the foot.

Turkey has also been prompt in providing extensive base facilities for U.S. military units deploying to the area. It has reinforced its own military forces opposite Iraq, moved them closer to the border, and is considering deployment of a naval contingent. Turkey deserves credit and allied assistance for its ready and costly response. Give Turkey an A-plus for its contributions.

## The Soviet Union

One other European country deserves special treatment here -- the Soviet Union. We have already pointed to that country's important role in building a new superpower relationship that has helped facilitate a unified international response to Iraqi aggression.

No one can argue about recent Soviet contributions to global security and stability in a broad sense. The Gulf crisis, however, has demonstrated that, for various reasons, the U.S.S.R. is not prepared to take on a full load of responsibilities for maintaining global security and stability. Its response has been high in political substance but very low in military and (understandably) financial terms.

Politically, Moscow joined its former superpower adversary in opposing the Iraqi invasion almost immediately. The tone of the Soviet-American message to Saddam Hussein was set at the Helsinki summit at which the two presidents published a joint statement that declared:

> We are united in our belief that Iraq's aggression must not be tolerated. No peaceful international order is possible if larger states can devour their smaller neighbors. . . . Nothing short of complete compliance with United Nations Security Council Resolutions is acceptable.

That message has been amplified repeatedly by both superpowers. For example, Soviet Foreign Minister Eduard Shevardnadze stated before the United Nations in late September that:

> This is a major affront to mankind. In the context of recent events, we should remind those who regard aggression as an acceptable form of behavior that the United Nations has the

0069

power to suppress acts of aggression. There is ample evidence that this right can be exercised. It will be, if the illegal occupation of Kuwait continues.

At least until the last few weeks, Moscow has continued to work closely with Washington and the other members of the U.N. Security Council to increase the pressures on Saddam Hussein. The Soviets provided a driving force in the U.N. deliberations on that organization's role in organizing military responses to this crisis. Except for its ill-advised repetition of its long-standing proposal of an international conference to deal with the "complex and interlocking problems" of the Middle East -- a proposal that was hastily offered and soon left to languish -- the Soviet political campaign in this crisis has been both responsible and responsive. That gaff put the Soviets in the same crowd with Presidents Bush and Mitterrand and their similar ill-conceived and disruptive speeches.

In the last few weeks, however, a gap appears to have opened between Shevardnadze, advocating continued work in harness with Washington, and President Gorbachev, who is flirting with some sort of compromise concept. The problem with the talk of a compromise settlement is that it reduces the pressure on Saddam to get out of Kuwait. The irony is that talk of avoiding war through compromise makes war all the more likely because Saddam is less likely to feel an urge to comply with the UN resolutions. Thus, the most recent political moves emanating from Moscow have not been at all helpful.

At considerable expense to its own financial standing, however, the Soviet Union has fully supported and complied with the embargo. Iraq for a long time was the Soviet Union's favorite non-Bloc customer. The Soviets were by far Iraq's leading arms supplier and those arms sales were on the upswing when Saddam invaded Kuwait. In fact, Iraq had placed orders for some of the most advanced and expensive equipment in the Soviet inventory. Baghdad currently owes Moscow about $6 billion for past deliveries and was paying off in oil that Moscow would then sell abroad for much needed hard currency. Despite this, Moscow suspended arms sales to Baghdad.

Yet, Moscow has not made a military contribution to the multinational defense effort. Several Soviet naval vessels have operated in the Gulf region and have coordinated with the allied embargo effort, but these were standard deployments and Moscow has announced it will not play a military role except under United Nations auspices. It is also true that Moscow was slow to begin withdrawing 150 to 200 "military technicians" and several hundred civilian advisors to the Iraqi defense industry, saying they were not providing any offensive training and all would be withdrawn upon the conclusion of their contracts. As it turns out, many of these Soviet personnel, among others of the 5,000 or so Soviet citizens in Iraq, have been denied exit visas by the Iraqi government and remain Baghdad's "guests."

0070

Moscow's position on military participation and the lack of a Soviet financial contribution to the multinational effort are driven largely by domestic realities. Economic and political strife in the Soviet Union along with considerable disarray in the Soviet armed forces have that country struggling and clearly limit Moscow's military and financial freedom of action in the Gulf. The Soviet Union is contributing only slightly below our standard of sharing responsibilities commensurate with national capabilities. Give the Soviet Union a B for its performance to date.

## The Arab World

Saddam Hussein is first and foremost a threat to the Arab world, which he itches not to lead but to command, in the sense of master, dictate and direct. But Saddam is no Saladin or Nasser. With the invasion of Kuwait, most Arab regimes recognized the threat Saddam poses to the very heart and sole of Arabism. Yet some still try to ride the wild horse of Saddamism as if it were a tame pony.

## Kuwait

Kuwait has suffered a brutal invasion and tragic loss of life, and is being plundered. It recognizes Saddamism for what it is. Kuwaitis have been fighting back in many ways. A considerable resistance to the Iraqi occupation began immediately and continues today, although the harsh and brutal tactics of the occupation forces have eroded the resistance significantly. Several thousand Kuwaiti military personnel escaped the invasion and are forming Kuwaiti units in Saudi Arabia.

The Kuwaiti government in exile agreed promptly to help pay the costs of the multinational effort against Iraq. It has pledged $5 billion to the effort, split between the United States military operation and the front-line states. In fact, the Kuwaiti government has already deposited $750 million in cash into the U.S. Treasury's Defense Cooperation Account established to accept direct foreign contributions to offset the costs of Operation Desert Shield.

The Kuwaitis, regrettably, missed the boat before the invasion, declining all offers from us that might have dissuaded Iraq from attacking. Still, since the Iraqi attack was launched, their performance has been nothing short of remarkable.

The Kuwaiti Air Force, for example, resisted admirably. Although the opening act of the war cratered the runway at Ali As-Salem airport, Kuwaiti airmen manhandled their aircraft to the neighboring highway, took off and attacked targets until the airfield was overrun a few hours later. Airmen at the other airfield flew missions for two days until their base was similarly overrun.

0071

Air units from both fields retired in order to Saudi Arabia, where the Kuwaiti Air Force still exists -- about 40 aircraft in all -- and is preparing for the next round. After the fall of Kuwait, a resistance developed immediately. And, although the Iraqis offered roles in the occupation government to numerous members of the political opposition, none took up the offer. There were no quislings to be found. The Kuwaitis get an A.

## Saudi Arabia

Saudi Arabia has also responded well. The Saudis have been leaders in the important tasks of countering Saddam's efforts to split the coalition confronting him and keeping him isolated within the Arab community. They were quick to invite multinational forces into their country and provide base facilities as well as most in-country needs such as fuel and water. Most significantly, they realized within days that the old "over the horizon" relationship with the United States had been demolished. The Saudi-American alliance is now out of the closet. And the Saudis have shown no qualms about proclaiming it -- at least for now.

The Saudi government has also pledged roughly $10 billion -- $4 billion to $5 billion to offset foreign military costs and over $5 billion to assist front-line states. And, of course, the Saudis have committed their more than 65,000 military personnel to the defense effort.

So, Saudi Arabia is doing a lot in this multinational operation. It can, however, certainly afford to do what it is doing -- and more. Given the rise in oil prices and in Saudi oil production, the Saudis -- conservatively -- stand to enjoy windfall profits of roughly $150 million a day.[2] At that rate, a $10 billion Saudi contribution to the multinational military effort would absorb less than 10 weeks of increased Saudi revenues. Since the confrontation with Saddam Hussein is now almost 15 weeks old, the Saudis have already earned significantly more than they have pledged to the effort.

---

[2] This is based on the following assumptions:

|  | Production (million barrels per day) | X Price (dollars per barrel) | = Income (million $ per day) |
|---|---|---|---|
| First-half 1990 | 5.5 | $16 | $ 88 |
| September 1990 | 7.5 | $32 | $240 |

The increase in income is thus $152 million a day. This is conservative since the October price has been substantially greater than $32 a barrel. But a conservative calculation is warranted given the volatile nature of the oil market.

0072

Money does not grow on trees, but in Saudi Arabia it does spew from derricks. More should be expected of Riyadh.

One of the fundamental issues in this confrontation is the security of Saudi Arabia. The world is helping the Saudis, and generously so. No one expects them to prostrate themselves before the armies that are coming to their rescue. But we have a right to state flatly that Riyadh should not make a profit out of this confrontation.

Ground forces from more than one dozen foreign nations have deployed to Saudi Arabia primarily to prevent an Iraqi invasion or intimidation of that country. Balancing Saudi Arabia's assets and its benefits from the multinational effort on the one hand with its contributions to the effort on the other, give the Saudis a B.

## Egypt

Egypt's response to the Iraqi aggression has also been commendable. Cairo sent 2,000 troops to Saudi Arabia shortly after the invasion and promptly committed a total of 30,000 ground troops -- more than any other country apart from the United States and Saudi Arabia itself. And, it seems clear that Egypt is prepared to maintain those deployments for the long haul -- Cairo is reconstituting units in Egypt to take the place of those sent to Saudi Arabia.

Financially, Egypt is one of the hardest hit by the crisis (along with Turkey and Jordan). In addition to its military expenses, estimates are that it will lose several billion dollars a year in revenues. This includes losses from the now prostrate tourist business, from the decline in Suez Canal revenues due to the embargo, and about $1 billion a year in hard currency remittances from Egyptian workers in Iraq and Kuwait who are being dumped onto the beleaguered Egyptian economy and who now become part of Egypt's pressing social problem rather than part of its solution.

Egypt has been an active political partner as well. It has worked hard diplomatically to secure additional international political, military and financial support for the joint effort. Egyptian President Hosni Mubarak has been firm in condemning Saddam Hussein's aggression as a violation of Arab as well as international law and helping isolate him in the Arab World.

Egypt is shouldering responsibility in this crisis fully commensurate with its capabilities and doing so in a responsive manner. So, give Egypt an A-plus.

## Syria

Syria has performed better than one should have expected. It is deploying about 15,000 troops to Saudi Arabia, including an armored division with more than 300 tanks. Interestingly, this division is being

0073

taken from the Golan Heights, a decision that may have significance beyond this confrontation. About 4,000 arrived in Saudi Arabia within the month after the invasion. The Syrians also called up reservists to replace the deployed forces.

In an unpublicized lapse in its performance, however, Syria has looked the other way while residents of its eastern border communities have continued their traditional trade with Iraqi towns across the border. This was the price paid for domestic peace in those communities.

Syria has not been as active as Saudi Arabia and Egypt in marshaling foreign participation in the effort, but Syrian President Hafez al-Assad has worked with Tehran in an attempt to bolster Iranian resolve in opposing Saddam and resisting Iraqi attempts to buy Iranian support. Of course, Assad is a long-time rival of Saddam's and has his own reasons for joining the multinational effort. Nonetheless, Syrian actions are clearly supportive of the joint effort and are probably just about commensurate with Syrian capabilities. And Syria also has to pay a domestic political and ideological price for its resolve. Damascus has earned a B-plus in this course (though still getting failing marks in other subjects, such as human rights compliance).

## Jordan

Jordan is between a rock and a hard place. The Jordanian economy is being devastated by the crisis, more so than any other country. Prior to the invasion, it was tied inextricably to the economies of Iraq and Kuwait, which bought about a third of Jordan's total exports, including more than two-thirds of its industrial output. The World Bank estimates that Jordan could lose a quarter of its gross national product as a result of the embargo. No other country is being asked to pay this kind of penalty.

In addition to its economic crisis, King Hussein faces serious political pressures stemming primarily from the fact that the majority of his country's population is Palestinian and supportive of Saddam Hussein as a strong Arab leader committed to the future of a Palestinian homeland. These economic and political pressures have resulted in mixed signals from Amman, some providing political succor to Saddam and some supportive of the U.N. Resolutions.

As any reading of the daily media shows, Jordan has not fully complied with the embargo. But given its constraints, Jordan's compliance has been more than satisfactory. Jordan's trade with Iraq is down to a trickle. The main problem for Jordan is that this trickle has regularly appeared on the evening news. The volume of goods crossing the Syrian and Iranian borders may even exceed that crossing the Jordanian border, but those regimes don't let anyone film their border posts.

0074

Hopefully, allied financial assistance and political support will enable Jordan to continue distancing itself from Iraq. Given the domestic political pressures on the king and the economic devastation resulting from enforcement of sanctions, Jordan's performance is excellent. Give Jordan a B-plus.

More than a good grade, however, King Hussein would undoubtedly prefer a little economic help from the Saudis and Gulf Arabs who have spent the last few months treating the king like a kickball and making it harder for him to help them! The goal here should be to encourage Jordan to help. Unfortunately, the Saudi propensity for punishing King Hussein for his initial non-compliance just makes it all the harder for him to be helpful in the future. That's one reason Jordan gets higher marks than the Saudis themselves.

## The rest of the Arab world

Looking at the rest of the Arab world, most countries outside the Gulf region get at best a C. Most have dodged and weaved, trying either to avoid the issue entirely or play both sides of the fence simultaneously.

But three Arab states need to be singled out -- Yemen, Libya and the Sudan, all of which get Fs because all of them are clandestinely trying to help Saddam Hussein evade sanctions. **Yemen** has a special role as the only Arab nation on the Security Council, where it has cast a string of abstentions. Yemen has a divided population, with residents of the capital favoring Iraq and the rest of the country generally anti-Iraqi. This can explain why its public diplomacy has swerved from one position to the other. Privately, however, it has cast its lot with Saddam Hussein. Yemen should not expect that to be forgotten. The **Sudan** could have sat this one out and no one would have complained given the country's political and economic chaos. But Khartoum didn't have the sense to sit it out and has instead exerted itself to help Saddam evade sanctions. As for **Libya**, no one expected much of Moammar Qadhafi -- and we haven't been disappointed.

## The Islamic Republic of Iran

Iran isn't capable of any appreciable military or financial contribution at this time since the revolutionary regime has spent the past decade running the Iranian economy and military into the ground. Yet, both self-interest and historical bitterness toward Saddam dictate that it do its utmost to cut Saddam Hussein down to size. But the revolutionary zealots of the Islamic Republic are still consumed more by their mythical visions of the Great Satan than by rational analysis. Fortunately, the current leadership team of President Ali Akbar Hashemi Rafsanjani and spiritual leader Ali Khamenei provide a veneer of rationalism. Of course, they must periodically nod in the direction of revolutionary myths -- and they are calculating.

The regime is not *grossly* violating sanctions. Oddly, the Bush Administration has made a point of repeatedly defending Tehran against charges of sanctions-busting. It is unlikely that Iran will allow a pipeline to be built across the border so that Iraq can export oil -- its sole source of income with which to pay the many business firms itching to bust sanctions for a profit. A pipeline would be too obvious, now that Tehran knows we are watching. But that does not mean Iran is simon pure. Iranian foodstuffs can be found in Baghdad. And Tehran recently leased 4,000 oil tanker trucks from Turkey!

Iran will look after itself -- and only itself -- in this confrontation. That means it will grab whatever money or other benefit it can from the confrontation. It will be restrained from selling to Iraq only by Iraq's ability to pay and Iran's fears of being caught. Common western wisdom says cooperation will stop when it comes to military supplies. Uncommon Iranian revolutionary wisdom, however, argues that Saddam cannot survive an American offensive -- and that the more American troops he kills on his way to oblivion the better for Iran. So, we shouldn't be surprised if the Islamic Republic of Iran even helps the Iraqi military. Iran gets a D.

## Israel

Israel is unique. The United States just wants it to audit this course or take it by correspondence. Class participation is not desired and is actively discouraged. Israel can best exercise its responsibilities by doing nothing that diverts attention from Iraq and aids Saddam Hussein in his effort to convince Arabs this is an Arab-versus-Israel dispute rather than the World-versus-Saddam.

Israel fully understands its role. We have asked it to be calm and quiet and to stay on the sidelines. It has done so. Unfortunately, Israel has fulfilled its role in a uniquely Israeli manner by frequently standing up on the sidelines, waving furiously at the press box and shouting, "See how quiet I'm being!"

The Temple Mount shooting has not helped either. The Israeli government did not plan that unfortunate incident and has suffered politically from it. But the fact remains that it distracted the United Nations from the Iraqi occupation for the better part of a month and has complicated the effort to manage a focused and unified response to Saddam's ambitions -- ambitions that threaten Israel in the long run.

0076

## Japan

Japan shares Germany's key strength as well as one of its key problems in this crisis, but does not suffer from the same crowded agenda or conflicting financial obligations. Let's begin with the key strength -- Japan's economy. It is the second largest in the world. It is larger than the combined economies of France, Britain and Italy. The core of that economy is a manufacturing sector that imports more than 99 percent of the oil it burns -- about 70 percent from the Persian Gulf.

Japan's defense budget is also sizable, now ranking fifth or sixth in the world. It has built a competent, well-equipped armed force totaling 250,000 personnel -- only about 55,000 fewer than British forces. And, it has a mutual defense treaty with the United States that finds almost 50,000 American troops stationed in Japan and helping protect Japanese security interests.

Yet, with so much capacity and with so much at stake in the Middle East, Japan has sent no forces to the Gulf. It pledged financial contributions well below its capabilities six weeks after the invasion and only after intensive browbeating from the international community, especially from the U.S. Administration and Congress.

Here again, we agree with the Japanese leader, Prime Minister Kaifu, when he told his people that Japan's status as a world economic power leaves it no choice but to take an active role in global politics as well. Unfortunately, the current crisis has not provided the time for that message to take hold in the Japanese government or populace. The international community has had to respond by putting people and money on the line for common security and the Japanese are way below the curve in doing their fair share.

What *has* Japan done? In mid-September, it responded to the pressures of the United States and other allies by pledging $4 billion -- $2 billion in logistical support to the multinational defense effort, and $2 billion to the relief of front-line states. The military logistics support is to come in the form of ships and aircraft transporting troops and supplies, equipment for desert use (for example, 800 4-wheel-drive vehicles) and medical personnel.

The Japanese have had real difficulty delivering even on this type of logistic support. Transfer of the off-road vehicles to the Gulf was delayed, for example, when Japanese shipping unions refused to handle them. The deployment of Japanese medical personnel to the Gulf has been held up because Tokyo has been unable to obtain sufficient volunteers.

We have only a partial fix on the $2 billion in assistance to front-line states. Some $600 million is to come in the form of emergency commodity loans at a 1 percent interest over 30 years. And, two Japanese airlines have provided wide-body jets to fly East Asian refugees from

0077

Jordan to their homelands. This is consistent with the Japanese track record in such matters -- providing loans rather than grants and ensuring that as much of the money as possible is spent in Japan.

Japan has a real and a serious constitutional impediment. The Japanese Constitution was imposed after World War II by the United States. The United States wrote the provisions that declare: "The Japanese people forever renounce war as a sovereign right of the nation;" and bar the threat or use of force as a means of settling international disputes.

Like Chancellor Kohl, Prime Minister Kaifu is committed to an effort to relax the restrictions on the use of Japanese military personnel. But Kaifu has not merely promised action later; he has already moved. He has submitted to a special session of the Japanese Diet a bill to create a "UN Peace Cooperation Corps." There are a lot of problems even with this new proposal. The Peace Cooperation Corps would operate only under UN auspices and would be non-combatant. It may be that in order to serve in this corps, military personnel would have to temporarily resign form the Japanese armed forces and, if deployed to a crisis area, they might even be withdrawn if armed conflict broke out. But even this minimalist proposal has run into a buzzsaw of opposition, underscoring the extreme Japanese fear (shared by many of Japan's neighbors) of any foreign policies that recall pre-war Japan's foreign adventurism. It's irrational. But it's real. And it inhibits what Kaifu can do.

The Japanese clearly have a great deal of homework to do before responsibly joining the post-Cold-War world. While awaiting that homework, the rest of the class has a right to expect Japan to contribute in the one way in which it is not politically inhibited -- financially. Give Japan a C.


## United States

The Bush Administration got off to a fantastic start. It recognized the threat to the world order posed by the Iraqi invasion better than any other government and moved with remarkable speed and agility to organize the world to confront Saddam Hussein.

Briefly, it got out ahead of the rest of the world, prompting the usual complaints about America's "cowboy" mentality and charges of over-reaction. But that has dissipated now. If anything, world public opinion may be ahead of American public opinion today. That is because President Bush has proven to be an inept communicator and has failed to convey to the public why we are in Saudi Arabia. Suggestions that we are deploying a quarter-million troops to shave a dime or two off the price of a gallon of gas have been allowed to fester.

The great start warranted an A-plus. But the Administration's performance has gotten a little ragged as the weeks have dragged on. So, give the United States an A-minus.

0078

## Conclusion

These are not final grades. This report card covers only the first quarter. Unlike most courses, none of us know how long this one will last or how demanding the final quarter will be. But, for now, virtually everyone can and should do more, and we must continue to work closely together to present a powerful, united front so we can resolve this crisis and be far better prepared for the next one.

# # # #

0079

## Table 1

## TABLE OF GROUND FORCE CONTRIBUTIONS TO MULTINATIONAL EFFORT

comprising ground troops located in Saudi Arabia
as of early November or expected reasonably soon

| | | | |
|---|---|---|---|
| U.S. Army | 120,000 | | |
| U.S. Marine Corps | 45,000 | | |
| U.S. subtotal[3] | | 165,000 | 57% |
| | | | |
| Saudi Arabia | 38,000 | | |
| Egypt | 30,000 | | |
| Syria | 15,000 | | |
| Kuwait | 7,000 | | |
| GCC[4] | 7,000 | | |
| Morocco | 1,500 | | |
| Arab subtotal | | 98,500 | 34% |
| | | | |
| United Kingdom | 9,000 | | |
| France | 5,000 | | |
| Europe subtotal | | 14,000 | 5% |
| | | | |
| Pakistan | 5,000 | | |
| Bangladesh | 6,000 | | |
| Senegal | 500 | | |
| Other Moslem subtotal | | 11,500 | 4% |
| | | | |
| GRAND TOTAL | | 289,000 | 100% |

| | | |
|---|---|---|
| Iraqi Army | | |
| in the Kuwaiti Theater | 430,000 | |
| elsewhere | 530,000 | |

[3] These figures include nothing for the added increment the Administration began discussing at the end of October.

[4] The Peninsula Shield force of units from the Gulf Cooperation Council member states not shown above, viz., Oman, the United Arab Emirates, Bahrain, and Qatar.

0080

## Table 2

## TABLE OF NATIONAL CONTRIBUTIONS

covering the nations described in this report

| NATION | MILITARY COMMITMENT | | | FINANCIAL COMMITMENT OR SACRIFICE (in $ millions) | EMBARGO COMPLIANCE | GRADE |
|---|---|---|---|---|---|---|
| | TROOPS TO SAUDI ARABIA | AIRCRAFT TO SAUDI ARABIA | SHIPS TO REGION | | | |
| Egypt | 30,000 | 20 | none | 8,000 - 10,000 (1) | Yes | |
| France | 6,050 (2) | 24 combat; 7 support | 13 | 40 | Yes | B |
| Germany | none | none | none | 2,100 | Yes | C |
| Iran | none | none | none | unknown losses and benefits | No | D |
| Japan | none (100 medical personnel) | none | none | 4,000 | Yes | C |
| Jordan | none | none | none | 1/4 of GNP (3) | Yes (4) | B+ |
| Kuwait | 7,000 | 40 | none | incalculable (5) | Yes | A |
| Libya | none | none | none | none | No | F |
| Saudi Arabia | 65,700 | 180 | 25 | 10,000 | Yes | B |
| Sudan | none | one | none | unknown | No | F |
| Syria | 14-15,000 | none | none | 7 (6) | Yes | B+ |
| Turkey | none | none | none | 4,100 (7) | Yes | A |
| United Kingdom | 10,000 | 30 (8) | 12 | 10 (9) | Yes | B+ |
| USSR | none | none | 2 | 800 (10) | Yes | B |
| Yemen | none | none | none | 2,500 in losses | No | F |
| US | >200,000 | 500 | 60 | ? (11) | Yes | A- |

N.B.    Footnotes will be found on the following page.

0081

Footnotes:

1. Egypt's losses in this estimate do not include costs associated with its military deployments; losses will be somewhat offset by debt forgiveness and direct aid. Gulf countries have forgiven about $8 billion and the U.S. $7.1 billion; Egypt is one of the primary recipients of aid from international financial contributions.

2. France, in addition to ground and air personnel in Saudi Arabia, has 1,550 naval personnel on the 13 ships involved in the region, 400 troops in the UAE, 200 in Qatar and the 4,500 troops permanently stationed across the Red Sea in Djibouti.

3. Jordan's economy is being devastated by the crisis. Pre-crisis, Iraq and Kuwait bought about a 1/3 of its exports including more than 2/3 of its industrial output; was dependent on Iraqi/Kuwaiti oil; World Bank estimates Jordan could lose 1/4 of its GNP as result of the embargo.

4. Initially, Jordan did not comply with the embargo; now, despite domestic political and economic pressures to the contrary, Jordan government enforcement has reduced trade with Iraq to a trickle. Allied assistance will help sustain compliance.

5. Kuwait has lost control of all domestic assets; Iraq is plundering Kuwait, removing much of its wealth, and exporting much of its citizenry (a Kuwaiti official estimates only about 1/4 of pre-invasion Kuwaiti citizens remain in the country; government-in-exile reportedly controls roughly $100 billion in assets and investments worldwide.

6. Syrian government claims it would have received $2 billion from Iraq if it had opened oil pipeline; had about 30,000 workers in Kuwait; costs of military deployments are unknown; but, has received almost $2 billion from Saudi Arabia and other Gulf states for its support; benefits financially from higher oil prices; EC has been considering dropping trade restrictions against it.

7. Estimated losses of $4.1 billion in one year would be from a total economy of about $100 billion; in shutting down the oil pipeline from Iraq, Turkey cut off an important export route for Saddam, along with about 70 percent of Turkey's oil supply. Scheduled to receive substantial international assistance.

8. Britain now has 30 Tornados in Saudi Arabia; 12 Jaguar ground-attack aircraft in Bahrain; maritime patrol aircraft operating out of Oman; several tankers in support.

9. London has pledged $10.3 million to refugee assistance; its contribution to the EC fund is unknown; it estimates a cost of $4 million/day to support its military deployments, along with a $180 million start-up cost.

10. Iraq owes the USSR about $6 billion for past arms sales; was paying in oil that Moscow sold for much needed hard currency; Moscow has suspended arms shipments and all other trade.

11. DoD estimates a cost of $15 billion for FY91 to sustain current deployments, of which as half might be offset by foreign contributions. CBO estimates U.S. FY91 costs at about $7.5 billion, with foreign contributions possibly offsetting those costs in full. U.S. is also forgiving Egypt's $7.1 billion debt and providing foreign aid to several countries in the region.

# Table 3

## TABLE OF NATIONAL CONTRIBUTIONS

covering nations NOT described in this report

| NATION | MILITARY COMMITMENT | | | FINANCIAL COMMITMENT OR SACRIFICE (in $ millions) | EMBARGO COMPLIANCE |
|---|---|---|---|---|---|
| | TROOPS TO SAUDI ARABIA | AIRCRAFT TO SAUDI ARABIA | SHIPS TO REGION | | |
| Argentina | 125-150 (1) | 2 (1) | 2 | none | Yes |
| Australia | none | none | 2 | 1 | Yes |
| Bangladesh | 6,000 | none | none | 3,500 in losses | Yes |
| Belgium | none (2) | none (2) | 4 | unk thru EC (3) | Yes |
| Bulgaria | none (4) | none | none | none | Yes |
| Canada | none | none (5) | 3 | 75 | Yes |
| Czechoslovak | 200 | none | none | none | Yes |
| Denmark | none | none | 1 | unk thru EC | Yes |
| Finland | none | none | none | 1-2 ? | Yes |
| Greece | none | none | none (6) | unk thru EC | Yes |
| Iceland | none (7) | none (7) | none (7) | 2.5 | Yes |
| Italy | none | none (8) | 4 | 150 (8) | Yes |
| Luxembourg | none | none | none | unk thru EC | Yes |
| Morocco | 1,200 | none | none | none | Yes |
| Netherlands | none | offer 18 (9) | 3 | unk thru EC | Yes |
| Norway | none | none | 1 | none | Yes |
| Pakistan | 5,000 (10) | offered (10) | offered (10) | 1,100 in losses | Yes |
| Poland | none | none | offer 2 (11) | none | Yes |
| Portugal | none | none | 1 (12) | unk thru EC | Yes |
| Senegal | 490 | none | none | none | Yes |
| South Korea | none (13) | none | none | 220 | Yes |
| Spain | none | none | 4 | unk thru EC | Yes |
| Sweden | none | none | none | 1-2 ? | Yes |
| Taiwan | none | none | none | 30 | Yes |

0083

Footnotes:

1. Argentina offered to send 125-150 Army personnel, 2 ships, 1 C-130 transport aircraft and 1 Boeing 707; ships are scheduled to arrive in the Gulf region in early November; ground and air assets are on hold pending invitation.

2. Belgium sent several C-130 transport aircraft to the region; at least 2 operated in Jordan ferrying refugees.

3. The EC has pledged $2 billion to the Gulf effort. We do not have information on the individual member contributions to that fund.

4. Bulgaria announce in late September it was prepared to send small military contingent (probably an engineer unit to clear land mines); no information on disposition.

5. Canada sent 18 F-18s and 2 C-130s to a base in Qatar from where they can fly in support of allied operations.

6. Greece did deploy 1 frigate to the Eastern Mediterranean.

7. Iceland has no military forces.

8. Italy sent 8 Tornados to a base in the UAE, from where they can fly in support of allied operations; unclear if Italy's pledge of $150 million is in addition to a contribution thru the EC.

9. The Dutch have offered to deploy 18 F-16s but Turkey declined to base them; continue to seek a base in the region.

10. Pakistan pledged 5,000 troops. Initially were being deployed in the UAE, final disposition unclear.

11. Poland has offered a hospital ship and a cargo ship, preferably for transporting Egyptian and Moroccan forces; no information on actual deployment.

12. Portugal pledged 1 transport ship for Gulf movements, sent 1 frigate to the Mediterranean, and chartered 2 merchant ships to the U.S.

13. South Korea announced intention to send a military hospital unit; no information on actual deployment.

0084

# 외 무 부

종 별 : 지 급

번 호 : USW-5199

일 시 : 90 1120 1813

수 신 : 장관(미북,미안,중근동)

발 신 : 주 미 대사

제 목 : 페만사태-의회 반응

1. 금 11.20 RANALD DELLUMS 하원의원(민주-캘리포니아)을 주동으로 미하원의원 45 명은 의회의 사전승인 없이 미행정부가 이락에 대해 선제무력공격 하지 못하게 하는 소송을 워싱턴 D.C. 연방지방법원에 제기하였음.

2. 상기 소송은 BUSH 대통령의 페만 주둔 미군의 추가 증강발표이후 추진되온 것으로 민주, 공화 양당 지도부는 상기 소송 제기는 페만 사태에 관한 미 정부 입장을 약화시키는것으로 반대 입장을 표명해 왔으며, 미연방법원은 상기 소송과 같이 헌법기관간의 권한 다툼에 대해서는 관례적으로 판결을 유보해 왔는바, 동 소송에 대해서도 관례를 적용할 가능성이 높은 것으로 전망되고 있음.

3. 상기 소송관련 보도자료 및 참가 의원 명단은 별전 FAX 송부함.

(대사 박동진-국장)

예고:90.12.31 까지

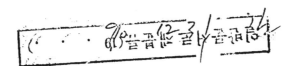

미주국     차관     1차보     미주국     중아국

PAGE 1

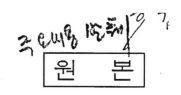

외 무 부

종 별 : 지 급

번 호 : USW-5292    일 시 : 90 1127 1810

수 신 : 장관(미북,미안,중근동)

발 신 : 주 미 대사

제 목 : 폐만사태 관련 청문회

1. 금 11.27 상원 군사위(위원장:SAM NUNN, 민주-조지아)는 JAMES SCHLESINGER 전 국방장관을 출석시킨가운데 US POLICY IN THE PERSIAN GULF 제하의 청문회를 개최하였음. 동청문회는 11.27(화)부터 12.3(월)까지 개최될 예정인바 일련의 폐만사태 청문회중 최초로 개최된것임.

2. 동청문회 NUNN 위원장은 11.8 BUSH 대통령의 병력 증파 발표 이후 폐만사태에 대한 미행정부 정책이 경제제재 및 외교적 해결에서 무력사용을 통한 해결로 돌연히 전환하고 있다고 지적하였으며, JOHN WARNER 간사(공화-버지니아)는 과거 200 년간 미국이 해외에서 무력을 사용한 회수는 215 건이나 이중 5 회에만 미의회에서 전쟁을 선포하였다고 말하면서 해외 무력사용이 반드시 미의회에서의 전쟁 선포를 필요로 하는것이 아니며, 의회에서는 예산권(POWER OF PURSE)을 통해 해외 무력사용을 통제할수 있다고 언급하였음. 다만 의회의 전쟁선포는 미국이 무력사용을 포함한 모든 수단을 동원해서 미국의 이익을 보호하겠다는 의지의 표현으로 볼수있으며, 금번 폐만사태의 해결에 있어 전쟁선포라는 미국의 의지 표현이 필요한지에 대해 각계인사의 견해를 들어 보는것이 필요하다는 요지의 발언을 하였음.

3. SCHLESINGER 전 국방장관은 청문회 증언을 통해 폐만사태는 무력사용보다는 지속적 경제제재를 통한 해결이 바람직하다는 요지의 발언을 하였는바 동요지 하기 보고함.

0 냉전시대 이후 국제정세는 국가 및 민족간의 반목과 경쟁, 종교적 분규로가득한 전통적 권력정치의 장으로 이해해야하며, 이라크의 쿠웨이트 점령 및 이에 대한 각국의 반응등은 이와같은 시각을 입증시켜 주고 있음.

0 미국이 폐만 지역에 대해 갖고 있는 이해는 석유의 전략적 가치, 사우디와의 전통적 우호관계 및 안보공약의 유효한 집행(기타 국가에 대한 미국의 안보공약의

| 미주국 | 장관 | 차관 | 1차보 | 미주국 | 중아국 | 청와대 | 안기부 | 대책반 |
|---|---|---|---|---|---|---|---|---|

유효성까지 포함)및 중동지역 전반의 안정임.

0    페만사태해결    방안으로서의    경제제재는    이락에    대해    경제적으로나
군사적으로(군사적으로는    현재    크게    곤란을    겪고    있지    않으나    장기적으로는
군사장비의부품    부족    등으로    곤경을    초래)타격을    주고    있으며,    미국등    우방국이
경제제재조치를    취함으로써    지불해야되는    댓가 (원유가격    상승등)는    이미    치루었는바,
지속적인    경제    제재    조치가    성공을    거둘것으로    보고    있음.    단,    경제제재    조치가
효력을    발생하기    위해서는    적어도    1    년정도    시간 (향후    6    개월    시간더    소요)이
소요되어야할것으로    보는바,    현단계에서    경제제재조치의    유효성을    판단하기는    시기
상조임.

0 페만사태    해결을    위한    무력사용의    경우에는    군사전략에    따라    상당한    사상자등
추가적    희생을    감수해야하며,    군사전략목표를    어디에    설정해야하느냐    등의    현실적
문제에    직면하게됨.

0 BUSH    행정부의    병력    증파    결정은    HUSSEIN 에    대한    압력을    가중시키기    위한
것이나    한편    무력사용의    가능성도    높이는    것임.

0 경제제재    및    무력사용외에    외교적    방안에    의한    해결    가능성은    거의    없음.    부쉬
행정부는    이락이    쿠웨이트에서    완전    철수하기전에는    이락과    대화를    가질    용의가
없음을    명백히밝히고    있고,    이락과의    대화자체는    미국    정책의    후퇴라는    인식을    주기
때문임.

4. 동청문회 질의응답시 한국과 직접 관련된 사항은 없었으나 대이락 전쟁시
미국의    동맹국이    어느정도의    기여를    할것인가라는    EXON    의원 (민주-네브라스카)
질문에    대해    SCHLESINGER    전    장관은    페만사태의    양상이    유엔의    지지를    받고    있다는
점에    월남전    보다는    한국전    양상에    보다    가깝고,    특히    전쟁    발발시에는
한국전에서와같이    전부력의    대부분을    미국이    담당하고    우방국으로부터는    형식적인
참여를    얻을    것이라는    답변한바    있음.

5. 관찰 및 평가

0    금번    청문회는    당초    CHENEY    국방장관과    POWELL    합참의장을    증인으로
출두시킬예정이었으나    BUSH    대통령이    무력사용에    대한    유엔    결의안을    추진하고
있는기간에    고위    행정부    관리가    청문회에서    증언하는것을    반대함에    따라    전직
각료를대상으로    실시되었음.

0    금번    청문회개최    직전    CHENEY    국방장관및    POWELL    합참의장이    12.3.    청문회에

출석가능하다는 입장을 재 봉보함에 따라 동인들을 대상으로 12.3. 청문회가 예정되었으며, 청문회의 대체적인 분위기는 참석 의원들이 페만사태해결전망 및 무력사용문제에 대한 자신들의 입장 및 우려를 표명하는데 그쳤고, 본격적인 질의 및 문제 제기는 12.3. 청문회시 거론될것으로 전망됨.

6. 동청문회 증언문 및 질의응답 요지는 별전 FAX(USW(F)-3215) 송부함.

(대사박동진-국장)

예고:90.12.31 까지

주 미 대 사 관

번호 : USW(F) - 3215

수신 : 장 관 (미북. 미안. 중근동)

발신 : 주미대사

제목 : 페만사태 청문회 (2매)

금 11. 27. 6천 군사위에서 개최된 페만사태
청문회 증언록 및 코의 증언 요지 늘 별첨 FAX
송부함.  끝.

13매>>

| 배부처 | 장관실 | 차관실 | 일차보 | 이차보 | 기획실 | 외전장 | 아주국 | 미주국 | 구주국 | 중아국 | 국가국 | 정책국 | 통상국 | 정문국 | 영교국 | 총우과 | 감사과 | 공보관 | 의연원 | 청와대 | 총리 5 | 악기부 | 정황 |
|---|---|---|---|---|---|---|---|---|---|---|---|---|---|---|---|---|---|---|---|---|---|---|---|
| 접수 | / | / | / | / | | | ② | | / | | / | | | | | | | | | / | / | / | |

## Notes from Hearing of the
## Senate Armed Services Committee
### on
### U.S. Policy in the Persian Gulf

**Witness:**
The Hon. James Schlesinger, Fmr. Secy. of Defense

**November 27, 1990**

Dr. Schlesinger stated at the outset that the basic reason why the United States must concern itself with the resolution of the Persian Gulf crisis is because of strategic concerns in the region--not because of "jobs," the economic rationale provided by the Bush Administration. He also stressed the importance of this crisis as a test case for U.S. resolve. In other words, the United States has committed itself to certain goals in the Gulf and must stand firm in its pursuit of them or risk looking indecisive.

He outlined three options for U.S. policy:

1. Let the economic embargo run Iraq into the ground. He said that he has heard that domestic production in Iraq has decreased by 40% since the sanctions took effect and that the country's supply of hard currency (necessary for smuggling) is dwindling. Dr. Schlesinger said that he believes that the 1 year timeframe for the sanctions to break Iraq seems reasonable given its results so far.

On this issue he added that contrary to some who argue that "Iraq should not be rewarded for his aggression, but should be punished," the sanctions **are** punishing Iraq--it has suffered a loss of $20 billion of foreign exchange already. He reminded the audience that military punishment is not the only effective way to punish. He also reminded those listening that a.) Saddam Hussein's current position is **not** enviable, b.) He has not been "rewarded" just because he has not yet suffered a military retaliation for his invasion of Kuwait, and c.) U.S. policy has **not** failed merely because there has not yet been a resolution to the crisis.

The price of keeping up with the economic embargo has been to nudge the world in the direction of recession, he said, but not to lead it over the edge as a full-scale war would likely do. He argued that the price of the sanctions has already been paid by the world--a loss of $100-200 billion in economic growth. However, this cost pales in comparison with the cost in growth and blood of a war. In effect, he said, the world can do without Iraqi and Kuwaiti crude oil.

1

325-2

2.   Seek a military solution.   Here Dr. Schlesinger argued that U.S. and allied forces could no doubt cripple Iraq by relying on air strikes and the mobility of their forces. He predicted that such an attack could be successfully concluded in 6-8 weeks. However, he cautioned, the Middle East would never be the same. The prestige of the United States would suffer greatly as it would have fought one Arab state from bases in another. Also, the non-combat costs (rebuilding, etc.) would be great. It is significant to note however, that Dr. Schlesinger added that it is only the threat that force might be used against him that has led Saddam Hussein to show any flexibility.

By eight months into the crisis, most of the cost of the sanctions will have been paid, but the cost of military action will have just begun.  In the near term, he stated, getting Iraq out of Kuwait (as President Bush has vowed to do) rests almost solely on the military option--however, most other members of the international coalition seek the resolution of the crisis through diplomatic means.

3. Seek a diplomatic solution.  This will be nearly impossible for the United States since it has stated that it will accept no communication with Iraq until it leaves Kuwait.  Third parties are willing to take the lead on this, but it could take several months for such a solution to gel.

The senators questioning Dr. Schlesinger were for the most part respectful of and in many cases fully supportive of his view that sanctions are the most cost-effective and prudent option. Some significant points from the questioning follow:

Senators James Exon (D-NE) and Strom Thurmond (R-SC) both argued strongly that some of the coalition members who are most dependent on imported oil, and particularly oil from Iraq and Kuwait, had been stingy in their support for the military presence in the Gulf in both men and money.

The senators who expressed ideas most in agreement with those of Dr. Schlesinger were Carl Levin (D-IL), Edward Kennedy (D-MA), John Glenn (D-OH) and Alan Dixon (D-IL).  For their part, Senators John McCain (R-AZ), William Cohen (R-ME) and Dan Coats (R-IN) expressed some concern that Dr. Schlesinger was too sanguine about the likely impact of sanctions and worried about the vulnerability of the troops in Saudi Arabia if they are forced to stay there for an extended period.

Chairman Sam Nunn (D-GA) asked two quite significant questions to Dr. Schlesinger. First, he wondered if the liberation of Kuwait

2

325-3

0091

is a vital American interest, to which Dr. Schlesinger replied that
Kuwait was not a vital interest when the invasion took place, but
that the Bush Administration has made it one by attaching our
national prestige to its fate. Second, he asked about the timeline
for Iraq's development of nuclear weapons.   Dr. Schlesinger
responded that the threat is there, but down the road five years
or so.  He added that the Bush Administration seems to be playing
on American fears by talking of an Iraqi nuclear weapon as an
immediate danger.

325-4

0092

STATEMENT BY
JAMES R. SCHLESINGER
before the
COMMITTEE ON ARMED SERVICES
UNITED STATES SENATE

November 27, 1990

Mr. Chairman, Members of the Committee:

I deeply appreciate the invitation to discuss with this Committee the challenge posed to American policy and, potentially, to America's armed forces by the developments in the Gulf. When last I addressed this Committee at the beginning of the year, I examined the implications for American policy, attitudes, deployments, and budgetary allocations implied by the collapse of the Warsaw Pact and the decline of the Soviet threat. In a sense today represents the continuation of that earlier testimony, for what we are to examine beyond the details of the Gulf crisis itself, is how this nation should grapple with the altered conditions in this post-Cold War environment.

Mr. Chairman, if you will permit, I shall deal initially with the shape of the post-Cold War world in which the sharp ideological divisions and the coalitions and alliances polarized to reflect those differences have now been muted. Some, stimulated by the response to the crisis in the Gulf, have expressed the hope that we are now engaged in fashioning a new international order -- in which violators of

0093

international norms will be regularly constrained or disciplined through the instrument of collective security. Put very briefly, Mr. Chairman, I believe that such aspirations for a Wilsonian utopia are doomed to disappointment. What is emerging is likely to resemble the somewhat disordered conditions before 1938 -- an era of old-fashioned power politics .-- marked by national and ethnic rivalries and hatreds, religious tensions, as well as smash and grab, and the pursuit of loot. Such elements clearly mark that catalyzing event, Iraq's seizure of Kuwait, and has marked the behavior of a number of players since August 2nd. To suggest that the international order will miraculously be transformed and that the players on the world scene will be motivated by a dedication to justice and international law strikes me as rather naive.

Mr. Chairman, you and Senator Warner have posed the question: what are America's interests in the Gulf. I shall mention three -- and leave it to the Committee to decide whether they are in ascending or descending order of importance.

First, is oil. There is no way of evading this simple reality. Oil provides the energy source that drives the economies of the industrial and underdeveloped worlds. Were the principal exports of the region palm dates, or pearls, or even industrial products, our response to Iraq's transgression

-2-

321-6

0094

would have been far slower and far less massive than has been the case. Nonetheless, this should not be misunderstood. Our concern is not primarily economic -- the price of gasoline at the pump. Were we primarily concerned about the price of oil, we would not have sought to impose an embargo that drove it above $40 a barrel. Instead, our concern is strategic: we cannot allow so large a portion of the world's energy resources to fall under the domination of a single hostile party. Any such party, even Saddam Hussein, would _ordinarily_ be concerned with the stability of the oil market, the better to achieve the long run exploitation of his economic assets. However, concern focuses on the extraordinary periods -- during which he might use his domination of these oil resources to exploit the outside world's vulnerabilities for strategic mischief.

Second, the United States has had an intimate relationship with the Kingdom of Saudi Arabia. It reflects a number of shared strategic objectives -- as well as Saudi efforts to stabilize the oil market, most dramatically in the period after the fall of the Shah. It is embodied in the Carter Doctrine which pledges military resistance to external assaults on the Kingdom, as well as the Reagan corollary which subsequently pledged resistance to internal subversion. Failure of the United States to honor such commitments would raise question about the seriousness of the United States, not only in the Middle East but elsewhere. It is notable that down

-3-

32/5-9

0095

through August 2nd Kuwait itself rebuffed attempts of the United States to provide similar protection -- though President Bush's remarks since that date have tended to establish a U.S. commitment to the security of Kuwait.

Third, since the close of World War II and, particularly, since the establishment of the State of Israel, the United States has had a generalized commitment to the stability of the Middle East and to the security of Israel. On numerous occasions this generalized commitment has led to U.S. diplomatic or military involvement in the region -- not always marked by complete success.

Let me turn now to the alternative strategies available to the United States and its allies. The first, of course, is to allow the weight of the economic sanctions, imposed in August, gradually to wear down the capacity and the will of Iraq to sustain its present position. The embargo, backed up by a naval blockade, is the most successful ever achieved aside from time of war. Early-on it was officially estimated that it would require a year for the embargo to work. It now appears to be working more rapidly than anticipated. In three months time civilian production is estimated to have declined by some 40%. Oil exports are nil -- and export earnings have dropped correspondingly. The hoard of hard currency, necessary to sustain smuggling, is dwindling away. The economic pressure can only grow worse.

-4-

While Iraq's military posture does not appear to have been seriously affected as yet, as the months go by that too will be seriously weakened. Lack of spare parts will force Iraq to begin to cannibalize its military equipment. Military industry, as yet significantly unaffected, will follow the downward path of civilian industry. In short, the burden on both Iraq's economy and her military strength will steadily increase.

We know that such burdens must ultimately affect political judgment and political will. In time, the original objectives of the United Nations will be attained. Already, Saddam Hussein shows a willingness, if not an eagerness, to compromise. One no longer hears that Kuwait is for all eternity the nineteenth province of Iraq. But for some ultimately may not be soon enough, and for others the original objectives may not be sufficient.

To the extent that those original objectives are augmented by demands that Saddam Hussein stand trial as a war criminal, that Iraq provide compensation for the damage it has done, that Iraq's military capacity must be dismantled or destroyed, or that Saddam Hussein must be removed from power, Saddam's determination to hang on will be strengthened. Some may prefer such a response in that it precludes a settlement and makes recourse to military force more likely. Nonetheless,

-5-

321-9

0097

if one avoids this list of additional demands and is satisfied
with the original objectives, the probability that the economic
sanctions will result in a satisfactory outcome is very high.
One should note that, since the original estimate was that the
sanctions route would require a year, it seems rather illogical
to express impatience with them, because they will not have
produced the hoped-for results in six months time.

In this connection one should also note the frequently
expressed view that Saddam Hussein must not be "rewarded" for
his aggression, but instead must be "punished". As an
expression of emotion it is understandable, but it must not be
allowed to obscure our sense of reality. Saddam Hussein is
being punished and punished severely. He has forfeited $20
billion of foreign exchange earnings a year -- indeed $30
billion at the current oil price. Iraq's credit is totally
destroyed, and the remnants of its hard currency reserves
dwindling. When Saddam looks across the border at Saudi
Arabia or the UAE, they are prospering because of his actions
-- from which he himself has derived no benefit. He is likely
to be consumed by envy. His own economy is rapidly becoming a
basket case.

Moreover, the position of preponderance that he had
earlier achieved in OPEC is now gone. He is diplomatically
isolated. His military position will slowly be degraded. His

-6-

3215-10

0098

pawns in Lebanon have been wiped out -- by his chief Baathist rival, Assad, who has immensely strengthened his own position. He has been forced to accept an embarrassing peace with Iran, and that nation's position relative to Iraq is slowly being improved. Sympathetic nations like Jordan and Yemen have been harshly treated -- and neither they nor he have any recourse. On the benefit side stands only the looting of Kuwait.

In brief, Saddam Hussein staked Iraq's position on a roll of the dice -- and lost. Only if he has a deeply masochistic streak can he regard himself as "rewarded". To allow our political rhetoric to obscure the severe punishment that has already been meted out or to suggest that our current policy is in some way unsuccessful and that Saddam's position is now or is potentially enviable strikes me as misconceived.

To be sure, imposition of the sanctions has not been painless. Given the limited spare production capacity for oil and the psychological reaction to the prospect of war, oil prices have shot up. At their peak they had more than doubled. The higher oil price along with the political and economic uncertainties have imposed a heavy burden on most national economies. Many, including our own, had already started or were tipping into recession. For most economies the Gulf crisis has either reenforced or initiated a further contraction.

-7-

325-11

0099

I do not want to understate the cost. (In the case of the American economy it will amount to $100-$200 billion in lost economic growth.) But that price has already been paid. The oil market, reflecting a sizable shrinkage of expected demand as a consequence of higher oil prices and the impact of recession, has now been brought into balance. The world is now able to do without Iraqi and Kuwaiti crude. Thus, to sustain the embargo, no further price must be paid. In effect, we can leave Iraq in isolation until it comes to its senses.

That brings us to the second alternative -- the military option.

There is little question that the United States and its allies can inflict a crippling military defeat on Iraq. It can eject Iraq from Kuwait; it can destroy Iraq's military forces and military industries; it can destroy, if it wishes, Iraq's cities. The question is at what cost -- and whether it is wise to incur that cost. Whenever a nation accepts the hazards of war, the precise outcome is not predetermined. Depending upon the military strategy chosen and the tenacity of Iraq's forces, there could be a considerable variation in the outcome. In the event of an all-out assault on entrenched Iraqi positions, the casualties may be expected to run into several tens of thousands. However, if we avoid that all-out assault, make use

-8-
3245-12

0100

of our decisive advantages in the air, and exploit the
opponent's vulnerabilities by our own mobility, the casualties
could be held to a fraction of the prior estimate. In between
four and eight weeks, it should all be over -- save for
starving out or mopping up the remaining Iraqi forces in
Kuwait. The question then becomes whether one goes on to
occupy Iraq, to destroy the balance of Iraqi forces, and the
like. That would be far more difficult and time consuming, but
circumstances may make it unavoidable.

I think it prudent to say no more about strategy and
tactics in this session. Suffice it to say that the immediate
price will not be small. American forces would be obliged to
carry a disproportionate burden in any struggle. This will
affect the attitudes of our public and the attitudes in the
Middle East regarding the United States.

I believe that the direct cost of combat -- including
that of a probable scorched earth policy in Kuwait -- will be
the lesser part of the total cost. The Middle East would never
be the same. It is a fragile, inflammable, and unpredictable
region. The sight of the United States inflicting a
devastating defeat on an Arab country from the soil of an Arab
neighbor may result in an enmity directed at the United States
for an extended period, not only by Iraq and its present
supporters, but ultimately among the publics of some of the

-9-
ヨ2ノㅏ-/ヨ

0101

nations now allied to us. To be sure, there are no
certainties, yet that risk must be born in mind. Moreover, the
United States will be obliged to involve itself deeply in the
reconstruction of the region in the aftermath of a shattering
war. .In brief, the non-combat costs of a recourse to war,
while not calculable in advance, are likely to be substantial.

On November 8 President Bush announced his decision to
acquire "an offensive military option" and nearly to double
U.S. forces deployed in the Persian Gulf. That announcement
altered the strategic, diplomatic, and psychological
landscape. The deployment of four additional armored divisions
implied that the United States might itself choose to cross
that "line in the sand" and forcibly eject Iraq's troops from
Kuwait. As the President indicated the earlier deployment in
August had been intended "to deter further Iraqi aggression".

One must recognize that to this point Saddam Hussein
has remained unmoved by either appeals or international
declarations. It is only the prospect that force might be used
against him that has brought forth any sign of a willingness to
compromise. The principal goal of the Administration in
deciding on these deployments may simply be to increase the
pressure on Saddam Hussein to withdraw from Kuwait.

-10-

325-1K

0102

Yet, the situation is more complicated. As Mr. Yevgeny Primakov, Mr. Gorbachev's special envoy, has indicated even if Saddam is prepared to withdraw from Kuwait he would require clear evidence that the sanctions would be terminated and that military force would not subsequently be employed against Iraq. In the absence of such commitments his incentive to withdraw is weak.

The new deployment might also point to an intention to resort to the military option. The deployment will peak in late January or early February -- and for technical reasons that deployment would be difficult to sustain. That, no doubt, adds to the pressure on Saddam Hussein, but it also increases the pressure to choose the war option and diminishes the immediate cost of going to war. It should also be pointed out that the time required to complete the additional deployments makes the first option, of relying on the sanctions, less costly. By the time the deployment is completed, military action is initiated, and the fighting ceases at least eight months of what was originally estimated to be the twelve months required for the sanctions to work will have elapsed. Even more of the time and cost involved in making the sanctions work will have thus already been incurred. At that juncture, however, only a modest part of the cost of exercising the military option will have been incurred.

-11-

325-15

0103

It should also be noted that Mr. Primakov's observations were confined to the original objective of forcing an Iraqi withdrawal from Kuwait and the restoration of the legitimate regime. Of late, to those original objectives, some additional goals have been hinted or stated: the elimination of Iraq's capacity to intimidate her neighbors, the removal of Iraq's military capability, the removal of Saddam Hussein from power, and the ending of Iraq's quest for a nuclear capability. The general effect is to paint Iraq as a rogue or outlaw state -- and that its menace to its neighbors and to the international order must be eliminated. To the extent that these additional objectives are embraced, either in appearance or reality, the prospect for a voluntary Iraqi withdrawal from Kuwait is sharply diminished. To achieve these objectives, there is really no alternative but to resort to war. Saddam Hussein's inclination to dig in will be stiffened -- and in all likelihood the willingness of Iraqi forces to resist will be strengthened.

Consideration of the military option will be influenced by attitudes within the international coalition that the United States has organized. By and large that coalition has revealed strong ambivalence regarding the military option and a preference for a diplomatic solution -- with those least directly involved most dubious about the military option. While the members of that coalition may be prepared to accept

-12

321-16

0104

military force to drive Iraq out of Kuwait, to this point they
have shown little inclination to embrace the sterner objectives
of policy that have been stated but never officially presented
or embraced.

    There is, of course, a third strategic alternative: the
possibility of a diplomatic solution.  Though it remains an
eventual possibility, I shall spend little time on it in this
hearing for two reasons.  First, the United States is probably
precluded from any negotiations with Iraq by the position that
it initially announced:  we will not have any direct
communication with Iraq until it has left Kuwait.  For the
United States itself to enter into negotiations would represent
too much of a diplomatic retreat.  To be sure, others have been
willing to serve the role of diplomatic intermediaries.  Since
August the possibility of an "Arab solution" has been raised on
several occasions.  The Soviets, the French, and others have
conducted explorations.  But, as the probability of recourse to
war rises, the probability of a diplomatic settlement, of
necessity shrinks.  That brings me to my second reason for
limiting discussion of this alternative: if there is to be a
diplomatic solution, it will be several months before the
outlines jell.  The United States, given its position, will be
obliged to appear merely to acquiesce in such an outcome -- out
of deference to pressures from other elements of the
international community.

-13
32/5-17

0105

There is something more, however, to be said about the diplomatic situation. In your letter of inquiry, Mr. Chairman, you and Senator Warner inquired about the durability of allied support for the multinational coalition. In regard to the original demands on Iraq and the use of sanctions, that support has been firmer than we might have anticipated. Saddam's appeal to the "hearts and minds" in the Arab countries seems to have peaked in September. There has been little restlessness elsewhere in the coalition -- no doubt, in large degree, due to the fact that the world can do without Iraqi and Kuwaiti crude. Moreover, the status quo includes authorization for the naval blockade, which can therefore be continued indefinitely. It would take a positive act of the United Nations to remove that authorization.

However, that coalition is likely to prove less durable, if combat takes place. Particularly would this be the case if the objectives turn out to be the new and sterner demands of war policy, reflecting the decision that Iraq has become an outlaw state that must be dealt with now. Needless to say, the international coalition has yet to embrace that line of reasoning.

Therefore, Mr. Chairman, I close with observations regarding two inherent difficulties in the emerging situation.

-14-

0106

First, if the United States conveys the impression that it has moved beyond the original international objectives to the sterner objectives that Saddam Hussein must go, that Iraq's military establishment and the threat to the region must be dismantled or eliminated, etc., then whatever incentive Saddam Hussein may presently have to acquiesce in the international community's present demands and to leave Kuwait will shrink toward zero. This may please those who have decided that the war option is the preferable one, but it makes it increasingly hard to hold together the international coalition, which we initially put together to bless our actions in the Gulf. That brings us to the second observation: the more we rely on the image of Iraq as an outlaw state to justify taking military action, the more we make holding together the international coalition inherently difficult, if not impossible. International approval of our actions is something on which the Administration has set great store. It has provided the desired legitimacy. To abandon it would mean the undermining of any claim to establishing a new international order.

Mr. Chairman, if you will allow me one final word that goes beyond the crisis in the Gulf. That crisis has preoccupied our attention for more than three months and is likely to do so for many months more. It has diverted our attention from subjects that may be of equal or even greater importance. Six months ago all of us were deeply moved by the

-15-

325-19

0107

developments in Eastern Europe and in the Soviet Union -- and with the prospect that those nations might move toward democracy and economic reform. Members of this Committee will recall our high hopes at that time. Yet, in the intervening period, with the diverting of our attention to the Gulf, those prospects have been dealt a grievous blow. First was the Soviet decision to force the former satellites to pay hard currency for their oil. Second, it was followed by the Gulf crisis that has sharply raised the international price of oil. The prospects and hopes for Eastern Europe, while our attention has been diverted, have been seriously damaged. Yet, to return to my original theme, in the shaping of the post-Cold War world it is not clear that the evolution of Eastern Europe and the Soviet Union may not be more important than developments in the Gulf.

# # #

-16-

0108

외 무 부

종  별 : 지 급

번  호 : USW-5315    일  시 : 90 1128 1925

수  신 : 장관(미북,미안,중근동)

발  신 : 주 미 대사

제  목 : 페만사태 관련 청문회

연:USW-5292

1. 상원 군사위는 연호 청문회에 이어 금 11.28 오전에는 DAVID JONES 및 WILLIAM CROWE 전 합참의장, 오후에는 HENRY KISSINGER 전 국무장관을 출석시킨 가운데 페만 사태에 관한 청문회를 개최하였음.

2. 금일 청문회는 작일 청문회 에서와같이 페만 사태의 해결 방안으로서의 무력사용 문제등에 관해 증언자들은 자신들의 개인 의견을 발표하였는바 동요지 하기 보고함.

(JONES 전 합참의장)

0 8.2. 이라크의 쿠웨이트 점령 이후 미 행정부가 취한 조치는 신속하고 적절한 대응이었음.

0 페만 사태의 해결을 위해서는 국제적 협력 및 미국내적 지지가 불가결한 요소이며, 국제적 협력을 확보하기 위해서는 보상, 후세인에 대한 재판 및 원자력, 화학무기 생산시설 철폐등으로 까지 페만사태 정책 목표를 확대 시키지 않는것이 바람직함.

0 최근 의 병력증강 조치는 이락에 대한 미국의 확고한 의지 표시로 볼수 있으나, 병력증강 자체가 성급한 무력사용을 유발시킬 위험성이 있음을 인식해야함.

(CROWE 전 합참의장)

0 대이락 경제제재 조치는 효력을 거두고 있으며, 확실한 성과는 1 년 내지1 년반의 기간을 소요할 것으로 보여짐. 중요한 점은 대이락 경제제재 조치가 효력을 거두고 있느냐 여부 보다는 제재 조치가 효력을 거둘때 까지 인내를 갖고제재 조치를 지속적으로 취할수 있느냐 하는것임.

0 중동지역에 대한 미국의 이해는 장기적 지역 안정을 유지하느냐 하는 점이며

| 미주국 대책반 | 장관 | 차관 | 1차보 | 2차보 | 미주국 | 중아국 | 정와대 | 안기부 |
|---|---|---|---|---|---|---|---|---|

PAGE 1

중동지역은 아랍- 이스라엘 분규, 팔레스타인 난민및 기타 국가간의 반목등으로 매우 복잡한 지역으로서 이러한 지역에서 미국이 군사적 행동을 취할경우, 중동지역의 안정을 해치고 분열을 더욱 초래할 가능성이 있음.

0 금번 페만 사태는 평화적 방법으로 해결을 모색해야 하며, 평화적 해결 가능성이 없다고 판단될때 비로서 군사적 해결 방안을 강구해야 할것임.

(KISSINGER 전 국무장관)

0 페만사태 관련, BUSH 행정부가 발표한 목표에 이라크의 군사공격 능력 (OFFENSIVE CAPABILITY)의 축소 (주변 국가의 공격 능력과 균형이 되는 수준까지)가요구됨. 이라크의 공격 능력이 감소되지 않는한, 페만 지역의 안정은 기대할수없음.

0 이락의 쿠웨이트 침공 직후 미국의 군사적 대응은 해군력을 중심으로 하고 상징적 억지력 으로서의 소규모 지상병력 배치가 바람직 하였으나 BUSH 행정부는 대규모 지상병력을 투입하였으며, 이는 오히려 지역 안정을 해치는 결과를 초래하였음.

0 경제봉쇄 조치와 군사적 해결을 연속적인 정책의 일환으로 제시한것은 현실적인 방안이 아니며, 봉쇄 조치가 효력을 거두지 못하고 있다는것이 확실해지는 시점에서는 효과적인 군사행동을 취할수 있는 여건이 형성되어 있지 않을 것임.

0 경제봉쇄 조치가 효과적일경우, 이라크는 항복 보다는 협상을 제시할것이고 협상문제가 거론되는 시점에서 제재 조치를 계속 취하기는 어려우며, 특히 이락의 공격능력이 감소되지 않는 상황에서는 주변국가는 이락과 개별적인 해결 방안을 추구할 가능성이 높음.

0 군사적 행동이 불가피할경우, 미국은 이락의 섬멸보다는 원자력, 화학무기 및 미사일 공격능력 제거를 목표로 해야함. 이경우에는 금번 페만사태 해결이후 페만 지역이 군사적 균형을 이룰수 있으며 또한 현재 취하고 있는 제재 조치의 성과를 촉진시키는 것임.

3. 동 청문회 질의 응답시 작일 청문회에서 처럼 부시 행정부의 병력증강 조치에 대한 우려 표명과 경제제재 조치가 효과를 거두고 있으므로 , 조급한 무력사용 조치를 경고하는 내용이 주된 논조였음. 다만 키신저 전 국무장관은 경제제재 조치를 통해 페만사태 정책목표를 달성할것으로 보지는 않으며 부시 행정부가 대규모의 지상병력을 투입한 현재 무력사용을 통한 해결방안 밖에는 현실적해결 방안이 없을 것이라는

내용의 발언을 한데 대해 KENNEDY 상원의원을 비롯한 민주계 의원들은 반박 의견을 표명하였음.

4. 상기 키신저 전 국무장관의 증언문 및 주요 질의응답 부분은 별전 FAX USW(F)-3239 송부함

(대사 박동진-국장)

예고:90.12.31 까지

주 미 대 사 관

번호 : USW(F) - 3239

수신 : 장 관 (미북, 미안, 중근동)

발신 : 주미대사

제목 : 페만 사태 청문회 (1000)

금 11. 28 상원 군사위 쿡관 페만사태 청문회

관계 자료를 별첨 FAX 송부함.

As Prepared for Delivery

STATEMENT OF

THE HONORABLE HENRY A. KISSINGER

BEFORE THE

SENATE ARMED SERVICES COMMITTEE

WEDNESDAY, NOVEMBER 28, 1990

1:00 PM

3239-2

0113

Mr. Chairman:

It is a pleasure to have an opportunity to speak to you today. To save time I would like to submit for the record the following adaptation of articles published in The Washington Post on August 19th, September 30th and November 11th as a basis for discussion.


## Objectives

American objectives have included fulfillment of stated UN goals of restoration of the status quo ante in Kuwait as well as the unconditional release of all hostages. But to contribute to President Bush's objective of stability in the Gulf, any solution to the crisis must also provide for a reduction of Iraq's offensive capability which now overshadows its neighbors. Without addressing this fundamental imbalance, a solution will

3239-3

0114

only postpone, and probably exacerbate, an eventual resolution of Gulf instability.

Were Saddam suddenly to accept the UN terms, he would in fact preserve the essence of his power, although it would represent a huge loss of prestige for him. Iraq would still retain its chemical and nuclear capabilities. Its large standing army would still preserve the capacity to overwhelm the area. Many nations in the Middle East might adjust to the perception that the mobilization of forces from all over the world cannot be repeated every few years.

Reducing Iraq's military potential is especially important if US forces are to be substantially withdrawn from the Gulf as I believe they should be. At the same time, it would be undesirable to reduce Iraq's armed forces below what is needed for equilibrium with its neighbors, especially in light of their past records, which attest to a low threshold of resistance to the temptations of a military vacuum.

3239-4

0115

## Early Choices

/    The United States had three choices in dealing with the
crisis of the Iraqi invasion of Kuwait:  it could passively
endorse whatever consensus emerged in the United Nations; it
could support whatever the industrial democracies--all of which
are more dependent on Mideast oil than the United States is--
were prepared to do in concert; or it could take the lead in
opposing Saddam Hussein and try to organize international support
for an effort in which the United States would bear the principal
burden.

     The Administration concluded that anything other than a
leadership role for the United States would have ended with
making Iraqi domination of Kuwait permanent and would lead to the
collapse of the moderate governments in the region including
Egypt.  Having committed the United States to a leadership role,
President Bush made another crucial decision.  The American
military role could have been confined to interdiction at sea and

2239-5

0116

a token force on the ground to make clear that an attack on Saudi
oil fields would lead to war with the United States. President
Bush and his advisers opted for a massive deployment. They
concluded that once they committed military forces, the best hope
of ending the crisis quickly was to assemble an overwhelming
force to overawe such a threat and to be able to go further if
necessary.

In short, early in America's involvement there was some
argument as to whether American vital interests justified a
massive deployment in the Gulf. That debate has since been
overtaken by the scale of our deployment and the number of
countries that have followed America's leadership in the Gulf.

The perception of American failure would shake international
stability. Every moderate country in the Middle East would be
gravely weakened by a debacle. Several Gulf states could not
survive it. Egypt, Morocco and even Turkey would face a tide of
radicalism and fundamentalism.

3239-6

0117

## Sanctions or Military Action?

The United States is approaching the point in the Middle East crisis where a choice must be made between a course relying on sanctions or, as a last resort, on a military course.

The two approaches have been presented as if they were successive phases of the same policy. In fact, they will prove mutually exclusive because by the time it is evident that sanctions alone cannot succeed, a credible military option will probably no longer exist.

To achieve the proclaimed objectives by sanctions, at least five hurdles must be overcome:

* The sanctions must bite.

* They must be maintained throughout any negotiations.

* Once the UN terms are achieved, arms control objectives must be addressed.

* The military option must remain intact psychologically, technically and diplomatically during the entire course of the negotiations.

3239-9

0118

● There must be no other upheavals to deflect the United

States or to rend allied cohesion.

/   To state these hurdles is to set forth the practical

obstacles to clearing them.

For one thing, upheavals in the Middle East are a way of

life.  In one recent week, the second highest ranking official in

Egypt was assassinated, Syria battled Christian forces in Beirut,

and 21 Palestinians died in Jerusalem.

If the sanctions do bite within a time frame relevant to

political processes, Iraq is more likely to offer to negotiate

than to yield.

In that case, pressures to ease the sanctions will be

difficult to resist.  Which democracy will want to be responsible

for starvation in Iraq and Kuwait once negotiations are under

way?

The fundamental dilemma is that the UN terms leave no real

room for negotiation--except perhaps the staging of the Iraqi

withdrawal.  Thus all so-called diplomatic solutions effectively

3239-8

0119

7

dilute the UN objectives while maintaining Iraq's war-making
potential and thus confirming Iraq as the supreme military power
of the Middle East.

For example, even if Saddam accepts the principle of
withdrawal from Kuwait, he has already hinted--and Soviet
presidential aide Yevgeny M. Primakov has confirmed--that he
would define Kuwait as excluding a strip of land containing a
major oil field as well as two islands controlling access to the
Shatt el-Arab.  And President Mitterrand has stated that only
agreement in principle to withdrawal is needed to bring about a
negotiation.

Saddam's Arab neighbors will surely note that none of the
proposals in the public discussion would reduce Iraq's military
pre-eminence of restore Kuwait completely.

If they conclude that they will be condemned to live with a
dominant Iraq, they will begin their own negotiations.  Recent

3239-9

0120

NOV.28 '90 19:37 KOREAN | SSY WASHINGTON DC                    P.013

8

remarks by Saudi Defense Minister Sultan suggest that the
haggling may already have begun.

But will the psychological basis for a military option still
exist after months of such inconclusive maneuvering? And without
a realistic military threat, how can the US/UN objectives be
achieved?

And having faced down the combined might of UN forces and of
the United States, Iraq would have little incentive to make
concessions to the fears of its neighbors in any subsequent arms
control negotiation.

## A Regional Security System?

Many who opt for sanctions-induced negotiations recognize
that sanctions will not be able to achieve a balance of power in
the Gulf. They propose to protect a settlement by a new regional
security system based on a significant American military presence
in Saudi Arabia.

3239-10

0121

걸프사태 : 미국 의회 동향, 1990-91. 전5권 (V.2 1990.10-12월)  297

I consider this a dangerous mirage.  If, after the adamant
pronouncements from Washington and the deployment of a large
expeditionary force, a regional balance of power could not be
reached, no Gulf state would easily entrust its fate to a long-
term American presence.

The often-heard argument that America proved its staying
power in Korea and Europe misses the point.  The issue in Arabia
is not American staying power but the host country's domestic
stability.

Conditions in the Gulf are not even remotely comparable to
Europe or Northeast Asia.  There, American forces contributed to
domestic stability; in Saudi Arabia they would threaten it.

A substantial American ground establishment would soon
become the target of radical and nationalist agitation.  Once
Iraq has faced down US and UN terms, such a force would sooner or
later become hostage to revolutionary Iraq, fundamentalist Iran
and events substantially out of our control.

3239-11

0122

Nor can the restoration of the military balance in the Gulf be left to subsequent arms control negotiations.  For having faced down the combined might of UN forces and of the United States, Iraq would have little incentive to make concessions to the fears of its neighbors in any subsequent arms control negotiation.

In short, the route of sanctions and the military option can be pursued up to a certain point simultaneously.  At some point, however, trying to pursue both courses will turn into an evasion incompatible with reaching what should be our objectives.  At that point the US must choose a strategy appropriate to its objectives or else choose objectives achievable by whatever policy we are willing to implement.


## What Military Strategy?

If war proved unavoidable it is to be hoped that military strategy remains related to realistic political objectives.

3239-12

Outsiders should not play field marshal.  But America has no national interest in weakening Iraq to a point where it becomes a tempting target for covetous neighbors.

If war does prove unavoidable, our objective should be not to destroy Iraq, but rather to raise the cost of occupying Kuwait to unacceptable levels while reducing Iraq's capacity to threaten its neighbors.

The destruction of the Iraqi military complex, especially its chemical and nuclear facilities as well as its air and missile forces, would improve the military balance in the Gulf and would speed up the effect of sanctions.

Such a strategy would rely on air and naval power and use ground forces primarily to overawe a response.  As the government of Iraq, which is after all a military dictatorship, sees its principal source of power erode, a negotiation more compatible with stated US objectives could result.

3239 -13

Even if one of the compromises sketched above came
eventually to be adopted—a contingency I would regret—the
setback would be eased by the reduction in the Iraqi military
threat.  I am extremely skeptical about a full-scale ground
assault.


Conclusion

In the process of overcoming the current crisis, the United
States must not emerge as the permanent defender of every status
quo.  But the path to peace and progress resides in success in
the Gulf.

Afterwards the United States, together with its Arab
partners, can demonstrate the benefits of cooperative action in
promoting the well-being of the Arab peoples.

Too, the United States should then seek energetically to
make progress toward a settlement of the Arab-Israeli conflict,
especially now that looming disaster might have brought all sides

3239-14

0125

second thoughts about both the nature of a peace and suitable
participants in peace negotiations.  But such a move cannot be
limited to the resolution of the current crisis for to do so
would turn Saddam into a hero in the Arab world.

It is to be hoped that a united America can find a way that
avoids both a military strategy of total destructiveness and a
diplomatic strategy committed to amassing UN resolutions—the
progressive disregard of which will at some point demonstrate the
UN's impotence rather than an international consensus.

But whatever our destination, we must arrive at it by design
rather than as captives of circumstances.

3239-15

0126

Notes From Hearing Of
Senate Armed Services Committee
On
U.S. Policy Toward the Persian Gulf

Witnesses:
Adm. William Crowe, Fmr. Chairman, Joint Chiefs of Staff
Gen. David Jones, Fmr. Chairman, Joint Chiefs of Staff
and
Dr. Henry Kissinger, Fmr. Secy. of State

November 28, 1990

In the morning session of this hearing, the two former Chairmen of the Joint Chiefs of Staff expressed quite similar opinions about the direction that the United States should take in the coming months to achieve the most advantageous resolution to the Persian Gulf crisis.

Both supported President Bush's immediate response to Iraq's invasion of Kuwait (i.e. the quest for an international coalition to help oust Iraq from Kuwait, the quest for United Nations resolutions condemning Saddam Hussein, and the immediate deployment of U.S. troops to prevent further Iraqi adventurism.) However, both also expressed the belief that progress should be sought first and foremost in this region through non-military means. Both acknowledged the usefulness of sanctions (as did Dr. James Schlesinger in his testimony before the committee yesterday) but the two former chairmen believe that there is a significant chance that sanctions alone might not succeed in achieving all the United States' stated objectives. In this case, the United States must be prepared to employ its military might in a way that will succeed in fulfilling our mission with a minimum of casualties and expense.

Additionally, the concern was expressed by both gentlemen that the November 8 declaration that the United States would double its current troop levels in the Persian Gulf could lead unintentionally to war. Gen. Jones expressed the worry that the buildup would be seen as an offensive action that would cause an escalation of tensions that could lead to fighting perhaps prematurely and unnecessarily. Gen. Jones further questioned the wisdom of the recent call for a troop buildup in that the support, training, morale, cultural, and readiness problems would increase greatly with such a huge deployment.

The questions of the senators largely focused on the sustainability of 400,000+ troops in the harsh desert conditions, the resolve of the American people and the international coalition to tolerate a protracted waiting period while sanctions take their "bite," the burdensharing issue, and the significance of the Iraqi nuclear capability. As yesterday, the senators split largely along party lines when commenting on the testimony of the two chairmen. Senators Carl Levin (D-IL), James Exon (D-NE), Edward Kennedy (D-MA), Robert Byrd (D-WV), Timothy Wirth (D-CO), Alan Dixon (D-IL)

3239-16

0127

John Glenn (D-OH) and Al Gore (D-TN) were the strongest supporters.

Senators Dan Coats (R-IN) and John McCain (R-AZ) voiced strong concerns with the hesitation of the chairmen to support the added deployment and the "military option." Senator McCain said that in order for all options to be available to the President, he must have the capability to launch an offensive if he deems it necessary. The additional troops will serve that purpose. For his part, Senator Coats expressed concern that the sanctions alone will not do the job of breaking down Saddam Hussein and liberating Kuwait. He seemed to suggest that people would tire of waiting for sanctions to crush Saddam Hussein and that therefore, an alternative must be relied upon--i.e. military power.

In his testimony, Dr. Kissinger outlined a somewhat more complicated and gloomy picture. He placed little stock in the ability of sanctions alone to get Saddam Hussein to give up Kuwait. He suggested that, contrary to many others, using sanctions to wear down Iraq for a while and then moving into a military offensive should the sanctions fail is not a policy based on reality. He believes that sanctions and military action are mutually exclusive options. He argued that by the time it is discovered that sanctions will not work, the military option will no longer be credible because there will be no clear point at which the sanctions will be effective. If Iraq starts crumbling internally, Saddam Hussein will not give Kuwait back, but will likely seek to negotiate. At this point, other nations in the region will start realizing that the United States will not destroy the warmaking capability of Iraq (even though it will be hampered by the sanctions) and will try to make bilateral agreements with Saddam Hussein. This will erode the international coalition.

Interestingly, Kissinger said that his ideal plan at the outset would have been to strike at Iraq's military targets with airpower immediately and place a small number of ground troops into Saudi Arabia to act as a deterrent. He seemed to be unconvinced of the wisdom of the President's policy of doubling the number of troops in the Gulf (which he sees as vulnerable and inefficient in battle) but he argued that since the Administration had committed itself to the deployment, it should be carried out because any perception of indecision would be damaging to U.S. credibility.

Senators Jeff Bingaman (D-NM), Edward Kennedy (D-MA) and Alan Dixon (D-IL) were most vociferous in their concerns about Dr. Kissinger's view that sanctions alone will not achieve U.S. objectives. Senator Kennedy worried that Dr. Kissinger's position was that war was the only option, Senator Bingaman worried that, credibility aside, the United States would be limiting its options if it continued with the enormous augmentation of its forces in Iraq. Senator Dixon expressed the view that with all the military and political power the United States has arrayed in the Persian Gulf, it should be willing to conduct successful negotiations.

3239-17

0128

# 報 告 事 項

報 告 畢

1990.11.29
美 洲 局
北 美 課(48)

題 目 : 페灣 事態 關聯 美 議會 聽聞會(1)

---

최근 부쉬 행정부의 대규모 병력 증파 결정을 둘러싸고 페만 사태 해결을 위한 무력 사용시 사전 의회 승인 여부에 대한 미 행정부와 의회간 의견 대립과 관련, 미 상원 군사위(위원장 : Sam Nunn, 民, GA)는 11.27(화)-12.3(월)간 '페르시아만에서의 미국 정책' 제하 청문회를 개최 중인 바, 동 청문회 참석 증언자들의 주요 언급내용 등 관련사항 아래 보고 드립니다.

---

1. 개 요

º 상원 군사위 청문회 증언자

   - 11.27(화) Schlesinger 전 국방장관

   - 11.28(수) Jones 및 Crowe 전 합참의장, Kissinger 전 국무장관

   - 12.3(월) Cheney 국방장관, Powell 합참의장 증언 예정

º 청문회 참석 의원들은 각자의 페만사태 해결 전망 및 무력사용 문제에 대한 우려를 표명함.

   - 질의 응답시 최근의 병력 증강 조치에 대한 우려 표명과 조급한 무력 사용을 경고하는 내용이 주 논조

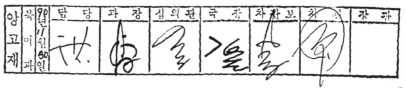

0129

## 2. 증언자 주요발언 내용

### 가. Kissinger 전 국무장관

ο 사태 해결후 주변지역 안정을 위해 이라크의 군사공격 능력 축소도
  미 전략목표에 포함되어야 함.
  - 주변국의 군사공격 능력과 균형유지 필요

ο 미국의 최초 군사적 대응은 해군력을 중심으로한 소규모 지상병력
  파견이 바람직 하였음.
  - 대규모 지상병력 배치는 페만 주변지역 안정을 해치는 결과 초래

ο 경제봉쇄 조치와 군사적 해결을 연속적인 정책의 일환으로 제시한 것은
  비현실적 방안이었음.
  - 경제봉쇄 조치 실패 인식 시점과 군사행동의 최적 시점은 불일치

ο 경제제재 조치가 효과적일 경우에는 이라크측은 항복보다는 협상을
  제안할 것임.
  - 협상 개시이후 미측의 제재조치 계속은 어려울 것이며, 주변국도
    이라크와 개별적 해결방안 모색 예상

ο 군사적 행동이 불가피한 경우에도 이라크의 섬멸은 바람직스럽지 못함.
  - 사태 해결이후 페만 주변지역 군사적 균형 고려
  - 원자력, 화학무기 및 미사일 공격능력 등만을 제거

ο 대규모 지상병력을 투입한 현 상황하에서는 무력사용을 통한 해결
  방안만이 현실적임.
  - 경제제재 조치만으로는 미 정책 목표 달성 불가능
  - Kennedy 의원등이 동 무력 사용 해결 의견에는 반대의사 표명

0130

나. Schlesinger 전 국방장관

　○ 냉전시대 이후 국제사회는 국가 및 민족간의 반목과 경쟁, 종교적
　　분규가 가득한 전통적 Power Politics의 장으로 이해해야 함.

　○ 페만 지역에 대한 미국의 이해로는 전략적 가치의 원유 공급선 확보,
　　사우디와의 전통적 우호관계 및 안보공약 유지 및 중동지역 전반의
　　안정임.

　○ 무력 사용보다는 대이라크 경제제재 조치의 지속적 시행을 통한 사태
　　해결이 바람직함.
　　- 경제제재 조치의 효력 발생에는 향후 6개월 소요 예상
　　- 무력사용시, 추가적 희생 감수 및 군사전략 목표 설정에 난관 직면

　○ 최근의 병력증파 결정은 후세인에 대한 압력 요소로도 작용하나 한편
　　무력사용 가능성도 높이는 조치임.

　○ 페만사태 양상은 UN의 지지를 받고 있다는 점에서 월남전보다는 한국전
　　양상에 가까움
　　- 무력사용시 한국전에서와 같이 전투력의 대부분을 미국이 담당 예상

다. Jones 전 합참의장

　○ 페만사태 해결을 위해서는 국제적 협력 및 미국내 지지가 불가결한
　　요소임.
　　- 국제적 협력 확보를 위해서는 페만사태 정책목표의 확대에 반대
　　- 최근 병력증강 조치는 무력사용 유발 가능성을 제고

0131

라. Crowe 전 합참의장

  ○ 대이라크 경제제재 조치는 효력 발생중이며, 확실한 성과는 향후 6개월
    내지 1년의 기간이 더 필요함.
    - 인내심을 가진 지속적인 추진 여부가 관건

  ○ 1차적으로 평화적 해결방법을 모색한 연후 군사적 해결방안을 강구해야
    함.
    - 군사적 행동시 중동지역 안정을 해치고 분열 초래 가능성 지적.  끝.

0132

# 외 무 부

종 별 :

번 호 : USW-5338                              일 시 : 90 1129 1848

수 신 : 장 관 (미북,미안,중근동)

발 신 : 주 미 대사

제 목 : 페만사태 관련 미 의회 특별회기 소집(언론보도)

1. BUSH 대통령은 12월초중 의회의 특별회기를 소집, 의회측으로 하여금 이락에무력사용을 허가하는 UN 안보리 결의안과 동일한 결의안을 채택토록 요청할 것으로 보도되었음.

2. 동 특별회기 소집방안은 당초 공화당 지도부측에서 제시되었으나 BUSH 대통령및 민주당 지도부 호응을 받지 못 하였음. 그러나 무력사용에 대한 UN 안보리 결의안이 봉과될 것이 확실시되고 이락에 대한 무력사용 가능성이 높아지고 있는 시점에서백악관측은 대 이락 무력사용 이전에 행정부의 페만정책에 대한 국내 정치적 입지를확고히 하고, 특히 민주당측으로 하여금 페만정책에 대한 책임의 일부를 담당케 하려는 정치적 고려에서 특별회기 소집을 고려하고 있는 것으로 알려지고 있음.

3. 민주당 지도부는 상기 특별회기 소집에 대해 상금 특별한 반응은 보이고 있지는 않으나, 민주당 지도부는 성급한 무력사용을 우려하고 있고 경제 제재조치가 성공을 거둘수 있도록 충분한 기간을 주어야 한다는 입장을 표명하고 있는바, 상기 특별회기가 개최되면, 오히려 BUSH 대통령의 의도와는 반대로 행정부의 정책을 견제하는 결과가 나올 가능성도 없지 않은 것으로 보여짐.

(대사 박동진- 국장)

---

| 미주국 | 1차보 | 미주국 | 중아국 | 통상국 | 정문국 | 안기부 | | 대책반 |
|--------|-------|--------|--------|--------|--------|--------|--|--------|

PAGE 1                                        90.11.30    10:08 FC

외신 1과 통제관

0133

외 무 부

종 별 :

번 호 : USW-5339

일 시 : 90 1129 1843

수 신 : 장관( 미북,미안, 중근동)

발 신 : 주 미 대사

제 목 : 페만사태 관련 청문회

연 USW-5315,5292

1. 금 11.29. 오전 상원 군사위는 JAMES WEBB 전 해군장관, EDWARD LUTTWAKCSIS 연구원 및 RICHARD PERLE 전 국방부 차관보를 출석시킨 가운데 페만 사태에 관한 청문회를 개최 하였음.

2. 금일 청문회는 연호 청문회와 같이 페만사태 해결방안, 경제제재 조치의성과, 무력사용 문제 및 최근의 미군 병력 증강 발표에 관한 소견을 발표 하였는바, 동 요지 하기 보고함.

(WEBB 전 해군 장관)

0 현재의 미군 총병력 수준 및 미군의 해외주둔 병력 수준을 고려하면, 사우디 주둔 미군 수준은 과도하고 장기적으로 현수준의 병력을 유지 하기 곤란하며, 과다한 병력 주둔은 결국 전쟁으로 치달을 위험이 있음.

0 만약 BUSH 대통령이 무력사용을 결정한다면 반드시 의회의 사전 승인을 얻어야 하고 현 수준의 사우디 주둔 병력을 유지 하기 위해서는 국민 개병제(DRAFT)를 실시하거나, 또는 사우디 주둔 미군 병력을 감축하고 그대신 동맹국으로 하여금 지상병력을 부입하는 조치를 해야 할것임.

(LUTTWAK 연구원)

0 WEBB 전 해군 장관의 분석에 전적으로 동감을 표하면서, 미국이 사우디에병력을 파견한것은 냉전시대의 시각에서 벗어나지 못하고 저가격 원유의 확보,소련과의 경쟁에서 비롯된 중동 지역의 중요성이라는 냉전시대 인식의 결과임.

0 페만사태의 근원적 해결을 위해서는 이락의 경제를 파탄에 이르게 하고 또한 군사산업 기반을 박탈할수 있는 장기적 경제제재 조치가 가장 유효하다고 보다 현재 사우디 주둔 미군 병력 수준을 고려하면, 장기적으로 경제제재 조치를취하기는

| 미주국 | 차관 | 1차보 | 2차보 | 미주국 | 중아국 | 청와대 | 안기부 | 대책반 |
|--------|------|-------|-------|--------|--------|--------|--------|--------|

현실적으로 어려움.

　　0 페만사태 해결을 위해 무력을 사용할 경우, 공군력으로 훌륭한 성과를 거둘수 있다고 봄. 사막의 지형을 고려하면 공군력으로 이락의 군사 시설을 마비시킬수 있고 지상병력의 이동을 효과적으로 봉쇄할수 있어 지상군의 교전은 회피할수 있을것임.

　　0 사우디 주둔 미군병력은 과다한 수준이며 이를 해결하기 위해서는 미군 주둔으로 반사적 이익을 얻고 있는 미국의 동맹국들로 하여금 병력을 파견 또는 증원하게 하는 것임.

　　(PERLE 전 국방부 차관보)

　　0 페만사태는 냉전시대 이후의 미국의 역할을 규정짓는 주요한 사건이며, 미국은 평화의 보루로서 역할을 계속 유지해야 함.

　　0 현재의 페만사태가 해결된 후에도 이락이 다시 지역 안정을 해치는 군사 강국이 되어서는 안되며 따라서 이락의 핵, 화학무기 생산 능력,-미사일 생산능력은 제거 되어야함.

　　0 이락에 대한 경제제재 조치로서는 페만사태에서의 미국의 정책목표를 달성하기는 어려울것으로 보며, 무력사용만이 유일한 방법일것임.

　　3. 금번 청문회 질의 응답시에도 사우디 주둔 미군 병력 수준, 페만 해결 방법으로서 무력사용 문제등이 주로 거론되었으며, 민주당 의원은 무력사용에 대한 우려를 표명한 반면, 공화당계 의원은 경제제재 조치의성과에 대한 의구심을 표명하였음.

　　4. 동 청문회시 한국이 직접 거론된 적은 없으나 미국이 사우디에 43 만명을 주둔시킬 경우 타지역에서의 돌발사태 에 대처할 능력이 있느냐는 NUNN 위원장의 질문에 대한 답변시 LUTTWAK 연구원은 돌발사태 발생 지역에 따라 다를것이나 만약 한국에서 사태가 발발하면 미국은 대규모의 병력 증원이 필요하기 때문에 사태 대처가 매우 어려울것이라고 답변 하였음.

　　(대사 박동진- 국장)

　　90.12.31. 까지

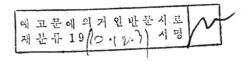

PAGE 2

외 무 부

종  별 :

번  호 : USW-5374

일  시 : 90 1203 1757

수  신 : 장관( 미북,미안,중근동)

발  신 : 주 미 대사

제  목 : 페만사태 관련 청문회

연:USW-5339

1. 금 12.3. 상원군사위는 DICK CHENEY 국방장관, COLLIN POWELL 합참의장을 출석시킨 가운데 페만사태에 관한 청문회를 개최하였음.

2. 동 청문회 개회 발언시 NUNN 위원장은 이락의 대사우디 침공을 억지하고 UN 의 경제 제재 조치를 뒤받침하기 위한 미군 병력의 사우디 주둔 및 행정부가 취한 일련의 대 UN 정책에 대해서는 광범위한 지지가 있으나, 사우디 주둔 미군의 규모의 적정성 및 대규모 병력에 대한 병참 지원 능력, 경제 제재 조치의 효과 및 바람직한 향후 정책방안등에 대한 논의가 필요하다고 발언하였으며, WARNER 공화당 간사는 UN 의 무력사용 결의안에 대해 미 의회가 지지를 표함으로써 이락에 대한 강력한 경고를 보내지 못하는것을 애석하게 생각한다 하면서 금번청문회를 통해 미 의회가 UN 및 행정부의 조치에 대해 일치된 입장을 갖고 있는다는 신호를 줄수 있기를 기대한다고 발언 하였음.

3. CHENEY 국방장관 및 POWELL 합참의장은 증언을 통해 사우디 주둔 미군 병력의 증강은 이락에 대한 공세전쟁을 대비한 조치이나 현재 무력 사용에 관한 어떠한 결정도 내린바가 없으며, 경제제재 조치는 이락 뿐만 아니라 동맹국에 대해서도 고통을 초래하는것으로 경제제재 조치의 성공을 위해 무한정 기다릴수는 없으며, 또한 경제제재 조치만으로 이락의 쿠웨이트 철수를 기대하기는 어렵다는의견을 표명 하였는바, 동 요지 하기 보고함.

(CHENEY 국방장관)

O 페만지역 및 사우디의 안보는 ROOSEVELT 대통령 이래 계속 미국의 주요 국가 이익의 하나로 천명되어 왔음.

O 이락의 쿠웨이트 침략이후 미국은 이락의 침략을 저지하고 사우디를 방어하며,

| 미주국 | 차관 | 1차보 | 미주국 | 중아국 | 정와대 | 안기부 | 대책반 |
|---|---|---|---|---|---|---|---|

PAGE 1

경제봉쇄 조치를 취하기 위해 파병하였고, 이락에 대항하는 국제적 협조 체제를 구축하였으나, 이라크는 국제적 협조 체제가 오래가지 않으리라고 믿고 있으며, 계속 대항 하는 자세를 취하고 있음.

0 이라크측에 대해 확실한 패배 의 전망을 심어주기 위해 11.8. 사우디 주둔 미군병력의증강을발표 하였으며, 이는 행정부가 이미 무력 사용 결정을 내렸다는 의미가 결코 아니고, 경제제재를 통한 평화적 해결 방안을 포기한것도 아님.

0 이라크는 경제 봉쇄로 부터 벗어나중 국제적 협조 체제를 와해시키기 위해 모든 노력을 기울이고 있는바, 경제제재 조치만으로서 이라크의 쿠웨이트 철수를 실현시키기 어렵다고 판단되며, 따라서 무력 사용이 필요하다고 판단되는 시점에서 무력을 사용할수 있도록 준비해야 함.

0 시간이 지남에 따라 국제적 협조 체제는 약화될수도 있고, 경제제재 조치는 이락뿐만 아니라 동맹국에게도 똑같이 피해를 주고 있으며, 경제제재 조치가 실패를 거두었을 경우에는 사우디등 주변국가의 안보에 심각한 영향을 초래할것임. 따라서 국제적 협조 체제가 확고하고 UN 에서무력 사용 결의안이 통과된 현 시점에서 이락에 대한 강력한 조치를 취하는것이 효과적임.

(POWELL 합참 의장)

0 군사적 전략 및 계획은 정치적 목표달성을 위한것이며, 금번 페만사태에 있어서 정치적 4 대 목표는 명백하기 제시 되었음.

0 페만 사태 목표 달성을 위해 방어 능력 뿐만 아니라 공세 능력을 갖추는 것도 중요하며, 미 합동 참모 본부는 이를 대통령에게 건의한바 있음.

0 혹자는 제한 폭격(SURGICAL AIR STRIKES)을 통해 소기의 목적을 달성할수있다고 주장하나 이는 이라크 측으로 하여금 대응책을 선택하는데 있어 주도권을 줄 우려가 있는바 공세 전쟁을 취할 경우 미군은 압독 우세를 점할수 있는 전략을 택해야 할것임.

4. 동 청문회 질의 응답시에는 경제제재 조치가 성공을 거두기 어렵다는 행정부의 판단에 대해 민주당 소속 의원들은 의구심을 표명하였고 , KENNEDY 상원의원은 의회의 전쟁선포권과 관련하여, 무력사용 이전 의회의 사전 승인이 필요하다는 의견을 발표한바, CHENEY 국방장관은 과거 205 회의 해외 무력사용시 의회의 전쟁 선포가 있었던 경우는 5 회에 불과하며, 금번 페만사태와같이 이락에 대한 국제적 조치를 취하고 있는 경우에 미국만이 전쟁선포를 하는 경우 국제적 조치를 양자간의 관계로 변질 시킬 우려가 있으므로 의회의 전쟁 선포는 바람직하지 않다는 의견을

제시하였음.

5. 동 청문회 CHENEY 국방장관 증언문 및 주요 질의 응답 요지는 별전 팩스송부함.

(대사 박동진 - 국장)

90.12.31 까지

대고문에 의거 일반문서로
재분류 19     . /    .      서명

주 미 대 사 관       보안<br>
                               통제   ㄴ

번호 : USW(F) - 3324

수신 : 장관 (미북, 미안, 중근동)

발신 : 주미대사

제목 : 페만사태 관련 청문회 (13매)

표 12.3 개최된 페만사태 청문회시 Cheney

국방장관의 증언문을 극요 결의능답요력 를

별첨 FAX 송부함. 끝

0139

### STATEMENT BY THE HONORABLE DICK CHENEY
#### Secretary of Defense
#### Concerning Operation Desert Shield
#### Before the Committee on Armed Services
#### United States Senate
#### December 3, 1990

Mr. Chairman, members of the Committee, I am glad to be here today with General Colin Powell, Chairman of the Joint Chiefs of Staff, to discuss Operation Desert Shield. A review of the events in the Persian Gulf region since early August clearly shows why we have arrived at the policy we're pursuing in the Persian Gulf.

In the early morning hours of August second, an Iraqi ground, air, and naval force of some 140,000 men launched a blitzkrieg attack against the small, peaceful country of Kuwait. Within a matter of hours, Iraqi forces were in Kuwait city. Within days they were arrayed on the Kuwaiti border with Saudi Arabia, deployed for further aggression. This unprovoked aggression was a blatant violation of the United Nations charter and all accepted principles of international relations. It directly threatened the stability and security of the entire Persian Gulf, a region in which the United States and the rest of the world have a vital interest.

On the sixth of August, I flew to Saudi Arabia at the President's direction to confer with King Fahd bin Abd Al-Aziz Al Saud. Following my meeting with the King and his senior advisors, the government of Saudi Arabia invited the United States to send troops, and the President ordered the commencement of Operation Desert Shield, a deployment of U.S. military forces unparalleled in recent times.

U.S. security interests in the Gulf region have been obvious to every administration since World War II, when the Allies recognized the importance of Persian Gulf oil resources to the war effort and the necessity of keeping those resources out of the hands of the Axis. Indeed, the establishment of a resident U.S. diplomatic mission in Saudi Arabia and the historic meeting aboard the USS Quincy between President Franklin D. Roosevelt and King Abdul Aziz were testimony to the importance of U.S. and Allied interests in the security of Saudi Arabia.

After World War II, it became apparent that the Persian Gulf was equally important to the economic and political welfare of the free world in peacetime. It soon became settled U.S. policy to ensure that no hostile power should dominate this vital area. President Truman told King Abdul Aziz in 1950 that "no threat could arise to your kingdom that would not be of immediate concern to the United States."

3324-2

0140

President Carter recognized the importance of the area in his 1980 State of the Union Address, when he pledged that "an attempt by any outside force to gain control of the Persian Gulf region will be regarded as an assault on the vital interests of the United States of America, and such an assault will be repelled by any means necessary, including military force."

After the Iranian revolution of 1979, it appeared that Iran might be able to dominate the region. But the principal threat is now Iraq. Even though threats to the region shift over time, what has not changed is the critical importance of the area to the United States and the rest of the world. President Reagan repeatedly assured the Saudis and the other moderate gulf nations of our determination to support their security. He deployed U.S. forces to protect free navigation in the Persian Gulf during the Iran-Iraq war. In 1984, he wrote King Fahd that "the security and well-being of Saudi Arabia are matters of vital interest for the United States."

And just last Friday President Bush, in noting the importance of the Persian Gulf to the free world, repeated what he has been saying since he first ordered troops to the region: "We're in the Gulf because the world must not and cannot reward aggression. We're there because our vital interests are at stake. And we're in the Gulf because of the brutality of Saddam Hussein."

The reasons that made the Gulf a concern of every President from Roosevelt and Truman to Carter and Reagan are equally compelling today: Persian Gulf countries possess nearly two-thirds of the world's proven crude oil reserves. Last year they accounted for more than one-fourth of the world's oil production and about one-third of the free world's. Oil is the source of more than half of global energy consumption and will probably become even more important over the next decade. It provides more than ninety percent of the energy needed by the ships, trucks, and airplanes that move food, raw materials, and industrial products to consumers, farms, and factories around the world. It is no exaggeration to say that the world's economy is fueled by oil.

Secure energy supplies are a fundamental interest of the entire world. The poorest countries are among the most seriously at risk from an unreliable supply. Putting Gulf oil supplies, or even a large share of them, into the hands of a single hostile power would pose a clear and present danger to the economic welfare and the political stability of regions as diverse as Sub-Saharan Africa, the Pacific rim, and newly liberated Eastern Europe.

It is simply not acceptable for any hostile country to be in a position to manipulate the availability and cost of energy, and so have the power to disrupt the world's economy and create political instability.

The response of the United States and the world community to Saddam Hussein's invasion must be seen in light of the world's dependence on the region's energy and in the context of the past forty-five years, during which U.S. policy has recognized the singular importance of this region. It has been in pursuit of this interest that one American president

2

3314-3

0141

after another, Democrat as well as Republican, has sought close military and political relations with Saudi Arabia and the other moderate countries of the Arabian Peninsula.

By the summer of 1990, Iraq had been at peace for less than two years, following the August 1988 cease-fire in its ten year war with Iran. While that war brought great destruction, it also left Saddam with a war-hardened military force -- disciplined, organized, and tough. Saddam proved he was willing to subject his forces to high levels of casualties for small gains. He had developed and used chemical weapons, developed biological agents, and continued to create a nuclear bomb.

Saddam Hussein also became increasingly vocal about the oil and financial policies of the other Arab states of the Gulf -- the very policies which kept world oil prices moderate and stable. Contrary to Iraq's claims, this was never a situation of "haves" versus "have-nots." With the world's second largest oil reserves, Iraq is, or should be, a very rich country. It has fifty times more oil in reserve, per person, than the United States. Yet under Hussein, the beneficiaries of this immense oil wealth have not been the Iraqi people. The country's wealth has been diverted to wage war, develop nuclear and other special weapons programs, commit aggression, and fuel Saddam's dreams of power and domination. By summer 1990, Hussein had actually driven his oil-rich country $60 billion into debt.

On June 26, he warned Kuwait and the United Arab Emirates that they must curb what he called "excess" oil production. The tone of the warning raised the specter that Iraq might use its military might against its neighbors -- ironically the same countries who supported Iraq in its war with Iran. Although the threats and intimidation continued to escalate, Hussein assured President Mubarak, King Fahd, and the world at large that he had no intention of invading Kuwait.

Even as Hussein provided these smiling assurances in late July, Iraq began moving troops to the Kuwaiti border and making more overt threats toward both Kuwait and the United Arab Emirates. In response, the UAE asked for, and President bush approved, the deployment of KC-135 tanker aircraft to enhance the effective range of the UAE's air defense fighters. But Kuwait itself did not respond militarily to Iraq's moves, fearing that its actions might be construed as a provocative, as Iraq's elite Republican Guards moved to the border.

At the same time, Iraq and Kuwait met in Jeddah to discuss Iraq's stated grievances. There, Saddam's representatives repeated their assurances that force would not be used. As we now know, this was merely an elaborate charade. Iraqi tanks were rolling toward the border before the talks were even broken off. It took the Iraqi army only a few hours to reach Kuwait City. Within a few days, Hussein's forces had effectively occupied the entire country.

The world response to the invasion was quick, severe, and virtually unanimous. Iraq's claims of an indigenous uprising and later its annexation of Kuwait were soundly rejected. On the very day of the invasion, the fifteen countries of the United Nations Security Council

3

3324-4

0142

passed Resolution 660, which condemned the aggression and called for Iraq's immediate withdrawal. The United Nations and its members continue to recognize and deal with Kuwait's legitimate diplomatic representatives. The Kuwaiti government in exile has been given control of its overseas assets.

The unanimity of world reaction is clearly expressed in the UN Security Council Resolutions condemning the invasion, imposing strict economic sanctions, authorizing the use of naval power to enforce the sanctions, condemning the taking of hostages and the mistreatment of the diplomatic missions in Kuwait, and taking a number of other measures. These culminated in the authorization last Thursday to use all necessary means to uphold and implement the previous resolutions and to restore international peace and security in the area.

Our response was equally decisive, and fully in keeping with the UN Charter and the actions of the UN Security Council. The President began by imposing immediate economic sanctions on Iraq, freezing Iraqi assets and protecting Kuwaiti assets so they could not be pilfered by Iraq or the bogus provisional government in Kuwait.

When I met with King Fahd in Jeddah on August 6, I assured him of four things: we would move quickly; we would deploy enough force to get the job done, not merely a token force; we would stay as long as necessary; and we would leave when the Saudi government asked us to go. In turn, the King explained to me the longstanding confidence he had in the U.S. government, a trust built up over decades of association between our two countries in political, economic, and military affairs.

From the first, President Bush clearly stated the objectives of U.S. policy:

- Achieving the complete and unconditional withdrawal of all Iraqi forces from Kuwait;

- Restoring the legitimate government of Kuwait;

- Protecting American lives; and

- Enhancing the security and stability of the Gulf region.

These objectives have not changed.

The mission the President gave the armed forces is equally clear: to deter further Iraqi aggression, to defend Saudi Arabia if deterrence failed, to enhance the indigenous military capabilities of friends in the region, and to enforce economic sanctions through a multinational interdiction effort.

4

0143

On August 7, Iraq's Army was on the Saudi border with nothing but the vastly
outnumbered Saudi and Gulf Cooperation Council forces to keep it from moving all the way
to Dhahran, Saudi Arabia. It was clear that Saddam Hussein's word was not to be trusted.

Something had to be done to put credible military force on the ground, and the only
country that could do that was the United States.

Having decided on the deployment of U.S. forces, we rejected the idea of a gradual,
calibrated buildup. We also rejected the concept of a modest trip wire force, since we did not
want to send just enough troops to provoke an Iraqi attack without being able to defend
against it. We intended to present a credible deterrent and to convey to Saddam Hussein that
we were serious.

At the same time, we were conscious that the United States should not and could not be
the only country to respond militarily. The President began immediately to work with Saudi
Arabia and the Kuwaiti government-in-exile to assemble a multinational force. Military forces
from 27 countries are now directly involved either in Desert Shield or in the maritime
enforcement of economic sanctions. All the Gulf Cooperation Council countries, including
free Kuwait, have ground forces in Saudi Arabia. Other countries, including Egypt, Morocco,
Syria, Pakistan, and Bangladesh have sent major ground forces as well. Saudi and other Arab
forces are on the front lines facing the Iraqi and Kuwaiti borders.

The United Kingdom and France and a number of our other allies have also dispatched
significant military forces to the region. The Soviet Union has cooperated at the United
Nations, ensuring unprecedented unanimity in the Security Council. An old friend in the
region, Israel, has acted coolly and responsibly despite repeated Iraqi provocations and has
avoided any action that could undermine the broad-based international coalition against Saddam
Hussein.

In addition to military contributions, there have been numerous pledges of financial
support for U.S. operations from countries in the region as well as from major industrial
states who have not been able to make a military contribution. These pledges and
contributions, running well into the billions of dollars, have helped offset the incremental
costs of Operation Desert Shield. Countries in the region have also assisted with financial
support. This has been a truly multinational effort. It is not the United States versus Iraq.
It is Iraq versus the world.

In the four months since August, we have completed the initial buildup of U.S. forces in
Saudi Arabia and the Gulf region. Forces from other countries continue to arrive. General
Powell will be describing this deployment in detail in his statement. I firmly believe that
without this operation Iraqi forces would not have stopped short of Dhahran, and we would
today be contemplating the liberation of Saudi Arabia as well as the liberation of Kuwait.

5

3324-6

0144

Despite the pain he is inflicting on his own people, there is no indication that Saddam Hussein is open to a peaceful resolution of the problem he has created. His repugnant hostage policy; his threats to use terror and chemical weapons against Saudi Arabia and Israel; the brutalizing of Kuwaitis and the looting of their country; and the continued mistreatment of diplomats all suggest that he does not yet realize that he cannot prevail.

It appears, in fact, that Saddam believes time is on his side. This view is reinforced by his continued efforts to find ways around the sanctions and his attempts to break the international consensus against him. He apparently believes that we and our allies do not have the staying power to see this crisis through to a successful conclusion. The trickle of hostage releases, his propaganda campaign against the presence of "infidels" in Saudi Arabia, and Saddam's manipulation of the well-meaning Western political figures who go to court him are obvious attempts to destroy the solidarity of the forces arrayed against him. At the same time, with every day of occupation, the Iraqi army continues the looting and destruction of Kuwait and continues to build up its military power.

It is therefore essential that we present him with the prospect of a serious Iraqi defeat. Thus on November 8, the President announced that it was necessary to deploy additional U.S. forces to the Persian Gulf region and sought to obtain Security Council agreement to the use of military force, should that prove necessary to eject Saddam Hussein from Kuwait. These steps do not mean that we have decided to go to war with Iraq. We hope that Saddam Hussein will see the light and settle this matter peacefully.

But to ensure that he fully understands the urgency of leaving Kuwait, and to be sure we have overwhelming power to deal with him if necessary, we are backing up our diplomatic effort with credible military power. We have not put any upper limit on deployments and we are basing our strength in the region on the advice of the commanders on the scene and the ever increasing size of Iraq's forces in Kuwait. And to achieve our required buildup, we have for now set aside the question of troop rotation.

The President's decision in early November was not a fundamental change in administration policy. It is a logical development from the principles he established at the outset of the crisis. Our objective remains the restoration of Kuwaiti independence under its legitimate government. Economic sanctions and diplomatic pressure are our preferred means of achieving this objective. But as the President has repeatedly stated, we are not ruling out any options.

The decision to put young men and women at risk has always been one of the most difficult our nation can make. In the end, our armed forces belong to the American people. For that reason, it is important that our citizens understand why American troops are in the Gulf. In any situation as complex as this, involving a host of American political and economic interests, there can be no single reason for our actions. The President and the international community have responded to Iraq's aggression against Kuwait because a constellation of conditions came together, involving matters of principle, interests, and military necessity.

6

3324 ㄱ

be satisfied. At the very least, Iraq would wish to hold sway over the politics and economics of the region.

We should remember that Iraq was willing to engage in a nearly decade-long war with Iran, and take approximately half a million casualties in the process. The gains from that conflict were so minimal that once the international community responded to Iraq's invasion of Kuwait, Saddam traded them away in an effort to secure his border with Iran, so he could concentrate on Kuwait.

Then there are the hostages. Iraq has been willing to take and use hostages on an extraordinary scale. Some hostages are used as human shields to protect Iraqi military assets, some are used as bargaining chips to help soften up members of the coalition and cause splits in the alliance. If Iraq is willing to use humans in this way, we have every right to wonder who or what it might choose to hold hostage in the future. Saddam's ballistic missile program gives him the option of one day holding entire cities hostage.

As for the hostages he now holds, Saddam should free them all immediately and unconditionally. And second, we hold him responsible for their safety and well-being. We will never forget or forgive if anything should befall our fellow Americans in his hands.

If Iraq's ambitions are not curbed today they will just grow stronger. But the next time we face this regime, its military power will be even greater. It will come armed not just with 5,600 tanks, a million man army, chemical weapons and ballistic missiles. In the future, Iraq could possess nuclear weapons and the long-range-missiles to deliver them.

Aggression begets aggression. We cannot afford to look the other way.

The second reason is the danger of Saddam Hussein's domination of world oil supplies.

The potential for Saddam Hussein to gain a dominant share of the world's oil is quite real. With Kuwait's oil assets, Iraq now controls more than ten percent of the world's oil production capacity and one-fifth of the world's proven oil reserves. With control or influence over Saudi Arabia and the smaller Gulf states, Iraq would dominate over sixty percent of the world's oil reserves. That is a powerful lever in the hands of a single regime, no matter what its political leanings, to manipulate the availability of petroleum.

There are, in fact, two reasons we must be concerned with Saddam's potential control of the Middle East's oil wealth.

First, is his control of supply. Because oil is fungible, it does not matter who gets oil from what source. What matters is the overall supply in relation to demand. In addition, the world economy is increasingly interlinked. When some nations' economies decline, others will also feel the pinch.

8

ㅋㅋㅋㅣㄷ -8

0146

Consider the impact Iraq could have on the world's economies. Threatened disruptions in supply could inspire buying panics, and actual disruptions could move some economies into recession. Iraq could create wild swings in prices, swings that would fit its current political intentions and economic needs. The mere ability to threaten such disruptions would enable him to blackmail the world.

The second reason concerns wealth. Iraq has used its wealth to build its military, not its economy, and there is every reason to think that pattern will continue. Counting just its own oil reserves, Iraq is a very wealthy nation. Before the invasion, Saddam was earning $20 billion a year from oil exports. This wealth went to pay for its war with Iran and build its military capability. It is reasonable to assume that increased oil wealth taken from Kuwait would be used to enhance Iraq's military arsenal, especially its chemical, biological, and nuclear capability.

So it is an error to look at our policy in the Gulf and see it as a reaction to oil prices. The fact is, for Hussein, oil is not so much a resource as a weapon of war.

The final reason we are in the Gulf is that Iraq's destruction of Kuwait strikes at the heart of the kind of world we are trying to build in the post-cold war era.

As the President said on November 8, when he announced additional troop deployments, "Iraq's aggression is not just a challenge to the security of Kuwait and other Gulf nations, but to the better world that we all have hope to build in the wake of the cold war." If Iraq can succeed in this kind of action, when virtually the entire world condemns it, a very strong signal will be sent to all aggressive regimes that brutality pays.

Invasions and aggressions far from our shores sometimes seem insignificant. They seldom are. In fact, the international response to aggression sets the tone of world politics for years to come. Just look at the weak response to Italy's invasion of Ethiopia in 1935. While there was generalized outrage, the League of Nations could only agree to impose relatively weak sanctions. The League failed to impose oil sanctions or to deny the movement of Italian troops and equipment through the Suez Canal. Essentially, Mussolini was given a free hand in Ethiopia. The world was to see a lot of that kind of aggression in the years to come.

Now, it is not necessarily the case that Iraq's occupation of Kuwait foreshadows a new world conflict. But it is clear that how we -- and the rest of the world -- react to naked aggression can set the stage either for greater peace and cooperation, or more violence.

Our interests and our goals are clear in this case.

From the first, our approach has been to liberate Kuwait by backing international sanctions with military force. Sanctions will have an effect, but they alone cannot be counted on to convince Iraq that its occupation of Kuwait is doomed, since Saddam's only concern

9

3324-9

would then be either how to get around the embargo, or how to break up the coalition that make sanctions effective. And what would be left of Kuwait after months of waiting while Iraq continued to loot and plunder? Not only do we need a military force in Saudi Arabia to deter and defend, we must have the ability to take offensive action if need be.

The Iraq Army and people should understand how grave a situation they have allowed Saddam to place them in and to see that they cannot win. At every opportunity, we will demonstrate renewed international unity and disrupt Saddam's strategy of "wait and divide." Finally, we will show those few countries that sympathize with Iraq that they, along with Saddam Hussein, are bound to be the losers in this confrontation. Each of these steps will contribute to making Iraq realize that the best possible solution is to withdraw peacefully now.

If, however, we take an approach of relying solely on sanctions, we would cede that initiative to Iraq. Such a policy would give Hussein a long breathing space in which he could concentrate his efforts. Because he could ignore the possibility of a military option, he could use the breathing space to work around the embargo, break up the alliance, enhance his military strength in Kuwait, and move ahead on his nuclear weapons program.

Those who would have us rely indefinitely on economic sanctions alone need to face the possibility that they will fail to achieve our aims. Such a failure will have very serious consequence and those consequences must also be faced.

The additional problem with the sanctions-only approach is that it has costs for us as well as Hussein. In some way, time works against a complex multi-national coalition. What's more, the economic impact of the embargo is felt by our friends as well as our enemy. And the nations that feel the economic effects first, such as Turkey, Egypt and the emerging democracies of Eastern Europe, may be the ones least able to absorb the shock. It is not so clear that time is altogether on our side.

It has been suggested in this regard that the United States is certainly strong enough to sustain sanctions for as long as we desire. Our strength, however, is not the issue. The issue is Saddam Hussein's willingness and ability to withstand an embargo and what steps he will be able to take during the time the embargo is in force. Moreover, we are not the only nation that must hold the line on sanctions. Again, time can work against a complex international coalition.

We must also be certain we understand what it means to say that sanctions are working. There is a difference, especially in a dictatorship like Iraq, between an embargo having an economic impact, even a severe one, and concluding that the embargo is working. Authoritarian regimes have a significant ability to withstand economic hardship, since popular discontent is easily stifled. Just because the Iraqi people may find certain staples hard to get, does not necessarily translate into a changed attitude on Saddam Hussein's part.

10

3324-10

0148

So we must not create a false dichotomy between sanctions and a military option: They are mutually reinforcing parts of a broad strategy to get Iraq out of Kuwait.

People sometimes underestimate both the patience and staying power of the American people. The fact that we stayed the course in Western Europe for forty-five years, even through dark periods when the experts said our struggle against communism was hopeless, proves that we can persevere when we must. But the nature of our democratic institutions and the open debates we conduct can convey serious misimpressions to those who do not understand that a free and democratic government is one of our nation's greatest strengths.

But having a capacity for patience does not mean we must remain patient when patience is not producing results. We must always have other options, and that is what the new deployments and the recent United Nations action are all about. They will broaden the options of the United States and its Allies and simultaneously narrow those of Saddam Hussein. They are a necessary next step toward the President's and the world's goal of restoring Kuwait to freedom and independence.

In closing, I want to say a word about the core of our military effort in the Gulf. I think all of us would agree that our greatest strength is our men and women in uniform. Their quality is our most fearsome weapon against tyrants like Saddam Hussein. I believe it represents the Pentagon's greatest success story since the end of the war in Vietnam. Having talked with the men and women in the Gulf, I know that they are prepared and willing to do whatever we ask of them. Our job, the job of this Administration and this Congress is to make sure that our decisions do not betray the trust our soldiers, sailors, airmen, and Marines have put in us.

Thank you, Mr. Chairman.

11

3324-11

0149

## Report on Hearing of the
## Senate Armed Services Committee
## on U.S. Policy in the Persian Gulf
Witnesses:
Dick Cheney, Secretary of Defense
Colin Powell, Chairman of the Joint Chiefs of Staff

### December 3, 1990

The main thrust of Secy. Cheney's testimony was aimed at clarifying the significance of the threat posed by Saddam Hussein to present and future stability in the Persian Gulf and laying out the reasons why the Administration must have total flexibility in determining its moves in the region. The latter refers to the oft-raised issue of waiting for sanctions to weaken Saddam Hussein, as opposed to initiating a military strike against him.

Secy. Cheney stressed that 70% of the world's proven oil reserves lie in the Middle East. 22% of those reserves are in Iraq and Kuwait. He warned that Saddam Hussein has shown in the past how he uses the vast wealth his oil affords him--by buying weapons of mass destruction. Secy. Cheney stressed that if left unchecked, Hussein could continue to threaten the world's economy even after the current crisis is resolved.

On the flexibility issue, Secy. Cheney stressed that the President must have the ability to use force in the region if he deems it necessary. In his view, sanctions alone cannot be relied upon to secure the goals that President Bush has outlined: 1.Achieving the immediate, unconditional withdrawal of Iraqi forces from Kuwait, 2.Restoring the legitimate government of Kuwait, 3.Protecting the lives of Americans abroad, 4.Restoring stability to the Persian Gulf region.

He showed little patience for the waiting game that would be the inevitable result of relying on sanctions. He argued that there are many factors that will work for Saddam Hussein unless action is taken early. Among them is the simple fact that Iraq is capable of withstanding tremendous amounts of hardship and Hussein will divert his resources to the army at the expense of the common citizens, enabling him to hold out even longer. Secondly, the longer the world waits before taking decisive action against Saddam Hussein, the more time he has to construct more formidable fortifications and to obliterate more fully Kuwait. Additionally, he said that the sanctions will do great harm to some of the friendly countries who did business with Iraq before the embargo.

For his part, Chairman Powell added to the testimony of Secy. Cheney the fact that this crisis can only be successfully resolved if the United States takes a "will win" attitude as opposed to a "hope to win" attitude. By this he meant that the United States should not allow Saddam Hussein to take the initiative for deciding what he will do. In his view, sanctions and limited air strikes when employed on their own, are two such flawed strategies.

3326-12

0150

Chairman Powell argued that the United States must be decisive in its actions against Iraq. Lest his rhetoric sound too belligerent, however, he reminded those present that President Bush asked for the option to go on the offensive, but he has not directed his generals to use it as of yet.

Chairman Powell also explained how the Nov. 8 decision was made to increase the number of ground troops in Saudi Arabia to over 400,000. He said that the initial deployment was adequate to carry out the primary mission of deterring an Iraqi attack on Saudi Arabia and defending the same if deterrence failed. Over time it became clear that there would not be enough troops to carry out an offensive should the need arise. Therefore, Phase II was initiated. He reminded the senators that assuring an offensive option is related directly to the Administration's political goal of ousting Iraq from Kuwait.

The question and answer period delved further into the validity of the Administration argument that the United States cannot wait for sanctions, but must seek a bolder solution. Many Democrats remained suspicious of that opinion. These included Senator James Exon (D-NE), Jeff Bingaman (D-NM), Alan Dixon (D-IL), John Glenn (D-OH), Al Gore (D-GA) and Robert Byrd (D-WV). They stressed the fact that the Administration may be selling short the damage that tough, relatively leak-proof sanctions can have.

Another issue of concern to both parties was that of consultation with Congress prior to the initiation of hostilities in the Persian Gulf. Senator Edward Kennedy (D-MA) was quite adamant in his demands for a declaration of war; the issue was also brought up by Senator Al Gore. In response to Senator Kennedy's call for a declaration of war, Secy. Cheney made the interesting point that the international coalition could be adversely affected if the United States entered into a unilateral war relationship with Iraq. Senator John McCain (R-AZ) argued for at least a special session of the Congress and expressed exasperation at President Bush and Congressional leaders for not calling one as of yet. Senator Robert Byrd also asked that the Congress be better informed by the President as to what his plans are in the Gulf.

A final issue brought up by the senators was moral support of U.S. policy in the Gulf. Senator Slade Gorton (R-WA) wondered how long high troop morale would last in the Gulf with no clear timeframe to look to. Chairman Powell assured him that he understands this difficulty and has done his best to encourage the troops to remain vigilant. Senator Dan Coats (R-IN) asked how significant gaining a national consensus is to U.S. success in the Gulf to which Secy. Cheney replied that deep divisions in the country would serve to reassure Saddam Hussein and make the job of wearing him down much tougher.

Jennifer Smith Mazarr     Congressional/Political     December 3, 1990

732F-13

0151

# 報 告 事 項

報 告 畢

1990.12.4
美 洲 局
北 美 課(49)

題 目 : 페만 사태 관련 미 상원 군사위 청문회(2)

---

기 보고드린 바와 같이 미 상원 군사위(위원장 : Sam Nunn, 민, GA)는
12.3(월) Cheney 국방장관 및 Powell 합참의장의 증언을 끝으로 페만 사태
관련 청문회를 종결하였는 바, 동 청문회시 주요 증언 내용등 관련 사항을
아래 보고드립니다.

---

1. 민주, 공화 당별 입장 개진

(Nunn 위원장)

ㅇ 미군 병력의 사우디 주둔 및 미 행정부가 취한 일련의 대 UN 정책에
   대해서는 광범위한 지지를 받고 있음을 인정함.
   - 사우디 주둔 미군 규모의 적정성, 대규모 병력에 대한 병참 지원
     능력, 경제 제재 조치의 효과 및 바람직한 향후 정책 방안 등에
     대한 논의 필요

(Warner 공화당 간사)

ㅇ 미 의회가 UN의 무력 사용 결의안 통과에 대해 지지를 표명함으로써
   이라크에 대한 강력한 경고를 보내지 못함을 애석하게 생각함.
   - 금번 청문회가 미 의회와 UN 및 행정부간 일치된 입장을 보여주는
     계기가 될 것을 기대

| 안 고 | 90년 12월 5일 | 단 당 | 과 장 | 심의관 | 국 장 | 차관보 | 차 관 | 장 |
|---|---|---|---|---|---|---|---|---|
| 미 주 과 | | | | | | | | 報告畢 |

0152

2. 증언자 주요 언급 내용

(Cheney 국방장관)

o 페만 지역 및 사우디의 안보는 1940년대 이래 미국의 주요 국가 이익의
  하나로 천명되어 왔음.

o 최근 대규모 병력 증파 결정은 이라크측에 확실한 패배 전망을 심어
  주기 위한 조치임.
  - 행정부가 이미 무력 사용을 결정한 것이 아니며, 경제 제재를 통한
    평화적 해결 방안을 포기한 것도 아님.

o 경제 제재 조치만으로는 이라크의 쿠웨이트 철수 실현은 어려울 것으로
  판단됨.
  - 적절한 시점에서의 무력을 사용할 준비 필요

o 시간 경과에 따라 국제적 협조 체제의 약화 가능성은 배제할 수 없음.
  - 경제 제재 조치는 이라크뿐 아니라 참가 동맹국에게도 피해 초래

o 국제적 협조 체제가 확고하고 UN에서 무력 사용 결의안이 통과된
  현 시점에서의 대이라크 강경 조치가 효과적임.

(Powell 합참의장)

o 기 표명된 4대 정치 목표 달성을 위해 군사적 전략 및 계획을 수립함.
  - 방어 능력뿐만 아니라 공세 능력도 갖추도록 건의

o 미군의 압도적 우세 확보를 위한 전략 선택만이 소기의 목적 달성을
  가능케함.

0153

3. 참고 사항

ㅇ 증언에 이은 질의 응답시, Kennedy 상원 의원이 무력 사용 이전 의회의
  사전 승인이 필요하다고 주장한데 대해, Cheney 장관은 의회의 대이라크
  전쟁 선포는 바람직하지 않다는 의견을 제시함.
  - 현재 국제적 협조하에 대이라크 제재 조치를 취하고 있어 미국만이
    전쟁 선포를 할 경우 국제적 조치를 양자간 관계로 변질 시킬 우려
  - 과거 205회에 걸친 해외 무력 사용시 의회의 선전 포고는 5회에 불과. 끝.

0154

# 채니 미 국방장관 12.3. 미 상원 군사위 증언 주요내용

報告畢.

90.12.4.
북 미 과

o 사담 후세인이 페르시아만 지역 안정에 미치는 위협 설명

  - 중동지역은 세계 총 원유 매장량의 ⅔를 점유하고 세계 원유 생산량의
    ¼을 생산
    따라서 이 지역은 세계 경제에 대해 사활적 중요성

  - 사담 후세인은 현 사태를 부국과 빈국의 대결로 호도하고 있으나 이는
    사실이 아님

    · 사담 후세인은 세계 제2의 원유 매장량 보유 국가인 이라크의 부(Wealth)
      를 핵 개발, 특수무기 개발 및 타국 침략 등 전비에 사용하므로써
      이라크를 1990년 여름 현재 600억불의 외채국으로 전락 시킴.

  - 금번에 사담 후세인을 억제하지 못할 경우, 그는 수년내 핵 무기와 장거리
    미사일을 보유하게 되어 중동지역 안정은 물론 세계 경제를 계속 위협할
    것이 분명

o 미국이 취할 조치에 대한 유연성(flexibility) 보유 필요성 강조

  - 경제적 제재 조치만으로는 부쉬 대통령이 제시한 이라크군의 무조건적인
    철수 등 4대정책 목표달성에 어려움

  - 경제적 제재조치가 효력을 나타낼 때까지 계속 기다릴 경우, 사담 후세인
    에게 무기개발 및 전력증강, 대이라크 제재를 위한 국제적 결속이완 기도
    등에 필요한 시간을 주게 되어 바람직하지 못함.

0155

- 따라서 필요하다고 판단되는 경우 페만 사태 해결을 위해 미국이 무력을
  사용할 수 있는 권한 및 능력 보유는 필수
  · 11.8. 부쉬 대통령의 병력 추가 파견 결정 및 UN안보리 결의 678호
    채택은 미국의 선택의 폭과 유연성을 증가시키고 사담 후세인의
    선택의 폭은 축소시키는 효과

o 미국의 단호한 의지 재강조
  - 미국의 민주적 제도와 공개 토론 등이 갖고 있는 속성을 오해, 미국의
    인내심과 힘을 과소 평가하는 오류에 대해 경고
  - 미국은 참고 견딜수 있는 힘을 보유하고 있으나, 인내를 통해 아무런
    결과도 얻을 수 없음에도 미국이 참을수 밖에 없을 것이라는 것은 커다란
    오산

0156

# 美議會의 폐灣 政策 聽聞會 結果

1. 美 上院軍事委(委員長 「샘넌」)는 11.27 - 12.3간 「美國의 폐灣 政策」題下 聽聞會를 개최하고 前·現職 行政府 高位官吏들로부터 證言을 聽取했음.

    ※ 證言者 : 「슐레진저」前 國防長官, 「키신저」前 國務長官, 「존스」前 合參議長, 「크로우」前 合參議長, 「웹」前 海軍長官, 「펄」前 國防次官補, 「루트워크」CSIS研究員, 「체니」國防長官, 「포웰」合參議長

2. 證言 要旨

【「슐레진저」前 國防長官(11.27)】

    ○ 폐灣事態는 지속적인 經濟制裁를 통한 해결이 바람직하며 經濟制裁가 實效를 거두기 위해서는 1년 정도 소요될 것임

    ○ 武力을 사용할 경우에는 상당한 死傷者등 追加犧牲을 감수해야하고 軍事戰略 目標를 어떻게 設定하느냐 하는 現實的 問題에 직면할 것임

31 - 6

0157

【「존스」前 合參議長(11.28)】

○ 페灣事態 해결에는 國際的 협력과 國內的 支持가 불가결한 요
소인 바 國際的 協力確保를 위해서는 페灣政策 目標를 「후세
인」에 대한 裁判, 이락의 核·化學武器 生產施設 撤廢 등으로
까지 擴大시키지 않는 것이 바람직함

○ 美 行政府의 兵力增強 措置는 이락에 대한 美國의 확고한 意
志表示로 볼 수 있으나 兵力增強 자체가 성급한 武力使用을
유발시킬 可能性이 있음을 認識해야 함

【「크로우」前 合參議長(11.28)】

○ 對이락 經濟制裁 조치는 效力을 거두고 있으며 확실한 成果는
1년내지 1년반이 소요될 것임

○ 美國은 인내를 갖고 經濟制裁를 持續해야하며 軍事的 行動은
中東地域의 안정을 해치고 分裂을 증대시킬 可能性이 있음

【「키신저」前 國務長官(11.28)】

○ 經濟制裁를 통해 페灣政策 目標를 달성할 수는 없으며 大規模
地上軍을 投入한 이상 武力使用을 제외한 현실적 解決方法은
없을 것임

○ 이락의 攻擊能力이 減少되지 않는 한 페灣地域 안정은 기대할

31 - 7

0158

수 없는 바 美 行政府의 政策目標에는 이락의 攻擊能力 縮小
가 포함되어야 함

【「웹」前 海軍長官(11.29)】

○ 사우디 주둔 美 軍事力 수준은 과다하고 長期的으로 현수준의
兵力을 維持하기가 곤란하며 과다한 兵力주둔은 결국 戰爭으
로 飛火될 위험이 있음

○ 부시 大統領이 武力을 사용한다면 반드시 議會의 事前承認을
얻어야하며 현수준의 兵力維持를 위해서는 徵兵制 실시 내지
同盟國의 地上軍 增派 조치가 요구됨

【「루트워크」CSIS 硏究員(11.29)】

○ 폐灣事態의 근원적 해결을 위해서는 長期的 經濟制裁 조치가
가장 유효하나 現 사우디 주둔 美軍수준을 고려하면 長期的
經濟制裁 조치를 취하기는 현실적으로 어려움

○ 사우디 주둔 美軍 수준은 과다한 바 同盟國들로 하여금 兵力
을 派遣케 해야하며, 武力을 사용할 경우 사막지형을 고려할
때 空軍力으로 效果를 거둘 수가 있을 것임

31 - 8

0159

【「펄」前 國防次官補(11.29)】

○ 經濟制裁 조치로는 美國의 政策目標를 달성할 수 없으며 武力
사용만이 유일한 해결방법임

○ 이락의 核·化學武器, 미사일 生産能力이 除去되어야함

【「체니」國防長官(12.3)】

○ 美國은 이락측에 대해 확실한 敗北展望을 주지시키기 위해 兵
力增派를 發表했음

○ 이락은 經濟封鎖로 부터 脫皮하고, 國際的 協助體制를 瓦解시
키기 위해 진력하고 있는 바 經濟制裁만으로 이락의 쿠웨이트
撤收를 실현시키기는 어려움

○ 시간이 경과함에 따라 國際的 協助體制가 약화될 可能性도 있
고 經濟制裁가 이락 뿐 아니라 同盟國에도 被害를 주고 있어
國際的 協助體制가 확고하고 UN에서 武力 사용 決議案의 통
과된 현시점에서 이락에 대한 強硬한 措置를 취하는 것이 效
果的임

【「포웰」合參議長(12.3)】

○ 페灣事態 관련 4대목표 달성을 위해서는 防禦能力 뿐 아니라
攻勢能力 確保가 重要함

31 - 9

0160

○ 攻勢的 戰爭을 택할 경우 美軍은 <u>壓倒的 優位</u>를 점할 수 있는 戰略을 택해야 할 것임

3. 評　價

　가. 이번 上院 軍事委의 聽聞會는

　　○ 부시 行政府의 對中東 美軍增派 결정(11.8)을 계기로 武力 使用 가능성이 증대됨에 따라

　　○ 經濟封鎖 및 外交努力을 통한 사태해결 가능성을 檢討하고 武力使用에 대한 議會의 立場을 정립할 목적으로 개최된 것임

　나. 전반적인 證言內容은

　　○ 사태발생이후 현재까지 行政府가 추진해 온 政策에는 대부분 支持立場을 表明하면서도

　　○ 향후 사태해결 方法과 관련해서는 經濟制裁의 持續을 강조하는 신중론과 武力行使의 불가피성을 강조하는 강경론으로 對立됨으로써

　　○ 사태해결을 위한 具體的 代案提示에 까지는 이르지 못한 것으로 評價

31-10

0161

다. 이같은 對立樣相은

○ 부시 行政府가 UN에서의 對이락 武力使用 決議案 채택등
   國際的 支持를 규합헀음에도 불구하고

○ 對內的으로는 폐灣政策에 대한 國民的 合意가 이루어 지지
   않고 있어 향후 對이락 軍事制裁 추진과 관련 制約要因이
   상존하고 있음을 示唆하는 것임.

31-11

0162

관리
번호 70-2258

원 본

외 무 부

종 별 :

번 호 : USW-5411    일 시 : 90 1204 1915

수 신 : 장관( 미북,미안,중근동)

발 신 : 주 미 대사

제 목 : 페만 사태 청문회

1. 금 12.4. 상원 외교위 (위원장 CLAIRBORNE PELL, 민주-로드아일랜드)는 ARTHUR SCHLESINGER 교수, ROBERT MCNAMARA 전 국방장관, JUDITH KIPPER 부르킹스 연구소 연구원 및 SAM ZAKHEM 전 주바레인 대사를 출석시킨 가운데 페만 사태에 관한 청문회를 개최 하였음.

2. 동 청문회시 PELL 위원장은 경제 제재 조치 성공을 거두기 위해서는 충분한 시간을 주어야 할것이라는 요지의 개회발언을 하였으며 동 청문회 증언자중ZAKHEM 전 바레인 대사를 제외하고는 증언자 전원이 경제 제재 및 외교적 수단에 의한 페만 사태 해결을 옹호하는 증언을 하였는바, 동 요지 하기 보고함.

(MCNAMARA 전 국방장관)

O BUSH 행정부측이 인내를 가지고 페만사태 해결 노력을 기울여야 하며, 신국제질서의 근간인 집단안보 체제의 구축을 위해 이락에 대항하는 국제적 협조 체제를 계속 유지하는것이 중요함.

O 미국이 국제적 협조 체제에 있어서 주도적 역할을 하고는 있지만, 페만사태 해결에 있어 동맹국간에는 균형있는 책임분담이 이루어 져야 하며, 이러한 책임분담은 향후 신국제질서의 주요 원칙이 되어야 함.

금번 페만 사태를 위해서는 경제제재 조치가 성과를 거둘수있도록 충분한 기회를 주어야 하며, 동시에 겨에 제재 조치를 뒷받침하기 위해 미국은 주사우디미군의 병력을 계속 주둔시켜야 함.

단, 주사우디 미군병력이 상당기간 주둔할수 있도록하기 위해서는 순환 근무제가 도입되어야하며, 순환 근무제가 없이 주사우디 미군이 장기간 주둔하게 될 경우에는 성급한 무력사용을 초래할 우려가 있음.

O 경제 제재 조치 및 모든 외교적 노력이 성과가 없다고 판단될때에는 무력사용의

| 미주국 | 장관 | 차관 | 1차보 | 2차보 | 미주국 | 중아국 | 청와대 |
|--------|------|------|-------|-------|--------|--------|--------|

PAGE 1

방법 밖에는 없을것임.

(SCHLESINGER 교수)

0 과거 히틀러에 대항할것인가에 대해 의회를 포함 미국내적으로 충분한 토의를 거친후 미국이 정책을 결정하였듯이 금번 페만사태에 대해서도 의회를 주축으로한 국내적 토의 과정은 반드시 거쳐야 할것임.

0 이락의 향후 군사능력을 파괴하기 위한 소위 예방전쟁(PREVENTIVE WAR) 주장은 과거 중국 및 소련에 대한 예방 전쟁 주장이 그릇된 주장이었듯이 잘못된것이며, 중동 지역은 종교적 분쟁, 국경분쟁 으로 점철된 역사를 갖고 있는 지역으로 이와같은 지역에 안정을 확립시키겠다는 미국 정책은 잘못된 것임.

(KIPPER 부르킹스 연구원)

0 사담 후세인은 영리하고 계산적인 사람이나 주변 보좌관들이 충분하고 정확한 보고를 해주지 않고 있음.

0 후세인은 금번 페만 사태가 어떠한 방향으로 해결이 되든지 아랍세계의 젊은 세대에게는 이스라엘을 지원하고 있는 서방 세계에 정면으로 대항했다는점만으로도 영웅으로 추앙될 우려가 있음.

0 금번 사태는 외교적으로 해결될수 있으며 전쟁은 회피되어야 할것임.

(ZAKHEM 전 바레인 대사)

0 후세인은 페만사태 정책에 대한 미 의회내 토의를 미 정부가 분열 되었다는 식으로 받아들일것이고, 대항하는 입장을 더욱 굳힐 것임.

0 후세인은 페만 지역에 있어서 패권을 추구하고 있으므로 미국은 모든 수단을 동원해서라도 이를 저지해야함.

3. 동 청문회 질의 응답시는 지난주 군사위 청문회에서와 마찬가지로 민주당측 의원들은 경제제재 조치를 통한 해결이 바람직하고, 무력 사용이 불가피한경우, 무력사용을 위해서는 의회의 사전 승인이 필요하다는 입장을 강력히 피력하였음.

(대사 박동진- 국장)

90.12.31. 까지

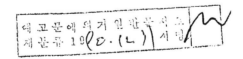

| 관리<br>번호 | 10-2363 | | 외　무　부 | | 원　본 |

종　별 : 지　급

번　호 : USW-5425　　　　　　　　　　　　일　시 : 90 1205 1805

수　신 : 장관( 미북,미안, 중근동)

발　신 : 주 미 대사

제　목 : 페만사태 관련 청문회

연:USW-5411

　1. 금 12.5. 상원 외교위는 JAMES BAKER 국무장관을 출석시킨 가운데 페만 사태관련 청문회를 개최 하였음.

　2. 동 청문회시 CLAIRBORNE PELL( 민주-로드아일랜드)  위원장은 무력사용의가능성이 높아지고 있는데 대해 우려를 표명하고 행정부의 정책이 첫째 경제제재 조치가 성공을 거둘수 있도록 충분한 기회를 주지 않고 있으며, 둘째 긴급한 조치의 필요성을 너무 강조하고 있으며 , 세째 사우디 주둔 동맹국 군사력에 있어서 미군이 차지하고 있는 비율이 너무 높다는 점을 지적하였고, JESSY HELMS(공화-노스캐롤라이나) 간사는 최근 10 여일 기간 페만 사태 정책에 대한 비난과추측들이 난무함에 따라 현시점에서 대통령이 가장 필요로 하고 있는 미국민의단합을 해치고 있고, 비공개로 심의되어야 하는 주요 사항들이 공개적으로 심의됨에 따라 주사우디 미군의 사기와 안전을 약화시키고 있다고 발언함으로써 최근 일련의 청문회 개최에 대해 심각한 반발을 표명하였음. 또한 페만사태 해결을위한 미군의 사우디 파병은 군의 최고 사령관으로서 대통령의 고유권한이며, 의회가 동권한을 제한하려고 해서는 안되고, 의회 다수당이 대통령의 권한을 통제하고자한다면 특별회기를 소집 하여 예산권한을 통해 대통령을 통제하여야 하며, 그러한 공시적 조치없이 대통령 권한 및 정책판단에 의문을 제기하는것은 국가를 불안정하게 하는 무책임한 것임을 강한 어조로 비판하였음.

　3. 동 청문회시 BAKER 국무장관은 이락의 쿠웨이트 침공이래 미국의 대 페만 사태 정책은 변화하지 않았으며, 11.8. 의 병력 증강 조치도 페만 사태의 평화적 해결을 위한 일련의 연속된 정책의 일환이라는 점을 강조하였고, 무력 사용과 관련, 무력사용 여부에 대해서는 상금 어떠한 결정이 내려진 상황이 아니나 경제제재 조치만으로

| 미주국 | 장관 | 차관 | 1차보 | 2차보 | 미주국 | 중아국 | 청와대 |

PAGE 1

이락의 쿠웨이트 철수등 4 대 정책 목표가 달성되기 어렵다는 판단이 점점 확고해 지고 있으며 , 따라서 무력사용 방안의 가능성에 대비하고 있다는 요지의 발언을 하였는바, 동 요지 하기 보고함.

O 페만 사태 해결의 기본 입장은 페만 사태의 4 대 정책 목표를 평화적으로그리고 가장 최소한의 희생으로 달성한다는 것이며, 만약 이러한 평화적 방법으로 해결될수 없다고 판단될 경우에는 무력사용도 불사한다는것임.

O 이락에 대한 경제 제재 조치는 이락으로 하여금 쿠웨이트로 부터 철수할수밖에 없을 정도로 커다란 댓가를 치루게 하는것이었으나 동 제재 조치가 4 개월 경과된 현시점에서 이락은 UN 결의안을 수용할 아무런 조짐을 보이지 않고 있으며, 오히려 쿠웨이트에 대한 약탈을 계속하고, 사우디 아라비아 및 이집트 등 주변국가 정부의 전복을 기도하고 있음.

O 최근 봉과된 UN 의 무력사용 결의안은 이락에 대해 사태의 평화적 해결을위한 마지막 기회를 제공하는것임.

O 혹자는 경제제재 조치만으로 페만 사태를 평화적으로 해결할수 있다고 판단하고 있으나, 경제제재 조치의 목표는 이락에 대해 경제적 피해를 주는것에 그치는것이 아니라 이락의 태도를 변화시키고 쿠웨이트로 부터 철수를 얻어내는것이며, 경제제재 조치가 4 개월 경과된 현재 경제제재 조치만으로 그 목표가 될성될수 있다고 확신하기는 어려움.

O 경제제재 조치가 성공을 거두도록 기다리는 정책은 후세인으로 하여금 제재 조치를 붕괴시킬수 있는 시간을 주는것이며, 또한 우리측에게도 피해를 입히는것임. 이락은 계속 인질 문제를 악화시키고, 국제적 협조체제의 와해를 기도하며 핵, 화학 및 세균 무기 개발을 추진할것이며, 기다리는 동안 국제적 협조 체제나 페만 사태 해결 의지를 약화 시키는 어떤 돌발 사태도 발생할수 있음.

O 미국은 무력 사용을 위한 만반의 준비를 하여야 하며, 이에 실패할경우에는 무력 사용의 위협을 통한 외교적 해결 가능성은 오히려 감소되고 이락의 쿠웨이트 점령을 묵인하는 결과를 초래하기 쉬우며, 만약의 무력 사용 사태 발발시 미국은 더욱 큰 사상자를 감수할수밖에 없을것임.

4. 동 청문회 질의 응답시에는 당노선에 따른 민주당 및 공화당 의원의 입장 차이가 크게 부각되었는바, 민주당 의원들은 지난주 군사위 청문회 및 금번 청문회시 대부분의 증언자들이 경제제재 조치가 12-18 개월 정도 지속되면 성공을 거둘것이며,

PAGE 2

0166

성급한 무력사용은 향후 페만 사태의 안정을 위해서도 바람직하지 않다는 증언 내용을 원용하면서 행정부가 경제제재 조치가 성과를 거둘수 있도록 충분한 시간을 주지않고 성급하게 무력사용을 준비하고 있는점을 신랄히 비난하였으며, LUGAR 의원등 공화당게 의원들은 의회측이 최근 UN 의 무력사용 승인결의안과 유사한 결의안을 채택할수 있도록 미 의회의 특별회기 소집 필요성을강조하였고, 페만사태 해결을 위한 행정부의 정책에 대한 지지를 표명하였음. 아울러, 주요 질의 응답 사항으로 1.15. 이후 무력사용 가능성에 대한 질문에 대해 BAKER 장관은 1.15. 이후 반드시 무력을 사용한다는것은 아니고 무력사용을 할수 있도록 원칙적 승인을 얻은것이며, 실질적 무력 사용은 동맹국과의 사전 협의를 거친후에 결정될 것이라고 발언 하였음.

5. 상기 BAKER 장관의 청문회에 이어 ZBIGNIEW BREZEZINSKI 전 카터 대봉령안보 보좌관등을 대상으로 청문회가 개최 되었으며(대부분의 공화당 소속 의원들은 붐참) , BREZEZINSKI 전 안보 보좌관도 무력사용은 향후 페만 지역의 안정을 크게 해친다는 점을 강조 하면서 경제제재 조치를 봉한 사태해결을 옹호 하였음.

6. 상기 BAKER 국무장관 및 BREZEZINSKI 전 안보보좌관 증언문 및 주요 질의 응답 사항은 별전 팩스 송부함.

USW(F)-3368

(대사 박동진-국장)

90.12.31. 까지

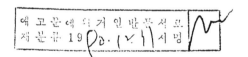

주 미 대 사 관

<table>
<tr><td>보안</td><td></td></tr>
<tr><td>통제</td><td></td></tr>
</table>

번호 : USW(F) - 3768

수신 : 장관 (미북, 미안, 름근봉 )

발신 : 주미대사

제목 : 페만 사태 청문회 (22매)

금 12.5 상원 외교위 특별 청문회 관계 자료를

불참 FAX 송부함.

1. Baker 국무장관 증언문

2. Brezezinski 전 안보보좌관 증언문 → 특기사항번해

3. 주요 질의 응답 요지        끝

Embargoed until Delivery
Expected at 10:00 a.m.(EST), December 5, 1990

America's Strategy in the Persian Gulf Crisis

Statement

By

The Honorable James A. Baker, III

Before

The Senate Foreign Relations Committee

December 5, 1990

336-2

Mr. Chairman:

Today, I come before you for the third time since August 2
to discuss Iraq's continuing occupation of Kuwait.

I have come here to consult with you because a very
dangerous dictator -- armed to the teeth -- is threatening a
critical region at a defining moment in history.  He must be
stopped -- peacefully if possible, but by force if necessary.

I would like to focus my prepared remarks on three aspects
of the situation:

- One, on explaining the President's strategy;

- Two, on detailing the reasons that preparations for the
  possible use of force -- and indeed a willingness to use
  force, if necessary -- remain essential to achieving a
  peaceful resolution; and

- Three, on presenting the compelling interests we have in
  seeing Saddam Hussein's brutal aggression undone.

336A-3

0170

-2-

## Strategy

From the outset, the international community has rallied
behind four objectives:

- First, the immediate, complete, and unconditional Iraqi
  withdrawal from Kuwait;

- Second, the restoration of Kuwait's legitimate government;

- Third, the release of all hostages; and

- Fourth, a commitment to the security and stability of the
  Persian Gulf.

The President has stated repeatedly that we seek to achieve
these objectives peacefully.  He has also made clear that we
seek to achieve them at least cost to ourselves and the other
members of the international coalition.

From the outset, our strategy to achieve these objectives
has been to make Saddam Hussein pay such a high price for his
aggression that he would quit Kuwait.  We have aimed to impose
costs on Saddam for his aggression by taking increasingly harsh
steps on a continuum of pressure and pain -- politically,
economically, and militarily.  On this continuum, economic
sanctions and military preparations are not alternatives, but
reinforcing and escalating steps of the same strategy.   3364-4

0171

-3-

Notwithstanding our desire for peace, from the outset we
have proceeded with the full realization that if these
objectives cannot be achieved peacefully, we must be prepared
to use force, given the vital interests at stake.

Thus, starting on August 2, an international coalition led
by the United States began to impose costs on Iraq for its
aggression.

The day of the invasion the Security Council passed
Resolution 660, calling for an immediate Iraqi withdrawal from
Kuwait. When this effort and the diplomatic efforts of the
Arab League were summarily rejected by Saddam Hussein, on
August 6 the Security Council imposed mandatory economic
sanctions to increase the pressure on Iraq and make it pay
greater costs for its aggression. The hope was that by
isolating Iraq politically and economically, Saddam Hussein
would withdraw.

While these diplomatic and economic steps were being taken,
military forces were deployed in the region to deter further
aggression and to support the Security Council Resolutions. As
of now, twenty seven nations have joined in this truly
unprecedented multinational force.

336A-5

To date, the international coalition has had considerable
success in isolating Iraq and making it pay high costs for its

0172

-4-

occupation of Kuwait.  We regret the pain this causes innocent
citizens of Iraq, a people with whom we have no quarrel.

But the question before us now is whether the costs we
impose on Saddam Hussein through sanctions alone will be high
enough to cause him to withdraw peacefully from Kuwait.

We have to face the fact that, four months into this
conflict, none of our efforts have yet produced any sign of
change in Saddam Hussein.  He shows no signs of complying with
any of the Security Council Resolutions.

Instead, he seems to be doubling his bets.  He has tried to
make Kuwait part of Iraq, systematically looting and
dismembering a sovereign Arab state.  He has been terrorizing
the population, his soldiers committing unspeakable crimes
against innocent Kuwaitis.  He has called for the overthrow of
King Fahd of Saudi Arabia and President Mubarak of Egypt.  He
has threatened to rain terror and mass destruction on his Arab
neighbors and on Israel.  He has been playing the cruelest of
games with hostages and their families and with our diplomats
in Kuwait.

## Preparing for War to Achieve Peace

After serious and sobering consultations, the United
Nations Security Council last Thursday passed by an
overwhelming majority a twelfth Resolution one that

336A-6

0173

-5-

authorizes all necessary means, including the use of force, to eject Saddam from Kuwait after January 15, 1991.  In passing this Resolution, the international community is giving Saddam yet another chance -- indeed, one last chance -- to come to his senses.

In passing Thursday's Resolution, the international community sends Saddam the following clear message: "We continue to seek a diplomatic solution.  Peace is your only sensible option.  You can choose peace by respecting the will of the international community.  But if you fail to do so, you will risk all.  The choice is yours."

To ensure that Saddam understands this choice, the President has invited the Foreign Minister of Iraq to Washington and has directed me to go to Baghdad.

Put bluntly, this is the last best chance for a peaceful solution.  If we are to have any chance of success, I must go to Baghdad with the fullest support of the Congress and the American people behind the message of the international community.

Let me be clear: This meeting will not be the beginning of a negotiation over the terms of the United Nations Resolutions.  Those terms are clear: a complete, immediate, and unconditional Iraqi withdrawal; the restoration of the legitimate Kuwaiti government; and the release of all foreign

336A-1

0174

-6-

Nor is this the beginning of a negotiation on subjects unrelated to Iraq's brutal occupation of Kuwait. I will not be negotiating the Palestinian question or the civil war in Lebanon. Saddam did not invade Kuwait to help the Palestinians. He did it for his own self-aggrandizement. As Eduard Shevardnadze has said, you do not enslave one people to free another.

Put simply, my mission to Baghdad will be an attempt to explain to Saddam the choice he faces: comply with the objectives of the Security Council or risk disaster for Iraq.

To give substance to these words, the President has directed the Secretary of Defense, the Chairman of the Joint Chiefs, and me to work with the other members of the international coalition to reinforce the multinational force in the Gulf and coordinate its efforts. Our aim is to ensure that if force must be used, it will be used suddenly, massively, and decisively.

Do the troop reinforcements and the Security Council Resolution mean that war is inevitable? Surely not. There is a peaceful outcome possible -- one that does not reward aggression -- and everyone, including Saddam, knows what it is. He can choose peace by withdrawing unconditionally from Kuwait and releasing all hostages.

*336 -A*

He will not make that peaceful choice, however, unless he

0175

-7-

be forced to comply.  That is the message we are trying to send
him.  That is the meaning of the steps the international
community has taken over the past month.  It is not a new
strategy but rather a continuation and reinforcement of the
strategy we have pursued since August.

I know that some here and throughout the country are uneasy
about the prospects of war.  None of us wants war.  Not you.
Not the President.  Not me.  None of us have sought this
conflict, and we are making every attempt to resolve it
peacefully, without appeasing the aggressor.

I know the arguments of those who believe that time and the
economic embargo alone will work to resolve this conflict
peacefully.  But we have to face some hard facts.

If sanctions are to succeed, they must do more than hurt
Iraq economically.  They must hurt Saddam so much that he
changes his behavior and withdraws from Kuwait.  That is the
criteria of success by which sanctions must be judged.

In considering the role of sanctions in our strategy, we
need to ask ourselves:

• Can economic sanctions alone compel a dictator like Saddam
  to make the politically difficult choice of withdrawing
  from Kuwait?

3368-9

0176

-8-

• Absent a credible military threat, will Saddam take the
  growing sanctions against seriously?

• Is there anything in Saddam Hussein's history that could
  lead us to believe that sanctions alone will get him out of
  Kuwait?


Let me try to answer these questions, based on the results
so far.  After four months of a stringent embargo, no one
doubts that sanctions are having some effect on the Iraqi
economy.  But we have to face the difficult fact that no one
can tell you that sanctions alone will ever be able to impose a
high enough cost on Saddam to get him to withdraw.  So far, all
available evidence suggests that they have had little if any
effect on his inclination to withdraw.


That's in part because Saddam, to a considerable extent,
can decide who in Iraq gets hurt by them.  And you can bet the
Iraqi people will feel the pain first and most deeply -- not
the Iraqi military or Saddam himself.  Saddam has a long
history of imposing great pain and suffering on the Iraqi
people.  It is not new for him to impose economic sacrifices on
the Iraqi people in pursuit of his ambitions.


We need to remember who we are trying to get out of
Kuwait.  Saddam is a ruthless dictator.  He has an inflated
sense of Iraq's leverage and a high pain threshold.  Saddam
undoubtedly believes he can endure economic sanctions.

0177

However, surely he understands more acutely the consequences of military force.

Waiting not only gives Saddam time to break the sanctions, but it imposes costs on us.

As we wait, Saddam will continue torturing Kuwait, killing it as a nation.

As we wait, he will continue manipulating hostages, attempting to break the coalition.

As we wait he will continue to stultify Kuwait, to build chemical and biological weapons, and to acquire a nuclear weapons capability.

As we wait, he expects other issues to deflect our attention, weaken our resolve, and dissolve the international coalition.

And as we wait, the burden of Saddam's crime weighs heavier on the world.

That is why we must make credible our preparations to use force.

The international community has clearly agreed that force will not be used before January 15 of next year, provided 2364-11

0178

Saddam does not provoke a response. Thus, Mr. Chairman, we
need to remind ourselves that for now, no one is making a
decision about going to war. Indeed, in asking me to go to
Baghdad, the President has made it clear that he will use the
next six weeks to exhaust all diplomatic opportunities.

Yet to support these diplomatic efforts, Mr. Chairman, the
President has also made it clear that we need continued support
for our military preparations to make credible an offensive
option to liberate Kuwait. While not prejudging any decision
whether force should be used sometime after January 15, I can
state unequivocally that failure to continue preparations now
has at least three dangerous consequences.

First, it would undercut our diplomatic leverage by
removing the other alternative to a peaceful withdrawal: use of
force. It would send Iraq exactly the wrong message -- that
is, "Continue to play for time. You will have lots of it
because the Security Council Resolution is just a bluff. The
international coalition is not even preparing the option to use
force, let alone take that option." That is a message we must
not send.

We must show Saddam that time is not on his side. He needs
to know that even if he believes he can withstand the
sanctions, and he may be right in this belief, we can and will
impose even greater costs on him through the use of force if
necessary.

336-12

0179

Second, failure to prepare a credible offensive military
option would only tend to reaffirm the status quo and
legitimize to some the brutal occupation that Saddam is now
carrying out against Kuwait and its people.

Third, failure to prepare adequately now would mean that
should conflict come, we would be irresponsibly risking greater
casualties -- putting the lives of those young Americans
already on the front lines in the Persian Gulf at greater risk
than they need be.  The President will not stand for that.  And
neither will the American people.

## What's at Stake

Mr. Chairman, we do not proceed along this path unaware of
the dangers and risks involved.  But let there be no doubt,
that succeeding in this endeavor -- hopefully in peace, if
necessary by force -- is in the vital interest of the American
people.

It is often said that there has been no clear answer given
to the question of why we are in the Gulf.  Much of this
results from the search for a single cause for our involvement,
a single reason the President could use to explain why the
lives of American men and women should be put in harm's way in
the sands of Arabia or the seas around it and in the air above
it.

3364-13

0180

-12-

Mr. Chairman, let us stop this search. Let us be honest with ourselves and with each other. There are multiple causes, multiple dangers, multiple threats. Standing alone, each is compelling. Put together, the case is overwhelming.

Put bluntly: <u>A very dangerous dictator -- armed to the teeth -- is threatening a critical region at a defining moment in history.</u>

It is the combination of these reasons -- <u>who</u> is threatening our interests, <u>what</u> capabilities he has and is developing, <u>where</u> he is carrying out aggression, and <u>when</u> he has chosen to act -- that make the stakes so high for all of us.

Let me explain.

<u>Strategically</u>, Saddam is a capricious dictator whose lust for power is as unlimited as his brutality in pursuit of it. He has invaded two neighbors, is harboring terrorists, and now is systematically exterminating Kuwait. Saddam uses poisonous gas -- even against his own people; develops deadly toxins; and seeks relentlessly to acquire nuclear bombs. He has built the world's sixth largest army, has the world's fifth largest tank army, and has deployed ballistic missiles.

<u>Geographically</u>, Saddam's aggression has occurred in a political tinderbox that is crossroads to three continents.

0181

His success would only guarantee more strife, more conflict,
and eventually a wider war.  There would be little hope for any
effort at peace-making in the Middle East.

Economically, Saddam's aggression imperils the world's oil
lifelines, threatening recession and depression, here and
abroad, hitting hardest those fledgling democracies least able
to cope with it.  His aggression is an attempt to mortgage the
economic promise of the post-Cold War world to the whims of a
single man.

Morally, we must act so that international laws, not
international outlaws, govern the post-Cold War world.  We must
act so that right, not might, dictates success in the post-Cold
War world.  We must act so that innocent men and women and
diplomats are protected, not held hostage, in the post-Cold War
world.

Historically, we must stand with the people of Kuwait so
that the annexation of Kuwait does not become the first reality
that mars our vision of a new world order.  We must stand with
the world community so that the United Nations does not go the
way of the League of Nations.

Politically, we must stand for American leadership, not
because we seek it but because no one else can do the job.  And
we did not stand united for forty years to bring the Cold War
to a peaceful end in order to make the world safe for the likes

0182

-14-

These then are the stakes.

If Saddam is not stopped now, if his aggressive designs are
not frustrated, peacefully if possible, or if necessary by
force, we will all pay a higher price later.

As the Security Council did last Thursday, this Congress
and the American people must tell Saddam Hussein in
unmistakable actions and words:

"Get out of Kuwait now or risk all."

Mr. Chairman, now -- more than at any time during this
conflict -- we must stand united with the world community in
full support of the Security Council Resolutions.

Simply put, it is a choice between right and wrong.

I believe we have the courage and fortitude to choose
what's right.

Thank you.

336A-16

0183

( Brzezinski 증언문)

MR. BRZEZINSKI: Thank you, Mr. Chairman. If I may, I would like to begin with a brief personal comment. As many of you know, I supported President Bush in the 1988 elections, and I have supported his foreign policy all along. Moreover, I do not subscribe to the notion that the use of force is altogether precluded in international affairs. I mention this at the outset because I would not want my views to be interpreted as motivated either by political or ideological biases.

Let me also say right off that I have supported and still support the initial decisions of the President regarding both troop deployments to deter any further Iraqi aggression and the imposition of sanctions on Iraq for the flagrant aggression that it did commit. The President and his team are to be commended for the skill with which the international coalition has been put together and for the impressively prompt deployment of American power. The policy of punitive containment of Iraq rightly gained almost universal international and domestic support.

Most Americans, I'm sure, share the hope that the President's recent and laudable decision to initiate a direct dialogue with the Iraqi government will lead to a serious and comprehensive exploration of a non-violent solution to the ongoing crisis. Wisely, the President indicated that the purpose of such a dialogue is not to merely convey an ultimatum but to convince Iraq that its compliance with the UN resolution is the necessary precondition for a peaceful settlement. It is thus not an accident that those who so fervently have been advocating war have promptly denounced the President's initiative.

To be meaningful, such a dialogue has to go beyond demands for unconditional surrender, but involve also some discussion of the consequences of Iraqi compliance with the UN resolutions. That means that Iraq, in the course of the ensuing discussions, will have to be given some preliminary indications of the likely political, territorial, and financial aftermath of its withdrawal from Kuwait.

I stress these points because those who favor only a military solution will now exercise pressure on the President to reduce the incipient dialogue essentially to a mere transmittal of an ultimatum. That, I trust, everyone recognizes would be pointless and counterproductive. It would simply accelerate the drift to war.

While it is premature to detail here the substance of a non-violent solution to the crisis that could emerge from the proposed dialogue, it is possible to envisage a series of sequential but linked phases, all premised on Iraq having satisfied the necessary preconditions regarding Kuwait.

336 ~ 17

0184

First, of course, is sanctions would be maintained until Iraq implements its willingness to comply with the UN resolutions regarding their withdrawal from Kuwait.

Two, binding arbitration by a UN-sanctioned body within a specified timeframe would be accepted by the governments of Iraq and Kuwait regarding territorial delimitations, conflicting financial claims, and other pertinent matters.

Three, an international conference would be convened to establish regional limitations on weapons of mass destruction, pending which a UN-sponsored security force would remain deployed in Kuwait, and perhaps in Saudi Arabia, to ensure needed security.

It is important to note, Mr. Chairman, that any dialogue to the above effect will be conducted while Iraq is being subjected to severe sanctions. The US would be, therefore, conceding nothing while conducting the talks. It is Iraq that is under duress, not us. It is Iraqi power that is being attrited, while ours is growing. It is Iraq that is isolated and threatened with destruction, not us.

Nor would any such outcome as the one outlined above be tantamount to rewarding aggression. Those who argue that do so because they desire only one outcome, no matter what the price to America -- the destruction of Iraq. Withdrawal from Kuwait would represent a massive setback for Saddam Hussein and a victory for the international order. It will be a dramatic reversal of aggression, humiliating and painful to the aggressor.

However, it is quite possible, perhaps even probable, that the talks will initially prove unproductive. In my view, that should not be viewed as a casus belli. Instead, we should stay on course applying the policy of punative containment. This policy is working. Iraq has been deterred, astrocized and punished. Sanctions, unprecedented in their international solidarity and more massive in scope than any ever adopted in peacetime against any nation -- I repeat -- ever adopted against any nation, are inflicting painful costs on the Iraqi economy.

Economic sanctions, by their definition, require time to make their impact felt. But they have already established the internationally significant lesson that Iraq's aggression did not pay. By some calculations, about 97 percent of Iraq's income and 90 percent of its imports have been cut off, and the shutdown of the equivalent of 43 percent of Iraq's and Kuwait's GNP has already taken place. This is prompting the progressive attrition of the country's economy and war-making capabilities. Extensive rationing is a grim social reality. Over time, all this is bound to have an unsettling effect on Saddam Hussein's power.

The administration's argument that the sanctions are not working suggests to me that -- in the first instance -- that the administration had entertained extrememly naive notions regarding how sanctions actually do work. They not only take time, they are by their nature an instrument for softening up the opponent, inducing in the adversary a more compliant attitude towards an eventual nonviolent resolution. Sanctions are not a blunt instrument for promptly achieving total surrender.

326A - 18

Worse still, the administration's actions and its rhetoric have conveyed a sense of impatience that in fact has tended to undermine the credibility of long-term sanctions.  Perhaps the administration felt that this was necessary to convince Saddam Hussein that it meant business, but the consequence has been to make the administration the prisoner of its own rhetoric, with American options and timetable thereby severely constricted.

The cumulative result has been to move the United States significantly beyond the initial policy of punitive containment with the result that the conflict of the international community with Iraq has become over-Americanized, over-personalized, and over-emotionalized.  The enormous deployment of American forces, coupled with talk of "no compromise" means that the United States is now pointed towards a war with Iraq that will be largely an American war fought predominantly by Americans, in which -- on our side -- mostly Americans will die, and for interests that are neither equally vital nor urgent to America, and which in any case can be and should be effectively pursued by other less dramatic and less bloody means.

Yet, to justify military action, the administration, echoing the advocates of war, has lately been relying on the emotionally charged argument that we confront a present danger because of the possibility that Iraq may at some point acquire a nuclear capability.  In other words, not oil, not Kuwait, but Iraq's nuclear program has become the latest excuse for moving towards war.

This argument deserves careful scrutiny.  But once subjected to it, this latest case for war also does not meet the tests of vitality or urgency to the American national interests.  First of all, it is relevant to note that when the United States was threatened directly by the far more powerful and dangerous Stalinist Russia or Maoist China, it refrained from engaging in preventive war.  Moreover, Israel already has nuclear weapons and can thus deter Iraq, while the United States has certainly both the power to deter or to destroy Iraq.  Deterrence has worked in the past, and I fail to see why thousands of Americans should now die in order to make sure that at some point in the future, according to experts some years from now, Iraq does not acquire a militarily significant nuclear capability.

Second, it is within our power to sustain a comprehensive embargo on Iraq to impede such an acquisition.  Unlike India or Israel, Iraq does permit international inspection of its nuclear facilities.  This gives us some insight into its program.  Moreover, much can happen during the next several years, including Saddam's fall from power.  Hence, the precipitation of war now on these grounds meets neither the criterion of urgency nor vitality.

More than that, war would be highly counter productive to the American national interest.  A war is likely to split the international consensus that currently exists, the United States is likely to become estranged from many of its European allies, and it is almost certain to become the object of widespread Arab hostility.  Indeed, once started, the war may prove not all that easy to terminate, given the inflammable character of Middle Eastern politics.  It could be costly in blood and financially devastating.

364-19

This prospect is all the more tragic —ause the United States would thereby be deprived of the fruits of its hard-earned victory in the Cold War. We stand today on the threshold of an historic opportunity to shape a truly cooperative world order based on genuine cooperation and respect for human rights. Yet, our over-reaction to the crisis in the Persian Gulf is now adversely affecting both our priorities and our principles.

In any case, Mr. Chairman, it is war that soon we may have to face because of the combined pressures resulting from Iraqi intransigence, the imposition of a deadline, the lack of patience in the application of sanctions, and the consequences of massive troop deployments. Given the possibility, therefore, that the United States might be plunged by presidential decision into a war with Iraq, I would urge this committee to examine carefully in its deliberations and to press the administration for answers regarding the following three clusters of critically important issues.

One, what are the political limits and the likely geopolitical dynamics of war once the President decides to initiate it? For example, we have to be concerned over the use of air power, that in order to mitigate casualties for US ground forces, the killing not only the hostages, but also thousands, perhaps tens of thousands or even more, of Iraqi civilians who are not to be held responsible for Saddam Hussein's flagrant misconduct might be required. Is this politically viable? Is this morally admissable?

Also, how does the administration envisage the termination of the war? Do we expect a total surrender, or are we counting on a negotiated outcome after a spasm of violence? Are we prepared to occupy all of Iraq, including the huge city of Baghdad? Are we logistically prepared for a war that is not promptly resolved by air power? And are we psychologically, for heavy American casualties?

And once war begins, Iran and Syria may not remain passive, and the war could thus spread.

One has to anticipate the possibility that Iraq will seek to draw Israel into the war. Does the administration have a contingency plan in the event that Jordan becomes a battlefield? What might be the US reaction if some Israeli leaders seek to take advantage of an expanded war to effect the expulsion of all Palestinians from their homes in the West Bank? The Gulf crisis and the Arab-Israeli conflict could thus become linked. Our efforts to the contrary notwithstanding.

I believe, Mr. Chairman, the administration is paying insufficient attention to these inherent uncertainties of war. The war could prove more destructive, more bloody, and more difficult to terminate than administration spokesmen, not to speak of sundry private advocates of war, seem to think. I also believe the administration has not given sufficient thought to the geopolitical disruptive consequences of a war in a region that is extraordinarily incendiary. An American military invasion of Iraq would be likely to set off a chain reaction that could bog America down in a variety of prolonged security operations in a setting of intensified political instability.

2264-20

0187

Secondly, what are the likely broader aftereffects of the war? The administration has yet to move beyond vague generalities regarding its concept of the postwar Middle East. Yet considerable anxiety is justified that subsequent to the war, the United States might not be able to extricate itself from the Middle Eastern cauldron, especially if, in the meantime, the Arab masses have become radicalized and hostile to the Arab regimes that endorsed the US military action.

How will that affect America's global position? I would think it likely that with the United States embroiled in the Middle Eastern mess for years to come, both Europe and Japan, free to promote their own agendas, will pursue the enhancement of their economic power. And in the region itself, it is probable that fundamentalist Iran will become the dominant power in the Persian Gulf and that terrorist Syria will inherit the mantle of leadership among the Arabs. It is also possible that the destruction of Iraq by America and the resulting radicalization of the Arabs might leave Israel, armed as it already is with nuclear weapons, more tempted to use its military force to impose its will in this volatile region.

How will all this affect the area's sensitive balance of power? I believe that none of the above possible developments would be in the American interest. Yet I do not sense that sufficient strategic planning has been devoted by the administration to an analysis of the wider shock effects of a war that is bound to be exploited by other parties for their own selfish ends.

Third and finally, what is being done to ensure that the worst burdens and sacrifices are more fairly distributed among its potential beneficiaries or participants if war must come? One cannot help but be struck by the relatively limited contributions of our allies. Moreover, as I understand it, some states with forces in Saudi Arabia have indicated that they will not participate in offensive operations.

The American public certainly is not satisfied with the financial support extended by Germany and Japan. Is the administration satisfied? What additional financial contribution can be expected from the Saudis and the Kuwaitis? It is noteworthy that Saudi Arabia has already benefited very substantially from the oil crisis and that the Emir of Kuwait and his family are in the forefront of those arguing for Americans to initiate military action.

Are we thus, despite all of our rhetoric about the new international order, not running the risk of becoming the mercenaries in this war, applauded and financed by others to do the fighting and the dying for them?

I believe that it is already evident that the principal sacrifices of war, both financial and in blood, will in fact have to be borne by America and to a massively disproportionate degree. Such evident unfairness would inevitably have a very adverse impact on American attitude toward its allies with deleterious consequences for American public support for the so-called "international order."

2360-21

These are tough issues, and unless the administration responds to them satisfactorily, the war will lack domestic support while generating polarizing political passions. Even worse, unless the administration thinks hard about such questions, it could embark on a course deeply damaging to our national interest.

Mr. Chairman, let me conclude with a brief word about the lessons of history. It is important to apply them with a sense of proportion. To speak of Saddam Hussein as a Hitler is to trivialize Hitler and to elevate Saddam. Iraq is not Germany, but a middle size country on the scale of, say, Romania, dependent on the export of one commodity for most of its income, unable on its own either to fully feed itself or to construct its own weapons. It is a threat to regional peace, a threat with wider global economic implications. But it is a threat we can contain, deter, or repel as the situation dictates. Therefore, in my view, neither an American war to liberate Kuwait nor a preventive war to destroy Iraq's power is urgently required, be it in terms of the American national interest or of the imperatives of world order.

President Bush's initial commitment to punish Iraq and to deter it remains the wisest course, and one which this nation can resolutely and in unity sustain over the long haul. By any rational calculus, the trade-offs between the discomforts of patience and the costs of war favor patience. Both time and power are in our favor, and we do not need to be driven by artificial deadlines, deceptive arguments, or irrational emotion, into an unnecessary war.

Thank you, Mr. Chairman.

0189

# Report on Hearings of the
## Senate Foreign Relations Committee
## on U.S. Policy in the Persian Gulf
### Witnesses:

Hon. James Baker III, Secretary of State
Hon. Zbigniew Brzezinski, Fmr. National Security Adviser

December 5, 1990

Secy. Baker attempted to do three general things with his statement: 1. explain the President's policy toward the Persian Gulf region, 2. give reasons for the possible use of force against Iraq, and, 3. outline the U.S. interests in seeing Saddam Hussein's action reversed. He stated that the President seeks a resolution to this crisis at the lowest cost in terms of life and money but that a successful resolution may require the use of all the tools available, including military force. He added that economic sanctions, diplomatic pressure and military force are not mutually exclusive tools, but all exist along one continuum and can all be used together as part of an effective policy. He lamented however, that after four months, sanctions do not appear to be moving Saddam Hussein in the desired direction and therefore the Administration may have to resort to force if he does not respond to the recent United Nations Resolution demanding his withdrawal by January 15, 1991. (He did not say that force is mandated after Jan. 15, only that it is authorized.) Should the United States and international coalition decide that it has no alternative, Saddam Hussein will be dealt a crushing blow by U.S. and allied forces which would be swift and overwhelming.

Secy. Baker stated that during his visit to Baghdad he will not negotiate on anything or allow discussions having to do with the Palestinians or Lebanon. It is the Administration's position that these issues should not be dragged into this crisis and that negotiations will not take place on any issue. Secy. Baker basically assured the Committee that he is going to Baghdad to inform Saddam Hussein of U.S. resolve to cause him to back down, not to negotiate a face-saving way out for him.

Further addressing the issue of waiting vs. acting, he echoed other Administration officials who have stressed that waiting for further stress from the sanctions will allow Saddam Hussein time to chip away at those very sanctions, to continue destroying Kuwait, to try to subvert the international coalition arrayed against him, and to manipulate those hostages that he has. He argued for military preparations for three reasons: 1. they will strengthen diplomatic leverage, 2. they will demonstrate unwillingness to tolerate the status quo and 3. they will save casualties if in fact fighting starts.

On the issue of reasons for U.S. involvement, he said that in the Persian Gulf at present we find a dangerous, well-armed

3368-28

0190

dictator threatening a vital region at a defining moment in history. The Middle East, he said, is the crossroads of three continents and Saddam Hussein's victory there would lead to a wider war which could threaten world recession or depression, mortgage economic growth to his own whims, and show that might can overcome right in the Post Cold War World.

Today the Republican senators were out in force and in most cases showed their support for the Administration's forceful position in this crisis. Senators Jesse Helms (NC), Richard Lugar (IN), Nancy Kassebaum (KS) and Rudy Boschwitz (MN) were the staunchest supporters. For his part, Senator Lugar complained that the Congress would not go into special session as he requested on August 14, 1990 so that it could send a clear message to the President. He expressed confusion that so many in Congress are asking for a role, yet no special session was called. Senator Helms expressed anger that open hearings were being held on what he considers to be sensitive matters that should not be accessible to Saddam Hussein through CNN.

Democratic Senators Christopher Dodd (CT), Paul Sarbanes (MD) John Kerry (MA) Paul Simon (IL) and Joe Biden (DE) all expressed their concern with the Administration's lack of faith in the same sanctions that just a few months ago it was supporting. They all stated that they think the Administration should show the patience it was encouraging the American people to have when sanctions were the main instrument for pressuring Saddam Hussein. The senators also expressed concern that this shift in policy occurred just after the November elections suggesting that for political reasons it was kept secret so that it would not hurt Republicans' chances for (re)election. They also expressed that if force is used precipitously and Americans die, they will regret that every peaceful avenue was not explored. Baker assured them that if military action against Saddam Hussein is initiated, it will only be after the high-ranking officials in all the governments of the countries making up the force have agreed to it.

In his testimony, Dr. Brzezinski showed a great uneasiness about the likely results of a military action in the Gulf led primarily by American troops. He argued strongly that President Bush's plan to give up on sanctions showed great naivete and an impatience that could do more to undermine international support than waiting out sanctions would. Dr. Brzezinski stressed that the war could easily widen to include Iran, Jordan or Syria and that radical elements could upset friendly regimes in Egypt, Saudi Arabia and Bahrain, for example. For this reason, he was much more sober in assessing the costs of a war in the Gulf than the Administration witnesses. His general position is that sanctions should be emphasized and that a dialogue should be held with Saddam Hussein allowing him to discuss his future after he withdraws from Kuwait. However, he acknowledged that the use of deadly force should not be precluded as an instrument of pressure against this atrocious dictator.

336ρ -2ρ

0191

To a question from Chairman Claiborne Pell (D-RI) he answered that a similar show-down from history was the Cuban Missile Crisis where President Kennedy showed resolve and firmness, but not shrill rhetoric and impatience. Dr. Brzezinski argued that it is just that same approach that would serve the world best in this crisis. He said that he fears that President Bush is over-personalizing, and over-emotionalizing this crisis and that such behavior could lead to an unintentional escalation into a war that no one wants.

To a question from Senator Frank Murkowski (R-AK) Dr. Brzezinski stated that he envisions a peace process wherein Iraq believes that the United States is serious and that it must concede Kuwait. This will only be achieved, in his view, if the United States is willing to go beyond merely transmitting ultimata to Saddam Hussein. Backing Saddam Hussein into a desperate corner, Dr. Brzezinski argued, is one of the surest ways to force him to fight.

When asked by Senator Sarbanes why he felt the Administration's policy has shifted, he answered that there could be four reasons: 1. the fear could be real that the coalition will not stand up over time, 2. the narrow decision-making process in the White House may have concluded that fighting is inevitable and there is no dissent among those at the top, 3. Bush has personalized this whole crisis too much and wants to go after Saddam Hussein, and 4. friends abroad may have influenced the Administration, i.e. Britain, Kuwait, Saudi Arabia, and possibly Israel.

Dr. Brzezinski made the significant statement that this is the first time that former American officials and military men have been so critical of a contemplated military action. He said that virtual unanimity among such people has existed going into all other wars and that the Administration should rethink its policy given that such support does not exist in this instance. He later added that entering into this military action without a Constitutional mandate and without sufficient political support could take this country back to the divisive days of Vietnam.

Jennifer Smith Mazarr
Congressional/Political
December 5, 1990

3368-25

# 외 무 부

종  별 :

번  호 : USW-5432

일  시 : 90 1205 1945

수  신 : 장관( 미북,미안,중근동)

발  신 : 주 미 대사

제  목 : 걸프사태관련 WEBSTER CIA 부장 의회 증언

연:USW-5410

1. 금 12.5. WILLIAM WEBSTER CIA 부장은 하원 군사위의 걸프 사태 관련 청문회에서 모두 발언을 통해 현재 실시중인 대 이락 경제 봉쇄의 성과 및 전망에관해 증언하였는바, 동 요지 하기 보고함(모두 발언 전문은 USWF-3369 로 팩스편 송부, 질의 응답은 비공개로 진행)

가. 대이락 경제 봉쇄의 성과

-쿠웨이트 침공 이전에 비해, 이락의 수출입 규모가 공히 90 퍼센트 이상 감소 (특히 , 외화 부족 심각)

-전체 산업이 어느정도의 영향은 받고 있으나, 발전소 및 정유 산업은 심각한 타격을 받지 않고 있음.

-주요 식료품은 일반 시장을 통해 구입 가능하나, 식료품 가격은 급등

의료, 위생분야 써비스 격감

-그러나, 현재 후세인 대통령 자신은 여사한 경제봉쇄를 극복해 나갈수 있는것으로 믿고 있음( 이락내 국내 정국 불안정 움직임도 상금 별무)

나. 전망

- 명년 봄이면 외화 보유고 고갈 예상

-늦어도 내년 여름이면 에너지 관련 분야 및 군수 산업이외의 모든 산업 분야가 거의 가동 중지될 것으로 예상

-명년 봄이면 설탕, 식용류 부족난 심각예상, 다만 5 월 수확기 이후 곡물류 재고는 어느정도 수준 유지 가능예상

-비전투 상황하에서, 지상군 및 공군력은 향후 약 9 개월간 현 수준의 임전태세 유지 가능 예상

| 미주국 | 장관 | 차관 | 1차보 | 2차보 | 미주국 | 중아국 | 청와대 |
|---|---|---|---|---|---|---|---|

라. 결론

-대이락 경제 봉쇄 조치가 언제, 어떤 방식으로 후세인 대통령의 심경을 변화 시킬수 있을지는 아무도 예상키 어려움(즉, 대이락 경제봉쇄 조치만으로는 이락군의 쿠웨이트 철수를 유도하기 어렵다는 점을 시사)

2. 한편 WEBSTER 부장뿐 아니라, BAKER 국무장관, CHENEY 국방장관등 미 행정부 지도층 인사들이 이구동성으로 의회 청문회 및 언론기자 회견등을 통해 대이락 경제 봉쇄만으로는 이락군의 쿠웨이트 철수를 유도할수없다는 점을 강조하고 있는바, 여사한 정보 판단의 밑바탕에는 사우디에 파견된 대규모 미군 병력의실제 작전투입 가능성을 이락측이 보다 더 심각하게 받아들이게 함으로써 금번사태의 평화적 해결을 도모하려는 의도가 깔려 있는것으로 분석됨( 특히 BAKER국무장관은 현재의걸프 사태관련 미국내 논의가 대이락 무력 사용가능성에 신빙성을 더해주는 목적으로 진행되어야 한다는 점 강조)

(대사 박동진- 차관)

90.12.31. 일반

PAGE 2

HEARING OF THE HOUSE ARMED SERVICES COMMITTEE/SUBJECT:  PERSIAN GULF
CRISIS, CHAIRED BY:   REPRESENTATIVE LES ASPIN (D-WI), WITNESS:
WILLIAM WEBSTER, DIRECTOR, CIA, 2118 RAYBURN,
WEDNESDAY, DECEMBER 5, 1990

     MR. WEBSTER:  Now, I appreciate the opportunity to address this
Committee on what the intelligence community believes the sanctions
have already accomplished and
what we believe the sanctions are likely to accomplish over time.

Of course, sanctions are only one type of pressure being applied on
Iraq, and their impact cannot be completely distinguished from the
combined impact of military, diplomatic and economic initiatives in
Iraq.  At the technical level, economic sanctions and the embargo
against Iraq have put Saddam Hussein on notice that he is isolated
from the world community and have dealt a serious blow to the Iraq
economy.

     More than 100 countries are supporting the UN resolutions that
impose economic sanctions on Iraq.  Coupled with the US government's
increased ability to detect and follow-up attempts to circumvent the
blockade, the sanctions have all but shut off Iraq's exports and
reduced imports to less than 10 percent of their pre-invasion level.
All sectors of the Iraq economy are feeling the pinch of sanctions
and many industries have largely shut down.  Most importantly, the
blockade has eliminated any hope Baghdad had of cashing in on higher
oil prices or its seizure of Kuwaiti oil fields.

     Despite mounting disruptions and hardships resulting from
sanctions, Saddam apparently believes that he can outlast
international resolve to maintain those sanctions.  We see no
indication that Saddam is concerned at this point that domestic
discontent is growing to levels that may threaten his regime or that
problems resulting from the sanctions are causing him to rethink his
policy on Kuwait.  The Iraqi people have experienced considerable
deprivation in the past.  Given the brutal nature of the Iraqi
security services, the population is not likely to oppose Saddam
openly.  Our judgment has been and continues to be that there is no
assurance or guarantee that economic hardships will compel Saddam to
change his policies or lead to internal unrest that would threaten his
regime.  Now, let me take a few minutes to review briefly with you
some of the information that led us to these conclusions as well as
to present our assessment of the likely impact of sanctions over the
coming months.

     The blockade and embargo have worked more effectively than
Saddam probably expected.  More than 90 percent of imports and 90
percent of exports have been shut off.  Although there is smuggling
across Iraq's borders, it is extremely small relative to Iraq's
pre-crisis trade.  Iraqi efforts to break sanctions have thus far
been largely unsuccessful.  What little leakage has occurred is due
largely to a relatively small number of private firms acting
independently.  And we believe that most countries are actively
enforcing the sanctions and plan to continue doing so.

          3269 —— 1

                                             0195

Despite these shut downs, the most vital industries, including electric power generation and refining, do not yet appear to be threatened. We believe they will be able to function for some time because domestic consumption has been reduced, because Iraqi and Kuwaiti facilities have been cannibalized, and because some stockpiles and surpluses already existed. The cutoff of Iraq's oil exports

and the success of sanctions have also choked off Baghdad's financial resources. This too has been more effective and more complete than Saddam probably expected.

In fact, we believe that a lack of foreign exchange will in time be Iraq's greatest economic difficulty. The embargo has deprived Baghdad of roughly $1.5 billion of foreign exchange earnings monthly. We have no evidence that Iraq has significantly augmented the limited foreign exchange reserves to which it still has access. And as a result, Baghdad is working to conserve foreign exchange, and to devise alternative methods to finance imports.

We believe Baghdad's actions to forestall shortages of food stocks, including rationing, encouraging smuggling and promoting agricultural production are adequate for the next several months. The fall harvest of fruits and vegetables is injecting new supplies into the market, and will provide a psychological as well as tangible respite for mounting pressures. The Iraqi population in general has access to sufficient staple foods. Other food stocks still not rationed also remain available. However, the variety is diminishing and prices are sharply inflated. For example, sugar purchased on the open market at the official exchange rate went from $32 per 50 kilogram bag in August, to $580 per bag last month. Baghdad remains concerned about its foodstocks, and continues to try to extend stocks and increasingly to divert supplies to the military.

In late November, Baghdad cut civilian rations for the second time since the rationing program began while announcing increases in rations for military personnel and their families. So on balance, the embargo has increased the economic hardships facing the average Iraqi. In order to supplement their rations, Iraqis must turn to the black market where most goods can be purchased but at highly inflated prices. They are forced to spend considerable amounts of time searching for reasonably priced food, or waiting in lines for bread and other rationed items.

In addition, services ranging from medical care to sanitation have been curtailed. But these hardships are easier for Iraqis to endure than the combination of economic distress, high casualty rates and repeate missile and air attacks that Iraqis lived with during the eight year Iran-Iran War.

During this war incidentally there was not a single significant public disturbance, even though casualties hit 2.3 percent of the total Iraqi population. About the same as the percentage of US casualties during the Civil War.

Looking ahead, the economic picture changes somewhat. We

3369 — 2

expect Baghdad's foreign exchange reserves to become extremely tight, leaving it little cash left with which to entice potential sanctions' busters. At current rates of depletion we estimate Iraq will have nearly depleted its available foreign exchange reserves by next spring.

Able to obtain even a few key imports, Iraq's economic problems will begin to multiply as Baghdad is forced to gradually shut down growing numbers of facilities in order to keep critical activities functioning as long as possible. Economic conditions will be noticeably worse and Baghdad will find allocating scarce resources a significantly more difficult task. Probably only energy related and some military industries will still be functioning by next spring. This will almost certainly be the case by next summer. Baghdad will try to keep basic services such as electric power from deteriorating.

The regime will also try to insulate critical military industries to prevent an erosion of military preparedness. Nonetheless, reduced rations coupled with rapid inflation and little additional support from the government will compound the economic pressures facing most Iraqis.

By next spring Iraqis will have made major changes in their diets. Poultry, which is a staple of the Iraqi diet, will not be available. Unless Iraq receives humanitarian food aid or unless smugglin increases, some critical commodities such as sugar and edible oils will be in short supply. Distribution problems are likely to create localized shortages. But, we expect that Baghdad will be able to maintain grain consumption, mainly wheat, barley, and rice, at about two-thirds of last year's level until the next harvest in May.

The spring grain and vegetable harvest will again augment food stocks, although only temporarily. To boost next year's food production, Baghdad has raised prices, paid the farmers for their produce, and decreed that farmers must cultivate all available land. Nonetheless, Iraq does not have the capability to become self-sufficient in food production by next year.

Weather is the critical variable in grain production, and even if it is good, Iraqis will be able to produce less than half the grain they need. In addition, Iraq's vegetable production next year may be less than normal because of its inability to obtain seed stock from abroad. Iraq had obtained seed from the United States, the Netherlands, and France.

Although sanctions are hurting Iraq's civilian economy, they are affecting the Iraqi military only at the margins. Iraq's fairly static defensive posture will reduce wear and tear on the military equipment and, as a result, extend the life of its inventory of spare parts and maintenance items.

Under non-combat conditions, Iraq ground and air forces can probably maintain near-current levels of readiness for as long as

3369 - 3

nine months. We expect the Iraqi air force to feel the effects of sanctions more quickly and to a greater degree than the Iraqi ground forces because of its greater reliance on high technology and foreign equipment and technicians.

Major repairs to sophisticated aircraft like the F-1 will be achieved with significant difficulty, if at all, because of the exodus of foreign technicians. Iraqi technicians, however, should be able to maintain current levels of aircraft sorties for three to six months.

The Iraqi ground forces are more immune to sanctions. Before the invasion, Baghdad maintained large inventories of basic military supplies, such as ammunition, and supplies probably remain adequate. The embargo will eventually hurt Iraqi armor by preventing the replacement of old fire control systems and creating shortages of additives for various critical lubricants. Shortages will also affect Iraqi cargo trucks over time.

Mr. Chairman, while we can look ahead several months and predict the gradual deterioration of the Iraqi economy, it is more difficult to assess how or when these conditions will cause Saddam to modify his behavior. At present, Saddam almost certainly assumes that he is coping effectively with the sanctions. He appears confident in the ability of his security services to contain potential discontent, and we do not believe he is troubled by the hardships Iraqis will be forced to endure. Saddam's willingness to sit tight and try to outlast the sanctions, or in the alternative, to avoid war by withdrawing from Kuwait, will be determined by his total assessment of the political, economic and military pressures arrayed against him.

Thank you, Mr. Chairman.

REP. ASPIN: Judge Webster, thank you very much. And we will now adjourn the meeting temporarily while we clear the room and continue the hearing in closed session. Thank you very much.

END

3369-4

0198

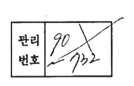

# 외 무 부

종 별 : 지급

번 호 : USW-5436

일 시 : 90 1206 1638

수 신 : 장관(미북,미안,중근동)

발 신 : 주미대사

제 목 : 페만사태 관련 청문회

연:USW-5425

1. 금 12.6 하원 외무위는 JAMES BAKER 국무장관을 출석시킨가운데 페만사태 청문회를 개최하였음.

2. BAKER 장관은 동 청문회시 작일 상원 외교위에서와 동일한 내용의 증언을 한후, 이락의 외국인 인질석방 발표에 언급, 현재 이락 정부측의 공식 입장을확인하고 있는 중이나, 인질석방 조치는 환영할만한 의미 있는 사태 발전으로서 동 발표가 실현되는것을 보기 원하고, 인질이 석방된다하더라도 페만 사태 해결에 대한 결의는 약화되지는 않을 것이며 인질석방 조치는 외교 및 군사적 수단을 통한 페만 사태해결이라는 정책이 성공을 거두고 있다는 것을 입증하고 있다고 발언하였음.

3. 금일 청문회 질의 응답시는 작일 상원 외교위 청문회 보다는 당노선에 따른 민주당과 공화당 입장 차이가 크게 부각되지 않았으며, 대부분의 민주당측 의원들은 무력 사용 승인 유엔 결의안 통과를 포함한 행정부의 대 유엔 외교의 성공등 행정부의 조치에 대해 치하를 한후 경제제재 조치를 통한 사태의 평화적 해결에 우선적인 노력을 기울이는것이 바람직 하다는 식의 의견을 조심스럽게 개진하였으며, BAKER 장관은 분위기를 압도해 가면서 행정부의 정책이 무력 사용의신빙성을 바탕으로한 사태의 평화적 해결이라는점을 강조하였음.

4. 민주당 의원중 SOLARZ 의원은 경제제재 조치로 이락의 쿠웨이트 철수라는 목표를 달성할수 있으면 좋겠으나 이락 국내 정세나 후세인의 정치적 입지등으로 보아 경제제재 조치만으로 정책목표 달성이 의심스러운바, 무력사용의 위협이라는 요소가 사태 해결에 큰 기여를 할것이라고 발언하면서 행정부 입장을 지지하였으며, PETER KOSTMAYER(민주-펜실바니아)의원은 페만사태의 정책목표가 중요하더라도 수천명의 미군의 생명을 희생하면서 까지 이를 달성할 필요성에 대해의문을 제기하면서

| 미주국 | 장관 | 차관 | 1차보 | 2차보 | 미주국 | 중아국 | 외연원 | 청와대 |
|---|---|---|---|---|---|---|---|---|

PAGE 1

무력사용에 반대하는 입장을 표명하였고, LAWRENCE SMITH(민주-플로리다)의원은 대이락 국제협조 체제에 시리아를 포함시키고 행정부 인사가 시리아 대통령을 만나고 쿠바 외상을 만난것은 미국 정책의 무도덕성을 드러내는 것이라고 비난하였음.

5. 주요 질의응답으로는 미국이 중동평화에 관한 국제회의를 지지하고 있다는 보도에 관한 질문에 대해 BAKER 국무장관은 행정부는 중동문제에 관한 국제회의가 적절한 시기에 개최되는것을 항상 지지해 왔으나, 아랍-이스라엘 분쟁에 대한 국제회의 개최는 반대해 왔음. 국제회의 개최에 관한 유엔 안보리 결의안에 대해 미국은 금번 페만사태와 아랍-이스라엘 분쟁을 연관시키는것에 항상 반대해왔고, 또한 현시점이 국제회의 개최에는 적절치 않다고 판단되기 때문에 지지를 하지 않고 있다고 발언하였으며, 금번 청문회종료시 BAKER 국무장관은 주이락 미국대사 대리가 이락의 외국인 인질석방 발표를 이락 정부에 공식 확인하였다는 발표를 하였음.

6. 금번청문회 주요 질의응답 요지는 별전 (USW(F)-3383)송부함.

(대사 박동진-국장)

주 미 대 사 관

번호 : USW(F) - 3383

수신 : 장 관 (미북. 미안. 음은홍)

발신 : 주미대사

제목 : 페만 사태 청문회        ( 3 매 )

금 12.6. 하원외무위에서 거취탄 페만사-태 청문회

주도 질의응답 요지를 별첨 송부함. 끝

## Notes From Hearing of the
## House Foreign Affairs Committee
## On U.S. Policy in the Persian Gulf
## Witness:

### Hon. James Baker III, Secretary of State

### December 6, 1990

Secretary Baker read the same statement that he presented to the Senate Foreign Relations Committee yesterday. (See report from the Senate Foreign Relations Committee; December 5, 1990.) He added at the end some brief remarks concerning Saddam Hussein's statement of this morning that he plans to release all foreign hostages. Secy. Baker stated that he did not at the time of the hearing have government-to-government confirmation of that announcement, but admitted that if true, it was a welcome and significant development. However, he stated that it should not be allowed to interfere with the quest to secure the other goals of the international coalition: assuring Iraq's immediate and unconditional withdrawal from Kuwait, restoring Kuwait's legitimate government, and assuring peace and stability in the Persian Gulf. Secy. Baker added that he believes that Saddam Hussein's announcement can be taken as a success for the policy of diplomacy and military pressure.

The questions were a combination of expressions of support (mainly from Republicans) and of wariness (mainly from Democrats) regarding the Administration's desire to maintain a credible offensive capability in Saudi Arabia in order to force Saddam Hussein out of Kuwait should he refuse to retreat willingly.

Rep. Lee Hamilton (D-IN) asked how the Secretary would respond to the testimony of Director of Central Intelligence, William Webster, who testified before the Committee yesterday that sanctions will likely cause Iraq to lose its military readiness in nine months. Secy. Baker responded that Dir. Webster is not in disagreement with him at all about the direction of policy. He reminded those present that sanctions may devastate Iraq, but if they do not remove it from Kuwait, then they will not have been successful. It is his main premise that they will not succeed no matter how much deprivation the Iraqi people and military suffer.

In concurrence with a statement by Rep. Robert Lagomarsino (R-CA) in which the Congressman claimed that sanctions have no hope of success, Secy. Baker said that diplomacy depends on the credibility of the military option. He also seemed to contradict earlier Administration reliance on sanctions by asking, "Do we really believe that sanctions will get the job done?" This rhetorical question reflects the change in emphasis of the

1

3383-2

Administration since Nov. 8 when it announced its plan to create
an offensive capability. Again, as in all previous hearings, the
answer to this question has been the key point of dissension on the
Administration's policy in the Persian Gulf.

Rep. Jim Leach (R-IA) raised the issue of Congressional
discordance on the Administration's Persian Gulf strategy and asked
what implications it could have for collective security in the New
World Order. Secy. Baker replied that it would be a tragedy if the
United States were the one to keep this operation from going
forward to reverse Iraq's aggression. He predicted that such
dissension would prove devastating for the New World Order.

Voicing a view at odds with most of his party, Rep. Stephen
Solarz (D-NY) said that he really does not trust sanctions to force
Saddam Hussein out of Kuwait without the absolute assurance that
devastating force will be used unless he does. For her part, Rep.
Olympia Snowe (R-ME) seemed slightly more cautious than her GOP
colleagues when she joined with her constituents who have written
to her to say that they are wary about the President's moves since
Nov. 8 when the doubling of the forces in Saudi Arabia was
announced. She urged the Secretary and thus the Administration to
better prepare the American people for U.S. actions in this
difficult crisis if they expect their support.

Rep. Larry Smith (D-FL) was another political maverick. In
his last day as a member of this Committee (he is joining the
Appropriations Committee starting in the 102nd Congress,) he
reminded Secy. Baker that the Foreign Affairs Committee had warned
the Bush Administration of the threat that Saddam Hussein posed to
the region long before this crisis, but that no one paid any heed.
He also questioned the idea of an international coalition wherein
the United States would be standing shoulder to shoulder with
unsavory leaders such as Hafez al-Asad of Syria. (Rep. Sam
Gejdenson (D-CT) expressed similar concern.) Rep. Smith
acknowledged, however, that he agrees with the Administration's
handling of the crisis and that the longer Iraq is allowed to hold
Kuwait, the less recognizable it will be once it is returned.

Rep. Doug Bereuter (R-NE) asked if the President wants the
Congress to act on legislation to grant him authority to use force
in the Gulf and if so, what form it should take. Secy. Baker
repeated the answer that he has given to all who raise this issue:
The President would warmly welcome such an initiative if it would
echo the United Nations Resolution authorizing the use of any means
necessary to remove Saddam Hussein from Kuwait if he doesn't go
willingly.

3383-3

0203

報 告 畢

1990.12.6.
美 洲 局
北 美 課(51)

# 報 告 事 項

題 目 :  페灣 事態 關聯, 美 上.下院 外交委 聽聞會

---

미 상.하원 외교위원회는 각각 12.4(화)-5(수)간 및 12.6(목) Baker
국무장관, McNamara 전 국방장관 등을 출석시킨 가운데 페만 사태 관련
청문회를 개최하였는 바, 동 청문회시 Baker 장관 증언내용 등 관련 사항을
아래 보고 드립니다.

---

1. 증언자

   가. 상원 외교위

      o  12.4(화)  :  Arthur Schlesinger 뉴욕대 교수

                      Robert McNamara 전 국방장관

                      Judith Kipper 브루킹스 연구소 연구원

                      Sam Zakhem 전 주 바레인 대사

      o  12.5(수)  :  James Baker 국무장관

                      Zbigniew Brezezinski 전 대통령 안보담당 보좌관

   나. 하원 외무위

      o  12.6(목)     James Baker 국무장관

0204

2. Baker 장관 증언내용 요지

(상.하원 공통)

o 페만사태 해결의 기본입장은 페만 사태의 4대 정책목표를 가장 최소한의
  희생으로 평화적으로 달성하는 것임.
  - 평화적 해결이 불가능하다고 판단될 경우 무력사용도 불사

o 대이라크 경제제재 조치 4개월 경과에도 불구, 동 UN 결의안 수용 조짐이
  없어 경제제재 조치만으로는 이라크측 태도 변화 기대가 난망시됨.
  - 오히려 대쿠웨이트 약탈 계속
  - 사우디 및 이집트등 주변국가 정부 전복 기도 계속

o 경제제재 조치의 성공만을 기다리는 정책은 이라크측에 동 제재조치의
  와해 공작을 위한 시간만을 제공하는 결과를 초래할 것임.
  - 인질문제 악화, 국제적 협조체제 와해 기도
  - 핵, 화학 및 세균 무기 개발 추진

o 최근 통과된 무력사용 결의안은 사태의 평화적 해결을 위한 최종 기회를
  이라크측에 제공하는 것임.

o 미국은 무력사용을 위한 만반의 준비를 해야 하며, 무력사용시 사상자
  발생 가능성도 감수해야 함.
  - 준비 실패의 경우, 무력사용 위협을 통한 외교적 해결 가능성은
    오히려 감소하며 쿠웨이트 점령을 묵인하는 결과 초래

o 91.1.15 시한 설정은 미측이 무력사용을 할수 있는 원칙적 승인일 뿐이며
  실제 무력사용시는 동맹국과의 사전 협의를 거쳐 결정 예정임.

0205

(하원 외무위)

o 중동문제에 관한 국제회의 개최 관련 UN 안보리 결의안 채택 움직임에
  대해서는 미국이 페만 사태와 아랍/이스라엘간 분쟁과의 연계를 반대해
  왔으며, 현 시점이 동 국제회의 개최에는 적절치 않으므로 지지하지
  않는다는 입장을 분명히 함.

o 이라크측의 인질석방 발표는 주 이라크 미국대사 대리가 공식 확인한
  사실임을 언명함.

3. 기타 인사 증언내용 요지

(McNamara 전 국방장관)

o 페만 사태 해결에 있어 동맹국간 균형있는 책임분담이 이루어져야 함.

o 경제제재 조치가 성과를 거둘수 있도록 인내심을 가져야 하며, 미국은
  동 조치를 뒷받침하기 위해 주 사우디 미군의 계속 주둔이 필요함.

(Brezezinski 전 안보 보좌관)

o 무력사용은 향후 페만 지역의 안정을 크게 해칠 것이며 경제제재 조치를
  통한 사태 해결이 바람직함.

(기    타)

o 각 의원 및 증언자들은 발언 또는 증언에 있어 당 노선에 따른 입장
  차이를 드러냄.
  - 민주당계 인사들은 경제제재 조치 성공을 위해서는 시간적 여유가
    필요함을 지적하고 성급한 무력사용은 중동지역 안정에 바람직스럽지
    않다는 견해 피력
  - 공화당계 인사들은 최근 UN의 무력사용 승인 결의안과 유사한 미
    의회내 결의안 채택을 위한 특별회기 소집 필요성을 강조하고, 부쉬
    행정부 정책에 대한 지지 표명

0206

관리
번호 90-2318

# 외 무 부

종 별 : 지급

번 호 : USW-5562　　　　　　　　　일 시 : 90 1214 1846

수 신 : 장관(미북,미안,중근동)

발 신 : 주 미 대사

제 목 : 페만 사태 관련 청문회

연: USW-5374

1. 금 12.14 하원 군사위는 DICK CHENEY 국방장관, COLLIN POWELL 합참 의장을 출석 시킨 가운데 페만 사태 에 관한 청문회를 개최함.

2. 금일 청문회시 CHENEY 장관및 POWELL 합참 의장은 12.3 상원 군사위 청문회와 동일한 요지의 증언을 하였으며, 증언시 경제 제재 조치가 이락측에게 큰피해를 주고 있지만 경제 제제 조치만으로는 이락의 쿠웨이트 철수라는 목적 달성을 기대하기 어렵다는점이 강조 되었음(상세 연호 USW-5374 참조)

3. 동 청문회는 민주당 소속의원이 대부분 참석한 가운데 진행되었으나(공화당 소속은 3 명만 참석), 전반적인 분위기는 주 사우디 주둔 미군 병력 수준및 무력 사용 가능성등과 관련하여 행정부 정책을 비난하기 보다는 동맹국의 비용분담 문제및 대규모 미군 주둔및 무력 사용 위협을 골자로 하는 행정부 정책 수행에 있어 제기되는 군사 비용 증가, 병력 운영및 군수 지원 문제등에 대한 사항에 대해 주로 논의되었음.

4. 동 청문회 주요 질의 응답 부문으로는 첫째, 미군 병력의 전반적 감축 이라는 장기 정책 목표(향후 5 년간 약 25 프로 수준 감축)가 페만 사태에 따른 병력 소요로 인해 어떠한 영향을 받을것이냐는 질문에 대해 체니 장관은 장기적 병력 감축 계획은 계속 추진될것이나, 페만 사태가 계속되는한 FY 91 년도 8 만명의 병력 감축 계획은 재조정되어야 할것이라 답변하였으며, 둘째, 대규모 미군의 사우디 주둔에 따른 주둔 비용의 충당 계획에 관한 질문에 대해 CHENEY 장관은 여타 지역에 있어서 미군의 군사 훈련을 축소 시키는것을 고려하고 있다고 답변하였고, 셋째, 사우디, 일본 , 독일등에 대한 비용 분담 증액 필요성에 대한 질문에 대해 동 장관은 동맹국이 비용 분담을 증액하는것은 항상 환영하나 현재의 동맹국 비용 분담 규모는 미국의 입장에서 보면 하찮은 규모일수도 있으나 동맹국의 입장에서 보면 상당한 규모라고 답변하였음.

| 미주국 | 차관 | 1차보 | 미주국 | 중아국 | 청와대 | 안기부 |
|---|---|---|---|---|---|---|

PAGE 1　　　　　　검 토 필 (1990 12.24)　　　　90.12.15　　10:10

외신 2과 통제관 BT

0207

5. 동 청문회 주요 질의 응답 부문은 별전 FAX 송부함.

(대사 박동진-국장)

90.12.31 까지

0208

주 미 덕 사 관          보안 등지  ᴄ

번호 : USW(F) - 2452

수신 : 장 관 ( 미안. 디북. 거럽 )

발신 : 주미덕사

지득 : 페 만 사태 공문회 득오린니 종안부등.

Notes on Hearing of the
House Armed Services Committee
on U.S. Policy in the Persian Gulf

**Witnesses:**
Dick Cheney, Secretary of Defense
Gen. Colin Powell, Chairman of the Joint Chiefs of Staff

December 14, 1990

The opening statements of the witnesses were essentially
identical to those they presented before the Senate Armed Services
Committee (see my report of December 3, 1990.)  As before, they
outlined U.S. interests in the Gulf and explained the
Administration's reasoning for not wishing to rely on economic
sanctions alone to resolve the crisis.  In doing so, they defended
the President's current policy of securing a credible offensive
option as part of his overall strategy.

The question and answer session saw very few new perspectives
and opinions originating from the Congressmen.  The following are
typical of the exchanges:

Chairman Les Aspin (D-WI) asked if the Administration was in
any way being pushed by its timeline to move toward offensive
action (the perennial use it or lose it argument.)  Both Secy.
Cheney and Gen. Powell denied that this is the case and stated that
it was important that Saddam Hussein feel a credible military
threat in order to realize that he must back down and leave Kuwait.
Gen. Powell added that the initial deployment of 200,000 troops was
only adequate for defensive purposes; the additional deployment was
necessary to pursue effectively the political goals the President
has outlined.

0209

Another issue of concern raised by Reps. Nicholas Mavroules (D-MA), Earl Hutto (D-FL), Ike Skelton (D-MO), Martin Lancaster (D-NC), and others was that of allied support for the efforts of the United States in trying to reverse the Iraqi occupation of Kuwait. Most were disgruntled that many allies do not seem to be offering enough money, and more still are unwilling to offer significant numbers of combat personnel. For his part, Rep. Mavroules warned that a U.S.-Iraqi conflict would be potentially devastating for future U.S. involvement in the region. He asked if other nations' troops would be operating side-by-side with those of the United States if it became necessary to invade Iraq. Secy. Cheney responded that the leaders of the nations involved will have to make that decision.

In a significant exchange with Rep. John Spratt (D-SC) who asked Secy. Cheney about where the Pentagon expects to get the money to support its activities in the Persian Gulf, the Secretary said that the U.S. Government may have to cut back on some of its exercises elsewhere in the world. He was not specific on which exercises or how much of a cutback they would face, however.

A final area on concern was raised by Rep. Ronald Dellums (D-CA). He spoke about the lawsuit he and 57 of his Congressional colleagues brought against the U.S. Government which sought to force the President to obtain a declaration of war before initiating any military action against Iraq. (The lawsuit was unsuccessful.) Rep. Dellums added that he believes all the Administration's talk about the many levels on which it is working misrepresents the truth. In his opinion, since Secy. of State Baker is not permitted to negotiate while meeting with Saddam Hussein in Baghdad, the diplomatic level is not part of the Administration's policy. Since Administration spokesmen say that sanctions will not work, the economic level is not part of the policy. Finally, only the military option remains.

3492-2

0210

# 정 리 보 존 문 서 목 록

| 기록물종류 | 일반공문서철 | 등록번호 | 2012090506 | 등록일자 | 2012-09-17 |
|---|---|---|---|---|---|
| 분류번호 | 772 | 국가코드 | US/XF | 보존기간 | 영구 |
| 명  칭 | 걸프사태 : 미국 의회 동향, 1990-91. 전5권 | | | | |
| 생 산 과 | 북미1과 | 생산년도 | 1990~1991 | 담당그룹 | |
| 권 차 명 | V.3 1991.1-2월 | | | | |
| 내용목차 | * 걸프사태 관련 미국 의회에서의 각종 논의, 법안, 결의안, 청문회 개최 동향 등 <br><br> * 1.12 상.하원, 페르시안 사태 관련 행정부의 무력 사용 승인 결의안 통과 <br> 1.17 상원, 대 이라크 참전 미군 및 대통령에 대한 지지 결의안 통과 <br> 1.18 하원, 상원 결의안(10.17자)과 동일한 내용의 공동결의안 채택 <br> 1.23 하원, 이라크의 이스라엘 공격 비난 결의안 및 이라크의 전쟁 포로 학대 비난, 학대 관련자 전범 처리 결의안 채택 <br> 1.24 상원, 상기 2건의 결의안 채택 | | | | |

0001

외 무 부

종 별 :

번  호 : USW-0009

일  시 : 91 0103 1802

수  신 : 장관(미안, 미북, 중근동)

발  신 : 주 미 대사

제  목 : 페만 사태-의회 동향

1. 금 1.3 BUSH 대통령은 페만 사태 관련 의회 지도부와 백악관에서 비공개회동을 가졌으며, 동 회동시 부쉬 대통령은 1.7-9 기간중 BAKER 장관과 AZIZ 이락 외무장관이 스위스에서 접촉을 갖도록 하는 제의에 대해 설명하였고, 특히 의회측이 무력사용 승인 UN 결의안과 유사한 결의안을 채택하는것이 바람직하다는 의견을 거듭 표시한것으로 알려짐.

2. MITCHELL 상원 민주당 원내 총무 및 FOLEY 하원 의장은 동 회동직후 가진기자 회견에서 의회측이 현재 여하한 내용의 결의안 채택에 대해 어떤 결정을 내리지는 않았지만, 부쉬 대통령의 희망대로 UN 결의안과 동일한 내용의 결의안을 채택 하기는 어렵다는 입장을 부쉬 대통령에게 전하였으며, 또한 금번 페만 사태의 중요성을 감안, 1.3-23 기간에는 관례대로 휴회 기간을 갖지 않고 필요하다고 판단이 되는대로 페만 사태에 대해 원내 토의를 가질 예정임을 밝혔음.

(대사 박동진-국장)

예고 : 91 12.31 까지에 예고 문에 의거 일반문서로 재분 됨

검토필 (1991. 6.20.)

---

미주국   장관   차관   1차보   2차보   미주국   중아국   안기부

91.01.04   08:27

외신 2과 통제관 BW

0002

외 무 부

종    별 : 지급

번    호 : USW-0081                                                일    시 : 91 0108 1840

수    신 : 장관(미안,미북,중근동)

발    신 : 주 미 대사

제    목 : 페만 사태-의회 동향

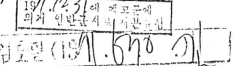

1. 1.3 개원한 미 의회는 1.9 예정된 BAKER-AZIZ 외상 회담 이전에는 페만 사태에 대한 토의를 자제한다는 민주당 지도부의 결정에 따라 PRO FORMA 회기를 갖고 있으나, BAKER- AZIA 외상 회담 직후인 1.10 이후부터는 상. 하원 공히 페만 사태에 대한 토의및 관련 결의안을 본격적으로 심의할 예정이며, 부쉬 대통령도 당초 의회측이 자체적으로 유엔 결의안과 유사한 결의안을 채택해주길 희망하나 의회측에 이를 요청을 하지는 않는다는 당초의 입장을 변경시켜, 유엔 결의안과 유사한 결의안 초안을 작성, 의회측에 동 결의안 채택을 요청하는 방안을 검토중인것으로 알려짐.

2. 상기와같이 의회측이 페만 사태에 대한 토의를 본격적으로 실시하게된 배경은

첫째, 진보적 성향의 민주당 의원 일각에서는 의회와 사전 승인없이는 무력상을 금지하는 결의안을 이미 제출한바 있고(상원에서는 HARKIN(민-아이오아),ADAMS(민-워싱턴), BURDICK(민-노스다코다)공동 명의로 결의안 제출, 하원에서는 DORGAN(민-노스다코다)등 5 명의원 공동 명의로 결의안 제출한바 동 결의안 별전 FAX 송부함)

둘째, 금번 페만 사태에 있어서도 의회측이 의견 표명을 위한 구체적 조치 없이 행정부측이 무력 사용을 취할 경우, 전쟁 선포권이라는 의회의 고유 권한은치명적인 타격을 입게되고, 향후 WAR POWERS 에 대한 행정부와의 권한 문제에 있어서 불리한 선례가 되며, 또한 국내 정치적으로 의회를 장악하고 있는 민주당측이 페만 사태 정책과 같은 중요 국가 정책 결정에 나름대로의 역할을 하지 못했다는 비난을 면치 못할 위험이 있기 때문인것으로 관측됨.

3. 1.10 이후 상. 하 양원에서 페만 사태 결의안이 심의될 경우 FOLEY 하원의장및 MITCHELL 상원 민주당 총무는 근소한 차이로 부쉬 대통령측이 원하는바와같이 유엔 무력 사용 결의안과 유사한 내용의 결의안이 민주당내 중도, 보수파 성향의 의원들의

| 미주국 총리실 | 장관 안기부 | 차관 | 1차보 | 2차보 | 미주국 | 중아국 | 신일 | 청와대 |
|---|---|---|---|---|---|---|---|---|

PAGE 1

지지를 얻어 채택될 가능성이 높은것으로 관측하고 있음.

　첨부 USW(F)-0062

　(대사 박동진-국장)

　예고:91.-12.-31-까지

번호 : USV(F) - 0062
수신 : 장관 (미안. 미북, 중근동)
발신 : 주미대사
제목 : 페만사태관련 결의안 (포지포함 4매)

( 하원 제출 결의안 )

# HON. BYRON L. DORGAN
### OF NORTH DAKOTA
### IN THE HOUSE OF REPRESENTATIVES
### Monday, January 7, 1991.

Mr. DORGAN of North Dakota. Mr. Speaker, I am introducing today with my colleagues Mr. MILLER of California, Mr. DURBIN, Mr. DELLUMS, and Mr. FOGLIETTA, a concurrent resolution which urges the President to request the establishment of a United Nations Military Command and Expeditionary Force in the Persian Gulf. Since the United Nations—not the United States—has authorized the framework for enforcing the resolutions designed to bring about an Iraqi withdrawal from Kuwait, it is the United Nations which should provide any needed military resources to achieve the goals of the international community.

The resolution also demands that the President obtain some real burden sharing agreements for the operation, that he seek the required authorization from Congress for any possible offensive operations, and that he first exhaust economic sanctions and diplomatic initiatives before committing the Nation to war.

If the international community has determined that Iraq is an outlaw, then the United Nations—not the United States—should bear the prime responsibility for restoring justice and stability to the Middle East.

That is not our current course.

### A MULTINATIONAL FIG LEAF

Presently, the United States has deployed the vast majority of military forces in the Persian Gulf region and has shouldered the main financial burden of paying for the deployment of these troops. The United States expects to send 400,000 troops to the region by the end of the month, while our NATO allies have provided less than one-tenth that amount.

It is true that Arab and Islamic States have sent several thousand troops to Saudi Arabia and nearby Gulf States. And Egypt deserves credit for its willingness to play a key role. However, many of these nations would not commit their troops to battle in the event that the United States initiated offensive action against Iraq.

So while the President asserts that the "anti-Iraq coalition" is bolstered by hundreds of thousands of troops from other nations and widespread financial backing, reality paints another picture. The fact is that the United States has again shouldered both the financial and military burden of defending the collective interests of other nations.

### CHEERLEADERS INSTEAD OF FOOT SOLDIERS

The other NATO nations—with the exception of Britain and France—have barely lifted a finger when it comes to military forces. You would think that the Belgians, the Dutch, the Spanish, the Canadians and others had not noticed that their vital interests were presumably at risk.

One can understand the constitutional reluctance of the Japanese and German Governments to deploy their own forces in other regions. However, there is no legal reason that the Germans could not deploy substantial forces to Turkey, a NATO ally which must defend its own border with Iraq against a possible attack. Yet the Germans have mustered the resolve to send only a few dozen planes to Turkey.

Nor have the Japanese found the creativity to send more than a handful of nonmilitary volunteers to support other coalition activities in the region. Japan's lone aid terms of seven doctors and nurses has quit and returned home. Japan's presence in this multinational operation now consists of two foreign ministry officials.

Neither have the Germans and Japanese willingly offered to pay what would be a fair share, a proportional amount, of the costs of the Desert Shield Operation. The Government of Japan only awakened to the chagrin of the American people on this score after Congress passed a tough measure mandating a greater Japanese contribution to mutual defense costs. The Germans are providing billions more in Deutsche marks in technical, housing and training aid to the Soviet Union than they are by way of contributions to reverse Iraqi aggression.

Even more remarkably, we have undertaken these responsibilities despite the fact that many other nations are relatively more dependent on Persian Gulf oil than we are. For example, the Japanese import 51 percent of their oil from the Middle East and the Europeans import 27 percent of their oil from the region, while the United States buys only 12 percent of the oil we consume from the Persian Gulf, according to the Congressional Research Service.

Most deplorable of all, Arab nations now making a windfall from increased oil production have not begun to pay their fair dues. And they do not even have the courage to publicly acknowledge their debt to the United States for saving their necks. They seem to believe that the Arab armada has turned the tide in the Persian Gulf and that a few billion dollars constitutes reimbursement for an operation now expected to cost United States taxpayers at least $30 billion in 1991.

### THE RISKS OF UNILATERALISM

Not only does the lack of real multinational action place an excessive burden on the United States, it also brings with it grave dangers. The first is the immediate threat to the anticipated 400,000 American men and women in uniform. We should be rotating our troops back and making way for other nations' forces.

Another danger is inviting terrorist attacks and recriminations against America and American citizens because the world sees Operation Desert Shield as a U.S. action in every respect. Should American forces take on Saddam Hussein, who is a hero to many poor nations, we can well expect to see more terrorism targeted against American citizens, embassies, and enterprises abroad.

Finally, the United States reacted to the Iraqi threat in the Persian Gulf because of our national interest in preserving the free flow of oil from the region. We also wanted the rule of international law to prevail in the post-cold war world order. That is why I and many Members supported the President's initial response to the Iraqi invasion of Kuwait. However, we have remained the dominant challenger to Iraq rather than assembling a genuine multinational force under United Nations auspices to do the job. I fear this may win short-lived points with some Arab governments who will seek to disavow the U.S. role in the future. This will hinder—not aid—our long-term position in the Middle East.

### THE UNITED NATIONS ROLE

I believe that we must request that the United Nations assume formal responsibility for military forces in the Persian Gulf. It may be that the United Nations would ask the United States to assume operational command of a multinational force—as it did during the Korean war. But that would be vastly preferable to the present unilateral position of the United States.

I would also contend that the establishment of a U.N. Military Command and Expeditionary Force would compel other nations to assume a fair and proportional share of the costs and military requirements of forcing an Iraqi withdrawal from Kuwait.

So I invite other colleagues to join us as cosponsors of a current resolution which urges the President to request an emergency meeting of the Security Council to establish a United Nations Military Command and Expeditionary Force for the Persian Gulf.

I reiterate that the resolution also urges him to seek more equitable burden sharing, to request the necessary authorization from Congress for any offensive action by U.S. troops participating in the U.N. force, and to permit economic sanctions and high-level diplomacy sufficient time to win a peaceful resolution of the crisis.

Whatever action the United States ultimately takes, however, it must do so as part of bona fide multinational effort and with the clear support of the Congress and the American people.

A text of the resolution follows:

H. CON. RES. —

Whereas the United Nations Security Council has condemned the occupation of Kuwait by Iraq and has authorized the United Nations member states, as part of the multinational effort to secure an Iraqi withdrawal, to employ sanctions, embargoes, and such other means as may be necessary;

Whereas the formation of a genuine multinational military force is essential to effective enforcement of the United Nations Security Council resolutions against Iraq, necessary for the achievement of short-term and long-term United States foreign policy goals in the Middle East, and critical for proportionately sharing the financial and military manpower obligations of the international community for the Persian Gulf operation;

Whereas the present military force arrayed against Iraq is not truly multinational since it is dominated by the United States and supported primarily with United States tax dollars; and

Whereas the United Nations Security Council already has in place a military committee to consider and oversee the establishment of a United Nations military command and force, such as was used in the Korean Conflict: Now, therefore, be it

Resolved by the House of Representatives (the Senate concurring), That the Congress urges the President to—

(1) request an emergency meeting of the United Nations Security Council to establish a United Nations Military Command and Expeditionary Force for the Persian Gulf;

(2) insist that such a force be constituted and supported in a manner by which the international community fairly shares the financial and military responsibilities of the operation;

(3) seek the necessary authorization from the Congress for any participation of the United States Armed Forces as part of such a United Nations force in any offensive military actions against Iraq; and

(4) give United Nations sanctions and high-level diplomacy sufficient time to bring about a peaceful resolution to the crisis.

0062-2

0006

(상원 제출 결의안)

102D CONGRESS
1ST SESSION

# S. CON. RES. _____

## IN THE SENATE OF THE UNITED STATES

Mr. HARKIN (for himself and Mr. ADAMS and Mr. BURDICK) submitted the following concurrent resolution; which was ___ _ ___ _. _ _ _____

# CONCURRENT RESOLUTION

Expressing the sense of Congress that Congress must approve
any offensive military action against Iraq.

1    *Resolved by the Senate (the House of Representatives*

2 *concurring),*

3 SECTION 1. APPROVAL OF INITIAL RESPONSE TO THE INVASION

4         OF KUWAIT.

5    The Congress supports the actions taken by the Presi-

6 dent to defend Saudi Arabia, demands that Iraq immediate-

7 ly withdraw from its illegal occupation of Kuwait, and

8 supports the President's diplomatic and economic initia-

9 tives to resolve the Persian Gulf crisis.

*0062-3*

0007

1  SEC. 2. REQUIREMENT OF CONGRESSIONAL AUTHORIZATION FOR

2        OFFENSIVE ACTION IN THE PERSIAN GULF.

3      The Congress finds that—

4          (1) the Constitution of the United States vests

5      all power to declare war in the Congress of the

6      United States; and

7          (2) any offensive action taken by the United

8      States against Iraq must be pursuant to an explicit

9      authorization by the Congress before such action

10     may be initiated.

11  SEC. 3. NOTIFICATION OF THE PRESIDENT.

12     The Secretary of the Senate shall transmit a copy of

13  this concurrent resolution to the President.

0062-4

0008

외 무 부

종 별 : 지급
번 호 : USW-0096
일 시 : 91 0109 1812
수 신 : 장관(미안,미북,중근동)
발 신 : 주 미 대사
제 목 : 페만 사태-의회 동향

연 USW-0081

1. 연호 관련, 1.8 부쉬 대통령은 상하원 지도부 앞으로 페만 사태 해결을 위해 무력 사용을 포함한 모든 수단을 사용하는것을 지지하는 결의안을 채택하여줄것을 요청하는 서한을 발송하였음.

2. 부쉬 대통령은 최근 여론 조사 결과 1.15 이후 무력 사용 문제에 대해서는 다수 여론이 형성되어 있지 않은 반면, 무력 사용에는 의회의 사전승인이 필요하다는 여론이 다수(N.Y.T-CBS 조사 60 프로, W.P-ABC 조사 66 프로)인점을 감안하고, 특히 페만 사태 해결이라는 중요 외교 문제를 다루는데 있어 의회의 지지를 구하고 또한 WAR POWERS 와 관련한 행정부와 의회와의 전통적 입장 차이로 인한 불필요한 국내 정치적 마찰을 해소하기 위해 상기 결의안 채택을 요청한것으로 관측됨.

3. 상기 요청 관련, 의회내 공화당 진영은 부쉬 대통령이 원하는 내용의 결의안 채택을 위해 민주당 중도.보수파 의원과 접촉을 강화하고 있으며, 민주당측은 의회의 전쟁 선포 권한을 강조하는 동시에 페만 사태 해결을 위한 최종적 수단으로서의 무력겨 사용은 배제하지 않으나, 무력사용은 아직 시기 상조이며 경제 제재 조치에 좀더 시간을 주어야한다는 내용의 결의안을 준비중에 있는것으로알려지고 있으나, 연호 보고와같이 무력사용을 지지하는 내용의 결의안이 채택될것이라는 전망이 지배적임.

(대사 박동진-국장)

91.12.31 까지

미주국  장관   차관   1차보   2차보   미주국   중아국   청와대   총리실
안기부

PAGE 1

91.01.10    09:07
외신 2과  통제관 BW
0009

(표지포함 2매) 홍

HLC

[January 9, 1991: 3 PM]

**102D CONGRESS
1ST SESSION**

H. CON. RES. _____

11007

## IN THE HOUSE OF REPRESENTATIVES

Mr. _____ submitted the following concurrent resolution;
which was referred to the Committee on _____

## CONCURRENT RESOLUTION

Regarding United States policy to reverse Iraq's occupation of
    Kuwait.

1    *Resolved by the House of Representatives (the Senate*
2    concurring), That (a) the Congress is firmly committed to
3    reversing Iraq's brutal and illegal occupation of Kuwait.
4        (b) The Congress authorizes continued use of American
5    military force to enforce the United Nations economic embargo

HR-1

0010

2

1 against Iraq; to defend Saudi Arabia from direct Iraqi

2 attack; and to protect American forces in the region.

3     (c) The Congress believes that continued application of

4 international sanctions and diplomatic efforts to pressure

5 Iraq to leave Kuwait is the wisest course at this time and

6 should be sustained.

7     (d) The Congress pledges its full and continued support

8 for sustaining the policy of increasing economic and

9 diplomatic pressure against Iraq; for maintaining our

10 military options; and for efforts to increase the military

11 and financial contributions made by allied nations.

12     (e) The Constitution requires the President to obtain

13 authorization from the Congress before initiating new

14 offensive military action or waging war against Iraq or Iraqi

15 forces. The Congress does not rule out the enactment by the

16 Congress at a later time of a declaration of war or other

17 Congressional authorization for the use of force should that

18 become necessary to achieve the goal of forcing Iraqi troops

19 from Kuwait. The Congress will consider any request from the

20 President for such an authorization expeditiously in

21 accordance with the priority procedures set forth in section

22 2.

23 SEC. 2. PRIORITY PROCEDURES.

24                 [To be added.]

M118-2

외　무　부

관리
번호 91-38

종　별 : 지급

번　호 : USW-0120　　　　　　　　　　일　시 : 91 01101957

수　신 : 장관(미안,미북,중근동)

발　신 : 주미대사

제　목 : 페만 사태 - 의회 동향

연 USW-0096

1. 금 1.10 상. 하원은 페만사태에 대한 전반적 토의및 관련 결의안에 대한심의를 시작하였으며, 명 1.11(금)에는 관계 결의안에 대한 토의를 계속하고 1.12(토)에는 표결을 할 예정임.

2. 금일 상원 본회의에서는 경제제재 조치가 효력을 거둘수 있도록 충분한 시간을 줄것을 요구하는 NUNN-PELL 결의안을 대상으로 토의가 진행되었으며, 동 결의안을 지지하는 민주당 의원들이 이에 반대하는 공화당 의원보다 빈번히 발언하였음. 동 결의안 지지 발언의 주요 내용은

첫째, 무력 사용은 마지막 해결 방안으로서 서둘러서는 안되며, 인내심을 갖고 경제 제재 조치가 성공을 거두도록 충분한 시간을 주어야하며, 둘째, 이락에 대항하는 국제 협조 체제는 명분에 지난지 않으며, 실질적으로는 미국이 대부분의 부담을 지고 있는바, 무력 사용의 경우, 미국측이 부당한 희생을 감수하게되고

세째, 무력 사용으로 사태가 해결될 경우에는 향후 페만 지역의 세력 균형및 안정이 저해될것이며, 또한 전세계적으로 미국민에 대한 테러 행위가 자행될 우려가 있다는것임. 이에 반해 동 결의안에 반대하는 공화당 의원들은

첫째, 경제 제재만으로는 이락의 쿠웨이트 철수라는 목표를 달성하기 어렵고, 둘째, 의회가 무려겨 사용을 포함한 행정부 정책에 대해 지지를 표시하지 못할 경우, 유엔 결의안은의미를 상실하게 되고, 침략에 대한 국제사회의 응징을근간으로 하는 새로운 국제 질서는 유명무실 해지며, 세째, 의회가 무력 사용을 지지함으로서 이락측에게 무력 사용 가능성에 대한 강력한 신호를 보내야만 오히려 사태의 평화적 해결 가능성이 높다는것을 강변하였음.

3. 금일 하원 본회의 토의시에도 상기 상원 트의시와같은 논지로 무력 사용을 둘러

| 미주국 안기부 | 장관 | 차관 | 1차보 | 2차보 | 미주국 | 중아국 | 청와대 | 총리실 |
|---|---|---|---|---|---|---|---|---|

PAGE 1

싸고 민주당 및 공화당 의원간의 논박이 있었으며, 금번 페만 사태에 대한 토의및 결의안 심의 일정에 대한 하원 규칙이 통과 되었음. 동 규칙에 의하면, 하기와같이 3 개의 결의안 외에는 새로운 결의안을 제출하지 못하며 동 결의안에 대해서는 12 시간의 토의를 갖은후 1.12(토) 수정안 제출을 허가하지 않고 표결을 실시 하기로 결정되었는바, 동 3 개 결의안 내용은 하기와같음.

O BENNETT(민-플로리다)-DURBIN(민-일리노이)결의안 이락에 대한 무력 사용은 사전 명시적인 의회의 승인을 거치도록 요구

O GEPHARDT(민-몬타나)-HAMILTON(민-인디에나)결의안 경제 제재 조치에 충분한 시간을 줄것을 요구

O SOLARZ(민-뉴욕)- MICHEL(공-일리노이)결의안 BUSH 대통령의 요청대로 무력 사용을 지지

4. 상기 하원의 3 개 결의안중 SOLARZ-MICHEL 결의안은 민주 및 공화당 의원이 함께 발의한것으로서 기타 결의안이 CONCURRENT RESOLUTION 인것에 반해 JOINT RESOLUTION 으로 발의되었으며, 상원의 경우에는 하원과같이 의사 규칙을 정할수 없는바, NUNN-PELL 결의안 외에 새로운 결의안이 제출될 가능성도 있음.

5. 상기 상원 NUNN-PELL 결의안, BENNETT-BURBIN 및 SOLARZ-MICHEL 결의안은 별전 FAX 송부함(기타결의안은 입수되는대로 송부 예정)

첨부 USW(F)-0093

(대사 박동진-국장)

91.12.31 까지

검토필 (1991. 6. 30. )

PAGE 2

홍

주 미 대 사 관

번호 : USW(F) - 0093

수신 : 장 관 ( 미안, (미북), 중근통 )

발신 : 주미대사

제목 : 페만사태 - 의회동향 ( 결의안 )

보안
등재  ㄴ

금 1. 10. 상·하원에서 심의된 페만사태

결의안을 하기와 같이 별첨 송부함

1. Nunn - Pell 결의안

2. Bennett - Durbim 결의안

3. Solarz - Michel 결의안

0014

# S. J. RES. ___

Mr. __Nunn, Byrd, Pell, Boren,__ Mitchell, and Levin, *luly, with* introduced the following joint resolution; which was

rend twice and referred to the Committee on _____

# JOINT RESOLUTION

Regarding U.S. policy to reverse
Iraq's occupation of Kuwait

1   *Resolved by the Senate and House of Representatives of the United*

2   *States of America in Congress assembled,*

That a) the Congress is firmly committed to reversing Iraq's brutal and illegal occupation of Kuwait.

b) The Congress authorizes the use of American military force to enforce the United Nations economic embargo against Iraq; to defend Saudi Arabia from direct Iraqi attack; and to protect American forces in the region.

c) The Congress believes that continued application of international sanctions and diplomatic efforts to pressure Iraq to leave Kuwait is the wisest course at this time and should be sustained, but does not rule out declaring war or authorizing the use of force at a later time should that be necessary to achieve the goal of forcing Iraqi troops from Kuwait.

d) The Congress pledges its full and continued support for sustaining the policy of increasing economic and diplomatic pressure against Iraq; for maintaining our military options; and for efforts to increase the military and financial contributions made by allied nations.

e) The Constitution of the United States vests all power to declare war in the Congress of the United States. Congress will expeditiously consider any future Presidential request for a declaration of war or for authority to use military force against Iraq, in accordance with the following procedures:

DD93.2

0015

(Bennett- Durbin 결의안)

# H. Con Res. 1
## CONCURRENT RESOLUTION

To express the sense of Congress that Congress must approve any offensive military action against Iraq.

1    *Resolved by the House of Representatives (the Senate*
2    *concurring)*
3
4    Section 1.    Approval of Initial Response to the Invasion of
5                        Kuwait.
6
7         The Congress supports the actions taken by the President of the
8    United States to defend Saudi Arabia, demands that Iraq
9    immediately withdraw from its illegal occupation of Kuwait, and
10   supports the President's diplomatic and economic initiatives to
11   resolve the Persian Gulf crisis.
12
13   Section 2.    Urgency of Congressional Authority for Offensive
14                        Operations in the Persian Gulf.
15
16       The Congress finds that the Constitution of the United States
17   vests all power to declare war in the Congress of the United States.
18   Any offensive action taken against Iraq must be explicitly approved
19   by the Congress of the United States before such action may be
20   initiated.

0093 -3

0016

H. J. Res. _____

Solarz - Michel 결의안)

IN THE HOUSE OF REPRESENTATIVES

Mr. Solarz (for himself, Mr. Michel, Mr. Fascell, Mr.
Broomfield, Mr. Montgomery, Mr. Aspin, Mr. Dickinson,
Mr. Murtha, Mr. Ackerman, Mr. Edwards of Oklahoma, Mr.
Berman, Mr. Gallegly, Mr. Levine, Mr. Gilman, Mr. McCurdy,
Mr. Hunter, Mr. Skelton, Mr. Hyde, Mr. Stenholm, Mr.
Leach, Mr. Torricelli, Mr. Lewis of California, Mr. Solomon,
Mr. Kyl) introduced the following joint resolution; which
was referred to the Committee on _____

_____           _ _           _____

JOINT RESOLUTION

To authorize the use of United States Armed Forces pursuant to
    United Nations Security Council Resolution 678.

Whereas the Government of Iraq without provocation invaded and
    occupied the territory of Kuwait on August 2, 1990; and

Whereas both the House of Representatives (in H.J. Res. 658 of
    the 101st Congress) and the Senate (in S. Con. Res. 147 of
    the 101st Congress) have condemned Iraq's invasion of Kuwait
    and declared their support for international action to
    reverse Iraq's aggression; and

Whereas, Iraq's conventional, chemical, biological, and nuclear
    weapons and ballistic missile programs and its demonstrated
    willingness to use weapons of mass destruction pose a grave
    threat to world peace; and

Whereas the international community has demanded that Iraq
    withdraw unconditionally and immediately from Kuwait and
    that Kuwait's independence and legitimate government be
    restored; and

Whereas the U.N. Security Council repeatedly affirmed the
    inherent right of individual or collective self-defense in
    response to the armed attack by Iraq against Kuwait in
    accordance with Article 51 of the U.N. Charter; and

Whereas, in the absence of full compliance by Iraq with its
    resolutions, the U.N. Security Council in Resolution 678 has
    authorized member states of the United Nations to use all

0093-4

0017

necessary means, after January 15, 1991, to uphold and
implement all relevant Security Council resolutions and to
restore international peace and security in the area; and

Whereas Iraq has persisted in its illegal occupation of, and
brutal aggression against Kuwait: Now, therefore, be it


Resolved by the Senate and House of Representatives of the
United States of America in Congress assembled,

SECTION 1.  SHORT TITLE.

This joint resolution may be cited as the "Authorization for
Use of Military Force Against Iraq Resolution."

SECTION 2.  AUTHORIZATION FOR USE OF UNITED STATES ARMED FORCES

(a)  AUTHORIZATION. -- The President is authorized, subject
to subsection (b), to use United States Armed Forces pursuant to
United Nations Security Council Resolution 678 (1990) in order to
achieve implementation of Security Council Resolutions 660, 661,
662, 664, 665, 666, 667, 669, 670, 674, and 677.

(b)  REQUIREMENT FOR DETERMINATION THAT USE OF MILITARY
FORCE IS NECESSARY. -- Before exercising the authority granted in
subsection (a), the President shall make available to the Speaker
of the House of Representatives and the President pro tempore of
the Senate his determination that  --

> (1)  the United States has used all appropriate
> diplomatic and other peaceful means to obtain
> compliance by Iraq with the United Nations
> Security Council resolutions cited in subsection
> (a); and

0093-5

0018

(2) that those efforts have not been and would not
be successful in obtaining such compliance.

(c)   WAR POWERS RESOLUTION REQUIREMENTS. --

(1)   SPECIFIC STATUTORY AUTHORIZATION. -- Consistent
with section 8(a)(1) of the War Powers Resolution, the
Congress declares that this section is intended to
constitute specific statutory authorization within the
meaning of section 5(b) of the War Powers Resolution.

(2)   APPLICABILITY OF OTHER REQUIREMENTS. -- Nothing in
this resolution supersedes any requirement of the War Powers
Resolution.

SEC. 3   REPORTS TO CONGRESS.

At least once every 60 days, the President shall submit to
the Congress a summary on the status of efforts to obtain
compliance by Iraq with the resolutions adopted by the United
Nations Security Council in response to Iraq's aggression.

0093-6

┌─── 걸灣 事態 關聯 ───┐
│ 美 行政府와 議會間 戰爭 遂行 權限 論議 │
└─────────────────────┘

1991. 1.

美 洲 局

0020

# 目     次

<table>
<tr><td>Ⅰ. 美 憲法 條項</td></tr>
</table>

Ⅰ. 美 憲法 條項

Ⅱ. 戰爭 授權法

Ⅲ. 쾨灣 事態 關聯 戰爭 遂行 權限 論議

Ⅳ. 展望 및 結論

添附 : 1. War Power Resolution

2. U.N. Resolution 678

0021

# I. 美 憲法 條項

## 1. 關聯 規定

### 가. 美 憲法 第1條 第8項

o 美 議會는 다음 權限을 가진다
"戰爭을 宣言하고 捕獲 認許狀을 授與하고 陸上 및 海上의 捕獲에
관한 規則을 정하는것"
(Article I Section 8

To declare War, grant Letter of Marque and Reprisal, and make
Rules concerning Captures on Land and Water)

### 나. 美 憲法 第2條 第2項

o 大統領은 合衆國의 陸軍, 海軍 및 現在 合衆國의 軍役에 복무하는
각주 민병의 총지휘관이 된다 ......
(Article II, Section 2)

The President shall be Commander in Chief of the Army and
Navy of the United States, ...... )


## 2. 論爭 沿革

### 가. 美 憲法 制定 當時 論議

o 制憲 議會에서는 당초 戰爭 遂行 權限을 당시 여타국 에에 따라
行政府에 부여키로함.

o 필라델피아 立憲會議(1987.8.17)시 절충끝에 戰爭 遂行權(to make
war)을 戰爭 宣布權(to declare war) 으로 수정, 戰爭 宣布 權限
만을 議會에 부여함.


0022

- 牽制와 均衡의 原則 適用

- 經驗, 先例 및 당시 時代 狀況등이 고려 요소로 작용

나. 議會의 宣戰 布告 事例

o 1812년 戰爭(1812-14), 멕시코 戰爭(1846-48), 미.스페인 戰爭
(1989), WW I 및 WW II 등 5차례에 불과함.

다. 宣戰 布告 없는 戰爭에 대한 論難

o 1950-53 韓國戰, 1958 레바논 事態, 1965 도미니카 共和國 事態
및 1965-73간 越南戰 등 이후 宣戰 布告 없는 戰爭에 대한 論議가
시작됨.
- 行政府는 과거 전례 원용(1946-75간 議會 宣戰 布告 없이 政治的
目的으로 美 軍事力 使用 事例는 215건)
- 宣戰 布告 方式은 奇襲 攻擊 대비 必要 및 核武器의 登場등으로
時代 錯誤的 制度라고 主張

라. 大統領의 戰爭 遂行權

o 大統領의 戰爭 遂行權의 背景으로서
- 軍 統帥權者로서의 責任
- 憲法을 保存, 保護 및 防禦한다는 就任 宣誓
- 緊急 攻擊으로 부터 國家를 保護해야 할 義務
- 行政府의 수반으로서의 固有 權限등을 主張

마. 議會內 決議案 通過 方式

o 合同 決議案(Joint Resolution) : 法案과 同一한 拘束力
- 통킹만 決議案(1964)

0023

· 軍 統帥權者인 大統領에게 美軍에 대한 攻擊 격퇴 및 추가 侵略 沮止를 위한 權限을 부여함.

· 1970.12. 議會는 동 決議案 폐기

o 一般 決議案 및 共同 決議案(Concurrent Resolution) : 上.下院內 특정 行政府 政策에 대한 찬.반 의견 또는 분위기 전달에 이용됨.

- 이란 人質 抑留 非難 決議案(1979)

- 리비아산 原油 輸入 禁止 贊成 決議案(1982)

- 越南戰 탈주자 사면 반대 決議案(1977) 등

0024

# II. 戰爭 授權法

## 1. 立法 背景

○ 제2차 世界大戰 이후 大統領이 議會의 승인없이 美 軍事力을 사용하는
事例 增加에 따라, 특히 越南戰 이후 美 議會內에서는 '美 國民의
安全과 利益에 影響을 미치는 결정에 대한 議會의 參與權 侵害' 라는
批判 여론이 增大됨.

○ 특히 越南戰의 長期化에 따라 닉슨 行政府의 軍事力 사용에 대한
재량권 확대 및 對議會 協議 소홀 사례 빈발로 1973.6. War Power
Resolution을 통과시켜 軍事力 사용에 대한 議會의 統制 增大를
도모함.
- 1973.10. 닉슨 大統領은 同 決議案이 위헌이며 最善의 美 國家
利益에 배치됨을 이유로 拒否權 행사
- 1973.11. 上.下院은 상기 大統領의 拒否權을 무효화(override)
함으로써 確定 通過

## 나. 戰爭 授權法 要旨(原文 別添 #1)

### (大統領의 對議會 協議 및 報告 義務)

○ 大統領은 가능한한(in every possible instance) 軍事力 使用前
議會와 협의해야 하며 軍事力 使用後에는 終了時까지 議會와
정기적으로 協議해야 함.

○ 大統領은 美軍이 宣戰布告 없이 ①敵對行爲 또는 임박한 敵對
行爲에 돌입하거나 ②戰鬪態勢로 他國 領內에 投入된 경우,
軍事力 使用을 必要케한 상황, 軍事力 使用의 法的根據 및
軍事力 使用 範圍와 時期에 대해 議會에 書面(in writing)
報告해야 함.

0025

(軍事力 使用 中止)

○ 議會가 軍事力 使用 報告 接受後 60일 이내에 ①宣戰 布告 決議
②軍事力 使用을 許可하는 法的 措置, 또는 ③美 領土에 대한
공격으로 議會의 召集이 물리적으로 不可能한 경우가 아니면
大統領은 軍事力 사용을 중단하여야 함.
단, 大統領이 불가피한 사유를 議會에 서면 통보하면 위 60일 시한을
30일 연장 가능

○ 議會의 承認없이 美軍이 領土밖에서 발생한 敵對 行爲에 개입된
경우, 上下院이 共同 決議(Concurrent Resolution)로 철수를 요구
하면 大統領은 軍隊를 撤收하여야 함.

다. 美 行政府의 W.P.R. 規定 履行 事例

○ 美 行政府가 W.P.R. 상 規定된 48시간내 보고 의무를 이행한 사례는
아래 5가지 경우임.
  - 1975.4. 포드 大統領은 다낭, 프놈펜 및 사이공으로 부터의
    美國人 및 난민 철수시 3차례 보고
  - 1975.5. 포드 大統領은 캄보디아군에 억류된 마야게즈호
    乘務員 39명 釋放을 위한 武力 使用時 報告
  - 1980.4.26. 카터 大統領이 이란내 人質 救出 作戰時 報告

라. 軍事 作戰의 祕密 유지 必要性과 國民의 '알 權利'間 相衝

○ 軍事 作戰의 基本 性格上 전격전의 필요성 등으로 W.P.R. 규정상
事前 協議 義務 이행에는 문제가 많다고 行政府側은 不平함.
  - 民主 國家에서 國民의 알 權利 保障과 軍事 作戰의 기밀 유지
    必要間의 相衝은 最近 제기된 딜레마
  - 파나마, Grenada 侵攻時 및 리비아 事態時등은 W.P.R.상 事前 協議
    義務 불이행

0026

# Ⅲ. 페湾 事態 關聯 最近 戰爭 遂行 權限 論議

1. 페湾 派兵의 法的 根據

   ○ 페湾 派兵 自體에 대해서는 90.10. 上·下院의 派兵 支持 決議案 探擇
     으로 法的 問題는 없음
     - 美 上·下院은 90.10.1. 및 10.2. 美 行政府가 취한 措置를 支持하는
       決議案(Joint Resolution) 通過
     - 現在 論難이 되고 있는 대이라크 軍事力 사용 문제도 議會의 사전
       承認 事項이 아님.

2. UN 安保理 決議의 性格

   ○ 73년 W.P.R. 통과 이후 先例가 없어 UN 軍事力 사용 허가의 美 國內
     法的 效果를 단정키는 곤란함.
     - UN 武力 使用 決議案 (別添 ＃2)

   ○ 그러나 대이라크 軍事力 使用에 대한 行政府의 法的·政治的 立場은
     크게 强化될 것으로 展望

3. 中間 選擧 前後 美 議會內 動向

   ○ 中間 選擧 以前 부쉬 行政府의 페湾 政策에 대한 높은 지지도에 따라
     民主黨側은 同 問題를 선거 이슈로 이용하는데 실패함.
     - 대 UN 긴밀 協調 體制에 비해 對議會 및 國民들과의 진지한 논의
       결여에 노골적 不滿 表示

   ○ 특히 中間 選擧 직후 부쉬 大統領의 페湾 駐屯 병력 증강 결정(90.11.8)
     시 증파 目的에 대한 對國民 설명 부족을 지적함.
     - 行政府의 페湾 戰略에 疑問 제기
     - 美國의 中東地域에서의 具體的 利益 設定 促求

0027

o 즉 中間選擧 以後 議會 휴회중 行政府가 議會의 承認없이 戰爭에
  돌입할 可能性에 대해 깊은 우려를 표명함.

  - 90.11.20. Dellums 議員(CA)등 45명의 民主黨 下院議員들은
    대이라크 武力使用時 의회 承認 必要 與否 決定을 요구하는
    소송을 워싱턴 D.C. 聯邦 地方 法院에 提起

  - 90.11.27-12.3.간 美 上院 軍事委 聽聞會 開催

  - 90.12.4.-12.5.간 및 12.6. 美 上.下院 外交委 聽聞會 開催

o Lugar, Dole 上院議員등 共和黨 중진의원들은 상기와 같은 민주당내
  반발 움직임에 대처하고 11.29. UN 安保理의 무력 사용 허가 決議案과
  동일한 決議案 채택을 위한 의회 특별회기 소집 필요성을 강조함.

  - 부쉬 大統領 및 民主黨 지도부의 미온적 반응으로 90년내 소집은
    무산


4. 最近 動向

o 부쉬 大統領은 91.1.8.자 의회앞 서한을 통해 이라크가 1.15. 이전
  철수 결정치 않을 경우 武力使用을 포함한 모든 수단 사용을 지지하는
  決議案을 美 議會가 통과시켜 줄 것을 정식 요청함.

  - 이라크군의 쿠웨이트로 부터의 撤收를 관철시키려는 美國의 결연한
    의지 傳達 目的

  - 1964. 존슨 大統領의 통킹만 決議案 통과 요청 이래 두번째 요청

o 同 決議案이 통과될 경우, 이라크에 대한 공격 개시 이전 의회의 간접적
  인 宣戰布告로 간주될 가능성이 높음

  - 美 行政府는 전쟁 수권법과 관련한 미 의회내 논란 종식에 이용
    豫想

  - 91.1.10.-1.12. 간 上.下院 特別會議를 통해 審議 豫定

  - 民主黨側은 문안 희석을 위한 지도부간 협의 계속


0028

° 1.9(水) Baker-Aziz 간 미.이라크 外務長官 會談 결렬과 관련, 美
  行政府의 대이라크 武力 制裁를 위한 최종 법적 보장 장치가 될
  것으로 예상됨.

° 民主黨内 일부 인사들 조차도 전쟁이외에는 事態 解決을 위한 현실적
  대안이 없으며 經濟 制裁 措置에의 의존은 커다란 전략적 실패를
  가져다 줄 수 있다는 주장(Haig 전 국무장관등)에 동조하고 있어 부쉬
  大統領 요청 決議案 통과는 낙관시됨.
  - Foley 下院議長(민주, WA)도 1.12.이전 決議案 通過 豫想
  - Les Aspin 下院 軍事委員長(민주, WIS) 등도 호의적

0029

# Ⅳ. 展望

## 1. 最近 輿論 調査 結果

가. NYT/CBS News 輿論 調査(1.5-1.7 간 미 전역 1,348명의 성인을
대상으로 전화 조사, 오차 ± 3%)

o 1.15. 이전 이라크가 쿠웨이트로 부터 撤收치 않을 경우 美國은
軍事 行動을 개시해야 하는가 ?

　　賛成 : 46%

　　反對 : 47%(경제 제재 조치 효과 계속 기대)

　　* 90.12월 輿論 調査 結果는 賛成 45% : 反對 48%

다. Times지/CBS News 輿論 調査

o 응답자의 57% 가 이라크와의 戰爭 勃發 可能性을 믿고 있음.
 - 90.12월의 경우 44%

o 응답자의 60%가 美軍 攻擊 개시전 의회는 宣戰布告를 해야 한다고
응답함.

o 1.9(수) 美.이라크 外務長官 會談과 관련해서는
51%가 實質 問題 討議를 기대하고, 36%는 쇼에 불과하다고 답변함.

## 2. 展望

o 부쉬 大統領이 의회에 요청한 武力使用 승인 決議案이 통과될 경우,
1973년 전쟁 수권법 제정 이후 美 軍事力 사용에 議會의 사전 승인을
받은 선례도 없으므로 戰爭 授權法을 위요한 議會내 論難은 종식될
것으로 예상됨.

0030

o 問題의 본질은 民主黨 중심의 議會와 共和黨 行政府間 對外 政策
  決定에 관한 주도권 다툼으로 政治的 解決이 모색될 것임.
  - 司法府도 상기 民主黨 下院議員들의 소송 제기에 대해서 동 문제를
    政治的 問題로 간주, 判決 留保 豫想

o 武力 使用 이후 結果에 따라 사태의 양상이 변하거나 武力 대치 상황이
  장기화될 경우, 戰爭 授權法에 대한 論議 再開 可能性이 있음.


添附 : 1. War Power Resolution 1 부
     2. U.N. Resolution 678 1 부.   끝.


0031

# War Powers Provisions

The 1973 War Powers Resolution :

o  Stated that the president could commit U.S. armed forces to hostilities
   or situations where hostilities might be imminent only pursuant to a
   declaration of war, specific statutory authorization or a national
   emergency created by an attack upon the United States.its territories
   or possessions, or its armed forces.

o  Urged the president "in every possible instance" to consult with Congress before committing U.S. forces to hostilities or to situations where
   hostilities might be imminent, and to consult Congress regularly after
   such a commitment.

o  Required the president to report in writing within 48 hours to the
   Speaker of the House and president pro tempore of the Senate on any
   commitment or substantial enlargement of U.S. combat forces abroad,
   except for deployments related solely to supply, replacement, repair or
   training ; required supplementary reports at least every six months
   while such forces were being engaged.

o  Authorized the Speaker of the House and the president pro tempore of
   the Senate to reconvene Congress if it were not in session to consider
   the president's report.

0032

o Required the termination of a troop commitment within 60 days after the president's initial report was submitted, unless Congress declared war, specifically authorized continuation of the commitment, or was physically unable to convene as a result of an armed attack upon the United States ; allowed the 60 day period to be extended for up to 30 days if the president determined and certified to Congress that unavoidable military necessity respecting the safety of U.S. forces required their continued use in bringing about a prompt disengagement.

o Allowed Congress at any time U.S. forces were engaged in hostilities without a declaration of war or specific congressional authorization by concurrent resolution to direct the president to disengage such troops.

o Set up congressional procedures for consideration of any resolution or bill introduced pursuant to the provisions of the resolution.

o Provided that if any provision of the resolution was declared invalid, the remainder of the resolution would not be affected.

0033

# U.N. Resolution 678

Following is the text of the resolution the U.N. Security Council adopted Nov. 29, 1990:

THE SECURITY COUNCIL,

RECALLING, AND REAFFIRMING its resolutions 660(1990) of 2 August, 661 (1990) of 6 August, 662(1990) of 9 August, 664(1990) of 18 August, 665(1990) of 25 August, 666(1990) of 13 September, 667(1990) of 16 September, 669(1990) of 24 September, 670(1990) of 25 September, 674(1990) of 29 October, and 677(1990) of 28 November,

NOTING THAT, despte all efforts by the United Nations, Iraq refuses to comply with its obligation to implement resolution 660(1990) and the above-mentioned subsequent relevant resolutions, in flagrant contempt of the Security Council,

MINDFUL of its duties and responsibilities under the Charter of the United Nations for the maintenance and preservation of international peace and security,

DETERMINED to secure full compliance with its decisions,

ACTING under Chapter VII of the Charter,

1. DEMANDS that Iraq comply fully with resolution 660(1990) and all subsequent relevant resolutions, and decides, while maintaining all its decisions, to allow Iraq one final opportunity, as a pause of good will to do so:

0034

2. AUTHORIZES Member States cooperating with the Government of Kuwait, unless Iraq on or before 15 January 1991 fully implements, as set forth in paragraph 1 above, the foregoing resolutions, to use all necessary means to uphold and implement resolution 660(1990) and all subsequent relevant resolutions and to restore international peace and security in the area;

3. REQUESTS all States to provide appropriate support for the actions undertaken in pursuance of paragraph 2 of the present resolution;

4. REQUESTS the States concerned to keep the Security Council regularly informed on the progress of actions undertaken pursuant to paragraphs 2 and 3 of the present resolution;

5. DECIDES to remain seized of the matter.

0035

외 무 부

관리
번호 M-39

종 별 : 지 급
번 호 : USW-0138
수 신 : 장관(미안,미북,중근동)
발 신 : 주 미 대사
제 목 : 페만 사태- 의회 동향

일 시 : 91 0111 1914

연 USW-0120

1. 금 1.11 상. 하원 은 페만 사태 관련 결의안에 대한 토의를 계속한바, 금일 토의시에도 무력 사용은 모든 평화적 수단의 해결 방안이 실패할 경우에 최종적으로 적용될 추산인바, 경제 제재 조치에 조금더 시간을 주어야 한다는 민주당측의 주류 의견과 경제 제재 조치만으로는 이락의 쿠웨이트 철수라는 목표를달성할수 없는바, 현 시점에서 무력 사용 또는 무력 사용의 위협만이 사맨 해결의 유일한 방안이라는 공화당 및 일부 민주당 하원의원의 의견이 작일 토의시와같은 논지로 강력히 제기되었음. 또한 민주당측의원들은 대이락 국제 협조 체제에 있어서 일본, 독일 및 EC 국가들의 책임 분담 노력이 부족하다는점을 빈번히지적하였으며, 이에 대해 공화당측 의원들도 반론을 제기하지는 않았음(한국이언급된적은 없음)

2. 금일 상원에서는 작일 제출된 MICHELL-NUNN 결의안(또는 NUNN-PELL 결의안으로 지칭, S.J. RES.1)을 대상으로 찬. 반 토의를 가졌으며, 조만간 공화당측은 작일 하원에 제출된 SOLARZ-MICHEL 결의안(H.J.RES 62)과 동일한 내용의 무력사용 지지 결의안을 제출할 예정임.

3. 금일 하원에서는 GEPHARDT-HAMILTON(상금 BILL NO. 미부여)결의안을 지지하는 민주당측과 SOLARZ-MICHEL 결의안을 지지하는 공화당 및 일부 민주당측간에 논박이 있었으며, BUSH 행정부의 입장을 지지하는 발언을 한 민주당 측 의원은 FASCELL(플로리다)외무위원장, MONTGOMERY(미시시피)원호 위원장, SKELTON(미주리)군사위 군사 교육 소위 위원장, ACKERMAN(뉴욕), TORRICELLI(뉴져지), LANTOS(칼리포니아)의원등 10 여명에 달하였음.

4. 페만 사태 관련 결의안은 예정대로 명 1.12(토)에 표결에 부쳐질 예정이며, 당지 언론 분석에 의하면 하원에서는 SOLARZ-MICHEL 결의안이 채택될 가능성이

미주국   장관   차관   1차보   2차보   미주국   중아국   총리실   안기부

PAGE 1

91.01.12   10:02
외신 2과  통제관 FE
0036

높으나, 상원에서는 어느 결의안이 채택될지 전망이 매우 불부명한것으로 나타나고
있음.

(대사 박동진-국장)

91.12.31 까지

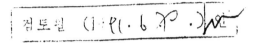

외 무 부

종 별 : 긴 급

번 호 : USW-0142                          일 시 : 91 0112 1647

수 신 : 장관(미안,미북,중근동)

발 신 : 주 미 대사

제 목 : 페만 사태 -의회 동향(결의안 표결)

연 USW-0318

1. 금 1.12(토) 상. 하원은 페만 사태 정책에 대한 결의안(상원 2 건, 하원3 건)에 대해 최종 심의 및 표결을 하였으며, 백악관측은 금번 표결에 앞서 대의회 지지 확보를 위해 대대적인 설득 노력을 기울였음. BUSH 대통령은 1.11(금) 108 명의 하원의원을 조찬회에 초청, 지지를 호소하였고, 퀘일 부통령, 체니 국방장관도 상하원의원들에 대한 개별 접촉을 갖고 지지확보에 최대한의 노력을 경주하였으며, 민주당측으로서도 상원 MITCHELL, 하원 GEPHARDT 원내 총무가 토의를 주관하였으며, FOLEY 하원 의장도 이례적으로원내 발언을 행하였음.

2. 금 1.12 결의안에 대한 표결 결과는 아래와같음.

(상원)

가.MICHELL-NUNN 결의안(S.J.RES 1)

-요지

. 경제 제재 조치를 수행하거나 사우디를 방어하고 사우디 주둔 미군을 보호하기 위한 무력사용은 승인

. 향후 필요하다고 판단될 경우 이락에 대한 무력 사용 방안을 배제하지 않으나, 현 단계에서는 경제제재 조치및 외교적 수단에 의한 사태 해결이 가장 현명한 정책임.

. 미 의회는 이락에 대한 경제 제재 조치및 외교적 압력 정책의 계속 적용을 지지하고, 무력 사용 방안을 유지하며, 동맹국의 군사적 재정적 책임 분담 증액을 지지함.

. 향후 무력 사용이 필요하다고 인정될 경우, 대통령의 요청에 따라 미 의회는 이락에 대한 전쟁 선포 또는 무력 사용 승인 문제를 신속 절차에 따라 24 시간 이내에 심의를 완료함.

| 미주국 총리실 | 장관 안기부 | 차관 | 1차보 | 2차보 | 미주국 | 중아국 | 정문국 | 청와대 |
|---|---|---|---|---|---|---|---|---|
| | | | | | | | | |

PAGE 1                                      91.01.13    08:25

-부표결과 찬성 46(민주 45, 공화 1), 반대 53 (민주 10, 공화 43)으로 부결됨.
(CRANSTON(민-캘리포니아)의원은 지병 관계로 불참)

-참고 사항 공화당 의원중 GRASSLEY(아이오아)의원만이 동 결의안에 찬성하였고, 민주당 의원중 10 명(BREAUX, BRYAN, GORE, GRAHAM, HEFLIN, JHONSTON, LIEBERMAN, REID, ROBB, SHELBY)이 반대 하였음.

나.DOLE-WARNER 결의안(S.J.RES 2)

-요지

. 페만 사태 관련 유엔 안보리 결의안을 수행하기 위해 유엔 결의안 678 의거, 미군사력을 사용하는 권한을 대통령에게 부여

. 대통령은 상기와 같이 미 군사력을 사용하기전 모든 외교적 및 평화적 수단을 행사 하였음에도 불구하고 이락측으로 하여금 유엔 안보리 결의안을 준수토록 하는데 실재 하였다는 사실을 하원 의장및 상원임시 의장에게 봉보해야함.

. 금번 결의안의 봉과에 따라 대통령은 WAR POWERS RESOLUTION 상의 권한을부여 받은것으로 간주함.

. 매 60 일 마다 적어도 1 회 이상 대통령은 이락의 유엔 안보리 결의안 이행을 위해 취한 조치에 대해 의회에 보고해야함.

-부표결과 찬성 52(민주 10, 공화 42), 반대 47(민주 45, 공화 2)로 가결됨(CRANSTON(민-칼리포니아)불참)

-참고 사항 공화당 의원중 GRASSLEY(아이오아), HATFIELD(오레곤) 2 명이 반대, 민주당 의원중 10 명(MITCHELL-NUNN 에 반대한 의원과 동일)이 찬성

(하원)

가. BENNETT-BURBIN 결의안(H.CON RES 1)

-요지 미국 헌법은 의회에 전쟁을 선포하는 권한을 부여하고 있으며, 이락에 대한 공세적 무력 사용(OFFENSIVE ACTION)은 미 의회의 사전 명시적 승인을 받아야함.

-부표결과 찬성 302(민주 260, 공화 41, 무소속 1), 반대 131 (민주 5, 공화 126), 기권 2(민주 2)로 가결됨.

나.GEPHARDT-HAMILTON 결의안(H.CON RES 33)

-요지 상원의 MITCHELL-NUNN 결의안과 동일

-부표 결과 찬성 183(민주 179, 공화 3, 무소속 1), 반대 250 (민주 86, 공화 164), 기권 2(민주 2)로 부결됨.

PAGE 2

0039

다.SOLARZ-MICHEL 결의안(H.J.RES 62)

-요지 상원의 DOLE-WARNER 결의안과 동일

-부표결과 찬성 250(민주 86, 공화 164), 반대 183(민주 179, 공화 3, 무소속 1), 기권 2(민주 2)로 가결됨.

3. 금후 절차

0 상하원에서 동일한 내용의 합동 결의안(JOINT RESOLUTION)이 통과 됨에따라 상하원 법안 심의 위원회(CONFERENCE COMMITTEE)의 조정을 거치지 않고대통령의 서명을 위해 즉시 행정부에 이송될 예정임.

0 BUSH 대통령은 동 결의안이 이송되는 대로 금일중 서명할것으로 보이며,서명 즉시 법률과 같은 효력을 발생함.

4. 당관 평가

가. 금번 부표 결과는 부쉬 대통령에 대한 신임 투표 성격의 표결로서 민주당의 상하원 지배에도 불구하고 페만사태 정책과 관련, 의회의 부쉬 대통령에 대하여 초당적인 지지를 명확히 하는 중요한 전환점을 마련하게된 것이며, 또한 최근 부쉬 행정부의 페만 사태 정책에 대한 찬. 반 논의 가운데 보여진 부쉬 행정부 정책에 대한 미국민의 지지도를 반영한것으로 볼수 있음.

나. 다만 의회의 선전 포고권을 인정하는 내용의 하원 BENNETT-BURBIN 결의안이 압도적으로 통과된것은 헌법상의 절차 문제에 대하여는 민주, 공화 양당의다수 의원들의 공통된 견해를 다시한번 재확인 한것이며, 결의안 형식도 대통령의 서명이 필요없는 CONCURRENT RESOLUTION 으로서 의회의 의사를 대외적으로표명한것에 불과함.(상원에서는 동일한 결의안이 심의되지 않았었음). 따라서금일 상하원에서 채택된 JOINT RESOLUTION 의 효력에는 아무런 영향을 미치지않는것으로 해석되고 있음.

다. 부쉬 대통령은 유엔 결의안에 따른 무력 사용 가능시한인 1.15 을 앞두고 무력 사용에 대한 국내 정치적인 장애를 제거함으롯 대이락 군사 공격을 포함한 페만 사태 해결을 위한 정책을 강력하게 추진할수 있게된 반면, 사담 후세인대통령은 미국을 포함한 국제적인 응징에 한걸음 더 직면하게 됨.

라. 당지 의회 전문가들에 의하면 금번 미 의회의 페만 사태 관련, 5 개 결의안(상원 2, 하원 3)심의를 위한 토론은 미 의회 사상 가장 훌륭한 내용의 하나로 기록될것으로 평가되고 있으며, 다만 부쉬 대통령이 이미 추진하고 있는 정책방향을

PAGE 3

0040

전환시키기에는 시기적으로 너무 늦었다는 점이 지적되고 있음.

　　마.　　금후　　의회의　　관심은　　금번　　토론　　과정에서도　　간헐적으로
나타난바와갑이동맹국들의 전쟁 수행 지원 문제로 전환될것으로 보이며, 동맹국에
대해 페만사태 관련 경비 지원 증액 및 병력 파견 증원 요청이 점증될것으로 전망됨.

　　(대사 박동진-국장)예고: '91. 12. 31 까지

美 議会 쾨湾事態 武力 使用 承認

1991. 1.

外 務 部

0042

美 上.下 兩院은 1.12(土) 폐灣事態 關聯 行政府의 武力使用을 承認하는 上.下 兩院 合同 決議案을 上院 52:47, 下院 250:183으로 通過시켰읍니다. 한편, 民主黨側이 提案한 現 對이라크 經濟制裁 措置 및 外交的 努力을 繼續할 것을 促求하는 決議案은 上.下院에서 共히 否決 되었는 바, 關聯事項 아래 報告드립니다.

## 武力使用承認 決議 要旨

* 提案 議員

. 上院 : 도올(共和, 캔자스) - 워너(共和, 버지니아)

. 下院 : 솔라즈(民主, 뉴욕) - 마이클(共和, 일리노이)

o 폐灣事態 關聯, 武力使用을 許容한 유엔 安保理 決議 第678號에 依據, 美 軍事力을 使用하는 權限을 大統領에게 附與함

- 금번 決議案 通過에 따라 大統領은 戰爭 授權 法上의 權限을 附與 받은 것으로 간주

- 大統領은 軍事力 使用前 外交的 手段을 포함한 모든 平和的 努力에도 不拘, 이라크측이 유엔 安保理 決議를 遵守토록 하는데 失敗하였음을 下院 議長 및 上院 臨時 議長에게 通報 必要

0043

o 大統領은 60日 마다 最小 1回以上 이라크의
유엔 安保理 決議 履行을 위해 취한 措置를 議會에
報告해야함

## 今後 節次

o 同 合同 決議는 大統領의 署名을 위해 즉시 行政府에
移送될 豫定이며 부쉬 大統領은 同 決議에 즉시
署名할 것으로 豫想됨

- 同 決議는 署名과 동시 法律과 동일한 效力 發生

## 評価 및 展望

o 금번 表決 結果는 부쉬 大統領에 대한 信任 投票의
性格을 가진 것으로서 부쉬 大統領의 페灣政策에 대한
議會의 超黨的인 支持를 明確히 하는 重要한 轉換点을
마련함

- 부쉬 行政府의 페灣事態 政策에 대한 美國民의
支持度를 反映

o 부쉬 大統領은 금번 決議 通過로 武力使用에 대한
國內 政治的인 障碍를 除去함으로써 對이라크 軍事
攻擊을 포함한 페灣事態 解決을 위한 政策을 보다
强力히 推進할 수 있게됨

0044

ㅇ 向後 폐灣事態 關聯 友邦國에 대한 分擔金 追加 支援
  및 兵力 派遣 要請이 增加될 展望임

  - 決議案 贊反 討議時 日本 및 獨逸의 微溫的
    支援 態度를 批判하는 議員 多數( 韓國에 대해
    言及한 議員은 없었음)

參考事項

ㅇ 금번 武力使用承認 決議는 1964年 존슨大統領이
  要請한 통킹灣 決議 通過以來 첫번째임

ㅇ 上記 決議와는 별도로 下院은 議會의 戰爭 宣布權을
  再確認하는 決議案을 302:131로 通過시켰는
  바, 이는 法的 拘束力이 없는 勸告的 性格임

                                                끝.

0045

# The Message, Stronger

Until yesterday, Saddam Hussein may have been unsure about the meaning of the debate in Washington over how to respond to Iraq's rape of Kuwait. Now that Congress has authorized President Bush to wage war in the Persian Gulf, Saddam Hussein cannot possibly misread America's message: Get out of Kuwait.

The vote sent other messages too. It reasserted Congress's constitutional war-making authority. It honored democracy. And, as a grateful and gracious Mr. Bush observed afterward, it honored Congress, which debated the supremely emotional question of war or peace honestly and decently.

The tally in the Senate was close, and neither house, as even Mr. Bush's supporters agreed, voted for precipitate action. The preferred solution is a peaceful solution. Congress has armed the President, first and foremost, for peace.

●

The Jan. 15 deadline established by the U.N. for Iraq's total withdrawal from Kuwait is a scant two days away. Many believe that in an effort to exploit the worldwide hunger for peace, Saddam Hussein will make a last-minute offer. But if peace now is to mean something more than war later, the world needs to be tough-minded in its responses.

Some European and Arab members of the anti-Iraq coalition are intrigued by hints of a "conditional" Iraqi withdrawal. Conditional on what? In the supple language of diplomacy, words like "conditional" and "linkage" can mean no more than allowing Saddam Hussein to save face as he removes all his forces from Kuwait.

But other meanings are clearly unacceptable. It would be unthinkable, for example, to give Iraq the blackmailer's leverage of keeping some of its forces in Kuwait while substantive discussions proceed about borders, oilfields or any other regional political question.

Full international sanctions, supported by allied military pressure, must be maintained as long as any Iraqi troops continue to occupy any part of Kuwait without Kuwait's consent. Even if Iraq fully withdraws, the embargo must continue to block any imports Baghdad might use to improve its military potential. As Secretary of State Baker has said, withdrawal would remove the threat of allied attack. And once Baghdad's withdrawal has been verified, restrictions on food and other consumer imports can safely be removed.

But the world asks for more than Iraq's withdrawal from Kuwait. It seeks a commitment to peace and stability. Thus the embargo on imports critical to Saddam Hussein's war machine cannot safely be removed until a satisfactory containment system is in effect. Containment requires some combination of weapons limitations, a system for inspection and verification, regional security agreements and a multinational peacekeeping force.

The same logic governs the embargo on Iraq's oil exports. Unless and until Iraq agrees to arms limitation, any relaxation of the oil embargo would let Iraq once more use its vast oil profits to acquire weapons of mass destruction that threaten the entire Middle East. Once arms control measures are in place, and verified, Iraq could re-enter normal world trade. But even then, it would be madness to resume unrestricted exports of highly sensitive technologies and materials.

Now that Congress has spoken, the world is understandably focused on the drama of Jan. 15. It prays for an Iraqi withdrawal without the need to shed blood. Yet what happens after an Iraqi withdrawal will matter just as much.

132-1

91.1.13 NYT

0046

# No Tonkin Gulf Vote

THIS WAS NO sudden, scared-up, uninformed Tonkin Gulf vote that Congress took on Iraq yesterday. Nor was it a hasty decision made simply on three intense days of floor debate. For no less than five months Congress has been profoundly immersed in this issue. In the end, it made a choice the weightier for all the time, information, scrutiny and debate that had gone into it. The choice was to add the warning of war to the embargo, diplomacy and buildup already being applied in order to strengthen the president's strategy of applying maximum pressure in the countdown to Jan. 15. In arming the president with legislative authority for his policy, Congress took the grave, responsible and necessary chance that this will help incline Saddam Hussein to quit Kuwait without war. President Bush struck the right note in his press conference after the voting in expressing the hope that this powerful new affirmation of American will would finally break through to the Iraqi leader.

As Jan. 15 nears, other countries and actors, including many who doubted the efficacy of American pressure, are using it to make a last-minute diplomatic surge. U.N. Secretary General Javier Perez de Cuellar has now brought to Baghdad the specific diplomatic charge of the European Community and the fervent hopes of many other nations and individuals. In the American threat to lead a coalition into battle, he has one tool of persuasion. He also carries positive incentives: American-supported offers to spare Iraq attack and to substitute peacekeeping forces for the foreign contingents now in Saudi Arabia, and a European pledge to call a regional peace conference.

It bears underlining, however, that the first ingredient for diplomatic progress—prompt unqualified Iraqi withdrawal, or as Mr. Bush said yesterday, instant large-scale commencement of it—is still missing. Saddam Hussein's aides churn out rumors of future compliance, but only the man himself counts, and he insists he will never yield Kuwait.

Between the European and American positions lie several variations. The Europeans, for instance, are readier to blur the no-linkage line: they would promise a conference on Israel and Palestine even before Iraq has agreed to withdrawal, let alone started or completed it. Whether the diplomats want Baghdad to notice these variations is uncertain. What must be made clear, however, is that no incentives can be made available to Iraq simply on the word of President Hussein. His concrete delivery on withdrawal must be the test.

The United States is long on record as supporting a "properly structured" international conference "at an appropriate time"—hedges inserted to satisfy Washington's essential concern for Israel and for its own credibility, if a conference would address the American interest in no-linkage Mideast peace. But the United States is also on record as rejecting any arrangement smacking of compensating Iraq for aggression. This defines the narrow space in which Mr. Perez de Cuellar must work in Baghdad.

wp

132 - 2

91. 1. 13 wp

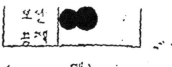

# Congress in Step

## After the Vote, Margins Are Ignored, But Potential Divisions Are Serious

### By ADAM CLYMER
#### Special to The New York Times

WASHINGTON, Jan 13 — A Congress that had seemed loath to deal with the Persian Gulf finally went ahead when its leaders despaired of getting President Bush to promise to ask formally for their support before attacking Iraq, some members of Congress and highly placed aides said today.

**News Analysis**

And a President who had previously told the leaders that he wanted action only if they could assure him the result would be overwhelming then went ahead and asked, and lobbied hard but won only a bare five-vote victory in the Senate.

Today no one was talking about the margins, or the history. President Bush said: "We went to Congress. Both houses of Congress affirmed the policy of this Government." The House Speaker, Thomas S. Foley of Washington, said, "It is clear that the Congress has spoken, and the exact size of the vote is irrelevant."

The Democratic leaders who had fought so hard for resolutions demanding continued reliance on economic sanctions had been quick to say, even before they lost the Saturday votes, that they would stand behind American troops if President Bush took them into battle, insisting that there would be no moves to cut off funds after Saturday's definitive vote.

### Potential Divisions

But even so, the voting patterns showed serious potential divisions. The partisan ones were obvious; 70 percent of the Democratic senators and representatives who voted Saturday opposed force and 98 percent of the Republicans favored it.

But the regional divisions were almost as sharp. Southern lawmakers voted 86 to 32 for force, and their senators in particular provided the Democratic votes that were essential to Mr. Bush's victory. Lawmakers from the Southwest favored force by 35 to 13. Mountain state lawmakers went 16 to 8 in favor of force.

But New Englanders, including a unanimous Massachusetts delegation, opposed force by 23 to 13. Midwesterners were narrowly opposed, 74 to 63, and lawmakers from the Middle Atlantic region favored force but only by 51

to 45. Pacific Coast lawmakers were almost evenly split, with 38 favoring force and 35 opposed.

Those differences, if there is war and it is not short, may divide the country more seriously than the party splits, for the Democrats on the losing side have been earnestly seeking to close ranks with the victors.

If there was a nearly universal area of agreement today, it was among lawmakers who felt proud that Congress had faced the issue and decided it, reasserting its prerogatives after decades of going along with Presidents who acted first and consulted later.

But institutional concerns were also a factor in its taking as long as it did to speak. Last fall, after Mr. Bush announced a doubling of troop strength to provide offensive capacity in the gulf, there were many calls from both Republicans and Democrats for Congress to return in special session. The leaders resisted, noting that there would be 49 new lawmakers in just two months. Instead, they held hearings from which one clear message was restraint.

Two other arguments were offered today. Mr. Foley said on the NBC News program "Meet the Press" that a vote even as recently as a month ago would have been seen by many members and outsiders as no more than "another quiver in the diplomatic armory." He said that if Congress was going to vote what he called "a real, practical equivalent of a declaration of war," then it should do so in absolutely clear focus, with no one in doubt about what the vote implied.

A complementary explanation for delay came from well-placed Congressional strategists. They said that the other possibility late last fall was a Congressional vote, with more Democrats than were with their leaders on Saturday calling for a reversal of the troop buildup. But with no prospect of a majority big enough to override a veto, that course would only have made the dispute ineradicably partisan.

As it happened, the vote was more partisan than the atmosphere. Senator Bob Dole of Kansas, the Republican leader, occasionally discerned party

motives among Democrats opposed to force. But few other Bush supporters did so, and it is rare for Congress to work so late into the night in as good a humor as was maintained late Friday and early Saturday.

### How the Action Unfolded

Even in the new Congress, action came more quickly than the leaders had expected. On Jan. 3, the first day of the 102d Congress, Mr. Foley and Senator George J. Mitchell of Maine, the Democratic majority leader, each promised Congressional action on the war issue, but each was vague about just when would be the appropriate time.

Liberal critics of Mr. Bush's policy demanded a vote before the Jan. 15 deadline, angrily on the Senate floor and more quietly in meetings in the House.

The leaders said they had hoped for a Presidential request for Congressional action before any conflict, but eventually gave up on it. On Friday, Jan. 4, Mr. Mitchell said the Senate would act before the deadline, and on Sunday, Jan. 6, Mr. Foley promised House action, and also predicted that Mr. Bush's side would win. Then, with his irons in the fire, Mr. Bush made the request and got busy lobbying.

And Monday, according to Marlin Fitzwater, the White House press secretary, he will sign the joint resolution authorizing him to go to war.

1. ' F. Sign

Jan. 14, 1991

NYT

0142-12

외 무 부

종 별 : 지 급

번 호 : USW-0246                                일 시 : 91 0117 1113

수 신 : 장관(미북, 중근동, 대책반)

발 신 : 주미대사

제 목 : 걸프 작전 (제16신, 미 의회 반응)

1. BUSH 대통령은 걸프 작전에 대한 의회의 지지를 구하기 위해 금 1.17. 아침의회 지도자들을 백악관에 초치함.

2. 당지 언론은 상원은 금일중, 그리고 하원은 내일중 걸프작전 지지 결의안을 채택할 것으로 전망하고 있음.

(대사 박동진- 국장)

| 미주국 | 장관 | 차관 | 1차보 | 2차보 | 중아국 | 중아국 | 정문국 | 정와대 |
|--------|------|------|-------|-------|--------|--------|--------|--------|
| 종리실 | 안기부 | 대책반 | | | | | | |

PAGE 1                                          91.01.18    01:43 CG

# 외 무 부

원 본

종 별 : 지 급

번 호 : USW-0248              일 시 : 91 0117 1128

수 신 : 장관( 미안, 미북, 중근동, 대책반)

발 신 : 주미대사

제 목 : 페만 사태 무력사용-의회 반응

1. 금 1.17. 오전 BUSH 대통령은 상하원 지도부 인사를 백악관으로 초청, 대이락공격 전황을 설명하고, 의회의 계속적인 협조를 당부 하였음.

2. 상기 회합 직후 FOLEY 하원의장, MITCHEL 상원 민주당 총무, DOLE 상원 공화당 총무는 기자 질문에 대한 답변을 통해 현재까지 거의 사상자가 없이 군사작전이 진행되고 있음에 대해 만족을 표하면서 페만 주둔 미군들의 전쟁 수행을 전폭 지원할 것임을 밝히고 초당적인 지원을 보내는 결의안을 채택할 것임을 아울러 표명하였음.

3. 상기 결의안 관련, 상.하원 지도부측에 탐문한바, 상원은 금 1.17, 하오, 하원은 명 1.18 중 동 결의안을 심의할 예정이라 함.

4. 관련 의회 동향 추보 예정임.

(대사 박동진- 국장)

| 미주국 | 장관 | 차관 | 1차보 | 2차보 | 미주국 | 중아국 | 중아국 | 정문국 |
|-------|------|------|-------|-------|--------|--------|--------|--------|
| 청와대 | 총리실 | 안기부 | 대책반 | | | | | |

# 외 무 부

종 별 : 긴 급

번 호 : USW-0262

일 시 : 91 0117 1719

수 신 : 장 관(민북,미안,중근동)

발 신 : 주 미대사

제 목 : 페만사태 무력사용-의회 반응

연: USW-0248

1. 금 1.17. 16:30 현재 민주당 및 공화당 지도부는 연호 결의안 문안에 대해 협의하고 있음.

2. 민주당및 공화당측은 공히 금번 군사작전에 참가하고 있는 미군에 대해 전폭적인 지지를 표하고 있으나, 결의안 문안중 대통령을 포함시키는 문제에 대해 민주당측은 반대하고있고, 공화당측은 미군의 봉수권자인 대통령에대한 지지 표시 없이 군인에 대해서만 지지를 표하는것은 논리상 문제가 있다는 이유를 들어 부시 대통령에대한 지지를 명확히 표시할것을 주장하고 있음.

(대사 박동진-국장)

| 미주국 | 장관 | 차관 | 1차보 | 미주국 | 중아국 | 중아국 | 안기부 |
|---|---|---|---|---|---|---|---|

PAGE 1

# 외 무 부

종 별 : 긴 급

번 호 : USW-0272

일 시 : 91 0117 1903

수 신 : 장 관( 미북, 미안, 중근동, 대책반)

발 신 : 주 미 대사

제 목 : 페만 사태 무력사용-의회 반응

연: USW-0248, 0242

1. 연호 미 상원은 금 1.17(목) 17:36 부터 30분간 대이락전에 페만에서 참전하고 있는 미군과 대통령의 정책에 지지를 보내는 내용의 결의안 (S.CON.RES 2) 을 심의한후, 만장일치 (찬성 98, 반대 0) 의 표결로 통과시켰음.

2. MITCHELL 민주당 원내총무와 DOLE 공화당원 내총무의 진행아래 발언에 나선 양당의원 17명 (민주 9명,공화 8명) 은 참전 미군에 대한 자부심과 최대한의 지지를 표하였으며, 또한 미 의회는 금번 페만 사태에 대한 대통령의 정책을 강력히 지지하고 있다는 내용의 발언을 하였음.

3.금번 결의안은 미 의회의 입장 (SENSE OF CONGRESS) 을 대외적으로 천명하는 공동 결의안 (CONCURRENT RESOLUTION ) 의 형식으로 채택 되었으며, 명일 1.18. 하원에서도 동일한 결의안이 채택될것으로 전망됨.

4.결의안 문안은 별전 팩시 송부함.

(USW(F)-208 1매)

(대사 박동진- 국장)

| 미주국 | 장관 | 차관 | 1차보 | 2차보 | 미주국 | 중아국 | 정문국 | 청와대 |
|--------|------|------|-------|-------|--------|--------|--------|--------|
| 총리실 | 안기부 | 대책반 | | | | | | |

PAGE 1

91.01.18    09:10 WG

외신 1과  통제관
0052

NT BY: XEROX Telecopier 7017; 1-17-81 ; 8:40PM ;                    202 797 0595;# 1

*attn: Noh*

S. CON. RESOLUTION 2
SUPPORTING THE UNITED STATES PRESENCE IN THE PERSIAN GULF

JANUARY 17, 1991

Whereas the President of the United States, with the
authorization of Congress, has ordered military action against
Iraq in an effort to force Iraqi armed forces from occupied
Kuwait;

Whereas 415,000 men and women of United States Armed Forces
are now involved in armed conflict;

Whereas 158,000 members of the Reserves and National Guard
have been called to active duty since August 22 and may become
involved in armed conflict;

Whereas Congress and the American people have the greatest
pride in the men and women of the United States Armed Forces and
support them in their efforts;

Now, therefore, be it resolved by the Senate (the House of
Representatives concurring),

That the Congress commends and supports the efforts and
leadership of the President as Commander in Chief in the Persian
Gulf hostilities.

The Congress unequivocally supports the men and women of our
Armed Forces who are carrying out their missions with professional
excellence, dedicated patriotism and exemplary bravery.

0053

외 무 부

종 별 :

번 호 : USW-0287

일 시 : 91 0118 1651

수 신 : 장 관(미안,미북,중근동)

발 신 : 주 미 대사

제 목 : 페만 사태-의회 반응

연: USW-0248, 0242, 0272

1. 연호, 미 하원은 금 1.18(금) 14:00 부터 100 분간, 작일 상원 결의안 (S.CON RES 2) 과 동일한 내용의 공동 결의안을 심의한후 찬성 398 (민주242,공화 156),반대 6 (민주 5, 기타 1) 의 압도적다수로 채택하였음.

2. GEPHARDT 민주당 원내 총무과 MICHEL공화당 원내 총무의 의사 진행 아래 50 여명의의원들이 발언한바, 미 행정부의 페만 정책과참전 미군들에 대한 출신 지역구민들의 강력한 지지를 전달하고, 분재의 조속한 해결을 위한 단합을 강조하였음.

(대사 박동진-국장)

| 미주국 | 장관 | 차관 | 1차보 | 2차보 | 미주국 | 중아국 | 중아국 | 정문국 |
|---|---|---|---|---|---|---|---|---|
| 청와대 | 안기부 | | | | | | | |

PAGE 1

91.01.19    09:05 WG

외신 1과 통제관

0054

# 외 무 부

종  별 :

번  호 : USW-0287               일  시 : 91 0118 1651

수  신 : 장 관(미안,미북,중근동)

발  신 : 주 미 대사

제  목 : 페만 사태-의회 반응

연: USW-0248,0242,0272

1. 연호, 미 하원은 금 1.18(금) 14:00 부터 100 분간, 작일 상원 결의안 (S.CONRES 2) 과 동일한 내용의 공동 결의안을 심의한후 찬성 398 (민주242,공화 156),반대 6 (민주 5, 기타 1) 의 압도적다수로 채택하였음.

2. GEPHARDT 민주당 원내 총무과 MICHEL공화당 원내 총무의 의사 진행 아래 50 여명의의원들이 발언한바, 미 행정부의 페만 정책과참전 미군들에 대한 출신 지역구민들의 강력한 지지를 전달하고, 분재의 조속한 해결을 위한 단합을 강조하였음.

(대사 박동진-국장)

| 미주국 | 장관 | 차관 | 1차보 | 2차보 | 미주국 | 중아국 | 중아국 | 정문국 |
|---|---|---|---|---|---|---|---|---|
| 청와대 | 안기부 | | | | | | | |

PAGE 1

# 외 무 부

종 별 : 지급

번 호 : USW-0376

일 시 : 91 0123 1806

수 신 : 장관(미안,미북,중근동)

발 신 : 주 미 대사

제 목 : 걸프전 분담금-의회 반응

1. 대통령의 무력사용에 관한 미의회의 승인이후 걸프사태가 실전으로 전개됨에 따라, 미의회는 상. 하원 공동결의안을 통해 걸프전에 임하는 미군과 대통령의 정책에 지지를 표명한바 있음.

2. 아울러 작 1.22 부터 정상적인 의회 일정에 돌입한 미의회는 상. 하원 예산위원회 주재로 걸프전이 미국 경제와 예산논의에 미칠 영향에 관한 일련의 청문회를 개최하고 있음.

3. 이와때를 같이하여, 하원 예산위원장 LEON PANETTA (캘리포니아)와 CHARLES SCHUMER (민, 뉴욕)의원은 걸프전의 소요경비와 동맹국들의 분담금에 관한 월레보고서를 미행정부 예산청(OMB)이 국무, 국방부와의 상의아래 의회에 제출토록하는 법안을 제안함.

4. PANETTA 위원장은 동법안이 걸프전 관련하여 동맹국들에게 정당한 역할 분담을 촉구할 목적으로 제안된 것임을 강조함.

5. 작년 8 월 이락의 쿠웨이트 침공이후 동맹국들의 역할분담에 관한 미의회의 반응이 대체로 일본과 독일의 기여가 미진함에 불만을 토로하는 방향으로 전개되었으며, 기타 국가들의 지원약속 이행이 불성실함에 또한 의회 논란의 촛점이 맞추어져왔음에 비추어 볼때 전시 상황에서의 분담금 관련 논란은 더욱 가속화될것으로 전망됨.

6. 현재까지 공식적으로 표명된 미행정부의 입장은 동맹국들의 참여도에 대체로 만족한다는 입장이나, 전쟁이 장기화될 경우 분담금 추가지원 요청은 불가피할것으로 예측하고 있음.

7. 이와관련, 1.20-21 간 뉴욕에서 개최된 서방 7 개국 재무장관회의에서 BRADY 미 재무장관은 전비의 1/3 은 미국이 분담하고, 1/3 은 사우디, 쿠웨이트가 , 너머지 1/3

| 미주국 | 장관 | 차관 | 1차보 | 2차보 | 미주국 | 중아국 | 정문국 | 정와대 |
|--------|------|------|-------|-------|--------|--------|--------|--------|
| 총리실 | 안기부 | | | | | | | |

은 기타 우방국들이 분담해야할것이라고 언급한바, 향후 분담금추가 요청도 전체전비 규모에 대한 산정방법과는 별도로 이러한 윤곽에서 이루어질것으로 예상됨.

8. 관련, 1.16. 당지를 방문한 EC COMMISSION 의 LEON BRITTAN 부집행위원장은 미국의 전비 부담이 과중함에 대한 이해를 표명함과 동시에, 12 개 EC 회원국들은 동구라파 사회주의 국가들의 경제 복구에 막중한 부담을 안고 있음을 강조함으로써 EC 의 제한된 참여에 관한 입장을 대변하였음을 참고 바람.

9. 상기 법안 추이는 추보예정인바 문안은 별첨 팩시 송부함.

첨부 USW(F)-0279(5 매)

(대사 박동진-국장)

예고:91.12.31 까지

PAGE 2

SCHUME050

USW(ド)- 0279
수신: 미안·미북·중근동
발신: 주미대사
제목: 유첨

(5부)  HLC

102D CONGRESS
1ST SESSION

H. R. ____

IN THE HOUSE OF REPRESENTATIVES

Mr. SCHUMER (for himself and Mr. PANETTA) introduced the
following bill; which was referred to the Committee on
_____

A BILL

To require regular reports to the Congress on the amount of
expenditures made to carry out Operation Desert Shield and
Operation Desert Storm and on the amount of contributions made
to the United States by foreign countries to support Operation
Desert Shield and Operation Desert Storm.

1    Be it enacted by the Senate and House of Representatives
2 of the United States of America in Congress assembled,

0299-1

0058

1  SECTION 1. REPORT ON COSTS OF AND CONTRIBUTIONS TO OPERATION

2         DESERT SHIELD AND OPERATION DESERT STORM.

3      (a) COSTS OF OPERATIONS.--(1) The Director of the Office

4  of Management and Budget, after consultation with the

5  Secretary of Defense, shall prepare periodic reports

6  specifying the total amount of obligations incurred and

7  expenditures made by the Department of Defense during the

8  period covered by each report to carry out Operation Desert

9  Shield and Operation Desert Storm.

10      (2) In determining pursuant to this section the amount of

11  obligations incurred and expenditures made by the Department

12  of Defense to carry out those operations, the Director may

13  not consider those expenditures that would have been made

14  regardless of the Iraqi invasion of Kuwait or the

15  implementation of Operation Desert Shield or Operation Desert

16  Storm.

17      (b) SPECIFIC COST AREAS.--Reports required by subsection

18  (a) shall specify the amount of obligations incurred and

19  expenditures made by the Department of Defense in each of the

20  following areas during the period covered by the report:

21         (1) Airlift costs directly related to the

22      transportation by air of personnel, equipment, and

23      supplies to and from the Persian Gulf region, including

24      maintenance, fuel, contractual support, and other

25      expenditures.

0279-2

0059

1    (2) Sealift costs directly related to the

2    transportation by sea of personnel, equipment, and

3    supplies to and from the Persian Gulf region, including

4    fuel, loading and unloading, merchant seamen contracts,

5    and other expenditures.

6    (3) Medical costs, including expenditures made to

7    activate hospital ships and purchase medical supplies.

8    (4) Costs associated with the call or order to active

9    duty of units and members of the reserve components of

10    the Armed Forces.

11    (5) Operation and maintenance costs, including

12    ammunition purchases and maintenance and fuel

13    expenditures required because of increased operating

14    tempo.

15    (6) Personnel costs, including pay and allowances of

16    members of the reserve components of the Armed Forces

17    called or ordered to active duty and increased pay and

18    allowances of members of the regular components of the

19    Armed Forces incurred because of deployment in the

20    Persian Gulf region.

21    (7) Costs of logistical support in the Persian Gulf

22    region, including expenditures for housing, water,

23    refrigeration, and sanitation.

24    (8) Fuel cost increases associated with increases in

25    the market price of oil.

0279-3

1        (9) Military construction costs, including

2    expenditures for additional billeting, mess, and supply

3    facilities.

4        (10) Other deployment costs not covered by a

5    preceding paragraph.

6        (c) CONTRIBUTIONS TO OPERATIONS.--(1) Reports required by

7    subsection (a) shall also specify the amount of financial

8    contribution made to the United States by each foreign

9    country that is making a financial contribution in support of

10   Operation Desert Shield or Operation Desert Storm. The amount

11   of each country's financial contribution during the period

12   covered by each report shall be broken down into categories

13   as follows:

14        (A) Contributions pledged as cash payments.

15        (B) Contributions pledged as in kind payments.

16        (C) Contributions received as cash payments.

17        (D) Contributions received as in kind payments.

18        (2) The Director of the Office of Management and Budget

19   shall prepare the information required by this subsection

20   after consultation with the Secretary of State and the

21   Secretary of Defense.

22        (d) SUBMISSION OF REPORTS.--The first report required by

23   subsection (a) shall be submitted to the Congress not later

24   than 14 days after the date of the enactment of this Act and

25   shall cover the period beginning on August 1, 1990, and

5

1 ending on the date of the enactment of this Act. Subsequent

2 reports shall be submitted to the Congress every 30 days

3 thereafter and shall cover the 30-day period beginning on the

4 day after the last day covered by the preceding report.

5 　　　(e) TERMINATION.--This section shall terminate one year

6 after the date designated by the President as the end of

7 Operation Desert Storm.

0279-5

0062

| 관리<br>번호 | 91-132 |
|---|---|

# 외 무 부

종 별 : 지급

번 호 : USW-0379

일 시 : 91 0123 1831

수 신 : 장관(미북,중근동,대책반)

발 신 : 주 미 대사

제 목 : 걸프전쟁-의회반응

연:USW-0359

금 1.23. 당관 임성준 참사관은 STANLEY ROTH 하원 아태소위 전문위원을 접촉, 한국군 의료단의 사우디 파견에 대한 국회 동의통과등 아국의 지원노력에 대해 설명하고, 걸프전쟁의 전망등에 관해 의견을 나눈바 동주요 내용을 하기 보고함.

(전쟁진행 상황에 대한 평가)

0 전쟁발발 직후 미국 언론의 보도 태도가 잘못되지 않았느냐하는 생각을 함. 전쟁개시 몇시간동안의 결과를 보고 미 언론이 너무 전쟁에 대해 낙관적인 보도를 하였고, 최근 이락의 스커트 미사일 공격 이후 미언론이나 미국민이 혼돈에 빠진 인상이 듬.

0 금번 전쟁이 순식간에 극적으로 종결될 가능성도 배제할수는 없음.

이락군부의 구테타도 상정할수 있고, 특히 사우디, 쿠웨이트 접경지대에 배치된 이락군이 최정예부대가 아닌바, 대규모 투항도 일어날수 있음.

0 현재까지 연합군은 합리적인 태도로 전쟁에 임해 왔다고 보며 연합군측, 특히 미측은 다소 사상자가 많더라도 전쟁을 가급적 조속히 종결하는 방안을 택할 것으로 생각함.

(걸프 전쟁 관련 의회 동향)

0 전쟁이 진행되고 있는 동안 의회가 어떤 적극적인 역할을 할수는 없으나, 전쟁이 장기화되고 사상자가 커지면 의회내 반전분위기가 고조될 가능성이 있음.

0 전쟁이 종료되면, 미의회는 전쟁 피해국에 대한 대외원조 문제, 전후 복구문제를 심의하게될것이며, 군사적으로 향후 무기체계 및 운영에 대해 전반적인재검토를 할것으로 전망됨.

(우방국의 책임 분담 문제)

| 미주국<br>안기부 | 장관 | 차관 | 1차보 | 2차보 | 중아국 | 정문국 | 청와대 | 총리실 |
|---|---|---|---|---|---|---|---|---|

PAGE 1

91.01.24  09:21

외신 2과 통제관 BW

0063

0 전쟁이 종결되면, 미의회내에서 미국의 우방국이 어떠한 기여를 하였는지에 대해 평가를 하려는 분위기가 있을 것이며 이경우 우방국의 기여에 대한 평가에 매우 감정적인 요소가 개입될 우려가 있을 것으로 봄.

0 일본의 경우, 일본정부가 40 억불이라는 막대한 금액을 분담하였음에도 불구하고, 일반 대중은 일본의 기여가 부족하다고 느끼고 있으며(일반 대중은 전쟁시 1 일 미국이 5-10 억불을 쓰고 있다고 생각)(300)이와같은 일반인의 생각은의회 논의시 그대로 반영될것임.

0 책임분담 문제와 관련해서 중요한 점은 우방국의 기여가 일반 대중의 눈에 드러나냐하는문제(VISIBILITY)이며, 상징적인 규모의 병력이라도 사우디에 군대를 파견하는것이 가장효과적인 방법이었을것임.

0 현재 미의회내 책임분담 관련해서 불만의 대상은 독일, 일본등이며, 한국이 크게 언급되지는 않고 있으나, 종전후 독일, 일본등에 대한 불만표출과정에서한국에 불이익이 돌아갈 가능성도 배제키는 어려울것임.(예: 미국의 해외주둔 병력의 일괄감축 결정시, 주한미군의 감축도 불가피할것임.)

(전쟁의 미국내 정치적 영향)

0 전쟁이 최소한의 희생으로 단기화되면, 92 년도 부시 대통령의 재선은 확실시될것이며, 민주당은 대통령 후보자를 내세우는것 자체가 어려운 상황이될것임.

0 전쟁이 막대한 희생으로 장기화되면, 상원 군사위 NUNN 위원장 처럼 전쟁을 반대한 의원의 발언권이 강화되고, NUNN 의원은 확실히 대통령선거에 출마하게될것임.

(대사 박동진-국장)

예고:91.12.31 까지

검토필 (1 . . .)인

9건

원 본

# 외 무 부

종 별 :

번 호 : USW-0380　　　　　　　　　　일 시 : 91 0123 1831

수 신 : 장 관(미북,중근동,대책반)

발 신 : 주 미 대사

제 목 : 걸프 전쟁- 의회 반응

　　1.금 1.23 하원은 걸프 전쟁 관련, 이락의 이스라엘공격 비난 결의안 (H.CON.RES 41 ) 및 이락의 전쟁 포로 학대 비난및 학대 관련자 전범 처리결의안 (H.CON.RES 48)을 각각 출석 의원만장 일치로 채택 하였음.

　　2.상기 관련, 상원은 명 1.24(목) 동 결의안 2건에 대한 표결을 할 예정 이며, 하원에서와 같이 만장 일치로 채택될 것으로 전망됨.

　　3.상기 결의안 2건은 FAX 송부함.( USW(F)-0285)

　　(대사 박동진-국장)

| 미주국 | 장관 | 차관 | 1차보 | 2차보 | 중아국 | 정문국 | 정와대 | 총리실 |
| 안기부 | 대책반 | | | | | | | |

PAGE 1　　　　　　　　　　　　　　　　　　91.01.24　　10:11 WG

외신 1과 통제관

0065

걸프사태 : 미국 의회 동향, 1990-91. 전5권 (V.3 1991.1-2월) 451

102D CONGRESS
1ST SESSION

# H. CON. RES. 41

Condemning the Iraqi attack against Israel.

---

## IN THE HOUSE OF REPRESENTATIVES

JANUARY 18, 1991

Mr. FEIGHAN (for himself, Ms. ROS-LEHTINEN, Mr. FASCELL, Mr. BROOMFIELD, Mr. GEPHARDT, Mr. SMITH of Florida, Mr. SOLARZ, Mr. OWENS of Utah, Mr. HOAGLAND, Mr. WAXMAN, Mr. PALLONE, Mr. ANDREWS of Texas, Mr. BURTON of Indiana, Mr. ANNUNZIO, Mr. BACCHUS, Mr. BORSKI, Mr. GINGRICH, Mr. WEBER, Mr. ZIMMER, Mr. CUNNINGHAM, Mr. PAXON, Mr. SCHUMER, Mr. ASPIN, Mr. CARDIN, Mr. HAMILTON, Mr. YATRON, Mr. STUDDS, Mr. WOLPE, Mr. LANTOS, Mr. KOSTMAYER, Mr. TORRICELLI, Mr. BERMAN, Mr. LEVINE of California, Mr. WEISS, Mr. ACKERMAN, Mr. UDALL, Mr. FUSTER, Mr. JOHNSTON of Florida, Mr. ENGEL, Mr. FALEOMAVAEGA, Mr. GILMAN, Mr. LAGOMARSINO, Mr. LEACH of Iowa, Mr. ROTH, Mr. HYDE, Mr. SMITH of New Jersey, Mrs. MEYERS of Kansas, Mr. MILLER of Washington, Mr. GALLEGLY, Mr. HOUGHTON, Mr. GOSS, Mr. FROST, Mr. FRANK of Massachusetts, Mr. FAZIO, Mr. McHUGH, Mr. SCHEUER, and Mr. LEHMAN of Florida) submitted the following concurrent resolution; which was referred to the Committee on Foreign Affairs

---

# CONCURRENT RESOLUTION

Condemning the Iraqi attack against Israel.

Whereas Iraq, without provocation, attacked Israeli civilian targets with surface-to-surface missiles;

Whereas Israel is a close democratic friend of the United States and a major non-NATO ally;

Whereas Iraq has threatened to "burn half of Israel" with chemical weapons;

0066

Whereas Israel has exhibited exceptional restraint in the face of those repeated threats;

Whereas Israel agreed to absorb this first strike and continues to support the implementation of United Nations Security Council Resolution 678 through the unprecedented international coalition of forces in the Persian Gulf; and

Whereas every country has the right to defend itself: Now, therefore, be it

1    *Resolved by the House of Representatives (the Senate*
2    *concurring),* That the Congress—

3            (1) condemns the unprovoked attack by Iraq on
4        Israel;

5            (2) expresses profound sympathy for the loss of
6        life, casualties and destruction;

7            (3) declares heartfelt solidarity with the people of
8        Israel;

9            (4) commends the citizens of Israel for their brave
10       and composed perseverance;

11           (5) recognizes Israel's right to defend itself;

12           (6) reaffirms America's continued commitment to
13       provide Israel with the means to maintain her freedom
14       and security; and

15           (7) commends the Government of Israel for its
16       restraint.

O

HCON 41 IH

ASPIN011

HLC

102D CONGRESS
1ST SESSION

H. CON. RES. 48

IN THE HOUSE OF REPRESENTATIVES

Mr. ASPIN (for himself, Mr. FASCELL, Mr. DICKINSON, Mr. BROOMFIELD, *MRS. BYRON, MR. BATEMAN* submitted the following concurrent resolution; which was referred to the Committee on _____

CONCURRENT RESOLUTION

Condemning the brutal treatment by the Government of Iraq of captured service members of the United States and its allies in the Persian Gulf conflict.

*0285 -3*

0068

AEPIN011

2

Whereas in the Convention Relative to the Treatment of Prisoners
  of War (done at Geneva, August 12, 1949; hereinafter in this
  resolution referred to as the ``Third Geneva Convention'')
  the international community has prescribed rules concerning
  the treatment of prisoners of war;

Whereas more than 160 nations, including Iraq, are parties to the
  Third Geneva Convention;

Whereas the Third Geneva Convention requires the humane treatment
  of prisoners of war at all times; prohibits acts of violence
  and intimidation against prisoners of war; prohibits physical
  and mental coercion against prisoners of war to obtain
  information of any kind whatever; provides that no prisoner
  of war may at any time be sent to or detained in areas where
  he may be exposed to the fire of the combat zone, nor may his
  presence be used to render certain points or areas immune
  from military operations; prohibits the public display of
  prisoners of war; and requires that a government that is
  holding prisoners of war permit representatives of the
  International Committee of the Red Cross to visit those
  prisoners of war;

Whereas beginning on January 19, 1991, captured United States and
  allied service members held prisoner by Iraq in the Persian
  Gulf conflict have been displayed and interrogated before
  television cameras;

Whereas these televised interrogations strongly suggest that

02A5-K

LGFIN011

3

those service members have been subjected to physical and

mental torture; and

Whereas the Government of Iraq has announced that it intends to

   hold captured United States and allied service members at

   potential military targets: Now, therefore, be it

1       Resolved by the House of Representatives (the Senate

2   concurring), That the Congress—

3           (1) condemns the abuse by the Government of Iraq of

4   captured United States and allies service members,

5   including the apparent use of physical and mental

6   coercion;

7           (2) condemns the Government of Iraq's stated

8   intention to disperse prisoners of war to potential

9   military targets;

10          (3) condemns the Government of Iraq's failure, thus

11  far, to permit representatives of the International

12  Committee of the Red Cross to visit and interview

13  prisoners of war;

14          (4) condemns the flagrant and deliberate violations

15  by the Government of Iraq of the Third Geneva Convention;

16          (5) calls on the Government of Iraq to comply fully

17  and immediately with its obligations and responsibilities

18  under the Third Geneva Convention; and

19          (6) urges the President, together with our partners

20  in the international coalition against Iraq and with the

draft-5

0070

: BY:OLC

ASPIN011

+++ E1____ OF KOREA       005
20222534===
202 226 0105:# 5

:12:05PM :

4

1   United Nations Security Council, to consider legal means
2   for bring to justice any individuals in Iraq who are
3   responsible for violating the rights of prisoners of war
4   under the Third Geneva Convention.

0071

# 외 무 부

종 별 :

번 호 : USW-0411 　　　　　　　　　　　일 시 : 91 0124 1851

수 신 : 장 관 (미북, 중근동, 대책반)

발 신 : 주 미 대사

제 목 : 걸프전쟁-의회반응 (우방국 역할 분담)

　　　작 1.23. PHILL GRAMM 상원의원 (공화-텍사스)은 전국 제조업 협회 주최 조찬회 연설시 금번 걸프전쟁 관련 하기와같이 언급하였음을 보고함.

　　　O 걸프전 발발이전 우방국은 걸프사태 소요 비용 (DESERT SHIELF 작전시)의 75 푸로를 부담하였으며, 이와같이 우방국으로 하여금 대규모의 역할 분담을 가능하게한 부시 대통령의 지도력을 높이 평가

　　　O 그러나, 걸프전쟁 발발이후 현재 미국 정계의 분위기는 우방국의 역할 분담액이 부족한바, 증액이되어야 한다는것임. 또한, 우방국간에 형평에 맞는 분담액 배분은 각국의 해외 원유 의존율에 따르는 것이라고 보며, 한국 및 대만은 역할 분담액을 증액해야할 국가로 생각함.

　　　O 걸프지역 국가는 금번 전쟁으로 인해 미국에 큰빚을 지게 되었으며 특히 사우디는 PLO 에 대한 일체의 지원을 중단하고, 이스라엘을 승인해야하며, 지역안정에 기여해야할것임.

　　　(대사 박동진-국장)

---

| 미주국<br>대책반 | 장관 | 차관 | 1차보 | 2차보 | 중아국 | 청와대 | 총리실 | 안기부 |
|---|---|---|---|---|---|---|---|---|

PAGE 1 　　　　　　　　　　　　　　　　　　　　　91.01.25　10:39 WG

　　　　　　　　　　　　　　　　　　　　　　　　외신 1과 통제관

　　　　　　　　　　　　　　　　　　　　　　　　　　　　　0072

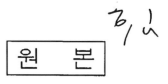

# 외 무 부

종 별 :

번 호 : USW-0423                       일 시 : 91 0125 1618

수 신 : 장 관(미북,중근동,대책반)

발 신 : 주미대사

제 목 : 걸프 전쟁-의회 반응

    작 1.24 상원은 이락의 이스라엘 공격을 비난하는 결의안( S.CON.RES 4) 및
이락측에게 전쟁포로의 인도적 대우에 관한 1949 제네바 협약을준수할것을 요구하는
결의안( S.CON.RES 5) 를각각 출석의원 만장 일치로 채택 하였음.

    (대사 박동진-국장)

| 종아국 | 차관 | 1차보 | 2차보 | 미주국 | 청와대 | 총리실 | 안기부 | 대책반 |
|---|---|---|---|---|---|---|---|---|
| 미주국 | | | | 중아국 | | | | |

PAGE 1                                          91.01.26    08:08 ER

외신 1과 통제관

0073

# 발 신 전 보

번 호 : WUS-0336    910128 2133 DA    종별 :

수 신 : 주    미    대사.총영사

발 신 : 장 관    (미북)

제 목 : 걸프전 관련 추가 세출안 심의

　　　　걸프 전쟁 발발 이후, 미 행정부는 전쟁으로인한 추가 예산을 의회에 요청
하고 이에따라 의회가 Supplemental Appropriation을 심의 통과시킬 것으로 예상
되는 바, 동 추가 세출안의 편성, 의회 심의절차, 심의일정 및 근거법령 등 관련
사항을 상세 조사 지급 보고바람.　끝.


　　　　　　　　　　　　　　　　　　　　　　　　(미주국장　반기문)


예 고 : 91.12.31.일반

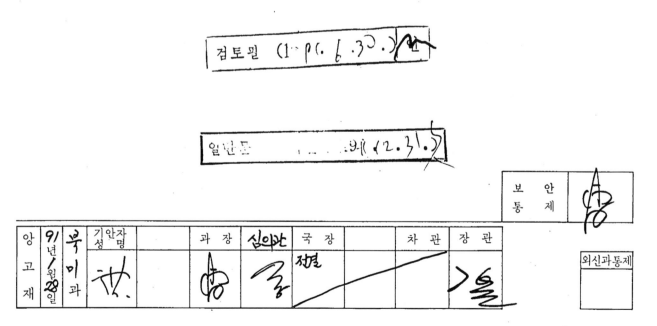

검토필 (1 PG. 6.30. )

일반문　　　　　　　　91 12.31.5

0074

관리번호 91-200

# 외 무 부

종　별 : 지 급

번　호 : USW-0463　　　　　　　　　　　일　시 : 91 0128 1702

수　신 : 장관(미북)

발　신 : 주 미 대사

제　목 : 걸프전 관련 추가 세출안

대 WUS-0336

1. 걸프 전쟁 발발 이후, 전쟁 수행 경비 충당을 위한 미 행정부의 노력은 최근 우방국들에 대한 추가 지원 요청과 더불어 1991. 회계 년도 예산에 추가 예산을 미 의회에 신청함으로서 구체화될것으로 예상됨.

2. 동 추가 예산은 2.4(월) 1992 회계년도 예산안에 첨부되어, 의회에 제안될 가능성이 높은것으로 의회 관련 인사들은 관측하고 있는바, 걸프 사태 이후 3개월간의 실전을 가정할때, 소요 경비가 약 600 억불로 추정하고(DARMAN 예산 청장 언급)그동안의 우방국 분담금 약속분이 300-400 억불에 상당한것을 감안,1991.회계 년도 추가 예산 규모는 잠정적으로 약 300 억불에 달할것으로 사료됨.

3. 일단, 의회에 요청된 추가 예산은 하원 세출위에서 정식으로 제안되어 군사 소위, 청문회 및 세출위 논의, 상원 관련 위원회의 심의와 상. 하원 합동위의 논의를 거쳐 기타 세출 법안과 동일한 절차에 따라 확정되게 되나, 사태의 심각성을 감안할때 추가 예산안 관련 청문회가 4 월에 개최되는 통례와는 달리, 의회에서의 논의가 신속히 진행될 가능성이 높음.

4. 미 행정부와 의회 지도부는 작년말 합의한 예산 적자 삭감안에 대한 수정을 가하거나, 신종 세금 부과 없이 전배를 충당할수 있을것으로 언급하고 있는바, 동언급은 우방국의 분담금에 대한 기대와 실질적 기여 촉구를 배경으로 한것으로 판단됨. 아울러 부쉬 대통령은 우방국의 기여도에 대한 의회내에서 불만을 무마시키기 위하여 1.29(화) 연두 교서 연설에서 우방국의 역할 분담에 대한 언급을 할 가능성도 있는것으로 당지 전문가들은 관측하고 있음.

(대사 박동진-국장)

91.12.31 일반

검토필 (1991. 6. 3. )

미주국　　장관　　차관　　1차보　　청와대　　안기부

PAGE 1

91.01.29　　08:10

외신 2과 통제관 BT

0075

외    무    부

종  별 : 긴  급

번  호 : USW-0557                                        일  시 : 91 0201 1745

수  신 : 장관(친전)

발  신 : 주 미 대사

제  목 : 미 상원의원 접촉

　　　　대 WUS-0354,0356
　　　　연 USW-0514

　　　　본직은 금 2.1(금) 하오 RICHARD LUGAR (공-인디아나) 상원의원을 방문, 대호 아국 정부의 지원과 관련한 걸프 전쟁 추이 및 한. 미 통상 문제등에 관하여 면담한바, 요지 아래 보고함 (당관 임성준 참사관 배석)

　　　　1. 대미 추가 지원

　　　　0 본직은 지난 1.16 걸프전 개전 이래 미국의 군사 작전이 크게 성공을 거두고 있음을 매우 기쁘고 다행스럽게 생각한다고 말하고, 우리 정부는 제 1 차 대미 지원및 군 의료단 파견에 이어 추가로 2 억 8 천만불에 달하는 지원과 군 수송단 파견을 결정하였다고 설명하였음.

　　　　0 이에 대하여 LUGAR 상원의원은 매우 반가운 소식(EXCELLENT NEWS)이며 깊은 사의를 표한다고 말한후, 우방인 한국으로 부터의 재정적 지원에 이어 인적 지원을 추가 하게 된것은 미국의 전쟁 수행에 큰 도움이 될것을 확신한다고 말함. 동 의원은 이어 작년 8 월 걸프 사태가 발생한후 얼마 안되는 시점에서 방한하여 노 대통령을 뵈었던바 미군의 사우디 병력 배치에 필요한 해상, 항공 지원을 약속하였던 사실을 고맙게 기억하고 있다고 말함.

　　　　2. 전쟁 추이

　　　　0 본직은 현재 순조롭게 진행중인 미 군사 작전이 신속하게 매듭지어 부쉬 대통령의 새로운 세계 질서(NEW WORLD ORDER)구축이 조속히 실현되기를 기원한다고 말하고 한국의 지원은 미국의 이러한 노력을 적극 지지하는 한국 정부의 기본입장을 반영하다는 점을 강조하였음.

　　　　0 LUGAR 의원은 지난 1.30(수) 저녁 백악관에서 BUSH 대통령, BAKER 국무장관,

장관  미주국  청와대 (외교안보)

CHEANY 국방장관, SCOWCRAFT 안보 보좌관, POWELL 합참 의장등이 참석한 회합에 초청받은 자리에서, POWELL 합참의장으로부터 전쟁 현황 보고를 청취한 요지를 아래 설명하였음 (상기 회합에는 작년도 방한 노대통령께서 접견한 HOWARDBAKER 전 공화당 총무도 참석 하였다함)

-미군의 군사 작전은 예상대로 순조롭게 진행 (UP TO THE SPEED)중에 있으며, 완전한 제공권 장악으로 이락군의 보급로를 90 프로 차단함으로서 이락군은 고립 상태에 있음.

-다만 정예 부대인 공화국 수비대만은 계속 되는 공중 폭격에도 불구하고 참호속에 잠복중 이므로 잘 견디고 있는듯하며, 타격을 입히는데 조금더 시간이 필요한것으로 보임.

-따라서 현재로서는 제공권 확보에 의한 보급로 차단과 공중 폭격으로 이락군의 항복을 받아내는데 주력하고 있으며, 지상군 부입 시기는 정하고 있지 않음(NOT TIME TABEL) 공군력으로 제압이 안되는 경우는 지상군 부입 전략을 마련해놓고 있음.

-최근 SAUDI 국경으로 침공한 이락의 지상군 공세는 미군에 대한 탐색전(PROBE)또는 저항 방커 잠복보다는 전투하는 편이 낫다는 판단인지 모르겠으나, 지상으로 노출되는 경우에는 동 지역이 사막이므로 미 공군력의 타격을 피할수 없을것임.

3. 전후 처리 문제

O LUGAR 의원은 전후 처리 문제와 관련, 사담 후세인이 유엔 결의 시한인 1.15 까지 철수를 행하였던라면, 사담으로서는 핵 개발 능력을 포함한 막강한 군사력을 그대로 유지하면서 중동 문제 처리에 유리한 위치(LEVERAGE)에 설수 있었을것이나, 전쟁이 발발한 현재로서 이락은 핵 능력은 거의 상실한 상태이며, 공군력도 대부분 파괴 될것이 명백 하므로 평화적 외교 교섭에 불응했던 것은 매우어리석은 판단이었다고 언급함.

O 미국으로서는 동지역에서 전쟁 종료후 평화와 안정을 확보하는것이 매우 중요한 목표이며 이를 대비하여 사전에 어떤 계획을 수립 해야 할것이기 때문에 현재 한편으로는 전쟁을 진행중이나 또 한편으로는 장래의 평화구조에 착안 하는노력도 병행중에 있음. 이러한 관점에서 우방들과도 긴밀히 협의해 나가는것이필요하다고 사견을 피력함.

4. 한미 통상 및 반미 감정 문제

PAGE 2

O 본직은 지난해 12월 조순 특사 방미시 동 의원이 한. 미 통상 문제와 관련, 솔직한 견해를 제시해 주어 조 특사 귀국후 노 대통령께 상세히 보고된바 있고, 그 이후 한. 미 경제 협의회, 실무 접촉등을 통해 한. 미 통상 문제가 건전한 방향으로 개선되고 있음을 다행하게 생각한다고 말함.

O LUGAR 의원은 조 특사 방미시에도 언급한바 있듯이 최근 한. 미 통상 문제와 관련, 한국 사회 일각에서 일고 있는 반미 감정은 양국간 우호 협력 관계를 매우 소중하게 생각하는 사람으로서 크게 염려 스럽고 (VERY DISTURBING)부당할뿐만 아니라(UNFAIR) 비생산적임을(UNPRODUCTIVE) 솔직히 지적하지 않을수 없다고 말하고, 미국의 입장에서 볼때는 그와같은 반미 감정이 팽배해 있는 분위기에서 한국 정부가 걸프 전쟁을 위한 대미 지원을 한다고 하여도 그 의미가 상실될수 있음(MAKE NO SENSE)을 충분히 인식하여 통상 문제등으로 인한 오해나 반미감정 확산의 방지를 위해 한국측이 계속 관심을 갖고 대처하는것이 좋겠다고 말함. 통상 관계 개선과 걸프 전쟁 지원 노력은 양자가 병행되어야 후자의 기여도을바른 평가를 받게 될것이라고 언급함.

참고 사항 본직은 2.5 PHIL GRAMM 상원의원(공-텍사스), JOHN MACAIN 상원의원(공-아리조나), GERALD SOLOMON(공-뉴욕) 하원의원과 2.6 CHALES ROBB(민-버지니아), THOMAS DASCHLE(민-사우스 다코다)상원의원 등과의 면담이 확정되어 있으며, 면담후 요지 보고 예정임.

(대사 박동진-장관)

91.12.31 일반

검토필 (1' 91.6 .9P . 안

PAGE 3

0078

외 무 부

종 별 : 지 급

번 호 : USW-0558                            일 시 : 91.0201 1745

수 신 : 장관(미북,미안,중근동,대책반)

발 신 : 주 미 대사

제 목 : 걸프전-의회 반응

1. BYRON DORGAN (민-노스 다코다)및 DAVID BONIOR (민주-미시간) 하원의원은 1.28 금번 걸프전 관련, 일, 독, 사우디, 쿠웨이트 4 개국을 대상으로 일정 비율의 걸프전 전비를 부담할것을 요구하는 합동 결의안 (H.J.RES 92)을 제출하였는바, 동 결의안의 주요 내용을 하기 보고함.

0 일본은 미국이 사용한 걸프전 전비의 25 프로(20 프로 이상), 독일은 15 프로, 사우디및 쿠웨이트는 각각 50 프로를 부담해야함.

0 행정부는 상기 4 개국가와 동 경비 부담에 관해 협의를 하며, 91.7.1 까지는 합의를 하여야함.

0 상기 4 개국과 91.7.1 까지 합의를 이루지 못할 경우 또는 상기 4 개국이합의 사항을 준수치 않을 경우에는 행정부는 동 국가로부터 수입하는 상품에 대해 특별 수입 관세를 부과하며, 수입 관세 총액이 동 국가의 전비 부담액에 상당할때까지 수입 관세를 부과함.

2. 상기 결의안은 미 의회내 (특히 민주당계) 우방국의 걸프전 전비 부담 노력에 대한 불만감의 표출로서 일부 민주당 진보파 의원들로 부터는 강력한 지지를 받을것이나 의회 통과는 어려울것으로 전망됨.

3. 동 결의안은 현재 하원 외무위와 세입위에 회부되어 있는바, 진전 사항 추보 예정임.

4. 동 결의안 내용및 관계 자료는 별전 FAX( USW(F)-411) 송부함.

(대사 박동진-국장)

91.12.31 까지

검토필 (1991. 6.?0. 까지)

| 미주국 대책반 | 장관 | 차관 | 1차보 | 2차보 | 미주국 | 중아국 | 청와대 | 안기부 |
|---|---|---|---|---|---|---|---|---|

## PERSIAN GULF WAR COST-SHARING ACT

(Mr. DORGAN of North Dakota asked and was given permission to address the House for 1 minute and to revise and extend his remarks.)

Mr. DORGAN of North Dakota. Mr. Speaker, the most important costs of the war in the Persian Gulf are the costs in human lives.

And we pray for the safety of our American troops serving in the gulf today, and the innocent civilians caught in the war.

But there is another cost, too. When the war is over, the enormous financial costs will have to be paid.

And who is going to end up paying the bill?

If history is our guide, our allies will want to charge it to the American taxpayers.

Today, Mr. Speaker, I am introducing a joint resolution (H.J. Res. 92) that will require the President to negotiate offset payments from our allies to cover most costs of the war in the Persian Gulf. My bill mandates cost-sharing agreements which the President must negotiate by July 1 with our allies.

Under terms of the Persian Gulf War Cost-Sharing Act, "Japan should bear 25 percent of the cost of the war; Germany 15 percent; the Saudi's and the Kuwaitis 50 percent. If these countries fail to agree to make payments to meet these shares, then tariffs will be imposed on the import of all goods from these countries to the United States to raise the money necessary to cover their specified contribution to this war.

It is time for our allies to pay up. No longer can American borrow money from our allies to turn around and pay for their defense. In the case of the war in the Persian Gulf, many of our allies are much more dependent on Persian Gulf oil than the United States.

If there truly is a new world order, let's impose that new order on the enforcement on the cost of the Persian Gulf war. It is no longer acceptable to have Uncle Sam bear the burden, carry the load, and pay the price while most of our allies sit on the sidelines bleachers as cheerleaders.

I am submitting the text of my bill to appear after my remarks.

### H.J. Res. 92

Whereas the United Nations has condemned the invasion of Kuwait by Iraq and authorized member states to use all means necessary, as part of a multinational effort, to secure the withdrawal of Iraq;

Whereas a multinational coalition has initiated military action against Iraq to bring about an Iraqi withdrawal from Kuwait;

Whereas the equitable sharing of the costs of the Operation Desert Shield and Operation Desert Storm is essential to the success of the war against Iraq;

Whereas the costs of Operation Desert Storm are estimated to be as high as $30 billion per month;

Whereas the military forces currently fighting Iraq are supported primarily with United States tax dollars;

Whereas the economic security of many nations is much more dependent on the success of Operation Desert Storm than is the economic security of the United States; and

Whereas many wealthy allied nations, particularly Japan and Germany, have not made proportional financial contributions to Operation Desert Shield and Operation Desert Storm: Now, therefore, be it

*Resolved by the Senate and House of Representatives of the United States of America in Congress assembled,*

SECTION 1. SHORT TITLE.

This joint resolution may be cited as the "Persian Gulf War Cost-Sharing Resolution".

SEC. 2. IMPOSITION OF ADDITIONAL IMPORT DUTIES ON PRODUCTS OF COUNTRIES NOT ENTERING INTO COST-SHARING AGREEMENTS OR THAT FAIL TO MEET OBLIGATIONS UNDER COST-SHARING AGREEMENTS.

(a) IN GENERAL.—

(1) Any duty imposed on any article under the authority of this seciton is in addition to any other duty that is, or may be, imposed on such article.

0080

(2) The duty imposed under subsection (b) or (c) on all articles of any country shall be of a uniform ad valorem rate.

(b) FAILURE TO ENTER INTO MANDATORY COST-SHARING AGREEMENTS.—

(1) If a country listed in section 3(a) does not enter into a cost-sharing agreement with the United States under section 3 before July 1, 1991, the President shall impose a duty on each article that is a product of that country and is imposed into the United States on or after that date.

(2) The rate of the duty imposed under paragraph (1) shall be calculated so as to result in the collection of revenues equal to the contribution that such country would have been required to make to the United States if a cost-sharing agreement that meets the requirements applicable to that country under section 3 had been entered into.

(c) FAILURE TO COMPLY WITH MANDATORY COST-SHARING AGREEMENTS.—

(1) If the President determines that a country listed in section 3(a) that entered into a cost-sharing agreement with the United States under section 3 is not complying with the terms of the agreement, the President shall impose a duty on each article that is a product of that country and is imported into the United States on and after a date determined by the President (but not later than the 60th day after the date of the determination of noncompliance).

(2) The rate of the duty imposed under paragraph (1) shall be calculated so as to result in the collection of revenues equal to the difference between—

(A) the contribution, if any, made by the country before the determination of noncompliance is made under paragraph (1); and

(B) the contribution that such country was required to make under such agreement before such determination.

(d) FAILURE TO COMPLY WITH NONMANDATORY COST-SHARING AGREEMENTS.—

(1) If the President determines that a country that entered into a cost-sharing agreement with the United States pursuant to section 3(b) is not complying with the terms of the agreement, the President shall impose a duty on one or more articles that are a product of that country and are imported into the United States on and after a date determined by the President (but not later than the 60th day after the date of the determination of noncompliance).

(2) The rate or rates of duty imposed under paragraph (1) shall be calculated so as to—

(A) encourage compliance with the terms of the agreement; or

(B) result in the collection of revenues equal to the difference between—

(i) the contribution, if any, made by the country before the determination of noncompliance is made under paragraph (1); and

(ii) the contribution that such country was required to make under such agreement before such determination.

(3) TERMINATION OR SUSPENSION OF DUTIES.—The President may terminate or suspend—

(1) the duty imposed under subsection (b) or (c) with respect to a country; and

(2) any duty imposed under subsection (d) with respect to a country;

after the President determines, and reports to Congress, that the purpose for which the duty with imposed has been achieved.

SEC. 3. COST-SHARING AGREEMENTS.

(a) MANDATORY COST-SHARING AGREEMENTS.—The President shall promptly undertake consultation for the purpose of entering into a cost-sharing agreement with the government of each of the following countries.

(1) Japan.
(2) Germany.
(3) Saudi Arabia.
(4) Kuwait.

(b) NONMANDATORY COST-SHARING AGREEMENT.—The President shall undertake consultations for the purpose of entering into a cost-sharing agreement with the governments of any country to which subsection (a) does not apply if the President considers that a contribution by such country to the United States for the Gulf War cost incurred by the United States is justified, taking into account—

(1) the economic or security benefit that accrued, or is accruing, to such country as a result of the efforts by the United States to compel the withdrawal of Iraqi forces from Kuwait; and

(2) the ability of such country to provide a contribution.

(c) DETERMINATION OF CONTRIBUTIONS.—

(1) A cost-sharing agreement entered into under subsection (a) or (b) with a country shall obligate that country to contribute to the United States, under such terms and conditions as may be mutually agreeable, its share, determined under paragraph (2), of the Gulf War costs incurred by the United States.

(2) The contribution which a country obligates itself to provide under a cost-sharing agreement is the product of the Gulf War costs incurred by the United States multiplied by a specified percentage (hereinafter referred to as the "cost-sharing percentage"). The President shall determine the cost-sharing percentage for each country, subject to the following requirement in the case of cost-sharing agreement entered into pursuant to subsection (a):

(A) The cost-sharing percentage for Japan may not be less than 20 percent.

(B) The cost-sharing percentage for Germany may not be less than 15 percent.

(C) The agreement of the cost-sharing percentage for the countries listed in subsection (a) (3) and (4) may not be less than 50 percent.

(d) NATURE OF CONTRIBUTIONS.—Contributions made under agreements entered into under subsections (a) and (b) shall be in the form of money, except to the extent otherwise agreed.

SEC. 4. REPORTS.

0081

(a) WHEN AGREEMENTS ENTERED INTO.—The President shall promptly submit to the Congress a report containing a description of each cost-sharing agreement that is entered into under section 3.

(b) PERIODIC IMPLEMENTATION REPORTS.— The President shall periodically (but not less than quarterly) submit to the Congress a report regarding the implementation of this Act, including—

(1) an assessment of the extent to which the obligations under each agreement entered into under section 3 are being complied with;

(2) with respect to any duties imposed under section 2—

(A) the reason for the imposition; and

(B) the amount of the revenues resulting from the imposition; and

(3) a current estimate of the extent to which the Gulf War costs incurred by the United States have been offset by contributions made under cost-sharing agreements.

## SEC. 5. CBO COST ESTIMATES.

The Congressional Budget Office shall—

(1) determine, and from time to time revise, the Gulf War costs incurred by the United States; and

(2) make such determinations and revisions promptly available to the Congress and the Executive branch.

## SEC. 6. DEFINITIONS.

As used in this Act—

(1) The phrase "Gulf War costs incurred by the United States" means the direct and indirect costs (as determined under section (5) to the United States—

(A) in carrying out those military, naval, air, and related operations known as Operation Desert Shield and Operation Desert Storm, and any successor operations related to compelling the withdrawal of Iraqi forces from Kuwait; and

(B) in implementing, after the cessation of such operations—

(i) the restoration of vital service in areas of allied countries in the Middle East that suffered damage or destruction,

(ii) the withdrawal of United States military personnel and equipment from the war area; and

(iii) the resettlement of refugees.

(2) The term "imported" means entered, or withdrawn from warehouse for consumption, in the customs territory of the United States.

0411-3

0082

BYRON L. DORGAN
_____ DAKOTA

___ CANNON BUILDING
WASHINGTON, DC 20515
(202) 225 2611

WAYS AND MEANS COMMITTEE

SUBCOMMITTEE
OVERSIGHT
SELECT REVENUE MEASURES

SELECT COMMITTEE ON HUNGER
CHAIRMAN INTERNATIONAL TASK FORCE

POSTING __ __
___ FEDERAL BLDG
THIRD AND ROSSER ___
P.O. BOX 2015
BISMARCK, ND ___
(701) 250 ___

112 ROBERTS ___
P.O. BOX ___
FARGO, ND ___
(701) 239 ___

# Congress of the United States
## House of Representatives
### Washington, DC 20515

January 30, 1991

## MAKE PERSIAN GULF COST-SHARING STICK

Dear Colleague:

We request that you join us as a cosponsor of the Persian Gulf War Cost-Sharing Resolution. This joint resolution gives the president the muscle needed to negotiate tough, binding cost-sharing agreements with key, wealthy allies in the Persian Gulf War.

The resolution creates a mandatory framework for negotiating cost-sharing agreements with four major allies: Japan, Germany, Saudi Arabia, and Kuwait. Under terms of the resolution, Japan would pay at least 25% of U.S. Gulf War costs and Germany would contribute 15% of total U.S. expenses. Saudi Arabia and Kuwait would share an additional 50% of our nation's war costs.

These four were selected to reflect their ability to pay, their relative dependence on the trade of Persian Gulf oil, and their actual military contributions to the Desert Storm operation. Japan and Germany are two of the world's three economic super powers and both import substantial quantities of Middle East oil. Saudi Arabia will likely reap a windfall of $40 to $50 billion from increased oil profits this year. And Kuwait reportedly holds up to $100 billion in foreign assets. Neither Japan nor Germany are now able to participate in direct military action.

Our legislation would require that the president seek to negotiate specific cost-sharing pacts with these four nations by July 1, 1991. If the president was not able to conclude an agreement by July 1, or if given nations reneged on their payments, the president would then have to impose an across-the-board tariff on all imported goods of the affected ally to raise enough revenues to pay for its share of the U.S. military costs in the Persian Gulf.

Let's not be lulled into complacency by allied promises of cost sharing. Despite all the hoopla about pledges, the Defense Cooperation Account has only received $4.7 billion in cold cash. That's barely enough to pay the U.S. costs of a Monday-to-Friday war in the Gulf.

With the persistent budget and trade deficits, a widening recession, and pressing domestic needs, this country can no longer afford to borrow from our allies to defend interests of greater importance to them than to us. It's time that we demand that others pay their fair share. Our resolution sets out the framework, the specific targets, and the mechanisms to make this happen.

Please ask your staff to call Douglas Norell or Susan Brophy at x52611 (Dorgan) to cosponsor H.J.Res. 92, or to obtain additional information.

Sincerely,

0083

David E. Bonior

Byron L. Dorgan

0841-5

0084

# ═ NEWS FROM ═

## U.S. CONGRESSMAN
## Byron L. Dorgan (North Dakota)

203 Cannon House Office Building ● Washington, D.C. 20515 ● (202) 225-2611 ●━━▶

FOR IMMEDIATE RELEASE                      CONTACT MARC KIMBALL
MONDAY, JANUARY 28, 1991                        (202) 225-2611

### DORGAN BILL REQUIRES ALLIES TO PAY FAIR SHARE OF DESERT STORM'S COSTS
### --SETS PENALTIES FOR COUNTRIES THAT DON'T CONTRIBUTE

WASHINGTON, D.C. -- President Bush would be required to negotiate
specific payments from Japan, Germany and wealthy Mideast oil-producing
countries to defray the cost of the Persian Gulf war and to penalize allied
countries that do not pay their share, under legislation introduced by
North Dakota Congressman Byron L. Dorgan today.

Dorgan said the cost in human lives is by far the most important
consideration in the conflict.  But, he said when the fighting ends, there
will be another cost: the war's huge financial burden which will fall on
the shoulders of the American taxpayers unless payments are required from
countries whose interests the United States is fighting to protect.

"I don't think taxpayers from North Dakota or any other state should
be required to carry the financial load for our allies when the war is
over," Dorgan said.  "We are fighting to protect the interests of our
allies, many of whom have much more at stake in the conflict than we do.
Those countries should be expected to share much of the financial burden."

Dorgan said only the British have made a major contribution to the
Desert Storm operations.  Virtually every other allied country has failed
to meet their responsibility in contributing to the effort, he said.

### DORGAN'S LEGISLATION

Dorgan's legislation mandates that the President negotiates specific
payments from U.S. allies to cover the expense of the conflict and it
imposes tariffs on imports from countries such as Japan and Germany if they
do not meet the payment thresholds described in the bill.  The tariffs
would raise the money required to pay those countries' share of the war's
costs.

Under the legislation, Japan would be required to share 25 percent of
the war's costs and Germany would share 15 percent.  Kuwait and Saudi
Arabia would share 50 percent of the costs.  The president would have the
authority to assign payment levels for other NATO countries and set targets
for other wealthy Mideast oil-producing countries.

(more)

0441-6

0085

DORGAN - PAGE TWO


    Dorgan said original estimates put the cost of the U.S. role in the
Persian Gulf at $35 billion if fighting did not break out.  Now that war
has begun, that cost will skyrocket.

    "Our economy is in a recession.  We are choking on federal debt, so it
is time we ask our allies to pay their fair share of the cost of defending
the free world," he said.  "If they refuse, we should collect the money
through a tariff."

                              --30--

0411-7                              0086

원 본

# 외 무 부

종 별 : 긴 급

번 호 : USW-0646                    일 시 : 91 0206 1912

수 신 : 장관(미북,미안, 중근동,동구일,대책반)

발 신 : 주 미 대사

제 목 : 하원 외무위 청문회( 걸프 사태 관련)

1. 금 2.6. 하원 외무위 (위원장:DANTE FASCELL, 민주-플로리다)는 BAKER 국무장관을 출석시킨 가운데 청문회를 개최하였음.동 청문회의 FY 92 년도 국제관계 예산 논의를 위해 개최 되었으나 실제로는 현재 진행되고 있는 걸프전과 걸프전 이후의 지역안정 방안, 대소관계등 최근의 주요 국제문제 전반에 대해 논의 되었으며, 특히 걸프전 우방국의 역할 분담 관련, BAKER 장관은 증언문 및 관련 질의 응답을 통해 우방국의 역할 분담 노력에 만족을 표하였으며, 걸프전 발발이후 한국은 일, 독, 사우디 , 쿠웨이트 등 주요 우방국과 함께 2.8 억불을 추가로 지원하였다고 발언 하였음.

2. 상기 관련, 금번 청문회시 BAKER 자오간의 증언 요지를 하기 보고함.

(걸프전 진전 상황)

0 금번 걸프 사태관련, 크게 주목해야할 점은 UN 이 당초의 의도대로 역할을 하게 되었다는것이고, 국제사회가 걸프전 전비 및 전선국가에 대한 경제원조에 있어서 책임분담을 하고 있다는것임. 미국의 우방국 들은 91.3 월 말까지 미국이 사용하게될 전비에 대한 지원을 약속하였으며 현재까지 500 억불 이상 규모의 군사비 부담 및 140 억불 이상 규모의 대 전선국가 경제원조를 공약하였음.

0 또하나의 주목사항은 미국의 군사전략이 금번 걸프사태 해결 목표라는 정치적 목표를 충실히 반영하고 있다는것이고, 미국은 정당한 전쟁을 정당한 방법으로 수행하고 있음.

0 이락의 생.화학 무기 사용 위협 관련, 미국은 생.화학 무기가 사용될 경우 당하고만 있지 않을것이라는 경고와 함께 만약 생화학 무기가 사용되면, 매우심각한 결과가 초래될것이라는 점을 명백히 하고 있으며, 또한 이락에 전쟁포로 대우에 관한 제네바 협약을 이행할 것을 강력히 촉구하고 있음.

| 미주국 종리실 | 장관 안기부 | 차관 | 1차보 | 2차보 | 미주국 | 구주국 | 중아국 | 청와대 |
|---|---|---|---|---|---|---|---|---|

(전후 걸프 지역 안정)

O 걸프전에서의 국제협조 체제는 전후 지역내 안정과 정의를 구축하는데에도 지속되어야 할것이며, 전쟁 자체 뿐만 아니라 전쟁이 종결되는 방법도 전후 지역 안정에 커다란 영향을 미칠것임.

O 전쟁으로 야기된 제문제를 풀어 나가는데 절제의 마음가짐(SENSE OF MODESTY) 이 필요하고, 걸프 지역 뿐만 아니라 중동지역 전체 국민의 주권이 존중되는 방안이 모색되어야 하며, 걸프 지역을 넘어 중동지역 전체의 평화를 정착시키는 노력이 필요함.

O 중동 지역 전체의 평화정착 목표에 대한 첫번째 도전은 걸프지역내 안전보장을 확보하는 방안임. 안전 보장 방안 수립에는 첫째 안전 보장 방안의 목표와원칙, 둘째 역내 국가 , 역내 조직 및 국제사회의 역할, 마지막으로 지역 안정이 확립될때 까지의 군사적 필요성을 감안해야 할것임.

O 걸프지역 안전 보장의 목표와 원칙으로서는 침략저지, 영토의 불가침성, 국가간 제분쟁의 평화적 해결이며, 이러한 원칙과 목표를 달성하는데는 역내 국가와 GCC 등 역내 국가 조직이 주독적 역할을 담당해야 하며, UN 및 역외 국가들은 역내 국가의 이러한 주도적 역할에 강력한 지원을 보내야 할것임. 미국은 TRUMAN 행정부 이래 걸프만에 해군을 배치하여 왔으며, 사우디등 역내 국가와의 양자관계를 강화시켜 나갈것이나, 미국은 전후 페만 지역내 지상병력을 유지시킬 계획은 없음.

O 전후 처리 과정에 있어서 지역안정을 위한 중요한 문제는 지역국가로 구성된 지상군을 구성, 역내에 배치하는것이 필요한지와 이와같은 지상군을 UN 의 산하에 두어야 하는지 또는 GCC 와같은 역내 조직의 산하에 두어야 하는지, 또한역외국가들이 동 지상군에 병력을 파견함으로써 역내 전쟁 억지력을 제고 시켜야 하는지등 중요한 문제들이 제기될것이며, 이러한 문제 해결에 있어 미국은 관계국과 광범위한 협의를 진행시킬것임.

O 중동지역 전체의 평화에 대한 두번째 도전은 역내 재래식 무기 및 대량 살상무기의 확산 방지임. 이를 위해 전후 이락의 대량 살상 무기 생산 및 보유 능력을 없애고, 역내 국가간에 무기 보유 경쟁을 억제시키며, 중동지역에 일종의신뢰구축 조치를 적용하는 방안이 검토되어 야 할것임.

O 세번째 도전은 경제복구 및 재건조치로서 쿠웨이트의 경제 복구에 협력을하고, 이락에 대해서도 보복을 하기 보다는 경제 복구를 지원해야 함. 더나아가서는

PAGE 2

0088

경제복구 이후 지역내 자유무역 및 부자를 확대하고 경제성장을 촉진하는경제정책 수립에 도움을 주는것이 필요하며, 특히 역내 국가의 수자원 개발에역점을 두어야 할것임.

ㅇ 네번째 도전은 이스라엘, 아랍국가 및 팔레스타인 민족간에 진정한 화해와 평화를 이룩하는것으로서 이는 상호간에 존중 및 신뢰를 기반으로 해야함. 걸프전으로인해 이스라엘과 팔레스타인 민족간의 대화는 전반적 평화정착 과정의 필수적 부분이며, 미국은 이를 위해 계속 노력을 경주할것임.

ㅇ 마지막 도전은 미국내 정책에 관련된 것으로 미국은 에너지 보존, 에너지보유량의 증대 및 대체에너지 개발에 큰 노력을 기울여야 함.

(대소관계)

ㅇ 소련과의 협력관계가 장기적으로 구축되기 위해서는 소련이 개방 정책을 성공적으로 수행하는것이 관건이나, 최근 소련은 경제 정책의 중앙집권화, 언론자유 봉제, 정부내 개혁주의자 축출 및 발틱 국가에 대한 무력 사용등 불안한 조짐을 보이고 있음.

ㅇ 발틱 국가와 관련, 미국의 목표는 발틱 민족의 여망을 성취하는 것을 도와주는 것이지 소련을 응징하는것이 아님을 명백히 밝혔으며, 소련측도 대화를 통한 동 문제해결 입장을 밝힌바 있으나, 미국은 발틱 사태를 예의 주시하고 있음.

ㅇ 소련의 지도부는 현재 교차로(CROSSROADS)에 서있으며, 현재로서는 성급히 어떤 결론을 내리기는 어려운 상황임.

3. 금번 청문회시 주요 질의 응답 내용을 하기 보고함.

(우방국 역할 분담)

ㅇ 1990 년중 미국의 군사비용 총액은 110 억불이며, 우방국 29 개국이 약 97억불 지원을 약속하였고, 현재까지 65 억불을 실제로 기탁 하였음.

ㅇ 91.1.16. 전쟁발발이후 전쟁 수행 비용으로 몇몇 우방국이 추가로 지원 약속을 하였는바, 쿠웨이트 및 사우디는 각각 135 억불, 일본 80 억불, 독일 55 억불, 한국 2.8 억불등 총 410 억불 상당에 달함.

ㅇ 전선국가에 대한 원조도 26 개국이 총 146 억불 지원을 약속하였으며, 이중 62 억불은 이미 집행되었음.

ㅇ 상기 우방국의 역할 분담 규모를 감안하면, 전반적으로 미국이 전비를 충당하는 문제는 전망이 매우 밝으며 , 미국의 우방국이 공정한 역할분담을 하고 있지 않다고

주장하기는 어려울것임.

(미.소 재래식 무기 제한 협정:2.6 자 NYT 기사 관련)

O 군축문제 관련 소련내 외무부 보다 강경 노선을 취하고 있는 국방부가 영향력을 장악하고 있으며, CFE 협정 대상으로 서방측이 생각해 왔던 소련의 기갑부대가 해군의 해안 방위 부대로 재편성 되어 협정 대상에서 제외 되었으며, 전략무기 제한협상은 기술적 문제로 난항을 거두고 있다는 NYT 기사 내용은 행정부의 일부 우려를 대체로 잘 반영하고 있음.

O 미국은 상기 우려를 소련측에 전달한바 있으며, 이러한 우려가 해소될때 까지는 CFE 협정에 대한 상원 비준 요청을 보류토록 건의할 생각임.

4. 관찰

O 금번 청문회는 걸프전쟁이 진행되고 있는중에 고위 행정부 인사를 대상으로 실시된 최초의 청문회로서, 금번 전쟁이 매우 낙관적으로 진행되고 있는점을 바탕으로 하여 전후처리 문제를 주로 언급한데 특징이 있음.

O 또한 , 우방국의 역할 분담 관련, 부쉬 행정부측은 의회 및 국민에게 우방국의 역할 분담 규모에 대해 만족을 표함으로써 금번 전쟁 관련 행정부의 정책전반에 큰 성공을 거두고 있는 점을 강조하고, 의회 및 국민의 계속된 지지를 확보하려는 노력으로 관측됨.

O 동 청문회 BAKER 장관 증언문 및 주요 질의 응답 요지는 별전 팩스 송부함.

(USW(F)-0481)

(대사 박동진- 국장)

91.12.31 까지

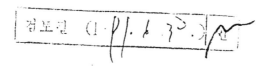

USW(F) - 0481

수신: 장관 ( 미복, 미안. 중근동. 동구일. 대책반)

발신: 주미대사-

제목: 하원 외무위 청문회 ( 걸프사태 관련) (24매)

#

TESTIMONY

BY

SECRETARY OF STATE JAMES A. BAKER, III

BEFORE THE

HOUSE FOREIGN AFFAIRS COMMITTEE

Wednesday, February 6, 1991

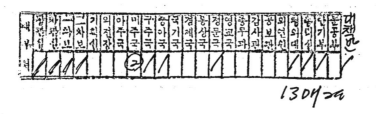

130매

0091

Mr. Chairman,

It is a privilege to appear before this Committee to testify on behalf of our Foreign Affairs funding proposal for FY 1992. With your permission, I would have my detailed written statement entered into the record. This year, even more so than most years, the funds requested should be seen as an investment in a better future -- a world of secure nations, free peoples, and peaceful change.

I realize that as armies fight in the Persian Gulf such a world seems far distant. Yet I believe that it is vitally important to see the challenges we face also as opportunities to build a more secure and just world order. And so, today I would like to make a few comments concerning our ideas about post-crisis challenges and arrangements.

## The Gulf War

The international coalition has been waging war against Iraq for three weeks now with very clear objectives: to expel Iraq from Kuwait; to restore the legitimate government of Kuwait; and to ensure the stability and security of this critical region. I want to make several observations about the course of the conflict so far.

First, the international coalition has held steadily to its purpose and its course. An outstanding achievement of the current crisis has been the ability of the United Nations to act as its founders intended. Before January 15, a dozen Security Council resolutions guided the United States and other nations as together we waged a concerted diplomatic, political, and economic struggle against Iraqi aggression. We did so because we all share a conviction that this brutal and dangerous dictator must be stopped and stopped now. Since January 16, in actions authorized by Security Council Resolution 678, we have been able to wage war because we are equally convinced that all peaceful opportunities to end Saddam's aggression had been explored and exhausted.

Let me give you some idea of those exhaustive efforts, both by the United States and other nations. In the 166 days between the invasion of Kuwait on August 2, 1990 and the expiration of the UN deadline for Iraqi withdrawal on January 15, 1991, I personally held over 200 meetings with foreign dignitaries, conducted 10 diplomatic missions, and travelled over 100,000 miles. For over six and one half hours, I met with the Iraqi Foreign Minister -- six and one-half hours in which the Iraqi leadership rejected the very concept of withdrawal from Kuwait, even the mention of withdrawal. As you know, many others also tried -- the Arab League, the European Community, the UN Secretary General, Kings, Presidents, and Prime Ministers.

0481-2

- 2 -

None succeeded because Saddam Hussein rejected each and every one.

Second, the coalition is sharing responsibility for the economic burdens of conflict. Support for U.S. military outlays covers both 1990 commitments for Desert Shield and 1991 commitments for the period of January through March for Desert Shield/Storm. In addition, funds have also been forthcoming to offset the economic costs confronting the front line states in the region.

To date, we have pledges of over $50 billion to support our military efforts and over $14 billion to assist the front line states and others with their economic needs.

Third, our unfolding military strategy fully reflects our political purposes. This is the place to restate, as the President has done so often, that we have no quarrel with the Iraqi people. Our goal is the liberation of Kuwait, not the destruction of Iraq or changes in its borders.

A thoroughly professional and effective military campaign is underway. Our young men and women and the forces of our coalition partners are writing new annals of bravery and skill. But the task is formidable, and no one should underestimate Saddam's military capabilities. Iraq is not a third rate military power. Billions have been diverted from peaceful uses to give this small country the fourth largest army in the world. Iraq has more main battle tanks than the United Kingdom and France combined. It has more combat aircraft than either Germany, France, or the United Kingdom. Ejecting Iraq from Kuwait will not be easy, but, as the President said, "So that peace can prevail, we will prevail."

We are also trying our best to wage a just war in a just way. Our targets are military, and we are doing all we can to minimize civilian casualties and avoid damage to religious and cultural sites. And as General Schwarzkopf has pointed out, the coalition forces are even putting themselves in danger to minimize the risk to innocent lives.

In shocking contrast, Saddam Hussein's conduct of the war has been not unlike his conduct before the war: a relentless assault on the values of civilization. He has launched missiles against Israeli cities and Saudi cities, missiles aimed not at targets of military value but fully intended to massacre civilians. He has abused and paraded prisoners of war and he says he is using them as "human shields" -- actions totally in violation of the Geneva Convention. And he has even attacked nature itself, attempting to poison the waters of the Persian Gulf with the petroleum that is the patrimony of the region's economic future.

외사 -3

- 3 -

We have heard, and we take at face value, Saddam's threats to use chemical and biological weapons. We have warned him -- and he would be well advised to heed our warning -- that we will not tolerate the use of such weapons. Any use of chemical or biological weapons will have the most severe consequences. And we will continue to insist that Iraq fulfill its obligations under the Geneva Convention with respect to coalition POWs.

I think that our conduct of the war is in itself a great strength, the strength that comes from doing the right thing in the right way. And Saddam's continuing brutality redoubles our resolve and the entire coalition's conviction about the rightness of our course. Ending Saddam's aggression will also be a blow to state-sponsored terrorism.

This is also the place to note our deep appreciation and great admiration for the extraordinary restraint of the Government of Israel. Israeli cities have been attacked by Saddam Hussein because part of his strategy has been to consolidate his aggression by turning the Gulf crisis into an Arab-Israeli conflict. Despite its clear right to respond, the Israeli government has acted with restraint and responsibility. The United States has been and will continue to be in close contact at the highest levels with Israel. We have offered and Israel has accepted batteries of Patriot missiles -- some with American crews -- to defend against Scud attacks. We continue to devote special military efforts to destroying the Scuds and their launchers.

Everyone should know: when we speak about our unshakeable commitment to Israeli security, we mean it.

The fourth observation I would make is this: the great international coalition that is now winning the war must also be strong enough to secure the peace. Winston Churchill once observed that "We shall see how absolute is the need of a broad path of international action pursued by many states in common across the years, irrespective of the ebb and flow of national politics." If we are going to redeem the sacrifices now being made by the brave men and women who defend our freedom with their lives, then we must fashion a peace worthy of their struggle. And that can be done if we can hold together in peace the coalition tempered by war.

I believe that when Congress voted the President authority to use force in support of the United Nations Resolutions, it voted also for peace -- a peace that might prevent such wars in the future. I believe that the American people support our role in the coalition not only to defeat an aggressor but to secure a measure of justice and security for the future.

0481-4

0094

- 4 -

### Post-War Challenges

Mr. Chairman, we and every nation involved in this conflict are thinking about the post-war situation and planning for the future. It would be irresponsible not to do so. At the same time, it would be both premature and unwise for us to lay out a detailed blueprint for the postwar Gulf or, for that matter, the region as a whole.

The war itself and the way it ends will greatly influence both the security of the Gulf and the rest of the area. The deepest passions have been stirred. The military actions now underway necessarily involve many casualties, great hardships, and growing fears for the future. Tough times lie ahead.

We should therefore approach the postwar problems with a due sense of modesty. Respect for the sovereignty of the peoples of the Gulf and Middle East must be uppermost. In any event, modern history has shown that no single nation can long impose its will or remake the Middle East in its own image. After all, that is partly why we are fighting Saddam Hussein.

Yet among all the difficulties we face, one fact stands out: The peoples of the Gulf and indeed the entire Middle East desperately need peace. I truly believe that there _must_ be a way, working in consultation with all of the affected nations, to set a course that brings greater security for all and enduring peace. We should therefore make every effort not just to heal the Persian Gulf after this war but also to try to heal the rest of the region which needs it so badly.

So I would like to discuss several challenges that I believe we must address in the post war period.

<u>One challenge will be greater security for the Persian Gulf</u>. After two wars in ten years, this vital region needs new and different security arrangements. In our view, there are three basic issues to be resolved: the purposes or principles of the security arrangements; the role of the local states, regional organizations, and the international community; and in the aftermath of the war, the military requirements until local stability is achieved, and thereafter.

I think we would find already a wide measure of agreement on the principles. They would include:

- Deterrence of aggression from any quarter.

- Territorial integrity. There must be respect for existing sovereignty of all states and for the inviolability of borders.

- 5 -

● Peaceful resolution of disputes. Border problems and other
disputes that have long histories -- and there are many
beyond the Iraq-Kuwait example -- should be resolved by
peaceful means, as prescribed by the U.N. Charter.

These principles must be put into action first and foremost
by the local states so that conflicts can be prevented and
aggression deterred. We would expect the states of the Gulf
and regional organizations such as the Gulf Cooperation Council
to take the lead in building a reinforcing network of new and
strengthened security ties. No regional state should be
excluded from these arrangements. Post war Iraq could have an
important contribution to play. And so could Iran as a major
power in the Gulf.

There is a role, too, for outside nations and the
international community, including the United Nations, to
encourage such arrangements and to stand behind them.

As for the United States, we have deployed small naval
forces in the Persian Gulf ever since the Truman Administration
in 1949. We had and continue to have very strong bilateral
ties with Saudi Arabia and other local states. And through the
years, we have conducted joint exercises with and provided
military equipment for our friends in the region. The
President has said that we have no intention of maintaining a
permanent ground presence on the Arabian Peninsula once Iraq is
ejected from Kuwait and the threat recedes.

Before security is assured, however, important questions
must be answered. We will be going through an important
transitional phase in the immediate aftermath of the war as we
try to establish stability. Let me list just a few of the
questions that need to be answered.

● Should there be a permanent, locally stationed ground force
made up of local troops under UN auspices or under regional
auspices, such as the GCC?

● How can the international community reinforce deterrence in
the Gulf, whether by contributing forces or through other
political arrangements, such as resolutions or security
commitments?

No one has the answers yet to these and other questions.
Some may never be answered. But however we eventually proceed,
we will conduct extensive consultations among all of the
concerned parties to such arrangements.

A second challenge will surely be regional arms
proliferation and control. This includes both conventional
weapons and weapons of mass destruction. The terrible fact is
that even the conventional arsenals of several Middle Eastern

0096

states dwarf those of most European powers. Five Middle
Eastern countries have more main battle tanks than the United
Kingdom or France. The time has come to try to change the
destructive pattern of military competition and proliferation
in this region and to reduce arms flows into an area that is
already overmilitarized. That suggests that we and others
inside and outside the region must consult on how best to
address several dimensions of the problem:

- How can we cooperate to constrain Iraq's post war ability
  to retain or rebuild its weapons of mass destruction and
  most destabilizing conventional weapons?

- How can we work with others to encourage steps toward
  broader regional restraint in the acquisition and use of
  both conventional armaments and weapons of mass
  destruction? What role might the kinds of confidence
  building measures that have lessened conflict in Europe
  play in the Gulf and the Middle East?

- Finally, what global actions would reinforce steps toward
  arms control in the Gulf and Middle East? These could
  include rapid completion of pending international
  agreements like the Chemical Weapons Convention, as well as
  much tighter supply restraints on the flow of weapons and
  dual-use technology into the region. And what implications
  does that have for arms transfer and sales policies?

A third challenge will be economic reconstruction and
recovery. An economic catastrophe has befallen the Gulf and
the nations trading with it. Kuwait has been looted and
wrecked. Hundreds of thousands of workers have lost jobs and
fled. Trade flows and markets have been disrupted.

I am confident that the people of Kuwait will rebuild their
country. As we have worked with the Kuwaitis in their moment
of trial so we shall look forward to cooperating with them in
their hour of recovery.

And no one should forget that for the second time in a
decade, the people of Iraq will be recovering from a disastrous
conflict. The time of reconstruction and recovery should not
be the occasion for vengeful actions against a nation forced to
war by a dictator's ambition. The secure and prosperous future
everyone hopes to see in the Gulf must include Iraq.

Of necessity, most of the resources for reconstruction will
be drawn from the Gulf. Yet, should we not be thinking also of
more than reconstruction? It might be possible for a coalition
of countries using both local and external resources to
transform the outlook for the region -- in expanding free trade
and investment in assisting development, and in promoting
growth-oriented economic policies which have taken root across
the globe.

*0097*

- 7 -

Any economic effort must have a special place for water development. Well over half the people living in the Middle East draw water from rivers that cross international boundaries or depend on desalination plants. We have all been incensed by Saddam Hussein's deliberate poisoning of the Gulf waters, which could affect a large portion of Saudi Arabia's desalinized drinking water.

Finally, we will want to consult with governments both from the Middle East and from other regions about specific arrangements that might best serve the purposes of region-wide economic cooperation. Such cooperation would surely be helpful in reinforcing our overall objective: reducing one by one the sources of conflict and removing one by one the barriers to security and prosperity throughout the area.

A fourth challenge is to resume the search for a just peace and real reconciliation for Israel, the Arab states, and the Palestinians. By reconciliation, I mean not simply peace as the absence of war, but a peace based on enduring respect, tolerance, and mutual trust. As you know, I personally had devoted considerable effort before the war to facilitating a dialogue between Israel and the Palestinians -- an essential part of an overall peace process. Let's not fool ourselves. The course of this crisis has stirred emotions among Israelis and Palestinians that will not yield easily to conciliation. Yet in the aftermath of this war, as in earlier wars, there may be opportunities for peace -- if the parties are willing. And if they really are willing, we are committed to working closely with them to fashion a more effective peace process.

The issues to be addressed are of course familiar and more challenging than ever.

- How do you go about reconciling Israelis and Palestinians? What concrete actions can be taken by each side?

- What will be the role of the Arab states in facilitating this process and their own negotiations for peace with Israel?

- How will regional arms control arrangements affect this process?

- What is the best diplomatic vehicle for getting the process underway?

Again, we will be consulting and working very closely with our friends and all parties who have a constructive role to play in settling this conflict.

A fifth and final challenge concerns the United States: we simply must do more to reduce our energy dependence. As the President has stressed, only a comprehensive strategy can

okAY -A

0098

- 8 -

achieve our goals. That strategy should involve energy
conservation and efficiency, increased development,
strengthened stockpiles and reserves, and greater use of
alternative fuels. We must bring to this task the same
determination we are now bringing to the war itself.

As you can see, Mr. Chairman, some of these elements are
political, some are economic, and some of necessity are related
to security. That suggests that we should view security not
just in military terms but as part and parcel of the broader
outlook for the region. We're not going to have lasting peace
and well-being without sound economic growth. We're not going
to have sound economic growth if nations are threatened or
invaded -- or if they are squandering precious resources on
more and more arms. And surely finding a way for the peoples
of the Middle East to work with each other will be crucial if
we are to lift our eyes to a better future.

## The Soviet Union at a Crossroads

Before closing, I would like to say a few words on another
challenge we face:  our relations with the Soviet Union.

The President has spoken often of a new world order in
which freedom and democracy might flourish, secure from the
fears of the Cold War. We have been hopeful about such an
order partly because of the growing cooperation between the
United States and the Soviet Union. In the fall of 1989, I
described that cooperation as a search for points of mutual
advantage. And this search has yielded good results.

Three examples will suffice. First, over the past year, a
democratic Germany, fully a member of NATO, was united in
peace. The Iron Curtain has vanished and with it the Cold
War. Second, the countries of Central and Eastern Europe have
emerged in their own right once more, free to pursue democracy
and economic liberty. Third, the Soviet Union has joined the
international coalition confronting Iraqi aggression. As
Foreign Minister Alexander Bessmertnykh reiterated last week,
the Soviet Union continues to completely support the full
implementation of the UN Security Council resolutions.

While we both have worked at finding these and other points
of mutual advantage, it has long been clear to both sides that
the potential for long-term cooperation or even partnership
between our countries would depend ultimately on the course of
the Soviet Union's domestic reform. That is why when last fall
I called for pathways of mutual advantage, not just discrete
points, I also announced our desire to see a broader democratic
dialogue with Soviet reformers. Not just economic reform but
essential political reform could transform the Soviet Union
into a very different society.

0481-9

0099

- 9 -

Over the course of several summits and numerous meetings, we have become much more familiar with the ups and downs of perestroika, the enormous and daunting difficulty of changing after seventy years a society's basic direction and many of its values.

In the last several months, however, we have seen a series of unsettling events. They include the tragic violence in the Baltics; an apparent turn toward economic re-centralization; a less free media; extension of army and KGB authority; and the resignation or departure from the government of key reform advocates.

These actions are completely inconsistent with the course of peaceful change, democratic principles, the rule of law, and real economic reform. There is simply no justification for the use of force against peaceful and democratically elected governments. Our hearts go out to the courageous people of the Baltic states who have acted throughout with dignity and restraint.

The President and I have had extensive discussions with President Gorbachev and other Soviet officials about these developments. We and our European allies have pointed out the inevitable consequences if the Soviet government continues on this path. And we have stated our belief that the Soviet Union cannot hope to succeed in meeting its own objectives if it should abandon perestroika, democratization, and glasnost.

On the Baltics, I could do no better here than to quote the President's words from the State of the Union address: "... our objective is to help the Baltic peoples achieve their aspirations, not to punish the Soviet Union."

We have had representations from the Soviet leadership about their continuing commitment to reform, to peaceful dialogue with the Baltics, and to creating a society ruled by law, not force. We're going to watch this situation closely to see whether these representations become enduring realities.

I hope that the Soviet Union will relearn quickly the lesson from its own hard experience: the old ways are not the right ways. Perestroika cannot succeed at gunpoint. Clearly, we cannot rule out the possibility that matters may still turn more for the worse. But at the same time, we must be careful not to jump to premature conclusions.

The Soviet leadership is at a crossroads. We have made clear that their last several steps have taken them down a path of no benefit for them or for us or for anyone else. For the sake of history and for the sake of the world, I hope they resume the march that has given the entire world hope of a better future.

0681-10

0100

- 10 -

Mr. Chairman, I want to sum up my comments today with this observation. When I appeared before you a year ago to review our overall foreign policy, we were well on the way to a whole and free Europe, secured by expanding U.S.-Soviet cooperation in resolving the continent's outstanding political and military problems. The possibility, even the idea, of this terrible conflict in the Gulf was beyond anyone's imagination. Yet now we face the challenges of hot war in the Gulf and growing uncertainty about the course of Soviet reform.

There can be different views of how to handle these situations. I look forward to your counsel and good words on both issues. Yet on one point I believe we are in very basic agreement: the need for American leadership. If we do not do our part, then Churchill's broad path pursued by many states in common will not be possible. And as Churchill warned, "the middle path adopted from desires for safety and a quiet life may be found to lead direct to the bullseye of disaster." More clearly than we could have ever imagined a year or even six months ago, the world emerging from the end of the postwar era will be shaped by the United States and its international allies. Our constant purpose must be to make of that world a fitting place for free peoples to live.

## Overview of our Funding Request

Let me turn to our foreign affairs funding request. For FY 1992, we seek $21.9 billion in discretionary budget authority for International Affairs Budget Function 150, an increase of $1.8 billion over levels appropriated for FY 1991. In addition, we are requesting a one-time appropriation of $12.2 billion as the U.S. share of a global quota increase for the International Monetary Fund.

In accordance with the terms of the Budget Enforcement Act, our request provides for specific, stringent limits on our spending levels, in spite of unprecedente. demands for U.S. leadership across the globe.

In order to achieve our worldwide objectives within these resource constraints, additional flexibility is needed. Last year, I appealed to this committee to make constructive consultation -- not earmarking -- the primary vehicle for achieving consensus on program objectives. I am pleased to note that we made some progress toward that goal last session.

Earmarking in our Economic Support Fund (ESF) declined from 82 percent in FY 1990 to just over 66 percent in FY 1991. In our Foreign Military Financing (FMF) account, the decline was less dramatic but still significant, from 92 percent to 87 percent. This is a welcome trend, one that we want to encourage and promote.

0681 -11

0101

- 11 -

But we still have a long way to go. To support our request this year, let me express the Administration's willingness to work in partnership with Congress to develop greater flexibility in our State operations and foreign assistance legislation. To guide this effort, let me suggest five broad objectives for our international cooperation programs, built around the five foreign policy challenges which I presented in my testimony before this Committee last year.

<u>First</u>, promoting and consolidating democratic values, including free and fair elections and respect for human rights. As the President noted in his State of the Union address, this fundamental American principle has stood as a beacon to peoples across the globe for more than two centuries.

Transitions toward democracy, however difficult, cannot be accomplished in isolation from the rest of the world. The essential ingredients of democracy -- respect for human rights, the rule of law, free and fair elections, and political and economic opportunity -- are also the basic building blocks of the new world order.

<u>Second</u>, promoting free market principles and strengthening U.S. competitiveness. Sustainable economic development cannot be separated from the pursuit of sound, growth-oriented policies; together, these can promote U.S. economic interests abroad. By fostering market forces through deregulation, privatization, and promotion of free trade and investment, reform-minded countries can establish an appropriate complement to building and securing democracy. They also can develop into thriving markets for U.S. exports and the jobs they represent. Indeed, U.S. exports to four aid graduates -- Colombia, Chile, Taiwan, and Korea -- total more than twice the value of our entire worldwide foreign assistance budget. Our long-run goal should be to graduate more countries from foreign assistance toward mutually beneficial trade and investment relationships with the United States.

<u>Third</u>, promoting peace by helping to defuse regional conflicts, strengthening the security of our regional partners, and pursuing arms control and nonproliferation efforts.

As the crisis in the Persian Gulf has demonstrated, there is no substitute for strong U.S. leadership. We continue to play a vital role in bolstering the security of regional allies around the world. Egypt and Turkey -- two long-standing beneficiaries of U.S. security assistance -- are bulwarks of the coalition against Saddam Hussein.

National and regional security are preconditions for democracy and free enterprise to flourish. Saddam Hussein's aggression is a dramatic reminder of the continuing need to protect the security of regional states of vital interest to

*0101-12*

0102

- 12 -

the United States and our allies. The proliferation of missile systems and chemical and biological weapons further sharpens our interest in promoting regional stability.

Fourth, protecting against transnational threats, especially to the environment and from narcotics and terrorism.

As I noted in my first statement to Congress two years ago, "The future of our civilization demands that we act in concert to deal with a new class of problems, transnational in nature." This includes curbing proliferation, protecting the environment, and countering terrorism and narcotics.

We have made progress in all of these areas. We have led the international effort to tighten nonproliferation export controls on a global basis. We continue to work to advance our environmental agenda. We are actively pressing state sponsors of terrorism in an effort to thwart terrorism around the globe. And our international narcotics efforts to counter supply are complemented by reports of declining demand at home.

But progress is sometimes slow, unheralded, and hard won. Iraq's conduct following its invasion of Kuwait is a brutal reminder of the danger posed by the interaction of these transnational threats. Saddam Hussein's most recent actions illustrate how traditional concepts of threats to national security need to be extended. Indeed, Iraq has combined:

c   A credible threat of the use of chemical and biological weapons.

c   A contemptible use of missile technology as a weapon of terror against innocent civilian populations.

c   Perhaps the world's first deliberate use of an environmental disaster as a wartime weapon, with unknown consequences for the entire region for years to come; and

•   A worldwide call for terrorist actions, sometimes supported by embassies abroad in flagrant violation of the basic principles of diplomacy.

These challenges to international order can all be defeated by a committed world community, supported by firm U.S. leadership and appropriate resources as needed.

Finally, meeting urgent humanitarian needs will continue to reflect deep and abiding concerns of the American people. America's record for responding quickly and substantially to alleviate severe suffering caused by natural and man-made disasters is unequaled. We salute the role played by American private voluntary agencies and private American citizens in this regard. Meeting the most pressing humanitarian needs with food aid, disaster relief, and refugee assistance will always be an essential component of U.S. assistance policies.

0481-13

- 13 -

    We are prepared to work with Congress on legislation that
builds on these basic objectives to provide more flexibility
and simplicity to our economic cooperation efforts.  Working
with our global partners, we envision the use of five principal
mechanisms to advance this agenda worldwide:

    One, more flexible and integrated bilateral assistance
authorities.  We seek more flexible account structures and
greater ability to transfer funds both within and among
accounts to meet pressing, unexpected needs.  We hope to move
toward an assistance program unified around a single set of
core objectives, along the lines of those outlined above.  As a
first step toward this goal, we have proposed a modest $20
million Presidential contingency fund in our FY 1992 budget
request.

    The need for flexibility is especially urgent at a moment
when developments in the world are moving so quickly and
unpredictably, while our ability to respond with additional
resources is severely constrained by budgetary realities.  The
Gulf crisis, the restoration of democratic rule in Nicaragua
and Panama, and the dramatic developments in Eastern Europe,
the Soviet Union, and South Africa over the past year
illustrate that when unprecedented demands for American
leadership are combined with limited resources, our need for
flexibility becomes all the more urgent.

    Two, we see scope for more creative use of multilateral
mechanisms to advance our objectives, through both the
international financial institutions and the United Nations
system.

    The Bretton Woods institutions have now admitted all the
Eastern European countries, and are playing a central role in
structuring sound, adequately financed programs to ease their
transition to market economies based on private initiative.
Should the Soviet Union move further along the path of
structural economic and political reform, we would expect the
IMF and the World Bank to play a role in facilitating its
transformation as well.  The European Bank for Reconstruction
and Development will promote the development of infrastructure,
environmental programs, and private sector development in the
reforming countries of Central and Eastern Europe.  Meanwhile,
through our Enterprise for the Americas Initiative, the Inter-
American Development Bank is expected to play a major role in
promoting sound investment policy in our own hemisphere.

    To support the efforts of these institutions, we are again
proposing full funding for the multilateral development banks
-- including all arrears -- plus a periodic quota increase for
the IMF.  This funding will allow these institutions to
leverage other contributions in support of our objective of
promoting sound, growth-oriented economic policies in the
developing world.

                        0461-14

                                                          0104

- 14 -

As President Bush noted in his State of the Union address, the United Nations has played a historic role in the Gulf crisis, one that is close to fulfilling the vision of its founders. The Security Council's twelve resolutions, which laid the basis for ending the crisis, symbolized the unity of the international community against Iraq's aggression and established the principle of collective security as a cornerstone of the post-Cold War era. At the same time, the humanitarian organizations of the U.N. system have assisted the hundreds of thousands of refugees fleeing from Iraqi aggression. The United States has a vital interest in strengthening this new, revitalized United Nations as a full partner in the building of a post-Cold War world where peace, stability, and prosperity prevail.

Three, we foresee greater reliance on creative responsibility sharing as we strengthen our global partnerships with the European Community members and Japan in particular. As many in Congress have noted, our own difficult budgetary situation makes such efforts especially important for the advancement of a common agenda with partners who share our values and interests.

No effort so well illustrates the collective response of the world community to defend world peace as our successful efforts to enlist worldwide support for Operations Desert Shield and Desert Storm, and for the front-line states whose economies have been set back by the effects of Saddam Hussein's aggression.

In 1990, our coalition partners pledged $9.7 billion to meet Desert Shield costs, representing 88% of the roughly $11 billion in total incremental expenses we incurred. As soon as hostilities broke out, our allies again responded promptly and generously to shoulder their fair share of coalition military expenses under Operation Desert Storm. Over the past three weeks, we have received unprecedented pledges totaling in excess of $40 billion from Saudi Arabia, Kuwait, the UAE, Japan, Germany, and Korea, to offset Desert Shield Storm expenses expected to be incurred during the first three months of 1991.

The world community has also responded swiftly and generously to the needs of the front-line states, especially Egypt and Turkey, as they incurred substantial costs in standing up to Saddam Hussein's aggression. Through the U.S.-chaired Gulf Crisis Financial Coordination Group, over $14 billion has been pledged by the Gulf states, Europe, Japan, and Korea to ensure that the economies of affected regional states are stabilized and that their commitment to stay the course is reinforced. The United States has played its part in this effort, supported by Congress, by canceling Egypt's $6.7 billion military debt, thereby relieving a heavy burden on a critical regional ally. Other countries have followed suit and canceled an additional $8 billion in Egyptian debt.

0105

- 15 -

Meanwhile, in Eastern Europe, the successful G-24 process chaired by the European Commission has mobilized more than $18 billion in pledges for Poland and Hungary, to ease their transition to market economies. And in the Philippines, the Multilateral Assistance Initiative (MAI) has been responsible for nearly doubling the level of international assistance to this struggling democracy. We are also looking to our worldwide partners to assist us in clearing arrearages of Panama and Nicaragua to the international financial institutions and to assist in the financing of the enhanced debt strategy. Finally, we are encouraging Europe and Japan to join us in pledging $100 million a year over five years to create a Multilateral Investment Fund for Latin America and the Caribbean. This Fund is a key part of the President's Enterprise for the Americas Initiative and will play a crucial role in enabling countries to move from aid to trade and private investment as the principal engines of economic growth.

In each case, both strong U.S. leadership and a community of interests are essential to catalyze a broad worldwide response.

Four, we envision more creative use of trade and investment policies as vehicles to promote U.S. interests in world economic growth, as well as to enhance our own economic strength.

Central to these efforts over the past four years has been our determination to pursue a successful conclusion to the Uruguay Round of trade negotiations. We continue to believe that the Uruguay Round has profound political as well as economic implications for the shape of the world in the next century. Successful conclusion of the round is essential for the economic growth and stability of the emerging Eastern European democracies, as well as the wide range of developing countries who will ultimately rely on expansion of world trade -- not aid -- as the primary vehicle to generate employment opportunities and sustainable economic growth.

In our own hemisphere, the President's Enterprise for the Americas Initiative represents a comprehensive effort to promote economic growth and stability in the region, combining free trade and investment -- the primary vehicles for growth -- with debt relief and environmental initiatives.

As an important step toward the eventual goal of hemispheric free trade, the Administration intends to seek a North America Free Trade Area with Mexico and Canada, which we are convinced promises important economic benefits for all three countries. Since the President's announcement last June of his desire to seek a free trade agreement with Mexico, we have engaged in extensive consultations with Congress and the private sector. Canada's participation in these talks will

- 16 -

establish a free trade zone throughout the world's largest
market, worth over $6 trillion and including more than 350
million consumers.  The resulting stimulus to exports and the
creation of new business opportunities would act as a
significant engine of growth and employment generation.

Meanwhile, the United States has worked actively with our
Asian partners in the Asia Pacific Economic Cooperation (APEC),
to advance market-oriented cooperation among member states.

Our Bilateral Investment Treaty program has been an
important vehicle in ensuring an open and liberal investment
climate for U.S. investors and exporters.  Over the past year,
we completed negotiations with Poland and Czechosolvakia and
are actively negotiating with nine other countries which are in
the process of undertaking economic restructuring programs.

Finally, we will be challenged to pursue more vigorous U.S.
diplomacy, in the context of a State Operations budget that
reflects an activist approach to the diplomatic challenges of a
changing world stage.  I would again reiterate our need for
funding flexibility, especially as it relates to our ability to
transfer funds among accounts within our very tight State
Department Operations budget.

## Bilateral Assistance

Bilateral military and economic assistance will remain an
essential tool in advancing U.S. interests through the 1990's,
assuming the necessary flexibility can be provided to meet
emerging needs.  No other vehicle at our disposal is as well
suited to provide timely support to our allies and friends
around the world.  Our interests in political pluralism,
market-driven economic development, peace-making, and
strengthening alliances -- all can be advanced by prudent use
of bilateral assistance resources.

For FY 1992, our request for discretionary budget authority
for bilateral assistance programs totals $13.1 billion.  That
marks a 6.5% increase over the $12.3 billion appropriated by
Congress for FY 1991.  Highlights of this request by category
are as follows:

- $4.65 billion in Foreign Military Financing (FMF),
  supporting a program level of $4.92 billion.

- $3.24 billion in Economic Support Funding, up from $3.14
  billion.

- $1.3 billion in development assistance, the same as the
  prior year.

- $800 million for the Development Fund for Africa.

*OKH-M*

- 17 -

- $400 million for Central and Eastern Europe, a slight increase the FY 91 appropriation.

- $160 million for the Multilateral Assistance Initiative for the Philippines.

- $1.3 billion for bilateral PL-480 food aid, supporting the export of 5.9 million metric tons of U.S. commodities.

- $171 million for anti-narcotics assistance, plus additional security and development assistance resources to support these efforts.

## Multilateral Assistance

For the multilateral development banks, we are requesting $1.7 billion in FY 1992 budget authority, up from $1.6 billion in FY 1991. This includes $1.1 billion in funding for the International Development Association, the soft-loan window of the World Bank, which provides concessionary financing to the world's poorest countries, as well as full funding for the European Bank for Reconstruction and Development and the other regional development banks.

Our FY 1992 budget request also contains $12.2 billion in budget authority for the proposed increase in the U.S. quota in the International Monetary Fund (IMF), as provided for in the Budget Enforcement Act. This is to ensure that the Fund has the resources necessary to fulfill its responsibilities as the world's principal monetary institution. In the Third World, IMF arrangements support market-oriented adjustment and underpin debt reduction operations in support of the Brady Plan. The Fund has also spearheaded economic reform in Eastern Europe, and responded vigorously to assist countries seriously affected by the Persian Gulf crisis.

In addition, we are seeking $250 million for voluntary contributions to international organizations including the U.N. Development Program ($115 million) and UNICEF ($55 million).

## Refugees and Other Assistance Programs

The United States continues to play a preeminent role in addressing the plight of the world's refugees -- through our international assistance and domestic resettlement programs, as well as our diplomatic efforts in support of permanent solutions to refugee situations.

For FY 1992, we are requesting $491 million for Migration and Refugee Assistance, up from $486 million in FY 1991.

For our refugee assistance programs overseas, we seek $233 million in FY 1992 funding, a $20 million increase over the FY 1991 level. These programs will continue to focus on basic

0481 - 18

0108

- 18 -

life-sustaining activities for the most vulnerable groups and
support lasting solutions through opportunities for voluntary
repatriation and local integration.

To finance refugee admission and resettlement, we seek $192
million in FY 1992 funding. This will cover the expenses of an
estimated 120,000 refugees -- about the same number as last
year. Most refugee admissions will be from the Soviet Union
and Vietnam, but there will also be admissions from Eastern
Europe, Africa, Latin America, and the Near East. Family
reunification will continue to be a priority, as will the
resettlement of persecuted religious minorities and former
political prisoners.

In addition, we request $20 million to replenish the
President's Emergency Refugee and Migration Assistance Fund, to
enable us to respond to unforeseen refugee and migration needs
worldwide.

Another important component of our international
development assistance request is our $200 million request for
Peace Corps operating expenses.

<u>Investing in Diplomacy</u>

The Gulf crisis provides a vivid demonstration of the
"front line" role played by the State Department in protecting
American citizens and defending American interests abroad.
This is an increasingly expensive responsibility, exacerbated
by the demands on the Department to expand operations to meet
new political and economic opportunities around the globe.
Fluctuations in exchange rates, higher rates of overseas
inflation, and the continuing need to enhance the security of
our posts and personnel abroad further magnify the problem.
Today we face a potential and worrisome weakening of our
foreign affairs infrastructure at a time when we are being
called upon to meet extraordinary and new challenges.

Since January 1989, we have placed a high priority on
strengthening our ability to manage scarce resources:

● To better match national interests to available resources,
we are taking steps to better integrate policy planning
with the budget process.

● To strengthen foreign service personnel management, we have
begun to implement key proposals made by the Bremer and
Thomas commissions.

● To conserve personnel and financial resources, we have set
up a new center in Rosslyn, Virginia, to process hundreds
of thousands of refugee and asylum applications from the
Soviet Union, which can serve as a model to meet future
consular and immigration demands.

*0481-19*

0109

o  To strengthen our physical plant abroad, we have put into
   place a professional property management system and begun
   implementation of a five year integrated plan which
   addresses new construction, rehabilitation, repair, and
   maintenance.

o  To enhance the cost-effectiveness of our security efforts,
   we have begun to implement reforms to link our wide-ranging
   efforts at over 250 posts abroad to country-specific threat
   profiles.

   For State Department salaries and expenses, we are
requesting $2.05 billion in budget authority for FY 1992, an
increase of $179 million over the current year. This is the
minimal level of resources we need to fund our overseas and
domestic operations: over two thirds of the increase
compensates for price increases and exchange rate changes. The
remainder will be used to support several specific funding
requirements:

o  Expanding our diplomatic presence in the Soviet Union and
   Eastern Europe ($25 million).

o  Responding to increased immigration processing requirements
   necessitated by passage of the Immigration Act of 1990 ($24
   million).

o  Strengthening our information and financial systems by
   improving our infrastructure ($13.5 million).

   In the Foreign Buildings account, we have requested $570
million in FY 1992 funding. Of this total, $440 million
represents the first installment of a five year, $2.35 billion
program to address the Department of State's most urgent
facility replacement priorities, including embassies in Bangkok
and Bogota. Our goal is to restore the safety, security, and
workability of our aging but valuable inventory of overseas
facilities.

   We are also seeking $130 million in funding for the Moscow
Embassy project. It is imperative that we make a decision now
on a new building so we can begin to operate as soon as
possible in appropriate, secure space.

## Contributions to International Organizations

   The President has emphasized the urgency of restoring
financial viability to the United Nations and other
international organizations. After several years of effort on
the part of Congress and the Administration, we are pleased to
report significant movement toward budgetary and administrative
reform within the U.N. and its affiliated agencies. No one who
has witnessed the response of the United Nations Security

0481-20

0110

Council to recent events in the Persian Gulf could deny the importance to U.S. interests of a financially healthy United Nations system.

We remain absolutely committed to full funding for U.S. assessed contributions, to the extent permitted by law, and to paying our prior year arrearages over the next four years. We appreciate the full funding we received for FY 1991, which included initial funding toward the necessary process of arrears clearance. For FY 1992, we are requesting $750 million in budget authority to meet our current assessments to international organizations, plus an additional $371 million for arrears clearance, to be paid out over the following four years. For international peacekeeping activities, we are requesting $69 million to meet our full funding obligations, plus $132 million for arrearages.

## Public Diplomacy

Public diplomacy will be one of our most valuable tools as we seek to encourage the worldwide tide of democracy and political pluralism. For the valuable work of the U.S. Information Agency and the Board for International Broadcasting, we are requesting $1.3 billion in FY 1992 funding, up slightly from the prior year. Within this level, a new emphasis will be placed on information and cultural programs in Eastern Europe, the Soviet Union, and the Islamic world.

## Conclusion

Thank you, Mr. Chairman. We look forward to working with you and the Members of this Committee in the coming months to mobilize the resources needed to carry out our ambitious foreign affairs agenda.

( 주요 질의 응답요지 )

In answer to a series of question by Chairman Fascell, Sec. Baker had this to say:

Israel has not forwarded any official request for and Israel Emergency Aid Supplemental. The U.S. has been generous and will consider a request if received.

29 countries have contributed. In calendar year 1990, we got pledges of around $9.7 billion, for direct military costs against real costs of $11 billion and have received to date, $6.5 billion. That is good.

For 1991 since the Jan. 16 outbreak, we have received pledges over 41 billion for our expense in desert storm including $13 1/2 from Saudi Arabia, 13 1/2 b. from Kuwait, 8 b. from Japan, 5 1/2 b. from Germany, 280 million from Korea, 1 1/2 billion from United Arab Emigrates.

26 members of coalition pledged $14.6 billion in aid to front-line states, (Egypt, Turkey, Jordan), of which $6.2 b. has been dispersed.

The U.S. is bearing the human loss costs and allies are not yet carrying their fair share.

The Mulford Coordinating Committee is an interagency organization co-chaired by Treasury and State and is concerned with coordinating the financial contributions for the front-line states. This committee works with our allies and oversees what we have asked in burdensharing from our coalition partners.

The administration is happy to let you know all of our expense and burdensharing information, and only certain military information is classified.

In response to question posed to him by Rep. Broomfield, Sec. Baker had this to say:

Today's article which you read from the front page of the New York Times regarding and arms accord with the Soviets reflects some of our concerns accurately. WE have spoken frankly to the Soviets and they are award or our concerns. We will not submit any conventional force reduction treaty for Senate ratification until we clean up these concerns we have about recent tensions in the Soviet Union.

We have spoken to the Soviets about withdrawal for troops from the Baltic regions and hope this will come about.

We have increased our contacts with the leaders of the Baltic republics.

0481-22

In response to question from Rep. Hamilton, Sec. Baker had this to say:

It is true that Iraq has made efforts to stir anti-Americanism in the Arab and Muslim world. There has been some response to him in North Africa, Jordan and Palestine. Egypt continues to follow President Mubarek and support the U.S. efforts. We suspected many outbreaks of violence in the Arab and Muslim world, even before the outbreak on Jan. 16. The stir of anti-Americanism has not been massive, rather much less than we predicted.

We are making it clear to the war region that the U.S> is waging war in a just way, not targeting civilians, avoiding religious institutions, and securing American abroad and at home.

We are furnishing our partners with classified reports on these outbreaks so they may understand the situation fully.

As for an irreversible reversal of perestroika, I am cautious. I thing that Gorbachev would argue that what he is doing is necessary to see his reform through and he has not abandoned perestroika and glasnost. However, nobody can tell what will happen and our polices reflect that.

Iran has conducted itself in a credible way. We have no knowledge of Iran exploring its role as a mediator nor an proposal from Iran to that end.

We have no plans to abandon the UN Security Council resolution.

We support a unified and democratic Yugoslavia.

The recently-released State Dept. report on human rights violation, contains allegation against, many countries, many of them our allies.


There would be the most severe consequences for use of chemical or biological warfare by Iraq. We are also very concerned over the treatment of our POWs, which violates the Geneva accord.

If we decide to adopt this issue as a war aim, we would first have to consult with our United Nations allies.


In the case of a cease-fire, we will not accept a simple promise from Hussein. I must be a promise followed by immediate action, and a substantial withdrawal of troops.

The administration came to a clear conclusion that economic sanctions alone would not drive this tyrant from Kuwait before making further decision.

*0년/-23*

The costs for State Dept. functions as a result of Desert Storm amount to around $50 million and have not been included in the FY92 budget and we have not yet decided how to cover them.

We have encouraged our allies to contribute to Israel. They have received $600 million from Germany in military support. The EC is now examining how to aid Israel. The U.S. provide military assistance to Israel.

We have neither encouraged nor discouraged aid to Syria. Some arab countries are contributing to Syria, and we did not broker those contribution.

In the budget we allotted the Enterprise for Americans to help Latin American nations, $410 million.

I will look at Pre. Lantos' legislation. i would not like to see the American taxpayer pay one thin diem for the Persian Gulf Wa, We should think carefully about any action to enlarge or enhance or war aims.

Douglass Herd's Trans Atlantic Accord with the U.S. calls for greater cooperation between the EC and the US to understand one another better.

The PLO has made a terrible mistake in their policy toward this conflict.

WE have concrete evidence that a truck convey travelling from Baghdad to Amman carried Scud missile equipment and have bombed the highway it was travelling on and in the process, may have taken out some trucks carrying oil to Amman.

We have encouraged aid to Jordan so as not to put King Hussein's government in jeopardy. Jordan's sanction have been good.

A pledge from Iraq to compensate victims and destroy weapons stockpiles will depend on the way in which the war is terminated, either by peace treaty or what is left on the ground.

As far as a collection timetable for the funds pledged by coalition partners, we have made it for some and not for others. Remember, countries have different ways for payment. Some can give all in one lump some and other must increment. I repeat, the pledges we have received so far are remarkable and we are confident they will all be fulfilled.

0114

SECRETARY'S FEBRUARY 6 TESTIMONY ON THE GULF

   THE FOLLOWING IS AN ORAL MESSAGE FROM THE SECRETARY TO
THE FOREIGN MINISTER, ALONG WITH THE GULF PORTION OF THE
SECRETARY'S TESTIMONY BEFORE THE HOUSE FOREIGN AFFAIRS
COMMITTEE.

BEGIN TEXT OF ORAL MESSAGE:

--  I WANT TO SHARE WITH YOU THE TEXT OF A STATEMENT I MADE IN
TESTIMONY BEFORE CONGRESS.  IN THE STATEMENT, I EMPHASIZED
SEVERAL POINTS:

--  FIRST, OUR COMMITMENT TO FULL IMPLEMENTATION OF THE UNSC
RESOLUTIONS RELATED TO IRAQ'S AGGRESSION AGAINST KUWAIT REMAINS
UNSHAKEABLE.  THE INTERNATIONAL COALITION CONTINUES TO HOLD
STEADILY AND RESOLUTELY TO THIS COURSE.

--  SECOND, THE COALITION IS SHARING RESPONSIBILITY FOR THE
ECONOMIC BURDENS OF THE CONFLICT.

--  THIRD, THE COALITION'S MILITARY EFFORT TO REVERSE
IRAQ'S AGGRESSION FULLY REFLECTS OUR POLITICAL PURPOSES.  WE
HAVE NO QUARREL WITH THE PEOPLE OF IRAQ.  OUR GOAL IS THE
LIBERATION OF KUWAIT, NOT THE DESTRUCTION OF IRAQ OR CHANGES IN
ITS BORDERS.

--  AND FOURTH, WE MUST ALL PUT JUST AS MUCH EFFORT AND
IMAGINATION INTO SECURING THE PEACE AS WE HAVE PUT INTO WINNING
THE WAR.

--  ON THE LAST POINT, I SOUGHT IN MY STATEMENT SIMPLY TO
HIGHLIGHT A NUMBER OF THE CHALLENGES THAT WE WILL ALL HAVE TO
ADDRESS ONCE IRAQ IS EVICTED FROM KUWAIT.  WHAT I OUTLINED WAS
NOT A BLUEPRINT FOR POSTWAR ACTION, BUT THE HIGHLIGHTS OF AN
AGENDA THAT WILL REQUIRE VERY CAREFUL CONSULTATION AND
COORDINATION AMONG US.

--  WE ARE WORKING TO DEVELOP OUR OWN THINKING, ALTHOUGH MUCH
OBVIOUSLY DEPENDS ON THE ACTUAL SHAPE OF THE OUTCOME OF THE
CRISIS.  I LOOK FORWARD TO STAYING IN TOUCH WITH YOU ON THESE
IMPORTANT QUESTIONS IN THE WEEKS AND MONTHS AHEAD.

--  IN THE MEANTIME, OUR FIRST PRIORITY REMAINS REVERSAL OF
IRAQ'S AGGRESSION AND COMPLETE IMPLEMENTATION OF THE UNSC
RESOLUTIONS.  WITH CONTINUED SOLIDARITY WITHIN THE
INTERNATIONAL COALITION, THERE CAN BE NO DOUBT ABOUT THE
OUTCOME.  END TEXT OF ORAL MESSAGE.

BEGIN TEXT OF GULF PORTION OF SECRETARY'S ORAL TESTIMONY:

MR. CHAIRMAN,

IT IS A PRIVILEGE TO APPEAR BEFORE THIS COMMITTEE TO TESTIFY ON
BEHALF OF OUR FOREIGN AFFAIRS FUNDING PROPOSAL FOR FY 1992.
WITH YOUR PERMISSION, I WOULD HAVE MY DETAILED WRITTEN    0115

STATEMENT ENTERED INTO THE RECORD.  THIS YEAR, EVEN MORE SO
THAN MOST YEARS, THE FUNDS REQUESTED SHOULD BE SEEN AS AN
INVESTMENT IN A BETTER FUTURE -- A WORLD OF SECURE NATIONS,
FREE PEOPLES, AND PEACEFUL CHANGE.

I REALIZE THAT AS ARMIES FIGHT IN THE PERSIAN GULF SUCH A WORLD
SEEMS FAR DISTANT.  YET I BELIEVE THAT IT IS VITALLY IMPORTANT
TO SEE THE CHALLENGES WE FACE ALSO AS OPPORTUNITIES TO BUILD A
MORE SECURE AND JUST WORLD ORDER.  AND SO, TODAY I WOULD LIKE
TO MAKE A FEW COMMENTS CONCERNING OUR IDEAS ABOUT POST-CRISIS
CHALLENGES AND ARRANGEMENTS.

THE GULF WAR
------------
THE INTERNATIONAL COALITION HAS BEEN WAGING WAR AGAINST IRAQ
FOR THREE WEEKS NOW WITH VERY CLEAR OBJECTIVES:  TO EXPEL IRAQ
FROM KUWAIT; TO RESTORE THE LEGITIMATE GOVERNMENT OF KUWAIT;
AND TO ENSURE THE STABILITY AND SECURITY OF THIS CRITICAL
REGION.  I WANT TO MAKE SEVERAL OBSERVATIONS ABOUT THE COURSE
OF THE CONFLICT SO FAR.

FIRST, THE INTERNATIONAL COALITION HAS HELD STEADILY TO ITS
PURPOSE AND ITS COURSE.  AN OUTSTANDING ACHIEVEMENT OF THE
CURRENT CRISIS HAS BEEN THE ABILITY OF THE UNITED NATIONS TO
ACT AS ITS FOUNDERS INTENDED.  BEFORE JANUARY 15, A DOZEN
SECURITY COUNCIL RESOLUTIONS GUIDED THE UNITED STATES AND OTHER
NATIONS AS TOGETHER WE WAGED A CONCERTED DIPLOMATIC, POLITICAL,
AND ECONOMIC STRUGGLE AGAINST IRAQI AGGRESSION.  WE DID SO
BECAUSE WE ALL SHARE A CONVICTION THAT THIS BRUTAL AND
DANGEROUS DICTATOR MUST BE STOPPED AND STOPPED NOW.  SINCE
JANUARY 16, IN ACTIONS AUTHORIZED BY SECURITY COUNCIL
RESOLUTION 678, WE HAVE BEEN ABLE TO WAGE WAR BECAUSE WE ARE
EQUALLY CONVINCED THAT ALL PEACEFUL OPPORTUNITIES TO END
SADDAM'S AGGRESSION HAD BEEN EXPLORED AND EXHAUSTED.

LET ME GIVE YOU SOME IDEA OF THOSE EXHAUSTIVE EFFORTS, BOTH BY
THE UNITED STATES AND OTHER NATIONS.  IN THE 166 DAYS BETWEEN
THE INVASION OF KUWAIT ON AUGUST 2, 1990 AND THE EXPIRATION OF
THE UN DEADLINE FOR IRAQI WITHDRAWAL ON JANUARY 15, 1991, I
PERSONALLY HELD OVER 200 MEETINGS WITH FOREIGN DIGNITARIES,
CONDUCTED 10 DIPLOMATIC MISSIONS, AND TRAVELLED OVER 100,000
MILES.  FOR OVER SIX AND ONE HALF HOURS, I MET WITH THE IRAQI
FOREIGN MINISTER -- SIX AND ONE-HALF HOURS IN WHICH THE IRAQI
LEADERSHIP REJECTED THE VERY CONCEPT OF WITHDRAWAL FROM KUWAIT,
EVEN THE MENTION OF WITHDRAWAL.  AS YOU KNOW MANY OTHERS ALSO
TRIED -- THE ARAB LEAGUE, THE EUROPEAN COMMUNITY, THE UN
SECRETARY GENERAL, KINGS, PRESIDENTS, AND PRIME MINISTERS.
NONE SUCCEEDED BECAUSE SADDAM HUSSEIN REJECTED EACH AND EVERY
ONE.

SECOND, THE COALITION IS SHARING RESPONSIBILITY FOR THE
ECONOMIC BURDENS OF CONFLICT.  SUPPORT FOR U.S. MILITARY
OUTLAYS COVERS BOTH 1990 COMMITMENTS FOR DESERT SHIELD AND 1991
COMMITMENTS FOR THE PERIOD OF JANUARY THROUGH MARCH FOR DESERT 0116
SHIELD/STORM.  IN ADDITION, FUNDS HAVE ALSO BEEN FORTHCOMING TO
OFFSET THE ECONOMIC COSTS CONFRONTING THE FRONT LINE STATES IN

THE REGION.

TO DATE, WE HAVE PLEDGES OF OVER $50 BILLION TO SUPPORT OUR
MILITARY EFFORTS AND OVER $14 BILLION TO ASSIST THE FRONT LINE
STATES AND OTHERS WITH THEIR ECONOMIC NEEDS.

THIRD, OUR UNFOLDING MILITARY STRATEGY FULLY REFLECTS OUR
POLITICAL PURPOSES.  THIS IS THE PLACE TO RESTATE, AS THE
FRESIDENT HAS DONE SO OFTEN, THAT WE HAVE NO QUARREL WITH THE
IRAQI PEOPLE.  OUR GOAL IS THE LIBERATION OF KUWAIT, NOT THE
DESTRUCTION OF IRAQ OR CHANGES IN ITS BORDERS.

A THOROUGHLY PROFESSIONAL AND EFFECTIVE MILITARY CAMPAIGN IS
UNDERWAY.  OUR YOUNG MEN AND WOMEN AND THE FORCES OF OUR
COALITION PARTNERS ARE WRITING NEW ANNALS OF BRAVERY AND
SKILL.  BUT THE TASK IS FORMIDABLE, AND NO ONE SHOULD
UNDERESTIMATE SADDAM'S MILITARY CAPABILITIES.  IRAQ IS NOT A
THIRD RATE MILITARY POWER.  BILLIONS HAVE BEEN DIVERTED FROM
PEACEFUL USES TO GIVE THIS SMALL COUNTRY THE FOURTH LARGEST
ARMY IN THE WORLD.  IRAQ HAS MORE MAIN BATTLE TANKS THAN THE
UNITED KINGDOM AND FRANCE COMBINED.  IT HAS MORE COMBAT
AIRCRAFT THAN EITHER GERMANY, FRANCE, OR THE UNITED KINGDOM.
EJECTING IRAQ FROM KUWAIT WILL NOT BE EASY, BUT, AS THE
PRESIDENT SAID, "SO THAT PEACE CAN PREVAIL, WE WILL PREVAIL."

WE ARE ALSO TRYING OUR BEST TO WAGE A JUST WAR IN A JUST WAY.
OUR TARGETS ARE MILITARY, AND WE ARE DOING ALL WE CAN TO
MINIMIZE CIVILIAN CASUALTIES AND AVOID DAMAGE TO RELIGIOUS AND
CULTURAL SITES.  AND AS GENERAL SCHWARZKOPF HAS POINTED OUT,
THE COALITION FORCES ARE EVEN PUTTING THEMSELVES IN DANGER TO
MINIMIZE THE RISK TO INNOCENT LIVES.

IN SHOCKING CONTRAST, SADDAM HUSSEIN'S CONDUCT OF THE WAR HAS
BEEN NOT UNLIKE HIS CONDUCT BEFORE THE WAR:  A RELENTLESS
ASSAULT ON THE VALUES OF CIVILIZATION.  HE HAS LAUNCHED
MISSILES AGAINST ISRAELI CITIES AND SAUDI CITIES, MISSILES
AIMED NOT AT TARGETS OF MILITARY VALUE BUT FULLY INTENDED TO
MASSACRE CIVILIANS.  HE HAS ABUSED AND PARADED PRISONERS OF WAR
AND HE SAYS HE IS USING THEM AS "HUMAN SHIELDS" -- ACTIONS
TOTALLY IN VIOLATION OF THE GENEVA CONVENTION.  AND HE HAS EVEN
ATTACKED NATURE ITSELF, ATTEMPTING TO POISON THE WATERS OF THE
PERSIAN GULF WITH THE PETROLEUM THAT IS THE PATRIMONY OF THE
REGION'S ECONOMIC FUTURE.

WE HAVE HEARD, AND WE TAKE AT FACE VALUE, SADDAM'S THREATS TO
USE CHEMICAL AND BIOLOGICAL WEAPONS.  WE HAVE WARNED HIM -- AND
HE WOULD BE WELL ADVISED TO HEED OUR WARNING -- THAT WE WILL
NOT TOLERATE THE USE OF SUCH WEAPONS.  ANY USE OF CHEMICAL OR
BIOLOGICAL WEAPONS WILL HAVE THE MOST SEVERE CONSEQUENCES, AND
WE WILL CONTINUE TO INSIST THAT IRAQ FULFILL ITS OBLIGATIONS
UNDER THE GENEVA CONVENTION WITH RESPECT TO COALITION POW'S.

I THINK THAT OUR CONDUCT OF THE WAR IS IN ITSELF A GREAT
STRENGTH, THE STRENGTH THAT COMES FROM DOING THE RIGHT THING IN 0117
THE RIGHT WAY.  AND SADDAM'S CONTINUING BRUTALITY REDOUBLES OUR
RESOLVE AND THE ENTIRE COALITION'S CONVICTION ABOUT THE

RIGHTNESS OF OUR COURSE.  ENDING SADDAM'S AGGRESSION WILL ALSO
BE A BLOW TO STATE-SPONSORED TERRORISM.

THIS IS ALSO THE PLACE TO NOTE OUR DEEP APPRECIATION AND GREAT
ADMIRATION FOR THE EXTRAORDINARY RESTRAINT OF THE GOVERNMENT OF
ISRAEL.  ISRAELI CITIES HAVE BEEN ATTACKED BY SADDAM HUSSEIN
BECAUSE PART OF HIS STRATEGY HAS BEEN TO CONSOLIDATE HIS
AGGRESSION BY TURNING THE GULF CRISIS INTO AN ARAB-ISRAELI
CONFLICT.  DESPITE ITS CLEAR RIGHT TO RESPOND, THE ISRAELI
GOVERNMENT HAS ACTED WITH RESTRAINT AND RESPONSIBILITY.  THE
UNITED STATES HAS BEEN AND WILL CONTINUE TO BE IN CLOSE CONTACT
AT THE HIGHEST LEVELS WITH ISRAEL.  WE HAVE OFFERED AND ISRAEL
HAS ACCEPTED BATTERIES OF PATRIOT MISSILES -- SOME WITH
AMERICAN CREWS -- TO DEFEND AGAINST SCUD ATTACKS.  WE CONTINUE
TO DEVOTE SPECIAL MILITARY EFFORTS TO DESTROYING THE SCUDS AND
THEIR LAUNCHERS.

EVERYONE SHOULD KNOW:  WHEN WE SPEAK ABOUT OUR UNSHAKEABLE
COMMITMENT TO ISRAELI SECURITY, WE MEAN IT.

THE FOURTH OBSERVATION I WOULD MAKE IS THIS:  THE GREAT
INTERNATIONAL COALITION THAT IS NOW WINNING THE WAR MUST ALSO
BE STRONG ENOUGH TO SECURE THE PEACE.  WINSTON CHURCHILL ONCE
OBSERVED THAT "WE SHALL SEE HOW ABSOLUTE IS THE NEED OF A BROAD
PATH OF INTERNATIONAL ACTION PURSUED BY MANY STATES IN COMMON
ACROSS THE YEARS, IRRESPECTIVE OF THE EBB AND FLOW OF NATIONAL
POLITICS."  IF WE ARE GOING TO REDEEM THE SACRIFICES NOW BEING
MADE BY THE BRAVE MEN AND WOMEN WHO DEFEND OUR FREEDOM WITH
THEIR LIVES, THEN WE MUST FASHION A PEACE WORTHY OF THEIR
STRUGGLE.  AND THAT CAN BE DONE IF WE CAN HOLD TOGETHER IN
PEACE THE COALITION TEMPERED BY WAR.

I BELIEVE THAT WHEN CONGRESS VOTED THE PRESIDENT AUTHORITY TO
USE FORCE IN SUPPORT OF THE UNITED NATIONS RESOLUTIONS, IT
VOTED ALSO FOR PEACE -- A PEACE THAT MIGHT PREVENT SUCH WARS IN
THE FUTURE.  I BELIEVE THAT THE AMERICAN PEOPLE SUPPORT OUR
ROLE IN THE COALITION NOT ONLY TO DEFEAT AN AGGRESSOR BUT TO
SECURE A MEASURE OF JUSTICE AND SECURITY FOR THE FUTURE.

POST-WAR CHALLENGES
-------------------
MR. CHAIRMAN, WE AND EVERY NATION INVOLVED IN THIS CONFLICT ARE
THINKING ABOUT THE POST-WAR SITUATION AND PLANNING FOR THE
FUTURE.  IT WOULD BE IRRESPONSIBLE NOT TO DO SO.  AT THE SAME
TIME, IT WOULD BE BOTH PREMATURE AND UNWISE FOR US TO LAY OUT A
DETAILED BLUEPRINT FOR THE POSTWAR GULF OR, FOR THAT MATTER,
THE REGION AS A WHOLE.

THE WAR ITSELF AND THE WAY IT ENDS WILL GREATLY INFLUENCE BOTH
THE SECURITY OF THE GULF AND THE REST OF THE AREA.  THE DEEPEST
PASSIONS HAVE BEEN STIRRED.  THE MILITARY ACTIONS NOW UNDERWAY
NECESSARILY INVOLVE MANY CASUALTIES, GREAT HARDSHIPS, AND
GROWING FEARS FOR THE FUTURE.  TOUGH TIMES LIE AHEAD.

0118

WE SHOULD THEREFORE APPROACH THE POSTWAR PROBLEMS WITH A DUE
SENSE OF MODESTY.  RESPECT FOR THE SOVEREIGNTY OF THE PEOPLES

OF THE GULF AND MIDDLE EAST MUST BE UPPERMOST.  IN ANY EVENT,
MODERN HISTORY HAS SHOWN THAT NO SINGLE NATION CAN LONG IMPOSE
ITS WILL OR REMAKE THE MIDDLE EAST IN ITS OWN IMAGE.  AFTER
ALL, THAT IS PARTLY WHY WE ARE FIGHTING SADDAM HUSSEIN.

YET AMONG ALL THE DIFFICULTIES WE FACE, ONE FACT STANDS OUT:
THE PEOPLES OF THE GULF AND INDEED THE ENTIRE MIDDLE EAST
DESPERATELY NEED PEACE.  I TRULY BELIEVE THAT THERE MUST BE A
WAY, WORKING IN CONSULTATION WITH ALL OF THE AFFECTED NATIONS,
TO SET A COURSE THAT BRINGS GREATER SECURITY FOR ALL AND
ENDURING PEACE.  WE SHOULD THEREFORE MAKE EVERY EFFORT NOT JUST
TO HEAL THE PERSIAN GULF AFTER THIS WAR BUT ALSO TO TRY TO HEAL
THE REST OF THE REGION WHICH NEEDS IT SO BADLY.

SO I WOULD LIKE TO DISCUSS SEVERAL CHALLENGES THAT I BELIEVE WE
MUST ADDRESS IN THE POST WAR PERIOD.

ONE CHALLENGE WILL BE GREATER SECURITY FOR THE PERSIAN GULF.
AFTER TWO WARS IN TEN YEARS, THIS VITAL REGION NEEDS NEW AND
DIFFERENT SECURITY ARRANGEMENTS.  IN OUR VIEW, THERE ARE THREE
BASIC ISSUES TO BE RESOLVED:  THE PURPOSES OR PRINCIPLES OF THE
SECURITY ARRANGEMENTS; THE ROLE OF THE LOCAL STATES, REGIONAL
ORGANIZATIONS, AND THE INTERNATIONAL COMMUNITY; AND IN THE
AFTERMATH OF THE WAR, THE MILITARY REQUIREMENTS UNTIL LOCAL
STABILITY IS ACHIEVED, AND THEREAFTER.

I THINK WE WOULD FIND ALREADY A WIDE MEASURE OF AGREEMENT ON
THE PRINCIPLES.  THEY WOULD INCLUDE:

O   DETERRENCE OF AGGRESSION FROM ANY QUARTER.

O   TERRITORIAL INTEGRITY.  THERE MUST BE RESPECT FOR EXISTING
SOVEREIGNTY OF ALL STATES AND FOR THE INVIOLABILITY OF BORDERS.

O   PEACEFUL RESOLUTION OF DISPUTES.  BORDER PROBLEMS AND OTHER
DISPUTES THAT HAVE LONG HISTORIES -- AND THERE ARE MANY BEYOND
THE IRAQ-KUWAIT EXAMPLE -- SHOULD BE RESOLVED BY PEACEFUL
MEANS, AS PRESCRIBED BY THE U.N. CHARTER.

THESE PRINCIPLES MUST BE PUT INTO ACTION FIRST AND FOREMOST BY
THE LOCAL STATES SO THAT CONFLICTS CAN BE PREVENTED AND
AGGRESSION DETERRED.  WE WOULD EXPECT THE STATES OF THE GULF
AND REGIONAL ORGANIZATIONS SUCH AS THE GULF COOPERATION COUNCIL
TO TAKE THE LEAD IN BUILDING A REINFORCING NETWORK OF NEW AND
STRENGTHENED SECURITY TIES.  NO REGIONAL STATE SHOULD BE
EXCLUDED FROM THESE ARRANGEMENTS.  POST-WAR IRAQ COULD HAVE AN
IMPORTANT CONTRIBUTION TO PLAY.  AND SO COULD IRAN AS A MAJOR
POWER IN THE GULF.

THERE IS A ROLE, TOO, FOR OUTSIDE NATIONS AND THE INTERNATIONAL
COMMUNITY, INCLUDING THE UNITED NATIONS, TO ENCOURAGE SUCH
ARRANGEMENTS AND TO STAND BEHIND THEM.

AS FOR THE UNITED STATES, WE HAVE DEPLOYED SMALL NAVAL FORCES
IN THE PERSIAN GULF EVER SINCE THE TRUMAN ADMINISTRATION IN
1949.  WE HAD AND CONTINUE TO HAVE VERY STRONG BILATERAL TIES

0119

WITH SAUDI ARABIA AND OTHER LOCAL STATES.  AND THROUGH THE
YEARS, WE HAVE CONDUCTED JOINT EXERCISES WITH AND PROVIDED
MILITARY EQUIPMENT FOR OUR FRIENDS IN THE REGION.  THE
PRESIDENT HAS SAID THAT WE HAVE NO INTENTION OF MAINTAINING A
PERMANENT GROUND PRESENCE ON THE ARABIAN PENINSULA ONCE IRAQ IS
EJECTED FROM KUWAIT AND THE THREAT RECEDES.

BEFORE SECURITY IS ASSURED, HOWEVER, IMPORTANT QUESTIONS MUST
BE ANSWERED.  WE WILL BE GOING THROUGH AN IMPORTANT
TRANSITIONAL PHASE IN THE IMMEDIATE AFTERMATH OF THE WAR AS WE
TRY TO ESTABLISH STABILITY.  LET ME LIST JUST A FEW OF THE
QUESTIONS THAT NEED TO BE ANSWERED.

O   SHOULD THERE BE A PERMANENT, LOCALLY STATIONED GROUND FORCE
MADE UP OF LOCAL TROOPS UNDER U.N. AUSPICES OR UNDER REGIONAL
AUSPICES, SUCH AS THE GCC?

O   HOW CAN THE INTERNATIONAL COMMUNITY REINFORCE DETERRENCE IN
THE GULF, WHETHER BY CONTRIBUTING FORCES OR THROUGH OTHER
POLITICAL ARRANGEMENTS, SUCH AS RESOLUTIONS OR SECURITY
COMMITMENTS?

NO ONE HAS THE ANSWERS YET TO THESE AND OTHER QUESTIONS.  SOME
MAY NEVER BE ANSWERED.  BUT HOWEVER WE EVENTUALLY PROCEED, WE
WILL CONDUCT EXTENSIVE CONSULTATIONS AMONG ALL OF THE CONCERNED
PARTIES TO SUCH ARRANGEMENTS.

2  A SECOND CHALLENGE WILL SURELY BE REGIONAL ARMS PROLIFERATION
AND CONTROL.  THIS INCLUDES BOTH CONVENTIONAL WEAPONS AND
WEAPONS OF MASS DESTRUCTION.  THE TERRIBLE FACT IS THAT EVEN
THE CONVENTIONAL ARSENALS OF SEVERAL MIDDLE EASTERN STATES
DWARF THOSE OF MOST EUROPEAN POWERS.  FIVE MIDDLE EASTERN
COUNTRIES HAVE MORE MAIN BATTLE TANKS THAN THE UNITED KINGDOM
OR FRANCE.  THE TIME HAS COME TO TRY TO CHANGE THE DESTRUCTIVE
PATTERN OF MILITARY COMPETITION AND PROLIFERATION IN THIS
REGION AND TO REDUCE ARMS FLOWS INTO AN AREA THAT IS ALREADY
OVERMILITARIZED.  THAT SUGGESTS THAT WE AND OTHERS INSIDE AND
OUTSIDE THE REGION MUST CONSULT ON HOW BEST TO ADDRESS SEVERAL
DIMENSIONS OF THE PROBLEM:

O   HOW CAN WE COOPERATE TO CONSTRAIN IRAQ'S POST-WAR ABILITY TO
RETAIN OR REBUILD ITS WEAPONS OF MASS DESTRUCTION AND MOST
DESTABILIZING CONVENTIONAL WEAPONS?

O   HOW CAN WE WORK WITH OTHERS TO ENCOURAGE STEPS TOWARD
BROADER REGIONAL RESTRAINT IN THE ACQUISITION AND USE OF BOTH
CONVENTIONAL ARMAMENTS AND WEAPONS OF MASS DESTRUCTION?  WHAT
ROLE MIGHT THE KINDS OF CONFIDENCE BUILDING MEASURES THAT HAVE
LESSENED CONFLICT IN EUROPE PLAY IN THE GULF AND THE MIDDLE
EAST?

O   FINALLY, WHAT GLOBAL ACTIONS WOULD REINFORCE STEPS TOWARD
ARMS CONTROL IN THE GULF AND MIDDLE EAST?  THESE COULD INCLUDE
RAPID COMPLETION OF PENDING INTERNATIONAL AGREEMENTS LIKE THE
CHEMICAL WEAPONS CONVENTION, AS WELL AS MUCH TIGHTER SUPPLY
RESTRAINTS ON THE FLOW OF WEAPONS AND DUAL-USE TECHNOLOGY INTO

0120

THE REGION. AND WHAT IMPLICATIONS DOES THAT HAVE FOR ARMS
TRANSFER AND SALES POLICIES?

3  A THIRD CHALLENGE WILL BE ECONOMIC RECONSTRUCTION AND
RECOVERY. AN ECONOMIC CATASTROPHE HAS BEFALLEN THE GULF AND
THE NATIONS TRADING WITH IT. KUWAIT HAS BEEN LOOTED AND
WRECKED. HUNDREDS OF THOUSANDS OF WORKERS HAVE LOST JOBS AND
FLED. TRADE FLOWS AND MARKETS HAVE BEEN DISRUPTED.

I AM CONFIDENT THAT THE PEOPLE OF KUWAIT WILL REBUILD THEIR
COUNTRY. AS WE HAVE WORKED WITH THE KUWAITIS IN THEIR MOMENT
OF TRIAL, SO WE SHALL LOOK FORWARD TO COOPERATING WITH THEM IN
THEIR HOUR OF RECOVERY.

AND NO ONE SHOULD FORGET THAT FOR THE SECOND TIME IN A DECADE,
THE PEOPLE OF IRAQ WILL BE RECOVERING FROM A DISASTROUS
CONFLICT. THE TIME OF RECONSTRUCTION AND RECOVERY SHOULD NOT
BE THE OCCASION FOR VENGEFUL ACTIONS AGAINST A NATION FORCED TO
WAR BY A DICTATOR'S AMBITION. THE SECURE AND PROSPEROUS FUTURE
EVERYONE HOPES TO SEE IN THE GULF MUST INCLUDE IRAQ.

OF NECESSITY, MOST OF THE RESOURCES FOR RECONSTRUCTION WILL BE
DRAWN FROM THE GULF. YET, SHOULD WE NOT BE THINKING ALSO OF
MORE THAN RECONSTRUCTION? IT MIGHT BE POSSIBLE FOR A COALITION
OF COUNTRIES USING BOTH LOCAL AND EXTERNAL RESOURCES TO
TRANSFORM THE OUTLOOK FOR THE REGION -- IN EXPANDING FREE TRADE
AND INVESTMENT IN ASSISTING DEVELOPMENT, AND IN PROMOTING
GROWTH-ORIENTED ECONOMIC POLICIES WHICH HAVE TAKEN ROOT ACROSS
THE GLOBE.

ANY ECONOMIC EFFORT MUST HAVE A SPECIAL PLACE FOR WATER
DEVELOPMENT. WELL OVER HALF THE PEOPLE LIVING IN THE MIDDLE
EAST DRAW WATER FROM RIVERS THAT CROSS INTERNATIONAL BOUNDARIES
OR DEPEND ON DESALINATION PLANTS. WE HAVE ALL BEEN INCENSED BY
SADDAM HUSSEIN'S DELIBERATE POISONING OF THE GULF WATERS, WHICH
COULD AFFECT A LARGE PORTION OF SAUDI ARABIA'S DESALINIZED
DRINKING WATER.

FINALLY, WE WILL WANT TO CONSULT WITH GOVERNMENTS BOTH FROM THE
MIDDLE EAST AND FROM OTHER REGIONS ABOUT SPECIFIC ARRANGEMENTS
THAT MIGHT BEST SERVE THE PURPOSES OF REGION-WIDE ECONOMIC
COOPERATION. SUCH COOPERATION WOULD SURELY BE HELPFUL IN
REINFORCING OUR OVERALL OBJECTIVE: REDUCING ONE BY ONE THE
SOURCES OF CONFLICT AND REMOVING ONE BY ONE THE BARRIERS TO
SECURITY AND PROSPERITY THROUGHOUT THE AREA.

4  A FOURTH CHALLENGE IS TO RESUME THE SEARCH FOR A JUST PEACE AND
REAL RECONCILIATION FOR ISRAEL, THE ARAB STATES, AND THE
PALESTINIANS. BY RECONCILIATION, I MEAN NOT SIMPLY PEACE AS
THE ABSENCE OF WAR, BUT A PEACE BASED ON ENDURING RESPECT,
TOLERANCE, AND MUTUAL TRUST. AS YOU KNOW, I PERSONALLY HAD
DEVOTED CONSIDERABLE EFFORT BEFORE THE WAR TO FACILITATING A
DIALOGUE BETWEEN ISRAEL AND THE PALESTINIANS -- AN ESSENTIAL
PART OF AN OVERALL PEACE PROCESS. LET'S NOT FOOL OURSELVES.
THE COURSE OF THIS CRISIS HAS STIRRED EMOTIONS AMONG ISRAELIS
AND PALESTINIANS THAT WILL NOT YIELD EASILY TO CONCILIATION.

0121

YET IN THE AFTERMATH OF THIS WAR, AS IN EARLIER WARS, THERE MAY
BE OPPORTUNITIES FOR PEACE -- IF THE PARTIES ARE WILLING.  AND
IF THEY REALLY ARE WILLING, WE ARE COMMITTED TO WORKING CLOSELY
WITH THEM TO FASHION A MORE EFFECTIVE PEACE PROCESS.

THE ISSUES TO BE ADDRESSED ARE OF COURSE FAMILIAR AND MORE
CHALLENGING THAN EVER.

O  HOW DO YOU GO ABOUT RECONCILING ISRAELIS AND PALESTINIANS?
WHAT CONCRETE ACTIONS CAN BE TAKEN BY EACH SIDE?

O  WHAT WILL BE THE ROLE OF THE ARAB STATES IN FACILITATING
THIS PROCESS AND THEIR OWN NEGOTIATIONS FOR PEACE WITH ISRAEL?

O  HOW WILL REGIONAL ARMS CONTROL ARRANGEMENTS AFFECT THIS
PROCESS?

O  WHAT IS THE BEST DIPLOMATIC VEHICLE FOR GETTING THE PROCESS
UNDERWAY?

AGAIN, WE WILL BE CONSULTING AND WORKING VERY CLOSELY WITH OUR
FRIENDS AND ALL PARTIES WHO HAVE A CONSTRUCTIVE ROLE TO PLAY IN
SETTLING THIS CONFLICT.

5  A FIFTH AND FINAL CHALLENGE CONCERNS THE UNITED STATES: WE
SIMPLY MUST DO MORE TO REDUCE OUR ENERGY DEPENDENCE.  AS THE
PRESIDENT HAS STRESSED, ONLY A COMPREHENSIVE STRATEGY CAN
ACHIEVE OUR GOALS.  THAT STRATEGY SHOULD INVOLVE ENERGY
CONSERVATION AND EFFICIENCY, INCREASED DEVELOPMENT,
STRENGTHENED STOCKPILES AND RESERVES, AND GREATER USE OF
ALTERNATIVE FUELS.  WE MUST BRING TO THIS TASK THE SAME
DETERMINATION WE ARE NOW BRINGING TO THE WAR ITSELF.

AS YOU CAN SEE, MR. CHAIRMAN, SOME OF THESE ELEMENTS ARE
POLITICAL, SOME ARE ECONOMIC, AND SOME OF NECESSITY ARE RELATED
TO SECURITY.  THAT SUGGESTS THAT WE SHOULD VIEW SECURITY NOT
JUST IN MILITARY TERMS BUT AS PART AND PARCEL OF THE BROADER
OUTLOOK FOR THE REGION.  WE'RE NOT GOING TO HAVE LASTING PEACE
AND WELL-BEING WITHOUT SOUND ECONOMIC GROWTH.  WE'RE NOT GOING
TO HAVE SOUND ECONOMIC GROWTH IF NATIONS ARE THREATENED OR
INVADED -- OR IF THEY ARE SQUANDERING PRECIOUS RESOURCES ON
MORE AND MORE ARMS.  AND SURELY FINDING A WAY FOR THE PEOPLES
OF THE MIDDLE EAST TO WORK WITH EACH OTHER WILL BE CRUCIAL IF
WE ARE TO LIFT OUR EYES TO A BETTER FUTURE.

0122

# 걸프事態 関聯 美下院 外務委 聴聞会


## 1991.2


## 外 務 部

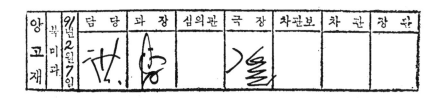

베이커 美 國務長官은 2.6(水) 美 下院 外務委
(委員長: 파셀 議員(民主, 플로리다) 聽聞會에 參席,
걸프戰 以後의 中東地域 安定 方案, 對蘇 關係等
最近의 主要 國際問題 全般에 대해 證言하였는 바,
同 長官 發言要旨等 關聯 事項 아래 報告드립니다.


## 證言 要旨


( 걸프戰 進展狀況)

o  금번 걸프戰 關聯 注目되는 점은 유엔이 제대로
   役割을 遂行하게 되었다는 점과 友邦國等 全 國際
   社會가 戰費 및 周邊國 經濟支援에 責任 分擔을
   하고 있다는 점임
   -  現在 500億弗 以上의 軍事費 및 140億弗
      以上의 經濟支援 約束
   한국이 ✓ 일본, 독일, 사우디, 쿠웨이트가 기여 2.8억불의 쉐어는 든 셰어은 민습

o  이라크側이 生化學 武器를 使用할 경우 매우 심각한
   結果가 招來될 것임을 警告함
   -  戰爭 捕虜 待遇에 관한 제네바 協約 履行도 促求


( 戰後 中東地域 安定 方案)

o  戰爭 勃發로 인해 惹起된 諸問題 解決을 위해서는
   節制의 마음 가짐이 必要함
   -  域內 國家의 主權 尊重 및 平和定着 努力 必要


0124

o  이라크軍  逐出後  美  地上軍은  永久  駐屯치  않을
   豫定임
   -  域內  國家들이  主導的  役割을  擔當  詳細事項은
      向後  美國과  關係國間  協議下에  決定

o  中東地域  安全  保障의  目標와  原則으로는  侵略  저지,
   領土의  不可侵性  및  國家間  紛爭의  平和的  解決임
   -  在來式  武器  및  大量  殺傷  武器의  擴散防止  方案
      講究도  必要

o  終戰後  쿠웨이트  經濟復舊에의  協力은  물론  이라크의
   經濟  再建도  支援해야  함
   -  이라크  및  이란의  建設的  役割  期待

o  相互  信賴를  基盤으로한  이스라엘,  아랍國家  및
   팔레스타인  民族間에  진정한  和解와  平和를  이룩해야
   함

( 對蘇  關係 )

o  長期的인  對蘇  協力關係  構築을  위해  蘇聯의  開放
   政策의  成功的  遂行을  支援해야  함

o  最近  발틱事態  關聯,  美國의  目標는  발틱民族의
   興望  成就를  支援하는  것임
   -  事態  銳意  注視中이며,  美.蘇間  對話를  통한
      問題  解決  立場  表明

0125

## 主要 質疑. 応答 內容

( 友邦國 役割 分擔)

o 90年中 美軍 戰費 110億弗中 友邦國 29個國이
97億弗 支援을 約束함( 現在 65億弗 寄託)
- 戰爭 勃發 以後에는 410億弗 約束
* 사우디, 쿠웨이트 各 135億弗, 日本 80億弗, 独逸 55億弗, 我国 追加支援 2.8億弗도 言及
- 對前線國家 經濟支援은 總 26個國이 146億弗
支援 約束( 現在 62億弗 執行)

o 美軍의 戰費 充當 展望은 밝으며 友邦國은 公正한
役割을 分擔中임


## 觀察 및 評価

o 금번 聽聞會는 順調로운 戰爭 進行 狀況을 바탕으로
주로 戰後 處理問題에 촛점을 맞춤

o 또한 부쉬 行政府側은 友邦國의 役割 分擔 規模에
대해 滿足을 表示하고, 금번 戰爭關聯 行政府의
政策 全般에 成功을 거두고 있음을 強調함
- 議會 및 國民의 繼續的 支持 確保 努力
- 끝 -

0126

관리
번호 71-293

# 외 무 부

종 별 :

번 호 : USW-0658                일 시 : 91 0207 1823

수 신 : 장관( 미북,미안,중근동,대책반)

발 신 : 주 미 대사

제 목 : 상원 외교위 청문회( 걸프사태 관련)

연:WUS-0646

1. 금 2.7. 상원 외교위는 작일 하원 외무위에 이어 BAKER 국무장관을 출석시킨 가운데"US FOREIGN POLICY AND THE FY92 BUDGET REQUEST" 제하의 청문회를 개최 하였음.

2. 금번 청문회시 BAKER 국무장관은 작일 하원 외무위에서와 동일한 내용의증언을 하였으며, 걸프지역의 전후 처리 과정의 일환으로 경제 재건 및 복구에관해 언급할시 하기 내용을 새로이 추가 하였음.

0 아시아, 아프리카, 미주 및 유럽에는 지역은행이 설립되어 있고, 1940 년대 전후 복구에 있어 세계 은행 및 IMF 가 중요한 역할을 수행하였던 점을 감안, 전후 중동지역의 재건과 개발을 위한 지역은행의 설립을 검토하는 방안을 제시할것임. 중동지역의 평화를 확고히 하기 위해서는 경제재건 및 개발에 다자간의 참여가 필요하다고 생각함.

3. 금번 청문회시 주요 질의 응답 내용은 하기와 같음.

(비용 분담 SARBANES 의원)

0 우방국의 역할 분담이 전쟁에 따른 추가 비용(INCREMENTAL COSTS) 만을 대상으로 하여 이루어진 관계로 총 군사비용의 일부에 불과하다는 지적에 대해, BAKER 장관은 전쟁추가 비용을 제외한 군사비용은 전쟁이 발발 하지 않았어도 미국이 부담해야 하는 금액이기 때문에 우방국의 분담 규모가 적다고 말하기는 어렵다고 답변함.

(전후 이락에 대한 경제복구 비용 조달:HELMS 의원)

0 전후 이락의 경제 복구 원조의 대부분은 걸프지역 국가가 부담해야할 것이며, 미국은 지역 전반이 평화와 안정을 회복시키는데 지도적 역할을 수행할것임.

| 미주국 안기부 | 장관 대책반 | 차관 | 1차보 | 2차보 | 미주국 | 중아국 | 정문국 | 청와대 |
|---|---|---|---|---|---|---|---|---|

PAGE 1

91.02.08    10:20

외신 2과  통제관 BT

0127

O SADDAM 이 집권하고 있는한 미국민의 돈이 이락에 지원될것을 기대하지 말라는 HELMS 의원의 발언에 대해, BAKER 장관은 이락에 대한 경제 복구 문제는 현 집권층이 계속 권력을 장악하게 되느냐 여부에 따라 달라질 것이라고 언급

(전범 처리)

O 종전후 전범재판 가능성 관련, 미국은 전범 재판의 선택 가능성을 배제하지는 않고 있음.

(전후 처리 과정에서의 PLO 역할 및 시리아- 이스라엘 관계:MCCONNELL 의원)

O PLO 가 기존 정책을 포기하고 평화를 위한 의지를 확고히 해야만 PLO 가 참여할수 있을것임.

O PLO 와 사우디와의 관계와 관련, 사우디는 PLO 에 대한 일체의 지원을 중단하였고, 지원이 조만간 재개될것 같지는 않음.

O 시리아와 이스라엘 관계 개선 가능성은 시리아측이 기존의 이스라엘과의 적대관계를 변경시키려는 정책적 노력에 달려있음.

(시리아에 대한 테러 국가 해제:PRESSLER 의원)

O 미국의 테러국가 리스트에서 시리아를 제외시키는 것은 현재 고려치 않고있음.

(요르단에 대한 원조 문제:MCCONNELL 및 PELL 의원)

O 2.6. 후세인 국왕 발언을 감안, 요르단에 대한 원조 제공 가능성에 대해,후세인 국왕이 잘못된 편에 서있으나, 요르단과의 대화 경로는 항상 열어 놓고있으며, 후세인 국왕에 대한 국내 내부의 압력은 잘 이해하고 있음. 후세인국왕이 축출되는 상황은 바람직하지 않다고 봄.

(대사 박동진- 국장)

91.12.31. 까지

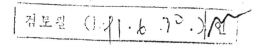

# 報 告 事 項

1991. 2. 26.
美 洲 局
北 美 課(12)

題 目 : 걸프 地上戰 開始後 美 議會 및 輿論 反應
_____

> 걸프 지상전 발발이후 전쟁 수행 및 후세인 정권 제거문제 등과 관련한
> 미 의회 및 여론 반응에 관한 미국의 언론 보도 요지를 아래 보고 드립니다.

## 1. 미 의회, 전쟁 수행 지지

○ 걸프 지상전 개시이후 다국적군의 조속한 승리가 예견되자 미 의회는 부쉬
   행정부의 전쟁 수행에 대해 전폭적인 지지 천명
   - Thomas Foley 하원의장(민주, 워싱턴), Les Aspin 하원 군사위원장(민주,
     위스콘신)등

○ 6주전에는 부시 대통령의 무력사용에 대해 반대하던 민주당원들도 이제는
   과거를 묻어두고 미국의 전후 입지 강화에 노력하여야 한다는 입장 표명
   - Lee Hamilton 하원 외교위 중동소위원장(민주, 인디애나)등

## 2. 후세인 제거 지지

○ 최근 WP-ABC 여론 조사에 의하면 70%가 후세인 축출 지지

o 이러한 여론을 반영, 많은 의원들이 종전후 후세인이 정치적으로 제기
  불가능하도록 하여야 한다고 주장
  - Alan Dixon 상원의원(민주, 일리노이), Joseph Biden, Jr. 상원의원
    (민주, 델라웨어), Joseph McDade 하원의원(공화, 펜실바니아)등

## 3. 후세인 제거 방법에는 이견

o Aspin 등 일부 의원은 이라크 영토 일부를 점령하고 종전후에도 경제 제재를
  계속함으로써 이라크가 후세인과 Baathist 당을 축출하도록 협상하자는
  의견 제시

o 그러나 일부는 미국의 전쟁 수행은 국제법 준수와 유엔 안보리 결의의 이행
  수단으로서 정당화된 것이므로 그 이상의 무력행사는 삼가되, 이라크가
  자체적으로 후세인을 축출할 것을 기대해야 한다는 의견
  - John Kerry 상원의원(민주, 메사추세츠), Albert Gore, Jr. 상원의원
    (민주, 테네시), Jim Leach 하원의원(공화, 아이오와)등

## 4. 전후 미군 잔류 등 반대

o 대부분 의원들은 걸프전 승리후 미국이 중동에서 주도적 역할을 수행할
  것으로 기대하나, 미군의 계속 주둔에 대해서는 반대
  - Hamilton 중동소위원장 등

o Foley 하원의장은 평화 유지군이 구성된다 하더라도 이는 주로 여타국
  군대에 의해 구성되어야 할 것이라고 주장하고, 의회는 걸프전 승리를
  위해 추경예산(150억불) 등 모든 필요한 지원을 제공할 것이나 국민들에게
  재정적 부담이 되는 대규모 전쟁 피해 복구사업 참여 등은 하지 않아야
  한다고 주장          끝.

0130

# Lawmakers Elated At Victory Prospect

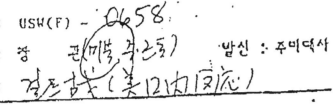

By John E. Yang
and David S. Broder
Washington Post Staff Writers

Lawmakers yesterday rejoiced at the prospect of a quick military victory in Kuwait and urged President Bush to press on until Iraqi President Saddam Hussein is removed from power.

"So far the news is very good," said House Speaker Thomas S. Foley (D-Wash.). "It's going better than one has a right to expect in any engagement of this kind involving huge numbers of forces."

House Armed Services Committee Chairman Les Aspin (D-Wis.) predicted the allied forces would need only four or five days to take complete control of both Kuwait and the southeastern corner of Iraq, just north of the border of the two countries.

But many lawmakers said it would not be enough to simply reclaim Kuwait from Iraq. It would be necessary, they said, to remove Saddam from power.

"You just can't let him go now," said Sen. Alan J. Dixon (D-Ill.), a member of the Senate Armed Services Committee. "My voters feel that strongly.... There's a lot of pent-up wrath and they don't want to let him stay in his shelter and then rule the country."

Rep. Joseph M. McDade (Pa.), the House Appropriations Committee's ranking Republican, warned that Saddam could find victory in a defeat. "We've got to be certain there's no way this fellow can convert a certain military defeat into political vindication and become larger than life," he said.

They appeared to be reflecting the growing public sentiment against Saddam. More than seven out of 10 of those questioned in the latest Washington Post-ABC News Poll said the U.S. objective should be to force "Saddam Hussein out of power."

Sen. Joseph R. Biden Jr. (D-Del.) said he thought "the American people figured out early ... the restoration of the emir of Kuwait was not worth one' life.... The ultimate goal was to render Saddam Hussein, not just incompetent, but impotent to conduct the affairs of his country."

These sentiments also marked a turnaround for Democratic lawmakers, a majority of whom voted only six weeks ago to deny Bush the authority he sought to go to war. "We lost that debate," said Rep. Lee H. Hamilton (D-Ind.), a co-sponsor of the House resolution that urged continued reliance on economic sanctions. "That's behind us. Let's now stand behind the president and the troops and see that the United States comes out of this in as strong a position as possible."

There was disagreement among lawmakers over how far the United States and its allies should go—or needed to go—in the military campaign to remove Saddam.

That goal could be achieved by other means, some lawmakers said. Aspin suggested that if Saddam were still in power when the fighting stops, the allies could use the seized Iraqi territory, along with continued economic sanctions, as leverage to drive the Iraqi president and his Baathist Party from power.

The forces should take "just enough part of Iraq to make the Iraqis want to get that back," Aspin said on CBS's "Face the Nation." "I think we stay there and negotiate a settlement."

Others cautioned against going beyond the objectives of the United Nations resolutions that have been the basis for the military operation in the Persian Gulf. "If you have to reach too brazenly beyond those resolutions, it could complicate the peace process," said Sen. John F.

Kerry (D-Mass.), a member of the Senate Foreign Relations Committee.

"The strength of George Bush's actions to date has been the strictest adherence to international law," said Rep. Jim Leach (R-Iowa), a member of the House Foreign Affairs subcommittee on the Middle East.

But if the Iraqi forces are routed, the question of what to do about Saddam may take care of itself. In that case, he could find himself "at the mercy of his own nation ... absolutely impossible to survive as leader, because of the extent of his humiliation," said Sen. Albert Gore Jr. (D-Tenn.).

While lawmakers said they believed an allied victory would allow the United States to play a major role in the Middle East, they also warned against a large American military presence in the region.

"My great hope is that we will be up to the challenge of translating what I think is going to be a clear military victory into a political triumph as well," Hamilton said on NBC's "Sunday Today." "We want stability in the region and that's what we've got to work for now."

But "a large ground presence would not play well with Congress, I don't think it would play well with the American people," said Hamilton, chairman of the House Foreign Affairs subcommittee on the Middle East.

"If there's a peacekeeping force, it ought to be largely composed of other countries," Foley told NBC News.

Neither should the United States play a large role in rebuilding the war-torn area, Foley said. "The American taxpayer should not be called upon to bear additional huge costs of the economic redevelopment of the region," he said.

This week, Congress is to take up Bush's request for $15 billion to pay the U.S. share of the war's cost. "He'll get whatever is needed to finish the campaign and to see that the troops get everything they need," Foley predicted.

*Staff writer Barbara Vobejda contributed to this report.*

Feb. 25, 1991    WP

END    0131

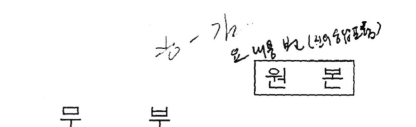

관리
번호 91-411

# 외 무 부

종 별 : 지 급

번 호 : USW-0947

일 시 : 91 0226 2022

수 신 : 장관(미북,미안,중동일,대책반,기정)

발 신 : 주 미 대사

제 목 : 상원 세출위 청문회(걸프전 추가 지출 법안)

1. 금 2.26 상원 세출위(위원장 ROBERT BYRD, 민-웨스트 버지니아)는 DARMAN 예산국장및 ATWOOD 국방부 부장관(당초에는 CHENEY 장관 출석 예정)을 출석시킨 가운데 걸프전 전비 관련 FY 91 국방 예산 추가 지출 법안에 관한 청문회를 개최 하였음.

2. 동 청문회시 DARMAN 예산국장은 90.10.1-91.3.31 기간중 걸프 사태로 인한 국방 추가 소요를 충당하기 위해 150 억불 규모의 추가 지출 예산을 요청하였으며, 동 자금은 일종의 BRIDGE LOAN 으로 국방부 장관이 OMB 의 허가를 얻어 우선정로 걸프전비에 충당하고, 동맹국 기여금(91.3.31 까지 나부 예정 총액 535 억불)은 접수되는대로 동자금 계정(WORKING CAPITAL ACCOUNT)으로 추가 시키는 방안을 설명하였음. 동 방안에 따르면 걸프전 전배는 금번 행정부가 요청한 150 억불 규모의 미 국방 예산에서 우선적으로 지출되고, 동 지출분은 동맹국 기여금에서 계속 보전 받는것으로 최종적으로 걸프전 전비가 동맹국 기여금( 535 억불)및 금번 추가 지출법안 금액(150 억불)의 합계에 못미칠 경우에는 금번 추가 지출법안 금액상에 잔고가 발생하게 되며, 동 잔고는 재무부로 이첩된다는것임.

3. 금번 청문회 질의 응답시에는 상기와같은 예산 운영의 경우에는 실제로 미의회가 예산에 대한 감독권을 행사할 여지가 없게 되는점에 대해 STEVENS 상원의원(공-알라스카)등 다수 상원의원이 반박하였으나, DARMAN 예산 국장은 첫째) 걸프전 전비 소요와 동맹국의 기여금을 일대일로 대응 시키는것은 실제로 거의 불가능하고, 둘째) 일국의 기여금을 복정 전비 소용에 충당할 경우, 동 국가로부터 반발도 예상할수 있어, 상기 방안이 가장 현실적이고 합리적이라는 의견을 제시하였음.

4. 동 청문회 질의 응답시, 동맹국의 기여금 수준과 관련, HOLLINGS

| 미주국 | 장관 | 차관 | 1차보 | 2차보 | 미주국 | 중아국 | 청와대 | 안기부 |
|--------|------|------|-------|-------|--------|--------|--------|--------|

91.02.27   11:36
외신 2과  통제관 BW

0132

상원의원(민주-사우스 캐롤라이나)는 한국, 일본및 독일의 기여금 수준에 대해 치하하고, 사우디, 쿠웨이트 및 UAE 등 직접 당사자 국가들의 기여금 수준은 불공평하게 낮은 수준임으로 동국가로부터 기여금을 더 받아내는 방안 수립이 필요하다고언급한바 있으며, 이와는 대조적으로 BUMPERS(민주-아칸소)상원의원은 고원유가로 야기될수 있는 손해를 감안하면 한국정부의 기여금 수준은 부족하다고 하면서 한국정부에 대해 압력을 가하는것이 필요하다는 요지의 발언을 하였음.

5. 동청문회 증언문및 주요 질의 응답 별전 FAX 송부함.

첨부 USW(F)-0692

(대사 박동진-국장)

91.12.31 까지

검토필 (1991. 6. 3.)

USW (F) - 0692
수신: 장관 (미북, 미안, 중동보, 미책반, 기정)          #
발신: 주미대사
제목: 상원 세출위 청문회 ( 걸프전 선비 관련 ) (17매)

EXECUTIVE OFFICE OF THE PRESIDENT
OFFICE OF MANAGEMENT AND BUDGET
WASHINGTON, D.C. 20503

THE DIRECTOR

INTRODUCTORY STATEMENT:
SUPPLEMENTAL REQUEST IN SUPPORT OF OPERATION DESERT SHIELD/STORM

BY

RICHARD DARMAN
DIRECTOR, OFFICE OF MANAGEMENT AND BUDGET

PRESENTED BEFORE THE
SENATE APPROPRIATIONS COMMITTEE
FEBRUARY 26, 1991

Chairman Byrd, Ranking Republican Senator Hatfield,
distinguished members of the Senate Appropriations Committee:

It is a pleasure to appear before you today.  I am pleased,
also, to be here with Secretary of Defense Cheney, who is able to
discuss issues of defense policy more authoritatively than am I.
With your understanding, I shall confine my remarks to budget-
related elements of Operation Desert Shield, which includes
Desert Storm.

As you know, the President transmitted to the Congress on
Friday a request for supplemental defense appropriations in
support of Operation Desert Shield/Desert Storm.

The requested supplemental is for the estimated incremental
costs of Operation Desert Shield/Storm for the period
October 1, 1990 through March 31, 1991.  It is comprised of two
basic elements:

(1) Working Capital:  $15 billion in budget authority to
establish and fund the Desert Shield Working Capital Account.

This account would be funded initially by resources from
the United States Government.  Its funds would be available
for transfer by the Secretary of Defense, with the approval
of the Office of Management and Budget, in order to
maintain continuity of payment for the incremental costs of
Operation Desert Shield/Storm.

0134

The Working Capital Account would be replenished by foreign contributions as funds become available from the Defense Cooperation Account.  Any balance in the Working Capital Account available after payment of all Desert Shield/Storm incremental costs would revert to the Treasury.

This $15 billion request is approximately equal to the (net) Desert Shield "placeholder" already included in the President's Budget and in the associated deficit estimates.

(2) Foreign Contributions:  Authority to transfer funds from the Defense Cooperation Account, the purpose of which is to receive current and anticipated foreign contributions.

Such transfers would be made by the Secretary of Defense, with the approval of the Office of Management and Budget, to reimburse defense appropriation accounts depleted by the incremental costs of Operation Desert Shield/Storm.

The Defense Cooperation Account currently holds $11.2 billion in foreign cash contributions received. Additional foreign contributions committed to Operation Desert Shield/Desert Storm, but not yet received, total $38.6 billion.

## Background

The Omnibus Reconciliation Act of 1990 provided that:

"The costs for Operation Desert Shield are to be treated as emergency funding requirements not subject to the defense spending limits. . . . Emergency Desert Shield costs mean those incremental costs associated with the increase in operations in the Middle East and do not include costs that would be experienced by the Department of Defense as part of its normal operations absent Operation Desert Shield."

In developing the Administration's supplemental request, we have attempted to live within the letter and spirit of this provision of law.  Applying the Desert Shield "incremental cost" standard, estimates have been developed for the following categories -- with incremental costs as noted:

2

0692-2                                              0135

|                                                      | Daily Rate | Total |
|------------------------------------------------------|------------|-------|
|                                                      | ($ billions)         ||

o  Return of personnel and
   equipment, as appropriate
   (including return of ready
   reserve fleet to non-deployed
   status and payment for
   reservist accrued leave) . . .            N.A.         5.2

Transfers from the Working Capital and Defense Cooperation
Accounts would be to accounts associated with each of the
foregoing categories, in the approximate order of their
presentation above.

Supporting detail for the estimates in each of these
categories has been provided directly to the Committee, and is
summarized here at Tables 1, 2, 3, 4, 5, and 6.  The
Administration has indicated that it is willing to provide
relevant cost (and foreign contribution) data to the Congress
routinely during Operation Desert Shield/Storm.

The incremental costs for the period October 1, 1990 -
March 31, 1991 (plus redeployment and return) total nearly
$40 billion plus the incremental costs of combat, which cannot be
definitively estimated at this point.

Total foreign commitments through March 31, 1991 total
$53.5 billion, including in-kind contributions.  (See Tables 7,
8, 9, and 10.)  If foreign commitments are fully honored, and if
hostilities end by March 31, the $15 billion Working Capital
account should be sufficient to cover the U.S. share of
incremental costs.  If these conditions are not met, however, it
may be necessary to seek additional foreign contributions and
U.S. appropriations.

It is important, for obvious reasons, that the Desert
Shield defense supplemental be enacted promptly.  Therefore, we
have not included non-defense or extraneous matters in this
supplemental request.  (We have submitted non-defense
supplemental requests separately for what we hope may be separate
legislative treatment.)

With that by way of introduction, please let me conclude by
thanking you again for inviting us to testify so soon after the
President submitted his request.  And let me try to respond to
your questions.

Attachments:  Tables 1-10.

4

0692-3                                                    0136

142 P10    LENINPROTOCOL                       '91-02-27  10:20

# TABLE 1

## CY 1990 DESERT SHIELD INCREMENTAL BASELINE COSTS

### ($ In Millions)

|  | CY 1990 |
|---|---|
| **Military Personnel** | |
| Reserve Callup | 742 |
| Imminent Danger Pay | 124 |
| Reserves on Active Duty | 253 |
| Other Guard/Reserve | -114 |
| Other MILPERS | 392 |
| Total MILPERS | 1,397 |
| **Operation and Maintenance** | |
| Transportation | 3,001 |
| Fuel - Incremental | 893 |
| OPTEMPO | 1,240 |
| In-Country | 1,035 |
| Equipment Procurement | 268 |
| Subsistence | 126 |
| RC Activation | 194 |
| Equipment Maintenance | 349 |
| Camouflage | 416 |
| Hosp./Supply Ships | 99 |
| Medical Support | 246 |
| Special Operating Forces | 8 |
| Comm./Map Production | 277 |
| Other MILPERS Support | -5 |
| Total O&M | 8,147 |
| MILCON | 133 |
| Investment | 367 |
| Stock Fund | 41 |
| Fuel - Price Increase | 1,009 |
| Grand Total | 11,094 |
| Less FY 1990 Appropriated Funds | -2,028 |
| OCT-DEC Incremental Cost Estimate | 9,066 |

069~ ᄯ 0137

## TABLE 2

### JANUARY - MARCH 1991
### DESERT SHIELD INCREMENTAL BASELINE COST ESTIMATE

#### (less combat)

($ in Millions)

| | |
|---|---:|
| **Military Personnel** | |
| Reserve Callup | 2,351 |
| Imminent Danger Pay | 152 |
| Reserves on Active Duty | 45 |
| Other Guard/Reserve | -325 |
| Other MILPERS | 498 |
| | |
| Total MILPERS | 2,721 |
| | |
| **Operation and Maintenance** | |
| Transportation | 1,505 |
| Fuel - Incremental | 474 |
| OPTEMPO | 1,704 |
| In-Country | 855 |
| Equipment Procurement | 243 |
| Subsistence | 812 |
| RC Activation | 750 |
| Equipment Maintenance | 905 |
| Camouflage | 148 |
| Hosp./Supply Ships | 28 |
| Medical Support | 300 |
| Special Operating Forces | 36 |
| Comm./Map Production | 290 |
| Other Guard/Reserve O&M | -223 |
| Other MILPERS Support | 152 |
| | |
| Total O&M | 7,979 |
| | |
| MILCON | 122 |
| | |
| Investment | 519 |
| | |
| Stock Fund | 301 |
| | |
| Fuel - Price Increase | 676 |
| | |
| Grand Total | 12,318 |

### Estimate Subject to Change

0691-5                    0138

## TABLE 3

### ESTIMATES FOR COMBAT

The following represent combat loss and cost estimates for notional days of combat in Desert Storm. The estimates include increased operating tempo; maintenance; prisoner support; medical transportation; ammunition; missiles; and replacement of aircraft, naval vessels, ground equipment and vehicles. Individually, they illustrate the effects of variations in factors such as the operational mission, conflict intensity and the level of participation of air and ground forces. In addition, the reliability of each approximation also depends on less predictable variables, such as weather, enemy intentions and capabilities.

Any attempt to combine individual estimates to compile a summary estimate of combat losses and costs is complicated by the nature of the operational plan, enemy initiatives and battlefield results taken on a daily basis.

|  | Daily Rate ($ Mil) |
|---|---|
| **Case 1:** Air campaign only. Losses include 1 F-15E and 1 F/A-18 plus the expenditure of munitions. | 200 |
| **Case 2:** Air campaign only. No aircraft losses, only the expenditure of munitions. | 150 |
| **Case 3:** Air campaign only. Losses include 1 F-117, F-16, 1 A-6, and 1 F-14, plus the expenditure of munitions. | 400 |
| **Case 4:** Ground campaign with associated air support. Losses include 1 A-10, 1 AV-8, 25 tanks, 22 IFVs, 32 APCs, 13 artillery pieces, 6 helos, 1 LCAC, and 1 AAV, plus the expenditure of munitions. | 800 |
| **Case 5:** Ground campaign with associated air support. Losses include 1 F-15, 1 A-10, 1 F/A-18, 1 F-16, 1 guided missile frigate (FFG), 44 tanks, 40 IFVs, 60 APCs, 25 artillery pieces, and 17 helos, plus the expenditure of munitions. | 1,650 |
| **Case 6:** Ground campaign with associated air support. Losses include 1 F-15E, 11 tanks, 10 IFVs, 15 APCs, 7 artillery pieces, and 4 helos, plus the expenditure of munitions. | 400 |

Legend:
   IFV    Infantry Fighting Vehicle (Bradley)
   APC    Armored Personnel Carrier
   LCAC   Landing Craft Air Cushioned
   AAV    Amphibious Assault Vehicle

0139

## TABLE 4

### FY 1991 DESERT SHIELD/STORM
Investment Supplemental
($ in Millions)

| | Accelerated Acquisition | Production Surge | Total |
|---|---|---|---|
| **Army** | | | |
| Aircraft Procurement | 35.7 | - | 35.7 |
| Missile Procurement | 128.0 | 1,152.8 | 1,280.8 |
| Procurement of Weapons & Tracked Combat Vehicles | 26.3 | - | 26.3 |
| Procurement of Ammunition | - | 1,248.7 | 1,248.7 |
| Other Procurement | 191.9 | - | 191.9 |
| RDT&E | 9.1 | - | 9.1 |
| Total | 391.0 | 2,401.5 | 2,792.5 |
| **Navy** | | | |
| Aircraft Procurement | 56.5 | - | 56.5 |
| Weapons Procurement | 12.0 | 1,920.1 | 1,932.1 |
| Other Procurement | 44.0 | 9.7 | 53.7 |
| Procurement, Marine Corps | 120.2 | 133.2 | 253.4 |
| Total | 232.7 | 2,063.0 | 2,295.7 |
| **Air Force** | | | |
| Aircraft Procurement | 111.2 | - | 111.2 |
| Missile Procurement | 30.0 | 540.0 | 570.0 |
| Other Procurement | 42.7 | 564.4 | 607.1 |
| Total | 183.9 | 1,104.4 | 1,288.3 |
| **Defense Agencies** | | | |
| Procurement | 47.2 | - | 47.2 |
| RDT&E | 6.7 | - | 6.7 |
| Total | 53.9 | - | 53.9 |
| **Grand Total** | 861.5 | 5,568.9 | 6,430.4 |

## TABLE 5

### ESTIMATED POST COMBAT PHASEDOWN COSTS

(<u>$ Bil)</u>

o  PERSONNEL SUPPORT.  Incremental cost of pay,
   and other military personnel costs including
   reservists on active duty and imminent danger
   pay for personnel in theater.                              3.9

o  TRAINING.  Training at reduced levels.  Reflects
   consumption of supplies and materials due to
   desert environment.                                         .3

o  TRANSPORTATION.  Movement of equipment dispersed
   throughout the theater of operation to staging
   areas for redeployment and transport of supplies
   such as repair parts, subsistence, and APO mail.            .6

o  MAINTENANCE.  All equipment will be inspected,
   fully repaired using in-theater spare
   parts/required services performed, and prepared for
   shipment.  For the Naval forces, emergent repairs
   and essential intermediate maintenance will be
   accomplished to ensure a safe redeployment.                 .6

o  SUSTAINMENT OF FORCES.  Includes base support
   infrastructure, medical support, morale, and
   welfare for troops and troop subsistence.                  1.2

o  SHIP DEPLOYMENT.  Naval forces called up from
   training status will continue to be deployed in
   the region during the phasedown period.                     .3

o  FACILITY DISMANTLEMENT.  Temporary structures
   and facilities will be dismantled.                          .1

Estimated Cost                                                7.0

## TABLE 6

## Return of Personnel and Equipment
### (Dollars in Millions)

### ARMY

Military Personnel, Army
    Requirements                      306.7
        Deactivation PCS       102.0
        Guard/Reserve Accrued Leave  204.7

Operation and Maintenance, Army
    Requirements                    3,586.4
        Transportation         3,000.0
        Reception of Units     123.8
        European Force Replacement   17.3
        POMCUS/War Reserve Replacement 445.3
TOTAL, ARMY                         3,893.1

### NAVY

Military Personnel, Navy
    Requirements                    46.4
        Deactivation PCS       26.4
        Navy Accrued Leave     20.0

Operation and Maintenance, Navy
    Requirements                    540.0
        Transportation         360.0
        Deactivation of RRF    180.0
TOTAL, NAVY                         586.4

### MARINE CORPS

Military Personnel, Marine Corps
    Requirements                    83.4
        Deactivation PCS       26.4
        Reserve Accrued Leave   57.0
TOTAL, MARINE CORPS                  83.4

### AIR FORCE

Military Personnel, Air Force
    Requirements                    75.2
        Deactivation PCS       26.0
        Guard/Reserve Accrued Leave  49.2

Operation and Maintenance, Air Force
    Requirements                    554.0
        Airlift              361.0
        Sealift             80.0
        AVPOL              94.9
        OPTEMPO           18.1
TOTAL, AIR FORCE                  629.2

GRAND TOTAL         0692-9         0142    5,192.1

TABLE 7

## DESERT SHIELD: CY 1990 AND 1991 FOREIGN COMMITMENTS TO THE U.S. 1/
(Millions of Dollars)

| | Commitments | | | Receipts | | | Future Receipts |
|---|---|---|---|---|---|---|---|
| | 1990 | 1991 | Total | Cash 2/ | In-kind | Total | |
| GCC STATES | 6,845 | 29,000 | 35,845 | 8,827 | 1,716 | 10,543 | 25,302 |
| SAUDI ARABIA | 3,339 | 13,500 | 16,839 | 4,457 | 1,566 | 6,023 | 10,816 |
| KUWAIT | 2,506 | 13,500 | 16,006 | 3,500 | 10 | 3,510 | 12,496 |
| UAE | 1,000 | 2,000 3/ | 3,000 | 870 | 140 | 1,010 | 1,990 |
| GERMANY | 1,072 | 5,500 | 6,572 | 2,432 | 531 | 2,963 | 3,609 |
| JAPAN | 1,740 4/ | 9,000 5/ | 10,740 | 866 | 457 | 1,323 | 9,417 |
| KOREA | 80 6/ | 305 | 385 | 50 | 21 | 71 | 314 |
| OTHERS | 3 | | 3 | | 3 | 3 | |
| TOTAL | 9,740 | 43,805 | 53,545 | 12,175 | 2,728 | 14,903 | 38,642 |

1/ Data compiled by OMB. Sources of data: Commitments — Defense, State, Treasury; Cash received — Treasury; Receipts and value of in-kind assistance — Defense

2/ $1 billion has been released from the Defense Cooperation Account to Defense in accordance with the FY '91 Appropriations Act.

3/ An additional amount above the $2 billion is under discussion.

4/ Japan pledged $260 million to other coalition forces for total contributions of $2 billion.

5/ Under consideration by Diet.

6/ Korea pledged $15 million to other coalition forces for total contributions of $95 million.

## TABLE 8

## DESERT SHIELD: CY 1990 FOREIGN COMMITMENTS TO THE U.S. 1/
(Millions of Dollars)

| | Commitments | Receipts | | | Future Receipts |
|---|---|---|---|---|---|
| | | Cash 2/ | In-kind | Total | |
| GCC STATES | 6,845 | 4,177 | 971 | 5,148 | 1,697 |
| SAUDI ARABIA | 3,339 | 807 | 854 | 1,661 | 1,678 3/ |
| KUWAIT | 2,506 | 2,500 | 6 | 2,506 | |
| UAE | 1,000 | 870 | 111 | 981 | 19 3/ |
| GERMANY | 1,072 | 272 | 531 | 803 | 269 4/ |
| JAPAN | 1,740 5/ | 866 | 457 | 1,323 | 417 4/ |
| KOREA | 80 6/ | 50 | 21 | 71 | 9 4/ |
| OTHERS | 3 | | 3 | 3 | |
| TOTAL | 9,740 | 5,365 | 1,983 | 7,348 | 2,392 |

| U.S. Share of CY 1990 Incremental Costs | 1,354 |
|---|---|

| Total CY 1990 Incremental Costs | 11,094 |
|---|---|

1/ Data compiled by OMB. Sources of data: Commitments for August – December 31 — Defense, State, Treasury; Cash received—Treasury; Receipts and value of in-kind assistance — Defense; Total cost for August – December 31 — Defense.

2/ $1 billion has been released from the Defense Cooperation Account to Defense in accordance with the FY '91 Appropriations Act.

3/ Cash reimbursement from Saudi Arabia and UAE awaiting bill from Defense. Saudi reimbursement includes enroute transportation through December for the second deployment and in-theater expenses for food, building materials, fuel, and support.

4/ In-kind assistance from Germany, Japan, and Korea. Orders made and receipt of goods expected soon.

5/ Japan pledged $260 million to other coalition forces for total contributions of $2 billion.

6/ Korea pledged $15 million to other coalition forces for total contributions of $95 million.

0692 — H

142 P18 LENINPROTOCOL '91-02-27 10:37

0145

## TABLE 9

## DESERT SHIELD MILITARY ASSISTANCE
## CY 1991 (JAN 1 – MAR 31) COMMITMENTS
(Millions of Dollars)

| | Commit-ments | Receipts | | | Future Receipts |
| --- | --- | --- | --- | --- | --- |
| | | Cash | In-kind | Total | |
| GCC STATES | 29,000 | 4,650 | 745 | 5,395 | 23,605 |
| SAUDI ARABIA | 13,500 | 3,650 | 712 | 4,362 | 9,138 |
| KUWAIT | 13,500 | 1,000 | 4 | 1,004 | 12,496 |
| UAE | 2,000  1/ | | 29 | 29 | 1,971 |
| GERMANY | 5,500 | 2,160 | 0 | 2,160 | 3,340 |
| JAPAN | 9,000  2/ | 0 | 0 | 0 | 9,000 |
| KOREA | 305 | 0 | 0 | 0 | 305 |
| OTHERS | | 0 | 0 | 0 | 0 |
| TOTAL | 43,805 | 6,810 | 745 | 7,555 | 36,250 |

1/  An additional amount above the $2 billion is under discussion.
2/  Under consideration by Diet

0692-12

걸프사태 : 미국 의회 동향, 1990-91. 전5권 (V.3 1991.1-2월)  531

0146

Table 10

Defense Cooperation Account
($ In Millions)

| | |
|---|---|
| Received | 12,175 |
| Interest | 70 |
| Total | 12,245 |
| Withdrawals | 1,000 1/ |
| Balance | 11,245 |

1/ Appropriated in the FY 1991 Appropriations Act.

Source: Department of Defense.

0692-13

142 P20    LENINPROTOCOL                    '91-02-27 10:29

MEMORANDUM of February 26, 1991

To:        Congressional Section

From:      Christine Hagedorn

Topic:     Senate Appropriations Committee Hearing, Supplemental
Costs of the Gulf War."  OMB Director Darman and Deputy Sec. of
Defense Atwood to testify (to replace Sec. Cheney who was called
to White House).

---

The committee met today to hear testimony on the
Administration's supplemental request for funds to cover the U.S.
portion of the cost for the Gulf War and its aftermath and to
discuss briefly the contributions of U.S. allies toward the effort.

This committee was very concerned with the reality of
collecting those contributions made by the coalition partners.

Director Darman spoke to the committee about two key elements
of President Bush's supplemental for estimated incremental costs.
The first, a working capital fund of $1 5 billion to be used as a
"bridge loan" to keep funds available to maintain continuity of
payment for incremental costs and to be replenished by allied funds
as they filter in .  The balance to revert to Treasury.  And the
second, foreign contributions, requiring DOD to be able to transfer
to reimburse Defense accounts depleted by costs of Gulf War.

The estimates for incremental costs were calculated under the
assumption that hostilities would run no longer than March 31,
1991.

Dep. Sec. Atwood listed priorities of the DOD in requesting
these funds:

1)    Wish to support supply costs of maintaining forces in the
Gulf.
2)    support costs of production of missiles , armor and
equipment needed by those forces in the Gulf.
3)    support costs of the phase down after hostilities cease.
4)    support costs of return  of personnell and equipment to
Germany and the U.S.

When asked by Chairman Byrd. when the witnesses feel this bill
should be passed, Darman replied that no later than May 1991, but
there is a disadvantage of waiting until that time, as Sec. Cheney
is now using the civil war food and forage act to budget for the
war, but that is a clumsy way of budgeting.  Therefore, it is the

0692-14                                    0147

hope of the administration to pass this supplemental bill as soon as possible.

When questioned about how to pay for immediate aftermath of war in terms of troops, Darman told Chairman Byrd that costs for an orderly phase down and return of troops have been included in this supplemental.

When asked if the Administration would come back to ask congress to pass another supplemental bill should the President decide to keep the troops in the desert past March 31st, Darman replied that if hostilities continue, there would be a need to come back. If hostilities do not continue after March 31st, that phase down is already included and will be no need to come back. Dep. Sec. Atwood added that if the Administration does need to come back after Mar. 31st, the size of the request of that additional supplemental would depend on the magnitude of the conflict at that time and he added that "the U.S. should want to show our contributing coalition partners that we have taken our action (in appropriating funds) as fast as we can," just as we expect them to do.

Senator Hatfield was the first of almost all of the committee members to ask" why do we give over the funds to the OMB? Why not do as with traditional supplemental cases and appropriate to the proper accounts? To this question, Darman explained for the first time in a series of explanations to follow, that this way was open to suggestions from Congress. OMB simply figured it was a neat and the best way to fund monies we had not yet received from coalition partners and that it was the only way in which to secure that left-over funds would revert back to Treasury.

[As an aside, there was quite a bit of anti-Japan sentiment regarding the timeliness of payment].

When asked why funds for munitions which appear to be a regular cost of DOD, are included in a supplemental that should only cover cost for Desert Shield/Storm costs, Atwood replied that the amounts for munitions are needed replenish inventory used in the war and to make sure enough are available for the soldiers over in the gulf. Munitions will be replaced to amount to those reduced levels the U.S. had envisioned as part of its overall reduction.

When questioned about the prospect that under the Geneva convention, we must provide $15 per day to feed U.S. POWs (same as we provide to our troops), Atwood explained that the supplemental requests include enough to support one million POWs and that adjustments will be made after hostilities cease for the funds not used to this end.

When questioned by Sen. Inouye about the fate of captured equipment , Atwood replied that no official plan for that as of now.

092-15

0148

Sen. Stevens harshly questioned Dir. Darman on "why have you submitted a request that calls for a basic changes in the law when it is such a time sensitive issue to pass this bill? The senator alleged that this bill requires two acts of Congress instead of one and attempts to set a new precedent for control of funds, taking the power of oversight away from congress. (Incidently, a few other members argued this same point).

Sen. Stevens also inquired as to what was the exact relationship of OMB to the working capital fund, and why should Congress not have that same relationship, Darman reiterated that the Administration in no way intends to use this bill to change policy, or gain control of funds but, rather to keep the process under control in a neat, orderly manner.

The supplemental requests additional patriots , MLRS and maverick systems which have all been scheduled for termination? Atwood was asked if this is DOD's underhanded way of reconsidering these programs and he replied that their inclusion in the supplemental is intended to replace the inventories we expected to have had the war not used up certain stockpiles. They are still scheduled for termination.

Sen. Hollings praised Japan ,Korea and Germany have for meeting "their fair share" of the war costs. He says we must put extra pressure on UAE, Saudi Arabia and Kuwait to agree to their fair share. Simply tell them what they owe and if these latter countries do not pay, we will simply put a tax on imports to pay for it that way. Sen. Specter seconded these sentiments in his remarks, asking the administration to "lay it on the line with UAE," before coming to congress to ask to use the American taxpayers money to fund the war.

In response to numerous questions regarding U.S. inclusions in the supplemental to reimburse Israel for losses, Darman, simply told that funding was not included in the supplemental and that the U.S. is working with the EC to arrange coalition supported-funding for Israel. He explained that the supplemental was for emergency funds and that the administration did not consider reimbursement to Israel an emergency.

When questioned by Sen. Leahy on how the U.S. will pay if a military presence must be maintained in the gulf region after the war is over, Atwoood replied that this issue needs to be discussed with coalition partners and no resolution of this issue has yet been made. He added that we have long held a naval presence in the region anyway which would likely continue. However, what ever those costs are in the future, they must remain within the mutually-agreed ceilings established by the Oct. 90 budget resolution.

*692-16*

0149

Sen Dominici chided Sen. Hollings for proposing a tariff on those countries who do not pay their "fair share" because the American taxpayer would ultimately pay for that tariff.  This Sen. also inquired as to the status of aid to Jordan and was told that it is under review by the President.

Sen DeConicini inquired as to why of all the government agencies included in the non-defense portion of the supplemental request, why customs got no funding and was told by Darman that customs would indeed get some money, but submitted its request on Feb. 22nd, so was not included.

Sen D'Amato was concerned about money from Japan and Darman assured him that receipt of the 9 billion was not the issue to be concerned with, rather where the funds would be tagged for , if at all requested by the Diet.  D'Amato alleged it was ridiculous for us to applaud the Saudi's for their $16 billion contributions when that is not nearly enough.

Sen Bumpers made specific mention of the fact that Korea's contribution is less than it could be and if the price of oil continues to go up, Korea's contribution will seem very small in comparison to what it can handle.  He suggested we put more pressure on Korea.

Sen Lautenberg made a huge case for Israel as a front-line state (so-declared by Sec. Baker) to receive reparations and was given the same answer Darman give to the other Israel-advocates, also citing that Israel would benefit from the structure of the peace in the new world order which will result from this war.

The senate broke for recess and C-Span went to the senate floor to broadcast live.

0692-17

0150

# 報 告 事 項

報告畢

1991. 2. 27.
美 洲 局
北 美 課 (13)

題 目 : 美 上院 歲出委의 걸프戰 戰費 支出 聽聞會

---

美 上院 歲出委(委員長 : Robert Byrd, 民主, WV)는 2.26(화) Darman 豫算
局長, Atwood 國防部 副長官을 出席시킨 가운데 걸프전 戰費 관련 FY 91 國防
豫算 追加 支出 法案에 관한 聽聞會를 開催하였는 바, 我國의 財政支援에
대한 言及等 관련사항 아래 報告 드립니다.

---

1. Darman 豫算局長 證言內容

º 90.10-91.3.期間中 걸프事態로 인한 國防費, 追加 所要 充當을 위해 150억불
규모의 追加 支出 豫算을 요청함.

- 일종의 連繫借用(Bridge Loan) 성격으로 걸프 戰費는 國防長官이 聯邦
豫算局 許可下에 소요 발생에 따라 우선 支出 執行

- 同盟國 寄與金 535億弗은 接受後 Working Capital Account에 入金, 事後
補塡

º 걸프 戰費 실제 지출액이 追加 支出金額 150億弗과 同盟國 寄與金 535億弗의
合計인 685億弗에 못미칠 경우, 剩餘 殘額은 美國庫로 移管 豫定임.

0151

(同盟國 寄與金 水準)

o Ernest F. Hollings 上院議員(民主, SC)

- 韓國, 日本 및 獨逸의 寄與金 水準 致賀("their fair share")

- 直接 當事者인 사우디, 쿠웨이트 및 UAE의 水準은 不公平하게 낮으므로
  더 寄與金을 받는 方案 樹立 必要性 指摘

o Dale Bumpers(民主, Ark)

- 高 原油價로 야기될 수 있는 損害 감안시, 한국의 寄與 水準은 부족함을
  指摘하고 對韓國 政府 壓力行使 필요성 언명

  * 同 議員은 89.6. 駐韓美軍을 1만명 수준으로 減縮하자는 法案을 提出
    한 바 있음.

(現 戰費 支出 計定)

o 걸프戰 關聯 戰費는 現在 內戰時 給食法(Civil War Food and Forage Act)상
  計定에서 臨時 支出中임.

- 91.5. 以前 追加 支出法案 通過 必要

- 事態가 3月末 以前 終了時 또다른 追加 支出 豫算案 提出은 不要

- 끝 -

0152

**외교문서 비밀해제: 걸프 사태 36**

**걸프 사태 미국 동향 3**

초판인쇄 2024년 03월 15일
초판발행 2024년 03월 15일

지은이 한국학술정보(주)
펴낸이 채종준
펴낸곳 한국학술정보(주)
주 소 경기도 파주시 회동길 230(문발동)
전 화 031-908-3181(대표)
팩 스 031-908-3189
홈페이지 http://ebook.kstudy.com
E-mail 출판사업부 publish@kstudy.com
등 록 제일산-115호(2000. 6. 19)

ISBN 979-11-6983-996-9 94340
       979-11-6983-960-0 94340 (set)